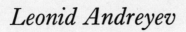

*Leonid Andreyev*

# Leonid Andreyev

## A STUDY

⁕

BY

JAMES B. WOODWARD

CLARENDON PRESS · OXFORD

1969

*Oxford University Press, Ely House, London W.1*

GLASGOW NEW YORK TORONTO MELBOURNE WELLINGTON
CAPE TOWN SALISBURY IBADAN NAIROBI DAR ES SALAAM LUSAKA ADDIS ABABA
BOMBAY CALCUTTA MADRAS KARACHI LAHORE DACCA
KUALA LUMPUR SINGAPORE HONG KONG TOKYO

PRINTED IN GREAT BRITAIN
BY W & J MACKAY & CO LTD, CHATHAM

# PREFACE

WITH the exception of Gorky, Russian prose writers of the early twentieth century have received scant attention in the West. Apart from the few associated with the symbolist camp, they tend to be treated in general histories of Russian literature under a single rubric as perpetuators of the traditions of nineteenth-century realism. Such a picture is misleading. Not only does it give an inadequate reflection of the intrinsic merits of some of the writers concerned; it also fails to convey their artistic and intellectual individuality and obscures the diverse processes which were taking place in prose fiction during this period. Perhaps no one has suffered more from this oversimplified approach than Leonid Nikolaevich Andreyev (1871–1919).

Regarded by the majority of his contemporaries as one of Russia's most original and talented writers, Andreyev displayed in his works almost from the outset an overriding preoccupation with problems of an abstract, philosophical nature and an artistic method or technique which at once distinguished him from other writers of the period. To no one else could the term 'realist', in the conventional sense of the term, be applied so inappropriately. Indeed, not the least of Andreyev's claims to our attention is the leading role which he played in promoting and reinforcing a counterbalancing romantic element in Russian narrative fiction and drama of the early twentieth century.

When Gorky, with his usual modesty, acknowledged the inferiority of his own artistic gifts to those of his friend, he was simply reiterating an opinion long held by most contemporary critics and *literati*, symbolists and 'realists' alike. Moreover, the general prevalence of this view, indicating that both camps found something to applaud in Andreyev's works, suggests that in certain important respects he may be considered a more widely representative figure than Gorky of Russian literary and intellectual life of the two decades before 1917. This probably explains why it is that after his death in 1919 his contemporaries tended to look back on him as a kind of symbol. The symbolist Georgiy Chulkov, for example, regarded his flamboyant, passionate, artistic personality as in a very real sense 'definitive of his age, of his time',[1] and a

---

[1] *Kniga o Leonide Andreyeve*, SPb.-Berlin, 1922, p. 64.

disillusioned and embittered Chirikov wrote in 1921: 'The terrible spiritual tragedy of Leonid Andreyev is our general Russian tragedy.'[1] Yet despite the fact that in his person and in his works he seemed to express, albeit in a highly distinctive manner, so much that was typical of his age, little attempt has been made to carry out a detailed analysis of his fiction against both the background of his times and of his own life in order to determine the extent both of his typicality and of his individuality.[2]

Within the wider context of seeking to familiarize the reader with the content of Andreyev's fiction and the personality of its creator, the primary purpose of the present study, which is based on part of a doctoral thesis completed at the University of Oxford, is to determine the mainsprings of his art and to provide an interpretation of his major works. Questions of style and technique are discussed only in so far as they contribute to this central purpose. A Bishop of the Orthodox Church truthfully remarked in 1908: '. . . even though the name L. Andreyev is so well-known and his works are so widely read, it cannot be said that many have understood his view of the world.'[3] It is hoped that our analysis may help to remedy this situation. With the assistance of hitherto unconsidered materials, the mass of articles and reviews which greeted almost his every work in the journals of the day, and a closer study of his fiction than has hitherto been undertaken, it is our aim to present an original interpretation of his thought, which, it is believed, is the only one which accords with the totality of facts and evidence forthcoming from his fiction, correspondence, diaries and recorded statements and which transforms the prevailing conception of him, and to cast in general much new light on an artist and thinker who, though so little discussed today, attained in his lifetime a degree of fame which equalled and momentarily even eclipsed that of Gorky.

There is no complete edition of Andreyev's collected works.

[1] E. Chirikov, 'Leonid Andreyev', *Russkie sborniki*, No. 2, Sofia, 1921, p. 73.
[2] The one exception is Alexander Kaun's book *Leonid Andreyev. A Critical Study* (New York, 1924), which is by far the most important work on the writer to have appeared thus far. Writing only five years after Andreyev's death, however, Kaun was unable to benefit from the wealth of materials which have since come to light, and many of his conclusions on both general and particular questions are no longer supportable.
[3] Episkop Innokentiy, 'Individualisticheskoe mirovozzrenie L. Andreyeva. (Literaturno-bogoslovsko-filosofskiy ocherk)', *Vera i razum*, 1909, No. 9–10, p. 285.

Two editions appeared between 1911 and 1913: the thirteen-volume edition of the publishing-house *Prosveshchenie* ('Enlightenment') and the eight-volume edition of A. F. Marks. The latter (*Polnoe sobranie sochineniy Leonida Andreyeva*), which was published as a premium to the journal *Niva* ('The Cornfield'), is the more complete and is used in this study for the works written by Andreyev before 1913. Volumes XIV–XVII of the other edition were subsequently published by different publishing-houses, and in preference to them I have used for Andreyev's works written after 1912 the almanacs and separate editions in which they first appeared.

The system of transliteration employed is the one recommended by *The Slavonic and East European Review*, published by the University of London, except that the Russian vowel *e* is transliterated as 'ye' only when it is preceded by another *e*; otherwise it is rendered as 'e'. In addition, a concession is made to conventional practice in the rendering 'Gorky'. The more accurate form 'Gor'kiy' is used only in the transliterated titles of references.

The transliteration of the names of journals, newspapers, almanacs and publishing-houses is preferred to their translation, though at the first mention of the name of each in the text and footnotes (not in references) the transliteration is followed by a translation in brackets. The reverse process is followed with the titles of Andreyev's works and those of other writers, except when the title consists of a proper name, in which case it is simply transliterated.

The places of publication of books are given in full, except for Moscow, St. Petersburg and Leningrad, which are indicated respectively by M., SPb., and L. Unless otherwise stated, all journals to which reference is made were published in Russia. Pre-Revolutionary dates are given in 'Old Style'.

Whenever reference is made to a book or article written under a pseudonym, the true name of the author is given where possible and the pseudonym is placed afterwards in brackets. This rule is not observed only when the author's real name was almost totally eclipsed by his pseudonym, e.g. Gorky, Veresaev, Serafimovich, Skitalets, Stanislavsky, Andrey Belyy.

I should like to express my gratitude to Professor S. Konovalov and Mr. J. S. G. Simmons of the University of Oxford for their advice in the early stages of the work. I also owe a special debt of gratitude to Professor James St. Clair-Sobell, Dr. W. J. Rose and Professor Valerian Revutsky of the University of British Columbia for their keen interest in the work and their many valuable suggestions. In conclusion, I would like to thank the editors of *Canadian Slavonic Papers*, *Études Slaves et Est-Européennes* and *Modern Drama* for their permission to use in this book material from my articles published in their journals.

J. B. WOODWARD

Swansea,
*August,* 1968

# CONTENTS

# LIST OF ABBREVIATIONS

BSN  V. V. Brusyanin, *Leonid Andreyev. Zhizn' i tvorchestvo*, M., 1912, 126 pp.

EMKT  N. E. Efros, *Moskovskiy Khudozhestvennyy teatr, 1898–1923*, M.-SPb., 1924, 450 pp.

FTV  N. N. Fatov, *Molodye gody Leonida Andreyeva. (Po neizdannym pis'mam, vospominaniyam i dokumentam)*, M., 1924, 368 pp.

KLA  *Kniga o Leonide Andreyeve*, SPb.-Berlin, 1922, 192 pp.

LN  *Literaturnoe Nasledstvo. Tom 72. Gor'kiy i Leonid Andreyev. Neizdannaya perepiska*, M., 1965, 630 pp.

MAMK  K. D. Muratova (ed.), 'L. N. Andreyev. Pis'ma k N. K. Mikhaylovskomu (1901–1902)', *Literaturnyy arkhiv*, vol. 5, M.-L., 1960, pp. 51–62.

MAMR  K. D. Muratova (ed.), 'L. N. Andreyev. Pis'ma k V. S. Mirolyubovu (1899–1907)', *Literaturnyy arkhiv*, vol. 5, M.-L., 1960, pp. 65–117.

PLA  *Pis'ma Leonida Andreyeva*, L., 1924, 47 pp.

PNA  P. N. Andreyev, 'Vospominaniya o Leonide Andreyeve', *Literaturnaya mysl'*, alm. III, L., 1925, pp. 140–207.

Rekviem  *Rekviem. Sbornik pamyati Leonida Andreyeva*, M., 1930, 276 pp.

VLA  V. L. Andreyev, 'Povest' ob ottse', *Russkie zapiski*, Paris, 1938, May, pp. 76–90; June, pp. 93–114; July, pp. 99–112; August–September, pp. 89–107; October, pp. 93–119; November, pp. 101–16; December, pp. 96–115.

VRSV  V. V. Veresaev, 'Leonid Andreyev', *Sochineniya v chetyryokh tomakh*, vol. 4, M., 1948, pp. 449–77.

Works  *Polnoe sobranie sochineniy Leonida Andreyeva*, 8 vols., SPb., A. F. Marks, 1913.

# PART I

## Introductory

# I

## THE FORMATIVE YEARS

ANDREYEV wrote two autobiographical sketches for publication in the course of his life. The first, entitled *From My Life* (*Iz moey zhizni*), appeared in January 1903 in the St. Petersburg monthly *Zhurnal dlya vsekh* ('A Journal for All')[1] and was subsequently republished in their works on him by the critics N. Gekker[2] and A. Izmaylov.[3] It was written in haste and gives only the barest outline of his life before 1898—the year which marks the beginning of his literary career, although he had written works of fiction previously. Some years later he confessed to Izmaylov: 'My attitude to the journal's demand was not serious enough and I did not fully appreciate the importance of that page.'[4] A number of his friends and associates in literary circles, including Gorky and Veresaev, expressed their dismay at its blatant inadequacy.[5] He received an opportunity to redeem himself in 1910 when Professor S. A. Vengerov, who at that time was compiling his *Critico-Biographical Dictionary* (*Kritiko-biograficheskiy slovar'*), requested a more substantial account of his early years. Andreyev responded with an *Autobiography* (*Avtobiografiya*) which was eventually published in 1911 in the miscellany *First Literary Steps* (*Pervye literaturnye shagi*), edited

---

[1] Andreyev presented it to Mirolyubov, the editor of *Zhurnal dlya vsekh*, in a letter of December 1902 (see *MAMR*, pp. 99–100).

[2] See N. Gekker, *Leonid Andreyev i ego proizvedeniya*, Odessa, 1903, pp. 6–8.

[3] See A. Izmaylov, *Literaturnyy Olimp*, M., 1911, pp. 241–3.

[4] Ibid., p. 243.   [5] See *MAMR*, p. 100.

by F. F. Fiedler,[1] and subsequently in *Russian Literature of the 20th Century, 1890–1910* (*Russkaya literatura* XX *veka, 1890–1910*), of which Vengerov was the editor.[2] Inevitably this sketch also leaves much unsaid. Of inestimable value for the biographer who wishes to trace the development of Andreyev's mind and character during his childhood and youth as a preliminary to the analysis of his fiction are the reminiscences of his relatives and a number of his contemporaries at the *gimnaziya* and university, which were collected and published in 1924 by N. N. Fatov.[3] Equally valuable are the reminiscences of the writer's brother Pavel, published in 1925,[4] in which highly revealing entries in Andreyev's early diaries are reproduced. In combination with these materials Andreyev's letters, his disclosures to Izmaylov[5] and his friend, secretary and fellow-writer Vasiliy Brusyanin,[6] the autobiographical content of certain of his early feuilletons and less important sources enable the critic to fill most of the gaps left by the autobiographies.

Leonid Nikolaevich Andreyev was born on 9 August 1871 in a house on the 2nd Pushkarnaya Street in the town of Oryol. His father, the son of an Oryol landowner and a peasant girl, had received a meagre education and occupied the modest post of land-tax surveyor; to supplement his inadequate income he also worked in a bank. Distinguished by his honesty and great physical strength, formidable will-power, purely pragmatic philosophy of life, and his congenital alcoholism, he dominated the Andreyev household. He also dominated life on the 2nd Pushkarnaya Street, where such qualities were held in the highest esteem. In later years, e.g. in the story *Bargamot and Garas'ka* (1898), his eldest son, Leonid, was to recall the 'Homeric' fights of which the street was so often the scene and in which his father played so conspicuous a part.[7] Pavel Andreyev writes:

This street also had its own moral code. Thus it was forbidden in a fight to strike a man when he was down. The street despised cowardice, hated the rich, 'foreigners', and had no respect for other people's property; hence the 'Pushkari' shut themselves off from unwelcome guests with

---

[1] *Pervye literaturnye shagi*, M., 1911, pp. 27–32.
[2] See S. A. Vengerov (ed.), *Russkaya literatura* XX *veka, 1890–1910*, vol. II, part 2, M., 1915, pp. 242–5.
[3] See *FTV*.  [4] See *PNA*.  [5] See Izmaylov, op. cit., pp. 243–50.
[6] See *BSN*.  [7] See *Works* VII, p. 233.

high, nailed fences and were constantly at war with other districts, thereby rearing their patriots. . . . When Leonid was older, he not only became a witness to all the scenes which were enacted on this street, but took a most active part in many of them.[1]

Such was the environment in which Andreyev spent his childhood and early youth. He inherited, in varying measure, all the noted qualities of his father except his pragmatism and, in addition, his abiding love of nature; '. . . he spent his whole life dreaming about the country,' he wrote of his father in 1910, 'but died in the town.'[2] But for the sources of his talent Andreyev looked to his mother's side.

Née Pockowska, his mother belonged to a branch of an old aristocratic Polish family which had moved to Russia centuries before and become fully russified—and impoverished. The complete opposite of her husband, modest, unassuming and almost illiterate, she nevertheless possessed a vivid imagination and with her endless repertoire of stories she plunged her son from his earliest years into a world of fantasy. An important feature of many of Andreyev's future works is foreshadowed in the following comments of his brother:

She was talented. The stories which she told were amazingly colourful, full of imagery and vivid. She loved to embellish a story and to fact added an incalculable amount of fiction. Truth in her stories was so closely interwoven with invention, fantasy, that it was impossible to separate the one from the other.[3]

She further stimulated her son's interest in the 'unreal' world by taking him regularly to the theatre and encouraging the passion for reading which he soon displayed. By the time he was 7 he already possessed a large library, and one form of punishment inflicted on him was deprivation of his books. Particularly conspicuous on his bookshelves were the works of Jules Verne, Mayne-Reid, Fenimore Cooper and Dickens—favourite authors among Russian children and adolescents at that time.[4] 'But I had no thought of becoming a writer,' he wrote subsequently, 'for almost

---

[1] *PNA*, p. 147.    [2] Vengerov (ed.), op. cit., p. 242.    [3] *PNA*, p. 145.
[4] A decade later Blok was reading works by the same authors. 'During these years,' writes Mochul'sky, 'Blok did not read much: the usual reading of young people in the nineties—Mayne-Reid, Fenimore Cooper, Jules Verne, Dickens' (K. Mochul'sky, *Aleksandr Blok*, Paris, 1948, p. 25).

from the time I was a baby I was passionately keen on painting.'[1] Again his mother was responsible for fostering this precociously displayed talent, even holding the pencil in his hand when he was too young to control it himself. He later blamed his failure to progress as a painter beyond 'fruitless dilettantism' on the absence of suitable schools and teachers in Oryol.[2]

Andreyev's relationship with his mother remained an extremely close one throughout his life. Although she had three other sons—Vsevolod, Pavel and Andrey—and two daughters, Rimma and Zinaida, her first thoughts were always for her 'Lenusha'. She idolized him—especially after the death of her husband in May 1888, when Andreyev, at the age of 17, assumed the responsibilities of head of the family. His own eldest son wrote half a century later:

For the 48 years of his life they parted rarely, a negligible number of times, and always pined without one another. . . . Not only we, her grandchildren, but even her children, my uncles and aunts, lived in the reflected light of this love. My grandmother loved us all, of course, but only my father enjoyed her unquestioning confidence. 'Lenusha said' was a law, a commandment, a gospel, and everyone who did not agree with Lenusha became her personal enemy.[3]

Andreyev's record in the Oryol *gimnaziya* is dated from 17 July 1882 and he studied there until 1891. He was a victim of the educational system, instituted in 1866, which laid an inordinate stress on teaching of the ancient languages as a means of curbing all potentially 'dangerous' inclinations. Grey and forbidding, staffed largely by Chekhovian 'men in cases', the typical *gimnaziya* was almost a microcosm of the Russia of the eighties. Every movement was closely supervised. 'At that time,' wrote Brusyanin in 1912, 'circles of self-education, as they were understood at the end of the last century, did not exist. *Gimnaziya* circles were restricted under conditions of vigilant observation by the class instructors.'[4] Andreyev, with the unusual strength of character and personality which he had inherited from his father, baulked from the beginning at this fetish for rules and regulations, of which he was subsequently to deliver scathing indictments in his early feuilletons. Yet at first he studied quite well and even received a certificate for good

[1] Vengerov (ed.), op. cit., p. 243.    [2] See ibid.    [3] *VLA*, May, p. 79.
[4] *BSN*, p. 36.

conduct[1]—an achievement which was not to be repeated. He progressed smoothly from class to class, but was hardly an exemplary student. He stood out against the grey student mass as a graphic protest. 'His gloomy, proud appearance, for which his comrades nicknamed him so aptly "the duke",' writes Fatov, 'his love of solitude, his contemptuous attitude to his studies at the *gimnaziya* and to the rules and teachers, which expressed itself in everything, beginning with his persistence in wearing his hair long, which was persecuted and punished by the authorities—all this sharply singled him out.'[2] He never completed his homework, and preferred to hasten to the *gimnaziya* early in the morning and participate in the 'co-operative' arrangement devised by a number of the students, according to which each performed for all the task for which he was best suited and which he most enjoyed. In accordance with this disposition, it frequently fell to Andreyev's lot to compose as many as six or seven Russian essays on the same topic. From the outset Russian composition was the one subject in which he excelled. Greek, Latin and mathematics were the main objects of his loathing. 'He had the reputation in the *gimnaziya*,' writes Pavel Andreyev, 'of a very capable, even talented student, but extremely indolent and reckless.'[3]

He was also conspicuous during his years at the *gimnaziya* for the unevenness of his temperament. His cousin Zoya Nikolaevna Pockowska recalls in her reminiscences: 'In a good mood he was gay, the soul of society, as they say, but suddenly he would become gloomy and at such times made everyone so miserable that it became quite unpleasant.'[4] When these serious moods descended upon him, he would take to his painting and books. ' "The despondent demon, the spirit of exile" with the face of the artist himself,' writes S. S. Blokhin, one of Andreyev's contemporaries at the *gimnaziya* and later at Moscow University, 'was the main theme of his sketches.'[5]

His passion for reading became more intense as the years passed, though his texts changed. 'Even during his years at the *gimnaziya*,' writes another contemporary, V. A. Elovsky, 'L. Andreyev began to read Hartmann, who was fashionable at that time, his "Philosophy of the Unconscious", and spoke a great deal about him at the *gimnaziya*.'[6] In the sixth class he also began to immerse himself in

---

[1] See *FTV*, p. 43.  [2] Ibid., p. 60.  [3] *PNA*, p. 149.  [4] *FTV*, p. 209.
[5] Ibid., p. 242.  [6] Ibid., p. 65.

Schopenhauer: 'And he quite tormented us,' writes Zoya Pockowska. 'You, he would say, think that the whole universe exists but this is only your idea, and perhaps even you yourself do not exist, for you are also only my idea.'[1] The conception of life which is reflected in his fiction was already in the process of formation.

By this time he had a wide knowledge of Russian and foreign literature and was well acquainted with the works of Russian critics and publicists—Belinsky, Pisarev, Dobrolyubov.[2] In Pisarev particularly he encountered that bold disrespect for traditional fetishes and institutions which was later to distinguish his own works. At the same time it is perhaps in his early reading of the works of the publicists of the sixties that we should seek the sources of his antipathy to the materialist, positivist view of the world—an antipathy which was, of course, fanned, to the subsequent chagrin of Gorky,[3] by his reading of Hartmann and Schopenhauer.

Thus the 'accursed questions' had already entered Andreyev's thoughts, and his fits of depression and excessive drinking caused him to regard them with a seriousness unnatural in a boy of his age. Bouts of drinking were invariably followed by periods of profound remorse, when he would conceal himself from the eyes of his family, and 'it demanded great efforts to return him to life again'.[4] Illustrative of his state of mind is the episode related by Brusyanin in which, at the age of 16, he lay beneath a train in order to 'test his fate'.[5] There were times when thoughts of suicide were never far from his mind. They were temporarily banished, however, by the death of his father when he was in the sixth class at the *gimnaziya*. The family was left with little more than the mortgaged house and Andreyev was compelled to devote his attention to more materialistic affairs. Like Pavel, the hero of his story *In Spring* (*Vesnoy*) (1902), he was momentarily 'resurrected' by the need to think of others; contact with sober reality was re-established.

Andreyev spent two years in the sixth class, and in the seventh his academic performance was worse than ever. The explanation is to be sought in another external circumstance—his first serious

[1] Ibid.    [2] See *PNA*, p. 149.

[3] Gorky wrote: 'Leonid Andreyev was intoxicated with the wine of Indo-Germanic philosophy. He succumbed under the weight of those books (i.e. Schopenhauer's *Die Welt als Wille und Vorstellung* and Hartmann's *Philosophie des Unbewussten*)' (A. M. Gorky, *Nesobrannye literaturno-kriticheskie stat'i*, M., 1941, p. 94).

[4] *PNA*, p. 152.    [5] *BSN*, p. 54. Cf. also *FTV*, p. 65.

romantic attachment. The girl in question was a student in the eighth class, who is referred to by memoirists as Zinaida Nikolaevna Sib-va. The romance had a significant effect on Andreyev's developing attitude to life. It gave him his first insight into and experience of the power of sex—an experience which was rendered all the more acute by the unpredictable, even cruel nature of Zinaida Nikolaevna. Here Andreyev made his first acquaintance with the seeming illogicality of the female mind, which was later to become an important theme in his fiction. He suffered greatly from his infatuation which outlasted his final two years at the *gimnaziya* and continued to plague him at the University of St. Petersburg. The source of his suffering was his sensitivity to the fact that he was no longer master of himself, that he was subject to the dispensation of a force which controlled the lives of men with a total lack of discrimination. The extent of his preoccupation with this problem is noted by his contemporary at the *gimnaziya* I. N. Sevast'yanov: '. . . questions of sex agitated Andreyev, and it can be said that in his personal life the problem of sex occupied an eminent, if not the dominant, role.'[1] Andreyev wrote in his diary on 29 March 1892:

Love is a great force. It summons to life all that is best in man. It awakens the desire to be perfect, to be better than others. It serves as a great stimulus to work and development. But unfortunately not all love has this effect; only love of the elevated and beautiful, whether it be a human being or an idea, is capable of elevating the lover and endowing him with beauty. But woe to man if his love is directed towards a base, vulgar object! In time the subject will resemble and merge with the object in its baseness and mediocrity. And it is indiscriminate. It acknowledges neither the elevated nor the base. It surrenders man indifferently to the power of the basest woman or the highest ideal. And this is little dependent on the qualities of a man. On the contrary, it is even accepted that intelligent men rarely love intelligent women and vice-versa. And life has surrendered me to the power of love—I will not say love of a vulgar, base woman, but a mediocre woman, a woman who is devoid of a reasoned and clearly conceived ideal. And I have been in the power of this woman for more than a year.[2]

This entry has been quoted at length, for it illustrates well the way in which Andreyev was wont, even at this early age, to expand

[1] *FTV*, p. 229.    [2] *PNA*, p. 153.

beyond his personal experience and come to far-reaching conclusions on fundamental problems of life. It exhibits the restless-
ness of his mind, his natural inclination to probe the fabric of life,
his perplexity in the face of the irrational. This relentless 'anatom-
ical' approach to life, combined with his assiduous reading of
German philosophy, was the embryo from which by degrees issued
the crystallized conception of life which constitutes the intellectual
framework of his fiction.

In the final analysis, excessive influence on Andreyev's intellectual development should not be ascribed to the *gimnaziya*,
except in so far as it enormously intensified his instinctive hostility
to every semblance of restraint which man sought to impose on his
opportunities for living a full and varied life. His development took
place in detachment from the *gimnaziya*; it was essentially a lonely
process of introspection, self-analysis and undisciplined reading.
Hence the remark which he made some years later to Brusyanin:
'. . . I recall the *gimnaziya* without animosity or sorrow. . . . The
"men in cases" did not kill my optimism.'[1] Though still under the
spell of Zinaida Nikolaevna Sib-va, he succeeded in the eighth
class, with the aid of a little prompting,[2] in passing the final examinations. The 'testimonial of maturity' (*attestat zrelosti*) which
he received in the spring of 1891 at once rendered him eligible for
a place at a university, and the following August he was admitted
to the Faculty of Jurisprudence in the University of St. Petersburg.

His choice of St. Petersburg as distinct from Moscow, where it
was more normal for Oryol students to proceed, is explained by the
presence there of Zinaida Nikolaevna Sib-va, who was attending a
series of courses. The two years which he spent there were in every
way disastrous and are best described in the words which he wrote
in his diary on 27 March 1892, i.e. towards the end of his first
year:

I have lived in this 'centre of intellectual life' for about a year, and when
I recently added up my acquisitions in the field of intellectual development, I was horrified. Not only have I not acquired anything—although
this environment at freezing-point is itself devoid of anything progressive
—but I have even lost much. . . . The reasons for the intellectual state
which I have called in myself obtuseness lie . . . in the fact that for the
last two years I have given myself wholly to a life of feeling, which has
completely suppressed and erased the life of my mind. The time which

[1] *BSN*, p. 18.    [2] See *FTV*, p. 61.

for others has marked the beginning of the flowering of all intellectual powers has been for me the beginning of an era of love in all its bad aspects.[1]

Almost the entire period appears to have been spent in agonizing and hopeless conflict with the 'dark power' which both fascinated and repelled him. The situation was not resolved until Zinaida Nikolaevna finally left him to marry an engineer with whom she subsequently departed for Siberia. Shortly afterwards Andreyev attempted to commit suicide. Her departure was unquestionably the main reason, rather than the oppressive 'social atmosphere' in which Brusyanin sought the explanation; Andreyev was much too confirmed an individualist to react so violently to social circumstance, although his environment and conditions of life in general certainly exacerbated his frustration and despair. 'Remorse, reproaches of the conscience,' he wrote in his diary some months later (5 April 1893), 'and, on the other hand, the illusory or real impossibility of changing my conduct, of halting on the downward plane, made my position inextricable. There was only one outlet—suicide.'[2]

In June 1893, after spending about eight months in Oryol, he was sent down from the university for failing to pay his fees and in the autumn he enrolled at the University of Moscow. Distance from St. Petersburg and all that he associated with it worked a temporary change in his mood. Attempting to explain his feeling of 'regeneration', he wrote in his diary:

Above all, the environment has disappeared. The question 'why?', which deprived me of all energy, has for a long time, more than a year, presented itself with increasing rarity, and six months have now passed without it presenting itself at all. . . . Due to the disappearance of the question 'why?', atheism and other disgusting views have lost their power. The second important sign of rebirth, which issues from the first, is a conscious desire to live. It began to appear a long time ago, but in fits and starts, and became constant only after the well-known (suicide) attempt. Finally, the third is a desire to work, which is still very weak. Evidently it complements the first two signs as the preparation for a whole world-outlook, and when it is effective it will mean that the rebirth has taken place. But this, it seems, will not happen at once, and I will have to remain for a very long time in the abominable

[1] *PNA*, p. 154.     [2] Ibid., p. 157.

state of transition until the fetters which bind my will to the past are finally rent asunder.[1]

His *modus vivendi* during his first two years in Moscow presented little evidence of this 'transition', however, and he soon abandoned himself to the round of debauchery in which so many students sought refuge in the eighties and early nineties—the life vividly portrayed in his works by Garin-Mikhaylovsky. 'Andreyev himself was a typical representative of this student-body,' writes Sevast'-yanov.[2] Again the immediate cause was an unrequited passion—on this occasion for a certain Antonova, a former *gimnazistka* at Oryol. In January 1894 he tried to shoot himself, but the bullet struck a button on his tunic and inflicted only a flesh-wound. Soon afterwards, in a state of intoxication, he attempted to cut his throat with a razor, but was saved, at considerable risk to himself, by a comrade, one Krechetnikov.[3]

In April and May 1894 he took and passed the mid-course examinations which he had not taken at St. Petersburg and then returned for the summer to Oryol. The autumn of that year witnessed the beginning of a new period in his life; his ties with Oryol were weakened when his mother moved with the children to Moscow. Looking back on this first period of his brother's life and endeavouring to give a balanced judgement of it, Pavel Andreyev writes:

. . . I must say that there were moments of cheerfulness and complete lightheartedness, and they were often of quite long duration. At such times our house was filled all day with laughter from his (Leonid's) jokes, witticisms and manifold pranks. It would be wrong to imagine him as a person who was gloomy in company and absorbed in himself. In society he was a gay, interesting and witty conversationalist. But social life was foreign to him. In the circles and fraternities of which he was one of the main members he frequently read papers and various kinds of report, always introducing interest and passion into his arguments. . . . Nevertheless, it should be mentioned that at that time he was little interested in politics. He was interested in questions of a quite different order—questions of a philosophical character.[4]

As at the *gimnaziya*, therefore, his intellectual development remained essentially an individual process and was little influenced

[1] Ibid., p. 158.   [2] *FTV*, p. 228.   [3] See ibid., p. 88.   [4] *PNA*, pp. 166-7.

by the intellectual life of the university. The ideas of Karl Marx, which in the mid-nineties began to fill the intellectual vacuum of student life, and the maturing conflict between Marxism and Populism failed absolutely to arouse his enthusiasm. Schopenhauer and Hartmann remained his principal intellectual nourishment.

His life changed radically with the arrival of his family. He became more settled and devoted much of his time to reading and writing. The family lived constantly under the threat of starvation and in reference to this period he wrote many years later: 'It should be remembered that I am a man who has been wounded' for ever . . . by poverty, which we experienced so acutely, and fear of it is firmly implanted in my subconscious, constantly giving birth to dark thoughts and images.'[1] In these thoughts and images lies the source of the powerful pictures of destitution which distinguish a number of his early stories and his plays *Tsar Hunger* (*Tsar' Golod*) (1907) and *Anathema* (*Anatema*) (1909). Moreover, it is noteworthy that it was hunger which had inspired his very first literary attempt—a story called *About a Hungry Student* (*O golodnom studente*), written in 1891–2 in St. Petersburg. 'My first literary experiment was prompted,' he stated in 1910, 'not by any inclination towards literature, but by hunger.'[2] Nevertheless, hi spirits were generally high during this third year in Moscow. 'Although we were cold and hungry,' writes his brother, 'I often remember Leonid gay and active.'[3]

It was in 1895 that a number of his stories appeared in print. After his first literary attempts had been rejected by the press of the capitals—by the journals *Severnyy vestnik* ('The Northern Herald'), *Nedelya* and *Niva*—he turned to the provinces, and one of his stories, entitled *He, She and Vodka* (*On, ona i vodka*), was

---

[1] Ibid., p. 168.

[2] Vengerov (ed.), op. cit., p. 244. The story was rejected by the editorial board of the journal *Nedelya* ('The Week'); '. . . they returned it to me,' recalled Andreyev, 'with a smile' (ibid.). But an entry in his diary of 17 April 1892, a letter of the same date to a close acquaintance in Oryol, Lyubov' Nikolaevna Dmitrieva, and a letter of 28 April 1892 to the same addressee indicate that it was published in the journal *Zvezda* ('The Star'). The Soviet scholar L. Iezuitova recently discovered in the one surviving number of the journal from this period— dated 19 April 1892—a story 'about a hungry student' entitled *In Cold and Gold* (*V kholode i zolote*) and adduces conclusive proof that it is the story to which Andreyev referred in 1910 (see L. Iezuitova, 'Pervyy rasskaz Leonida Andreyeva', *Russkaya literatura*, 1963, No. 2, pp. 184–5).

[3] *PNA*, p. 168.

accepted by *Orlovskiy vestnik* ('The Oryol Herald'),[1] one of the
most progressive provincial newspapers of that time. Two more of
his works were published by the same paper in 1895: on 25
October appeared a sketch entitled *A Students' Concert (Studen-
cheskiy kontsert)*[2] and a month later—a long story called *The
Mystery (Zagadka)*.[3] All these stories were largely autobiographical.

At this time Andreyev was in his fourth year at the university
and the following spring he was due to sit for the state examinations. He felt so incompetent, however, despite his regular attend-
ance at lectures, that he decided to postpone his attempt until the
following year. The decision was prompted partly by the fact that
the examinations had been brought forward and were scheduled to
extend from March until 5 May, so that they would not clash with
the coronation of Nicholas II. April 1896 found him in excellent
spirits. He wrote to Sof'ya Dmitrievna Panova on the 21st of that
month: '. . . there are no bounds to my good conduct. I have
drunk no vodka since the first day of Holy Week. I am not in love.
I feel very gay. I am sketching endlessly. I have painted as many
as ten very successful portraits and I am receiving orders. I go for
strolls. I drink tea. My teeth are aching.'[4] The sketches to which he
refers were an invaluable source of income for the struggling family.
At first he charged three to five roubles per portrait and later, when
he improved, ten or even twelve.[5] He also earned a further thirty
copecks a day by working in the inquiry office of the newspaper
*Russkoe slovo* ('The Russian Word').

In June 1896 he was heartened by the publication of yet another
of his stories in *Orlovskiy vestnik*—an unfinished work called *The
Odd Fellow (Chudak)*.[6] He spent the summer of that year giving
private lessons in a *dacha* at Tsaritsyno, situated about twelve miles
from Moscow, and it was there that he met Aleksandra Mikhaylovna Veligorskaya, another former *gimnazistka* at Oryol, who six
years later was to become his wife.[7] Despite the remarks which he

[1] It appeared in *Orlovskiy vestnik*, 1895, 9 September, No. 240, and was
signed 'L.A.'.
[2] *Orlovskiy vestnik*, 25 October 1895, No. 285.
[3] *Orlovskiy vestnik*, 21, 24–25 November 1895, Nos. 312, 315–16.
[4] *FTV*, pp. 109–10.
[5] Cf. Andreyev's autobiographical sketch of 1903: *MAMR*, p. 100.
[6] *Orlovskiy vestnik*, 29 June 1896, No. 169.
[7] Through an aunt Aleksandra Mikhaylovna was distantly related to the
Ukrainian national poet Taras Shevchenko.

made in his letter to Sof'ya Dmitrievna Panova, however, more than a year passed before he finally succeeded in shaking off his infatuation with Antonova. He came to see her as a symbol of death, while associating Aleksandra Mikhaylovna with life and light.

He completed the state examinations of 27 May 1897. Although he received the mark 'excellent' (*ves'ma*) in six out of the ten papers, he was awarded the status of *deystvitel'nyy student*—a title which denoted the equivalent of a second-class degree. Almost immediately he found employment in Moscow as assistant to the barrister Pavel Nikolaevich Malyantovich, who twenty years later was to become Minister of Justice in Kerensky's government.[1] Paradoxically it was this appointment which set him on the path to literary fame.

Towards the end of August 1897 Malyantovich received an invitation to contribute accounts of cases in the courts to the newspaper *Moskovskiy vestnik* ('The Moscow Herald') from its secretary, I. D. Novik. As the circulation of the paper was small and it could afford to pay no more than two copecks a line, the barrister offered the task to his young assistant. Andreyev was finding it increasingly difficult to support his family on his salary and meagre supplementary earnings and he gratefully accepted. His unorthodox reports were immediately successful; Novik describes them in the following words:

L(eonid) N(ikolaevich) kept to a specific manner. He ignored the protocol aspect and concentrated his whole attention on the general picture of the court-sittings. He was interested not in the dead process, but in the living face of the defendant. The court, the prosecutor and the barrister occupied a secondary position in his reports. The whole attention of the reader was concentrated on the defendant, on the circumstances which had brought him to the dock and on his experiences during the trial itself. In the end, a psychological study was obtained in which everything of primary importance in the trial from the point of

---

[1] Six years later (9 September 1903) Malyantovich was to defend Andreyev himself in court against the charge of arranging a literary soirée (on 12 December 1902) for charity, enabling Skitalets to read his poem *The Psaltery Player* (*Guslyar*) which had not been passed by the censor; the events of that evening are described in Skitalets (S. G. Petrov), *Povesti i rasskazy. Vospominaniya*, M., 1960, pp. 429–30. Andreyev was acquitted, but a protest was lodged and the case was reopened in 1904; on this occasion he was fined 25 roubles 'for disturbing the peace' (see *MAMR*, p. 77).

view of the conflicting parties was left in the shade and served only as a background for the hero of the trial—the defendant.[1]

Soon afterwards Novik informed him that an event was about to take place which could transform his entire career. A new paper, *Kur'er* ('The Courier'), larger and more wealthy than *Moskovskiy vestnik*, was being organized under the editorship of Ya. A. Feygin,[2] and he, Novik, had been invited to assume the post of secretary of the editorial board. He invited Andreyev to work for *Kur'er* in the same capacity as he was working for *Moskovskiy vestnik*. Andreyev accepted and the first edition of the paper, dated 6 November 1897, carried one of his reports.

For a time he continued to perform simultaneously the duties of barrister's assistant and reporter, spending six or seven hours a day in the courts and the nights at the editorial office and printing-house reading proofs. He summed up his legal career in the following brief paragraph in his autobiographical sketch of 1903: 'Through lack of time, I did not succeed in achieving a legal practice. In all, I had only one civil case which I lost on all points, and a few un-remunerated criminal defences.'[3] This description creates a false impression of incompetence and almost apathy. In fact, he took the work no less seriously than he did everything else and performed with a measure of success. The extent to which the work intrigued him is conveyed by the following entry in his diary of November 1898:

Soon I am due to act as defending-counsel. If only they knew the full meaning of this word: 'defending-counsel'! From nought to infinity. And fear, and a kind of underground faith in oneself, in one's powers, a thirst for renown, fame—a thousand devils fight in my head when I think of what will happen.[4]

But the work did not satisfy him. Devoting his time to the problems of others, he had little time to think of the problems which constantly filled his own mind. He also took exception to his fellow-members of the profession who, for the most part, were narrow specialists temperamentally foreign to him. He felt increasingly the

---

[1] I. D. Novik, 'Leonid Andreyev. (Materialy dlya biografii)', *Russkiy emigrant*, Berlin, 1920, No. 3, p. 14.

[2] Yakov Aleksandrovich Feygin (1859–1915) was well known not only as an editor but also for his translations of Bjornstjerne Bjornson, Schnitzler and Mirbeau. In 1900 he also published a critical study of Ibsen.

[3] *MAMR*, p. 100.     [4] *PNA*, p. 183.

powerful attraction of literature in which he could raise the mightiest questions. At the same time he was conscious of the value of the experience which he was acquiring in the courts; some years later he confided to Brusyanin:

In my youth I was generally lacking in public spirit, but the court, constant intercourse with people, observation of them in an unusual environment and, finally, the secrets of others' lives which were revealed in the course of the trials—all this unfurled before me the secrets of living people. Dramas and comedies in court showed me the lives of those people whom we know in the form of a crowd, *en masse*.[1]

Thus he valued the work primarily for the insight which it afforded him into the psychology of the average man. It narrowed the gap which had always existed between himself and the life of society at large, introducing him to a variety of types and situations. In addition, his writing of reports taught him to focus his whole attention on a single question; it disciplined him and compelled him to concentrate and compress his style. In short, it was a valuable school for the budding writer, even though he soon came to find it tedious and burdensome.[2]

He continued for a short period to work both for *Moskovskiy vestnik* and *Kur'er* and then went over entirely to the latter. His reports quickly made an impression both on the reading-public and on his colleagues at the offices of *Kur'er*. 'To me personally, through whose hands passed all L(eonid) N(ikolaevich)'s remarks,' writes Novik, 'it was quite clear that we had before us not a legal chronicler, but an artist—a writer who still did not know himself.'[3] Early in January 1898 Novik asked him whether he had committed any 'literary misdemeanours', to which Andreyev replied in the negative. This was, of course, a plain falsehood, even if we do not count the works which he had had published in *Orlovskiy vestnik* and those which had been rejected. Despite his busy life of affairs, he had still found time to write, and Osip Volzhanin, the head of the editorial board of *Moskovskiy vestnik* in 1897-8, recalls a number

---

[1] *BSN*, p. 57.

[2] Bewailing the shortage of time at his disposal for the writing of stories, he remarked to Mirolyubov, for example, in a letter of 17 August 1900: 'But it is regrettable that the daily scribbling for *Kur'er* gives me no opportunity to work and exhausts me' (*MAMR*, p. 76). For a similar comment on his attitude to the work see his letter to Mikhaylovsky of 31 October 1901, *MAMK*, p, 51.

[3] Novik, loc. cit., p. 14.

of stories which Andreyev showed to him during this period.[1] It is not surprising, therefore, that a few days later he presented Novik with a tattered exercise-book containing one such 'misdemeanour'. By 1921, when he wrote his reminiscences, Novik could recall little about it. 'I remember only,' he writes, 'that the content of the story was fantastic. The action took place somewhere between heaven and earth. The hero of the story reasoned for a very long time about something and aspired to something elevated.'[2] He advised Andreyev to 'descend to earth'. But the appearance three years later of Andreyev's stories *Laughter* (*Smekh*) and *The Wall* (*Stena*) caused him to regret that he had not kept this early work. 'It was the embryo, as it were,' he states, 'of his later works.'[3]

Andreyev soon became one of the most active collaborators on the paper and veered further and further from his purely legal career. Quite often two or three of his articles appeared in a single edition. A revealing, though somewhat biased, picture of life at the editorial office is given by P. A. Kogan, who after 1917 became Professor of Literature at the University of Moscow and was at this time one of the principal members of the sizeable Marxist group of workers on the paper:

. . . among the collaborators there was a firmly united ideological group of Marxist young men—myself, Fridman, V. M. Friche, V. Shulyatikov, and others. Our 'idealism' expressed itself mainly in our determined struggle to avoid the tone of a 'gutter newspaper' and our attempts to achieve equality with *Russkie vedomosti*. As a result, the paper began to enjoy undoubted success among the left-wing intelligentsia and especially among the students. . . . Andreyev did not enter our Marxist group and not only did not contribute to our struggle to make the tone of the paper more serious, but even hindered it sometimes, for so far as tone was concerned he generally experienced no scruples. There were often stormy arguments on the editorial board, especially when the collaborators were merry, and certain members of our Marxist group were also guilty of this sin. I remember, for instance, a heated argument between L. Andreyev and V. Shulyatikov on the question of whether Andreyev was a pessimist or not. Andreyev endeavoured to prove that he was not; Shulyatikov, who had drunk a great deal, shouted and swore and maintained that Andreyev had arrested the course of progress by $1\frac{1}{2}$ months.[4]

[1] Cf. O. Volzhanin, 'L. N. Andreyev na zare literaturnoy deyatel'nosti', *Vestnik literatury*, 1920, No. 3, pp. 2–5.
[2] Novik, loc. cit., 1920, No. 4, p. 10.    [3] Ibid.    [4] *FTV*, pp. 307–8.

Russian literature was Shulyatikov's province, while Friche wrote regular articles on foreign literature. Other contributors were V. A. Gol'tsev, a member of the editorial board of the journal *Russkaya mysl'* ('Russian Thought'), P. A. Sakulin, the future Professor and historian of Russian literature, Lunacharsky, Chekhov, Gorky, Veresaev, Chirikov, Ivan Bunin, Zaytsev,[1] Serafimovich,[2] Meyerkhol'd, Mamin-Sibiryak, Gusev-Orenburgsky, Skitalets, Teleshov, Bal'mont, Chulkov, Nemirovich-Danchenko, and Anastasiya Verbitskaya.

Andreyev did not have to wait long for his next opportunity to write a purely literary work. Towards the end of March 1898 he was asked by Novik to contribute an Easter story. He wrote *Bargamot and Garas'ka*, which was immediately accepted and published.[3] From this time onwards he contributed stories at quite regular intervals and also small, topical feuilletons published under the general title of *Impressions* (*Vpechatleniya*) and usually signed 'L-ev'. On Sundays he wrote larger feuilletons which were signed 'James Linch'.[4]

His literary career is usually dated from the appearance of *Bargamot and Garas'ka*. The editorial board was delighted with the work and on the first anniversary of the paper he was honoured together with the 'celebrities'. According to his brother, his own opinion of the story was not too high and he was surprised by the praise that was heaped upon it.[5] But it had already made an

---

[1] The help which Andreyev gave to Zaytsev in the early stages of his literary career is comparable to that which he himself received from Gorky. Impressed by his first literary efforts, which were sent to *Kur'er*, Andreyev put him in contact with Mirolyubov (who did not publish any of his works, however, until 1906 when *The Factory* (*Zavod*) appeared in the fourth number of *Zhurnal dlya vsekh*) and subsequently introduced him to the 'Wednesday' group (see *MAMR*, pp. 87–8).

[2] It was Andreyev who invited Serafimovich to come to Moscow from the south in order to work for the paper (see A. Serafimovich, 'Vospominaniya o Gor'kom', in *M. Gor'kiy v vospominaniyakh sovremennikov*, M., 1955, p. 63). Their association quickly developed into a close friendship (see I. A. Belousov, *Literaturnaya Sreda. Vospominaniya, 1880–1928*, M., 1928, p. 127). Like Zaytsev, Serafimovich was subsequently introduced by Andreyev to the 'Wednesday' group.

[3] It appeared in *Kur'er*, 1898, No. 94, 5 April.

[4] Andreyev's most common pseudonyms were A., A-ev, A-ev L., James Linch, L.A., and L-ev.

[5] See *PNA*, p. 192. When the story was republished four years later in the journal *Narodnoe blago* ('The National Good'), Andreyev changed the sentimental ending of the first redaction.

impression in another quarter. Its appearance coincided with the suspension of the newspaper *Nizhegorodskiy listok* ('The Nizhniy-Novgorod News-sheet')[1] to which Gorky subscribed. The request of the paper's editorial board that *Kur'er* be issued to its subscribers was granted and in this way Andreyev's first successful literary effort for *Kur'er* fell into the hands of Gorky, who at that time was at the height of his fame. Gorky reacted at once. 'In the Easter number of the Moscow paper *Kur'er*,' he wrote to Mirolyubov, 'there is a story "Bargamot and Garas'ka" by Leonid Andreyev—you should bear this Leonid in mind.'[2] Shortly afterwards Andreyev was informed at the editorial offices of *Kur'er* that a letter from Gorky had been delivered by the publicist and critic N. P. Asheshov, who worked for the paper, inquiring about the identity of the writer who used the pseudonym 'Leonid Andreyev'. The long and stormy friendship of Andreyev and Gorky and also Andreyev's rapid climb to fame can be dated from his reply to this letter. Through Gorky he made three highly important contacts.

The first was with Mirolyubov, whose attempt to provide in *Zhurnal dlya vsekh* a journal of the highest quality for the nominal annual subscription of one rouble had won the active support and encouragement of most progressive writers of the time. By September 1898, when Mirolyubov became co-editor with the journal's founder D. A. Genika, its circulation figure was 15,000 and was rapidly increasing.[3] In April 1899 Gorky suggested to Andreyev that he send a story to Mirolyubov.[4] Illness resulting from his heavy work for *Kur'er*, however, prevented Andreyev from acting on this advice until 30 July when he sent to Mirolyubov a new story entitled *Pet'ka at the Dacha* (*Pet'ka na dache*) which was published in *Zhurnal dlya vsekh* two months later (September). This was the first of the many stories by Andreyev which Mirolyubov was to publish in his popular journal, and Andreyev's letter of 30 July which accompanied the manuscript marked the beginning of their copious correspondence. It was a relationship which

---

[1] The suspension lasted from 9 February to 9 May 1898.

[2] *M. Gor'kiy. Materialy i issledovaniya*, III, edited by S. D. Balukhatyy and V. A. Desnitsky, M.-L., 1941, p. 24.

[3] See *MAMR*, p. 66. Mirolyubov assumed complete control over the journal in February 1899. By 1904 its circulation had reached 90,000.

[4] See 'Novyy tom "Literaturnogo Nasledstva". Neizdannaya perepiska. A. M. Gor'kiy i Leonid Andreyev', *Literaturnaya gazeta*, 1957, No. 73, 18 June, p. 2; and *LN*, p. 64.

Andreyev prized almost as highly as that with Gorky. He wrote to Mirolyubov on 23 March 1900: 'In general, fate has not stroked me on the head, but this time it surprises me: from the beginning I have encountered such great support as you and Aleksey Maksimovich.'[1] The acute and sometimes mercilessly critical comments of Mirolyubov on his stories were welcomed by the young writer, and the more severe they were, the more he esteemed them. 'Judge it a little more severely,' he wrote in the same letter of 23 March 1900 in reference to his story *On the River* (*Na reke*) which was published in *Zhurnal dlya vsekh* the following May.[2]

The second valuable contact which Andreyev made through Gorky was with the so-called 'Wednesday' (*Sreda*) group of writers formed in 1899 by N. D. Teleshov at whose apartment they met every Wednesday. It was the heir of a similar group formed, with the name of 'The Parnassus' (*Parnas*), by Teleshov in the mideighties.[3] The importance of the latter lies simply in the fact that it was the antecedent and prototype of the 'Wednesday' group which played a significant role in Russian literary life in the years leading up to the revolution of 1905–6. It continued to exist until 1918. Regular members of the group, besides Teleshov, were Ivan and Yuliy Bunin, Veresaev, Gol'tsev, Serafimovich, I. A. Belousov, Razumovsky, N. I. Timkovsky, S. S. Gologoushev[4] and Naydyonov. There were also periodic visits by writers from other cities: by Gorky and Korolenko from Nizhniy Novgorod, Kuprin, Garin-Mikhaylovsky and Chirikov from St. Petersburg, Chekhov and Elpat'evsky from the Crimea, and A. M. Fyodorov and Yushkevich from Odessa. Shalyapin, Rachmaninov and actors of the Moscow Art Theatre not infrequently attended, and older writers like Zlatovratsky and Mamin-Sibiryak made occasional appearances. Even Bryusov and Bal'mont were sometimes seen among this gathering of 'realists'.

The purpose of the meetings is described by Veresaev:

Writers read in the circle their new works, which were then subjected to the criticism of those present. It was a basic condition that opinions

---

[1] *MAMR*, p. 75.   [2] Ibid., p. 74.

[3] See I. A. Belousov, *Literaturnaya Sreda. Vospominaniya, 1880–1928*, M., 1928, p. 107.

[4] Sergey Sergeyevich Gologoushev (1855–1920) was a doctor of medicine and a literary and art critic who used the pseudonym 'Sergey Glagol' '. He was to become one of Andreyev's closest friends.

be expressed with complete frankness and a basic demand that no criticism be taken amiss. And the criticism was often cruel, crushing, with the result that certain more conceited members avoided reading their works at the 'Wednesdays'.[1]

Skitalets refers to the meetings as a 'purgatory through which passed each new work of the participant before it went to press' and mentions Yuliy Bunin as a particularly severe and penetrating critic.[2] Political and social questions were also discussed, but rarely and with the reluctance of most of the members.

The election of new members was carried out with great care. 'Before accepting any writer into their comradely society,' writes Belousov, 'the old members of the "Wednesdays" inspected him and made his acquaintance at the so-called extraordinary "Wednesdays" which assembled at the apartment of S. S. Goloushev.'[3] Andreyev does not appear to have undergone this ritualistic examination. Gorky simply wrote to Teleshov on 20 November 1900: 'I would like you to draw him closer to you. In my opinion he is an excellent fellow and talented,'[4] and soon afterwards introduced him to the members at one of their normal meetings. Andreyev took with him a story called *Silence* (*Molchanie*). He was too nervous to read it himself and the duty was performed by Gorky. Teleshov offers the following version of what happened afterwards:

Mirolyubov, who was amongst us . . ., went up to Andreyev, took the exercise-book from him and put it in his pocket. Andreyev's eyes gleamed. There was a great difference between publication in Mirolyubov's journal with its good reputation and huge number of subscribers and readers and publication in the insignificant Moscow newspaper *Kur'er*, on which he had worked up to that time.[5]

---

[1] *VRSV*, p. 453.

[2] Skitalets, *Povesti i rasskazy. Vospominaniya*, M., 1960, p. 422.

[3] Belousov, op. cit., p. 110.

[4] *M. Gor'kiy v vospominaniyakh sovremennikov*, M., 1955, p. 175.

[5] N. D. Teleshov, 'Pro Leonida Andreyeva', in his *Vsyo prokhodit. Iz literaturnykh vospominaniy*, M., 1927, p. 64. It appears that Teleshov was unaware that Andreyev had known Mirolyubov by that time for more than a year and had already had stories published in *Zhurnal dlya vsekh*. Moreover, for several months before this Mirolyubov had known of the existence of *Silence*; Andreyev had informed him that the work was complete three months previously in a letter of 20 August (see *MAMR*, p. 76). Nor did Andreyev grasp quite so eagerly as Teleshov implies at the chance to have the story published in *Zhurnal dlya vsekh*; he considered it to be worth more than Mirolyubov was accustomed to pay and in a letter of September to the latter he suggested that they discuss the matter (see ibid., p. 79). Early in October, however, he wrote another letter to

From this time onward Andreyev hardly missed a meeting and they were frequently held at his apartment.[1] All the works which he wrote in Moscow passed through the 'purgatory' and he listened attentively and without taking offence to the severest criticism. Some conception of the importance which he attached to it is conveyed by the fact that he did not publish those works to which the members took especial exception.[2]

By the spring of 1901 a number of Andreyev's stories had been published in *Kur'er* and *Zhurnal dlya vsekh* and he expressed the desire to have them collected and published as a separate volume. As early as October 1900 he had asked Mirolyubov if he could suggest a St. Petersburg publisher.[3] His request was difficult to meet. He was still little known outside the literary circles of the capitals and his name was still unfamiliar to the main publishers. He was introduced, however, to the publisher I. D. Sytin who paid him 350 roubles for the manuscript[4] and placed it in reserve. The months passed and still it did not appear. While it lay in the publisher's hands the co-operative publishing-house *Znanie* ('Knowledge') was formed in St. Petersburg with K. P. Pyatnitsky at its head. Gorky, who, as well as being the main contributor and an important investor in the concern also played a prominent part in its management and administration, introduced Andreyev at once and an agreement was made to publish the book. An important role in engineering its publication was also played by V. A. Posse,

---

Mirolyubov containing profuse apologies for his materialistic approach (see ibid.), and on receiving from him a few days later an understanding letter he immediately considered the matter closed. Thus the destination of the story was already decided before the episode described by Teleshov and it appeared in the December (1900) number of *Zhurnal dlya vsekh* (pp. 1427–38) with a dedication to E. M. Dobrova, the sister of Aleksandra Mikhaylovna Veligorskaya.

[1] There was a vogue among the members of the group of giving one another nicknames. The new recruit Andreyev was named *Bol'shoy Novoproektirovannyy Pereulok* ('Big Newly-Planned Lane'), perhaps because of his striking originality and the hopes which were laid on him (see N. D. Teleshov, 'A. P. Chekhov', in *Chekhov v vospominaniyakh sovremennikov*, M., 1954, p. 443).

[2] Cf. V. L'vov-Rogachevsky, *Dve pravdy. Kniga o Leonide Andreyeve*, SPb., 1914, p. 213.

[3] Cf. *MAMR*, p. 82.

[4] Cf. Andreyev's letter to Mikhaylovsky of October 1902, *MAMK*, p. 60. Teleshov mistakenly states in his reminiscences that the sum was 500 roubles (cf. Teleshov, 'Pro Leonida Andreyeva', p. 65); this is the sum that was afterwards offered to Andreyev by *Znanie* together with all the profits from sales (cf. *LN*, p. 408).

the editor of *Zhizn'* ('Life') and a shareholder in *Znanie*, who assisted Gorky in the editing of publications. On repayment of the 350 roubles, the manuscript was reacquired from Sytin and immediately dispatched to the printers.

The book came out on 17 September 1901 with a dedication to Gorky; it cost eighty copecks and contained ten stories: *The Grand Slam (Bol'shoy shlem), The Little Angel (Angelochek), Silence, Valya, The Story of Sergey Petrovich (Rasskaz o Sergeye Petroviche), On the River, The Lie (Lozh'), By the Window (U okna), Once upon a Time There Lived (Zhili-byli)* and *Into the Dark Distance (V tyomnuyu dal')*. Its success exceeded Andreyev's highest expectations. He was to write a year later: 'Today it is a year since I published the volume and it is already in its fourth edition—the eighteenth thousand'![1] Instead of the 350 roubles offered by Sytin he received from *Znanie* in the course of that year the regal sum of 6,000 roubles.[2] Criticism was almost unanimously favourable. His triumph was crowned by the long letter of congratulation which he received from Mikhaylovsky and the eulogistic article, devoted entirely to the volume, which the latter published in the November number of his journal *Russkoe bogatstvo* ('Russian Wealth').[3] At that time a complimentary article by Mikhaylovsky was a major goal of every young writer. A further mark of Andreyev's success was the offer which he received from Mirolyubov in that same month (November) to become co-editor of *Zhurnal dlya vsekh*—an offer which he was forced to decline because of his family's commitments in Moscow.[4] Another venerable critic who acclaimed the appearance of the 'new star' in the firmament of Russian literature was Yasinsky who, like Mikhaylovsky, was struck by the refreshing originality of the stories.[5] Shortly afterwards the Moscow Art Club

[1] Letter to Mikhaylovsky of September or October 1902, *MAMK*, p. 58.
[2] See ibid., p. 60. Gorky had predicted a sum of 1,200 roubles (cf. *LN*, p. 94).
[3] N. K. Mikhaylovsky, 'Literatura i zhizn'. Rasskazy L. Andreyeva. Strakh smerti i strakh zhizni', *Russkoe bogatstvo*, 1901, No. 11, pp. 58–74.
[4] See Andreyev's letter to Mirolyubov of 18 November 1901, *MAMR*, p. 91.
[5] See I. I. Yasinsky (M. Chunosov), 'Nevyskazannoe', *Ezhemesyachnye sochineniya*, 1901, No. 12, pp. 377–84. It was perhaps in memory of this laudatory article that a decade later Andreyev sent a telegram to Yasinsky congratulating him on his completion of forty years as a critic, writing somewhat floridly: 'I bow low to the beauty of your grey hair, the beauty of your mind and heart. Spend this day radiantly and joyously' (G.L.I., 'Torzhestvennoe chestvovanie I. I. Yasinskogo. (Po sluchayu 40-letiya ego literaturnoy deyatel'nosti)', *Istoricheskiy vestnik*, 1911, No. 2, p. 704). Even by the time that he wrote the article in 1901 Yasinsky, who was responsible for the publication of the newspaper

did Andreyev the honour of devoting an entire meeting to a discussion of the book.[1] On 4 February 1902 he wrote in jocular vein
to Oryol: '. . . now my every step is becoming known the following day and is distortedly commentated.'[2] In the same letter he
informed his relatives that the first edition of the collection of stories
had already sold out and that it was due to be reprinted. When the
second edition appeared, it contained stories that he had written in
the interim—*The Tocsin* (*Nabat*), *The Abyss* (*Bezdna*), *In the Basement* (*V podvale*) and *The Wall*—and also *Pet'ka at the Dacha* and
*Laughter*. The momentous impact of this second edition on critical
and public opinion will be described later.

Thus Andreyev's debt to Gorky was very considerable and he
subsequently acknowledged it on numerous occasions. Gorky's
service was not confined to the introduction of the young writer to
influential figures and groups in the Russian literary world; it
consisted also in the constant encouragement and advice which he
gave to him, all of which served to increase his self-confidence and
to nurture in him a feeling of responsibility and respect for his
work. 'Before my conversations with him,' Andreyev confided to
Izmaylov ten years later, 'I had never regarded my work and my
gift so seriously.'[3] He wrote to Pyatnitsky on 12 May 1902: 'He
[Gorky] awoke in me the spirit of self-criticism, made me adopt a
stricter attitude towards myself. . . .'[4] Even after sharp differences
of opinion had brought their relationship to an end, Andreyev was
never reluctant to express his gratitude. He remarked to the critic
Kleynbort in 1914: 'One can never forget the support which he
gave me. . . .'[5]

---

*Birzhevye vedomosti* ('The Stock-Exchange Gazette'), had come to be identified
with reaction by the socialist parties, as Andreyev was fully aware (see his letter
to Mirolyubov of 30 August 1900, *MAMR*, p. 77), and this reputation became
consolidated with the years; Andreyev's telegram, in consequence, was taken as
tangible proof of his political irresponsibility and he brought on himself a stern
reprimand from Gorky (cf. *LN*, p. 319).

[1] See P. Yartsev, 'Pis'ma o literature. Leonid Andreyev', *Teatr i iskusstvo*,
1902, No. 40, p. 724.
[2] *FTV*, p. 181.    [3] A. Izmaylov, *Literaturnyy Olimp*, M., 1911, p. 249.
[4] 'A. M. Gor'kiy v perepiske sovremennikov', *Voprosy literatury*, 1958, No.
3, pp. 79–80.
[5] L. Kleynbort, 'Vstrechi. Leonid Andreyev', *Byloe*, 1924, No. 24, p. 174.
The *Autobiography* of 1910 contains a similar acknowledgment (see Vengerov
(ed.), op. cit., p. 245).

Of no less importance for Andreyev than his astonishingly swift literary success was the transformation which took place in his personal life. On 10 February 1902 he married Aleksandra Mikhaylovna Veligorskaya. It has been seen that a transformation had been slowly maturing in him ever since he met her in 1896. Teleshov aptly called her his 'good genius',[1] while Andreyev himself was wont to refer to her as his 'Guardian-Angel'.[2] The unprecedented tranquillity which she introduced into his life is a factor of cardinal importance in relation to the evolution of his thought and attitude to life. The disorderly life which he had led at Oryol and during his student years in St. Petersburg and Moscow had left its mark on both his physical condition and his mind. We have seen that the concomitants of this life were attacks of profound depression, a nagging guilt-complex and a tendency to exaggerate the dark aspects of life. He wrote on one occasion in his diary: 'Very strong is the feeling of fear, or rather horror, which comes at times. It is difficult to determine the cause of this horror. Probably my body is afraid of what is happening in it.'[3] Yet in normal circumstances his attitude to life was fundamentally optimistic and his protests against Shulyatikov's charge of pessimism were undoubtedly sincere. Aleksandra Mikhaylovna, who seemed to him to personify all that was radiant in life, was largely responsible for creating the conditions which enabled him to maintain this optimism and give it a philosophical basis.

In 1938 Andreyev's eldest son, Vadim, came into possession of his father's personal copy of the 1901 *Znanie* edition of his first volume of stories. Andreyev gave the copy to Aleksandra Mikhaylovna, as his most valuable and cherished possession, on 4 February 1902—six days before they were married. Enclosed in it were four additional pages in which he described to her the transformation which had taken place in his life since he had met her. It is fitting that we precede our analysis of his fiction with some extracts from this acknowledgment:

My life was a desert and a pot-house, and I was lonely and had no friend in myself. There were days, radiant and empty, like a holiday that was not mine, and there were nights, dark and frightful, and at night I would think about life and death and fear life and death and not know which

[1] Teleshov, 'Pro Leonida Andreyeva', p. 66.    [2] See *FTV*, p. 215.
[3] *PNA*, p. 191.

I wanted more—life or death. The world was limitlessly vast, and I was alone—a sick, yearning heart, a tempestuous mind and an evil, powerless will. . . .

I always loved the sun, but its light is terrifying for the lonely, like the light of a lantern over an abyss. The brighter the light, the deeper the abyss, and terrible was my solitude before the bright sun. And it gave me no joy—this sun which I love and which is so merciless.

My death was already close. And I know—I know with my whole body which shudders from the recollections—that the hand which now steers the pen would be in the grave if your love had not come—the love for which I waited so long, about which I dreamed so very much and wept so bitterly in my hopeless solitude.

A perishing man heard a voice of love and desire from another, radiant world to which his soul had eternally aspired—and is he perishing now? Are not the doors of his prison thrown open—the prison in which languished his heart, tormented and outraged, dishonoured by people and by him himself? Am I lonely? And does not that sun, which before only scorched me, now shine joyfully for me?[1]

[1] *VLA*, October, pp. 96–7.

# II

# IDEAS AND INFLUENCES

THE analysis of Andreyev's thought will be considerably
facilitated by a brief preliminary delineation of the principal
ideas and concepts which constitute the philosophical substratum of his fiction and by some mention of the role played by
influences in their formation. The need for such an introduction
is prompted, above all, by that preponderance in his early works
of the critical element which induced the critic Evgeniy Lyatsky to
declare in 1907 in reference to their positive content: 'Few writers
present so vast a field for diverse interpretation as Leonid Andreyev
. . .'[1] A preliminary inquiry into his positive beliefs will enable us
to understand more clearly the full implications of and motives for
his *critique*.

The remark of Lyatsky raises the question of whether it is even
legitimate to speak of Andreyev's positive beliefs. Not a few critics
failed to perceive any consistent philosophy in his works and pronounced him devoid of one. Such was the verdict, for instance, of
the well-known theatre director Vasiliy Sakhnovsky who, in an
article of 1916 entitled *A Writer without a Dogma* (*Pisatel' bez
dogmata*), lamented the feeling of emptiness with which Andreyev's
works leave the reader:

Responsive and sad, highly sensitive, nervous and worn out by suffering,
he entered Russian literature with the frightful conviction that nothing
exists. With his passionate desire to make his own contribution to the
world in a doctoral voice, he can say nothing because no dogma lives
in his soul.[2]

Andreyev's achievement, according to Sakhnovsky, is limited solely
to 'vague contours, outlines of ideas and sentiments'.[3] Five years

---

[1] E. Lyatsky, 'Mezhdu bezdnoy i taynoy. ("Eleazar", "Iuda Iskariot" Leonida
Andreyeva)', *Sovremennyy mir*, 1907, Nos. 7–8, p. 61.
[2] V. Sakhnovsky, 'Pisatel' bez dogmata. (Osnovnye motivy tvorchestva
Leonida Andreyeva)', *Novaya zhizn'*, alm. I, M., 1916, p. 186.
[3] Ibid., p. 169.

earlier the critic M. Morozov had commented on his works: 'There is no faith, no conviction, no aim.'[1] Similarly, the Marxist critic V. V. Vorovsky stressed in 1910 the absence in Andreyev's works of a 'necessary criterion' in the name of which he conducted his criticism of contemporary beliefs, his 'transvaluation of values';[2] and three years before that another critic wrote: '. . . Andreyev, like Chekhov, is devoid of clear positive ideals . . .'[3] Similar judgements continued to be expressed after Andreyev's death. In 1929, for instance, Pozner came to the same conclusion: 'The writer was incapable of all synthesis; even in one and the same work he would affirm mutually exclusive truths.'[4]

The contention of these five critics and the many who agreed with them will be disputed in this analysis, as it was by Andreyev himself. He expressed his reaction to Sakhnovsky's article in a letter to Goloushev of 15 December 1916, in which he wrote: 'In general, this article is not of three dimensions, but only one. He has examined me attentively from only one angle and has failed to turn the corner . . .'[5] With equal justification Andreyev could have responded thus, had the remarks of the critics concerned been directed solely against the predominantly 'critical' works of the pre-1905 period. It is perfectly true that during this period Andreyev, despite his newly acquired fame, vastly improved material situation and happy marriage, continued to display a certain instability of mood. Symptomatic is the extract from his diary: 'Yesterday I felt happy, laughed and joked. Today I woke in the same carefree, joyous mood, but some two hours later I felt that I was the most unhappy man in the world.'[6] But the evidence forthcoming from his works of this period is that his convictions were unaffected thereby. Notes of despondency and discontent certainly punctuate isolated confessions in his letters, such as that addressed to Veresaev in July 1904: 'I am thinking a lot about myself, about my life—partly under the influence of the articles on V. Fiveysky.[7]

---

[1] M. Morozov, *Ocherki noveyshey literatury*, SPb., 1911, p. 1.
[2] See V. V. Vorovsky, 'Leonid Andreyev', in his *Literaturno-kriticheskie stat'i*, M., 1948, p. 149.
[3] N. Krasin, 'Nravstvennye nachala (printsipy) noveyshey russkoy khudozhestvennoy literatury', *Vera i razum*, 1907, No. 5, p. 630.
[4] V. Pozner, *Panorama de la littérature russe*, Paris, 1929, p. 215.
[5] *Rekviem*, p. 132.
[6] *PNA*, p. 191. Cf. the remarks of Andreyev's mother in *BSN*, p. 28.
[7] Andreyev is referring to *The Life of Vasiliy Fiveysky* (*Zhizn' Vasiliya Fiveyskogo*) which he wrote in 1903.

Who am I? To what unknown and terrible bounds will my negation extend?'[1] But even this effusion does not testify to a fundamental instability of convictions or to a vain quest for a positive view of life. Ignoring the evidence already furnished by Andreyev in his fiction, the majority of critics failed to perceive that he was rather bewailing the poverty in contemporary life of values and convictions which could withstand the attacks conducted by him in the name of an already existing *Weltanschauung*.

Perhaps, however, it will be argued that the strongest evidence of instability in the works of his early years is the vacillation which seems to be reflected, for example, in the transitions from the sentimental *A Theft Was Imminent* (*Predstoyala krazha*) (1902) to the tragic *In the Fog* (*V tumane*) (1902); and from the faith in man proclaimed in *The Marseillaise* (*Marsel'eza*) (1903) to the tedium of life depicted in *At the Station* (*Na stantsii*) (1903). It will be seen, however, that the diversity of mood here and the alternation of light and gloom are determined not by changes of conviction but rather by the diversity of angles from which Andreyev repeatedly affirms the same basic truths. There is no evidence whatever of any significant vacillation in Andreyev's fundamental beliefs before 1906; and even then his lapse into despair, motivated by tragic events in his personal life, was of short duration and culminated only in the stronger affirmation of his positive convictions.

In a letter to the critic Korney Chukovsky Andreyev wrote in 1901: 'It is true that I am a philosopher, though for the most part completely unconscious.'[2] His fiction gives expression to an intuitive understanding of life rather than to a carefully elaborated philosophical system; for the latter he was by temperament totally unsuited. 'He never proceeds from a book,' writes the actress Beklemisheva,[3] 'never quotes the sages of east and west, never refers to authorities in order to prove the correctness of his views. His sphere is not scientific knowledge of life, but its intuitive comprehension.'[4] Nevertheless, there can be little doubt that this 'intuitive comprehension' was influenced, in part, by the philosophical systems which he is known to have studied.

---

[1] *VRSV*, p. 459.

[2] K. Chukovsky, 'Leonid Andreyev', in his *Iz vospominaniy*, M., 1958, p. 258.

[3] Beklemisheva, who knew Andreyev well, was the mother of Yuriy Krymov, the author of the novel *The Tanker Derbent* (*Tanker Derbent*).

[4] *Rekviem*, p. 256.

Almost from the beginning his works show a dualistic conception of reality, a polarization of metaphysical unity and harmony
and phenomenal diversity and discord. His preoccupation with
this distinction between two realities, two levels of life, is confirmed
not only by his fiction, but also by numerous passing remarks in
his correspondence, typical of which is the following in a letter
recorded by Boris Zaytsev: 'With every passing year I become
increasingly indifferent to the first reality, for in it I am only a slave,
husband and father. . . .'[1] The term 'first reality' is employed by
Andreyev to denote the ephemeral, the world of man's empirical
existence, a world dominated by the principle which Schopenhauer
termed the *principium individuationis*. On this plane man is a
prisoner within the walls of his individuality, and his intellect is the
instrument by means of which he endeavours to pierce them. But
its struggles are eternally frustrated; its powers do not extend beyond the 'first reality'. The whole impetus of Andreyev's thought
is towards the establishment of contact with the 'other plane', the
transcendence of the empirical *ego*. In his endeavour to bring his
heroes to this state lies the single basic theme which Chukovsky
denies to his fiction.[2]

Are we, then, justified in pinning the label of 'mystic' on
Andreyev? Is he concerned 'only with that soul of the soul, that life
of life, with which the day's doings have so little to do', to use
Arthur Symons' definition of the mystic?[3] Andreyev himself was
beset by some doubt on this point—above all, through ignorance
of the meaning of the term. He made the following remarks in a
letter of 1913 to the critic and feuilletonist A. V. Amfiteatrov:

Who am I? A mystic? I do not know. And in the final analysis I simply
do not understand and—forgive me!—do not accept this division; it
seems to me ridiculous. . . . I know our 'Christians', theosophists,
aesthetes, shallow acmeists, philosophical scoundrels like Rozanov, vulgar
pessimists, I know X and Y—and they are all profoundly repugnant to
me, but not because they are 'mystics' and 'symbolists' or 'realists'.
They are repugnant to me because they like in life that which I do not

[1] *KLA*, p. 141.
[2] Cf. K. Chukovsky, *Leonid Andreyev bol'shoy i malen'kiy*, SPb., 1908, p. 35.
According to Beklemisheva, Andreyev considered Chukovsky the most talented
of contemporary critics, but at the same time accused him of instability (cf.
*Rekviem*, p. 257).
[3] A. Symons, *The Symbolist Movement in Literature*, New York, 1908, pp.
168-9.

and love that which I cannot endure. . . . But mystic? . . . What is a mystic?[1]

His belief in the existence of an ulterior, truer reality beyond the concrete reality in which we live certainly gave him an affinity with so undoubted a mystic as Maeterlinck; moreover, an undeniably mystical element manifests itself in his works from 1899 (*The Grand Slam*) onward. But decidedly uncharacteristic of Andreyev is the mystic's spiritual self-withdrawal from contingent life; on the contrary, his overriding concern is always with the *malaise* of the contingent world, with the detachment of the 'first reality' from the ulterior unity and harmony, with the reconciliation of man and nature, consciousness and unconsciousness.

Andreyev employs no specific term for the designation of his metaphysical principle; indeed, he rarely uses philosophical terminology. Identifying, however, the intellect and individuation, as stated, with empirical reality, he postulates, like Hartmann, a cosmic life-force of which the subconscious world of man is part, so that the term 'subconscious' is perhaps most apt. He conceived the individual as a momentary objectification of the life-force and as the passing heir to the complex of elements which constitute his subconscious world. In Ibsen's play *When We Dead Awaken*, to which he responded in 1902 with a homonymous article, he found material for the development of his thought on this question of the 'accumulative subconscious', the element of eternity and immortality which lives in the individual. In the figure of Irena he saw the symbol of this force which lives in Rubek, which seeks revenge when neglected and, when cherished, bears man to the highest peaks. He writes:

Each of us has his Irena. It is that which has no name, which each conceives and feels in his own way, which summons him to the mountains, now loves, now abandons, now gives the joy of creation, now menacingly and tormentingly reproaches. It lives in us but remains even for us a symbol, a mystery, the fact that we exist, but something which we cannot define and communicate in words to others.[2]

---

[1] *Rekviem*, p. 260.

[2] *Works* VI, p. 328. Whether Ibsen attached a comparable symbolic value to Irena is certainly debatable, but at any rate Andreyev's interpretation is considerably more convincing than that of a more recent Ibsen student who writes: 'In this play . . . Ibsen clearly reveals the symbolic use of names: . . . Irena means "peace", the blessing which Rubek has lost and which only she can give'

It was Andreyev's belief that if man is to achieve well-being and spiritual freedom in his empirical life he must live in obedience to the promptings of his subconscious, which is possible only if he is aware of its infinitely superior wisdom to that of his intellect—in short, if he recognizes his own subconscious as part of the spirit which informs the whole of nature, and thought as merely a faculty of his ephemeral individuality. Examples of this supreme enlightenment are encountered in his works for the most part, though not exclusively, from 1905 onwards.

The life-force of which he conceives is not Schopenhauer's chaotic, all-devouring will; for Andreyev the will, like the intellect, is phenomenal, peculiar to the 'first reality'. Knowledge of ultimate reality does not presuppose for him, as it does for Schopenhauer, its rejection; he sees the achievement of such knowledge not simply as the conquest of death, but as the sole foundation for an abiding love of life. The critic Nevedomsky has noted well the growth of vitality in those of Andreyev's heroes who attain to this level of cognition.[1] Andreyev also differs from Hartmann in that he does not dwell on the goal of the world-process; he reveals simply a faith in the gradual amelioration of life—a faith which is perceptible in his remarks in an article entitled *The Wild Duck* (*Dikaya utka*), which he wrote in 1902 after watching a performance of Ibsen's play at the Moscow Art Theatre: 'Neither truth nor falsehood will conquer; it is that which is in alliance with life which will triumph. There remains only that which is useful for life; everything harmful to it will sooner or later perish—perish fatally, inevitably.'[2] He is stating here that only that which contributes to the enrichment of life in its endless evolution, which does not seek to halt its course or run counter to its laws, can hope to survive. The cosmic process appeared to him as a continuum of such enrichment.

In a letter to Goloushev of late 1913 or early 1914 he wrote that the whole pivot of his thought 'lies in my incredible rapture before

---

(J. Northam, *Ibsen's Dramatic Method. A Study of the Prose Dramas*, London, 1953, p. 211). It is evident that she symbolizes a more dynamic force than 'peace' —a castigating force which is inseparably linked with Rubek's slumbering genius; the dagger with which she is armed is surely the most tangible proof of this.

[1] Cf. M. Nevedomsky, 'Leonid Nikolaevich Andreyev', in *Istoriya russkoy literatury XIX v.*, edited by D. N. Ovsyaniko-Kulikovsky, vol. 5, M., 1910, p. 269.

[2] *Works* VI, p. 335.

life, my affirmation of life, my thirst for life',[1] and this glorification of life received artistic expression as early as 1897—in an unpublished story which he wrote after the summer spent with Aleksandra Mikhaylovna at Tsaritsyno. In it he painted the following picture:

Mid-day; thick, fragrant grass; droning; coolness in the shade of a birch-tree; solitude; the soul dissolving in nature; life, profound, unfathomable, gigantic, for it has merged with all the billions of lives which exist in nature. Complete, indestructible peace; pure, peaceful joy, an unintelligible joy without cause—the joy of life.[2]

Andreyev did not renounce contingent life, as the critic, theatre director and actor S. Brailovsky claimed,[3] but, like Hartmann, called on man to reform his life on the basis of superior knowledge. It was only when his hopes for such reformation seemed to him impossible of fulfilment—before the spectacle of life in St. Petersburg from 1912 onwards—that he began to abstract his heroes from their corrupt environment; but his remark to Goloushev cited above testifies that his worship of cosmic life was not diminished by this disenchantment.

In addition to that of the two German philosophers, Andreyev acknowledged the influence on his thought of Russia's two greatest novelists. Both Dostoevsky and Tolstoy had a vision of the profound unity which underlies individuation. Engel'gardt has defined Dostoevsky's conception of the 'ulterior reality' in the following words:

It is the higher reality and at the same time the world in which passes the earthly life of the spirit which has attained to a state of true freedom. . . . This third realm is the realm of love and thus of complete freedom, the realm of eternal joy and happiness.[4]

It was a conception which brought Dostoevsky to the vision of mankind as one man and the individual as the whole of mankind. He conceived the guilt of one to be the guilt of all. Guilt and

---

[1] *Rekviem*, pp. 94–5.     [2] *PNA*, p. 175.

[3] Cf. S. Brailovsky, 'Zaklyatyy talant. Istoriko-literaturnyy ocherk po povodu desyatiletiya khudozhestvennoy deyatel'nosti Leonida Nikolaevicha Andreyeva (1898–1908)', *Filologicheskie zapiski*, 1911, No. 5, p. 689. Brailovsky played the role of Onufriy in his own production of Andreyev's play *The Days of Our Life* (*Dni nashey zhizni*) in the 1909–10 season at the Winter Palace in Penza.

[4] Cf. B. M. Engel'gardt, 'Ideologicheskiy roman Dostoevskogo', in *F. M. Dostoevsky. Stat'i i materialy*, edited by A. S. Dolinin, vol. 2, M.–L., 1924, p. 93.

redemption are the twin themes which dominate his fiction and they are interpreted in terms of the divine unity. Guilt is apostasy, self-detachment from the whole, the illusory metaphysical self-sufficiency which brings in its wake moral deformity and spiritual bankruptcy. The path to redemption is the path of self-transcendence and re-integration with the metaphysical unity of the people. The brotherhood of boys founded by Alyosha Karamazov on the memory of Ilyusha is the expression of Dostoevsky's faith in the restoration of the spiritual unity of mankind.

Andreyev felt himself to be much closer to Dostoevsky than to Tolstoy. He remarked in a letter to Belousov of 1914: 'I am a Petersburger—that is a fact—and I always was. Note: Moscow is Lev Tolstoy; Petersburg is Dostoevsky. And from whom am I descended?'[1] He shared with Dostoevsky a more intense interest in philosophical-ethical problems and the metaphysical bases of life than the ethical-social questions which claimed the attention of Chekhov and Gorky. 'The problem of being,' he wrote in one of his first letters to Nemirovich-Danchenko, '—it is to this subject that my thought is irrevocably dedicated and nothing will force it to turn aside.'[2] He also admired Dostoevsky as a 'rebel' and 'teacher of action' and chastised Gorky for his ignorance of these attributes of the great novelist.[3] It is important, however, to note the time when the statement to Belousov was made, for it is his first explicit acknowledgment of Dostoevsky's influence. In September 1903 he informed Gorky: 'I love Dostoevsky, but I do not always understand him and he is alien to me,'[4] and the novelist is conspicuously absent from the influences to which Andreyev confessed in 1908 in a letter to the critic L'vov-Rogachevsky;[5] but two years after the statement to Belousov he confided to the Dostoevsky scholar Leonid Grossman: 'Of past Russian writers Dostoevsky is closest of all to me. I consider myself his direct pupil and follower.'[6] Thus the evidence is that he was more conscious of Dostoevsky's influence in the later years of his life—from 1912 onwards, when he was almost exclusively preoccupied with what he termed the 'pan-psychic drama'. Moreover, his plays of that period contain evidence of his interest in the mythical-religious substructure of

[1] *Rekviem*, p. 71.   [2] *EMKT*, p. 294.   [3] Cf. *LN*, p. 334.   [4] Ibid., p. 179.
[5] Cf. V. L'vov-Rogachevsky, *Dve pravdy. Kniga o Leonide Andreyeve*, SPb., 1914, p. 24.
[6] L. Grossman, *Bor'ba za stil'. Opyty po kritike i poetike*, M., 1927, p. 271.

Dostoevsky's novels. Before this, the influence appears to have been rather of an unconscious nature, born of the points of similarity between their attitudes to life and between the types of problem which they approach. The problems of 'apostasy' and self-will occupy a no less prominent position in Andreyev's fiction than in that of his predecessor. It is true that he does not give them Dostoevsky's religious interpretation and that the mystical unity of which he conceived is ontological rather than Christian; but his faith in this unity as the only true reality has all the fervour of a religious faith and brings him to an identical conception of the fate of apostasy.

It is this similarity of philosophical-ethical point of departure, therefore, that primarily explains Andreyev's affinities with Dostoevsky from the beginning of his literary career; there is no evidence which suggests that Dostoevsky exercised any radical influence on the actual *formation* of his philosophy of life. Thus it is impossible to agree, for example, with the statement of the critic Tsetlin that Dostoevsky 'poisoned' Andreyev.[1] He was receptive to nothing more in Dostoevsky than that which accorded with and reinforced his own view of life.[2]

It is well known that both Schopenhauer and Dostoevsky exercised a powerful influence on the 'second generation' of Russian symbolists, whose interest in the philosophical side of symbolism brought them much closer to German than to Gallic culture. Belyy fell quickly under the influence of Schopenhauer's aesthetics and based his own theories on the latter's insistence on intuitive perception as the only true source of artistic creation. His reference to music as 'the unconditioned foundation of life (the will)'[3] is paralleled by Vyacheslav Ivanov's definition of it as 'the very soul of art'[4] and Blok's definition of intuition, in his well-known letter to Belyy of 3 January 1903, as 'the voice of music singing within'.[5] Blok gave the clearest expression to his 'musical perception' of the cosmic force in a lecture delivered two years before his death—

[1] See M. Tsetlin, 'O tvorchestve Leonida Andreyeva', *Gryadushchaya Rossiya*, Paris, 1920, No. 2, p. 250.

[2] For a survey of some of these areas of receptivity see: R. L. Jackson, *Dostoevsky's Underground Man in Russian Literature*, The Hague, 1958, pp. 84–101.

[3] A. Belyy, 'Maska', *Vesy*, 1904, No. 6, p. 9.

[4] V. Ivanov, *Po zvyozdam; stat'i i aformizmy*, SPb., 1909, p. 268.

[5] *Letopisi gosudarstvennogo literaturnogo muzeya. Kn. 7-aya. Aleksandr Blok i Andrey Belyy. Perepiska*, M., 1940, p. 3.

*The Collapse of Humanism* (*Krushenie gumanizma*) (1919)—in which he wrote:

There are, as it were, two times, two dimensions: one historical, chronological, the other incalculable, musical. Only the first time and the first dimension are invariably present in civilised consciousness; we live in the second only when we feel our proximity to nature, when we surrender ourselves to the musical wave which emerges from the world's orchestra.
. . . For this we need, above all, a healthy body and a healthy spirit, for the world's music can be heard only by the whole body and the whole spirit in unison.[1]

There is no evidence that Andreyev was familiar with this lecture,[2] but if he was, he certainly found in it an exposition of his own dualistic conception of life and the universe and also an echo of his own insistence on an equilibrium of mental and physical attributes as the prerequisite for the attainment of true knowledge. Even though the philosophical-ethical questions which occupied Andreyev's thoughts were transformed by Belyy and the 'Argonauts' into philosophical-religious questions and symbolism became an increasingly esoteric aesthetic-religious cult, one would have expected a degree of actual contact to have emerged from the similarity of their philosophical premises, and it will be necessary to return to the question of why it did not.[3]

Andreyev's attitude to the Christian dogma is expressed in his reaction to Tolstoy's *In What Lies My Faith?* (*V chom moya vera?*):

. . . I did not accept Tolstoy's faith in full. I did not accept the positive part of his teaching—faith in God, the perfection of one's individual life for a single purpose—God, and I discarded it as something foreign to me; there remained only that which was rejected by Tolstoy up to the bounds of his positive teaching.[4]

To certain basic philosophical tenets of Tolstoy, however, Andreyev could not have remained wholly indifferent—particularly his belief in the essential unity of life and matter in all their phenomenal

---

[1] A. Blok, 'Krushenie gumanizma', *Sobranie sochineniy v vos'mi tomakh*, vol. 6, M.-L., 1962, pp. 101-2.

[2] Andreyev died on 12 September 1919. Blok's lecture was not actually published until 1921, when it appeared in the January–March number of *Znamya* ('The Banner'), but it was first delivered in public before Andreyev's death—on 9 April 1919 at a meeting of the collaborators of the publishing-house *Vsemirnaya literatura* ('World Literature').

[3] See Chapter X.     [4] *BSN*, p. 53.

diversity, which he expressed in the principal exposition of his acutely anti-individualistic metaphysical beliefs, *Concerning Life* (*O zhizni*) (1887). It is noteworthy that Tolstoy also underwent the influence of Schopenhauer in the sixties. 'Schopenhauer, recommended to him by Fet, was his only (philosophical) food,' writes Chicherin.[1] This influence is perceptible both in Tolstoy's attitude to death, as expressed, for example, in *Three Deaths* (*Tri smerti*) and *The Death of Ivan Il'ich* (*Smert' Ivana Il'icha*), and in his conception of that metaphysical unity which in his treatise on Dostoevsky and Tolstoy Veresaev called the unity of the 'living life', taking the term from Dostoevsky's 'underground man';[2] he writes further:

For Tolstoy the living life does not know mistakes. It is blessed and great. A powerful, instinctive force is laid by it deep in man, which leads him to well-being. And woe to him who goes against this force, who does not obey his soul, however arduous and difficult this might be. 'Vengeance' inevitably falls upon him and he perishes.[3]

There is a clear similarity between the latter part of this statement and the words quoted from Andreyev's *The Wild Duck*. Both Andreyev and Tolstoy shared that belief in 'eternal justice' which lies at the basis of Schopenhauer's ethical theories, as expounded in Book IV of *The World as Will and Idea*, and displayed a similar conception of egoistic pursuit of the will's objectives as a crime incurring its vengeance.

It is the number of these acts of 'vengeance' in Andreyev's works, particularly before 1906, which has served to identify his name with gloom and pessimism, and to blind critics to whatever else these works disclose. Hence the reputation of 'arch-pessimist' with which he had to contend during his lifetime, and which has survived his death. The principal challenges to this view came from Chukovsky,[4] Brusyanin,[5] Nevedomsky,[6] Professor V. N. Speransky[7]

[1] B. Chicherin, *Vospominaniya. Moskva sorokovykh godov*, M., 1929, p. 217.
[2] Cf. F. M. Dostoevsky, *Sobranie sochineniy*, vol. 4, M., 1956, p. 240.
[3] V. V. Veresaev, 'Zhivaya zhizn' ', *Sochineniya v chetyryokh tomakh*, vol. 2, M., 1947, p. 590.
[4] K. Chukovsky, *Leonid Andreyev bol'shoy i malen'kiy*, SPb., 1908, 136 pp.
[5] *BSN.*
[6] M. Nevedomsky, 'Ob iskusstve nashikh dney i iskusstve budushchego', *Sovremennyy mir*, 1908, No. 1, pp. 162–82, and No. 3, pp. 165–90.
[7] V. N. Speransky, 'Ideya tragicheskoy krasoty i Leonid Andreyev', *Novyy zhurnal dlya vsekh*, 1908, November, pp. 71–9.

and V. F. Botsyanovsky,[1] though their general similarity of opinion by no means precluded radically different interpretations of important individual aspects of Andreyev's thought. Unfortunately the views which they expressed exercised no perceptible influence either on the majority of contemporary critics or on their Soviet successors. Generally speaking, Soviet appraisal of Andreyev's thought has not proceeded beyond the stress laid on his 'social pessimism' by Vorovsky.[2]

Andreyev's most definitive statement on the question of pessimism is again to be found in *The Wild Duck*:

> Pessimism has its fateful limit at which it passes most innocently into optimism. By denying everything you come to faith in things. By rejecting the whole of life you appear as its involuntary apologist. I never believe in life so much as when I read the 'father' of pessimism, Schopenhauer: a man thought in this way—and lived! This means that life is powerful and invincible.[3]

Correct understanding of this statement is impossible without reference to Andreyev's dualistic conception of reality. Botsyanovsky, who emerged in his critical-biographical studies of Gorky, Veresaev and Andreyev as a propagandist of the views of the *Znanie* group, writes on this question:

> However gloomy his colours, however great the sorrow aroused in him by various phenomena of life, it concerns not life, not its essence, but

[1] V. F. Botsyanovsky, 'Leonid Andreyev i mirovaya garmoniya', *Biblioteka teatra i iskusstva*, SPb., 1910, No. 10, pp. 36–72; and ' "Sut' " L. N. Andreyeva', *Teatr i iskusstvo*, 1909, No. 1, pp. 7–10.

[2] Cf. Vorovsky, op. cit., pp. 145–68. À propos of the Soviet attitude to Andreyev, he benefited, like many other writers, from the more liberal climate which followed the death of Stalin. The appearance in 1957 of a volume of his stories (Leonid Andreyev, *Povesti i rasskazy*, M., 1957) and, in 1959, of a collection of his plays (Leonid Andreyev, *P'esy*, M., 1959) are concrete evidence of this improvement. There is also a marked difference of tone between the comments on him in the *Bol'shaya Sovetskaya Entsiklopediya* of 1950 and the *Malaya* of 1958: in the former he is described as 'one of the most characteristic representatives of the bourgeois *decadentism* of the beginning of the 20th century' (*Bol'shaya Sovetskaya Entsiklopediya*, vol. 2, M., 1950, pp. 430–1), while in the latter criticism is tempered by reference to his 'protest against autocracy and sympathy for the revolutionaries' (*Malaya Sovetskaya Entsiklopediya*, vol. 1, M., 1958, p. 406). 'Bourgeois', 'pessimistic' and 'decadentistic' still remain, however, the most common epithets applied to him, though a more sympathetic attitude is found in K. D. Muratova's well-documented article 'Maksim Gor'kiy i Leonid Andreyev' in *LN*, pp. 9–60.

[3] *Works* VI, p. 335. Cf. Andreyev's letter to Gorky of 4 August 1904, *LN*, p. 218.

only those reflections in which life, real life, is refracted in the ordinary
grey and vulgar existence of various people. . . .[1]

In other words, that which criticism has almost unanimously
declared symptomatic of Andreyev's pessimism—the 'horror and
madness' which distinguish many of his most important works—is
related to a plane of reality which to the author himself was wholly
superficial—a distorted mask of that which he considered beautiful,
immortal and life-giving. The horror of his works is exclusively the
horror of the mask.

The meaning of our former assertion—that the apparent changes
of mood in Andreyev's early stories afford no grounds for a charge
of pessimism and instability—now becomes clear. The alternation of
radiance and gloom, joy and despondency, salvation and destruction, is determined by the phenomena of life in the 'first reality'
of which the author is treating, by the presence or absence of contact
which he perceives between these phenomena and the 'living life',
the 'higher reality'. The preponderance of gloom, despondency and
destruction is simply a testimony to the monstrous distortion of the
'mask', as Andreyev saw it, in the Russia of the first two decades of
the twentieth century. Failure to recognize this truth is primarily
responsible for the perplexity with which contemporary criticism
reacted to Andreyev, for the conflicting verdicts pronounced on
him, for Chulkov's despairing remark that Andreyev 'not only did
not construct but was incapable of constructing a harmonious
world-philosophy'[2] and that his undeniable talent was 'absolutely
devoid of any guiding ideas'.[3]

Equally clear becomes the true significance of Andreyev's so-
called 'transvaluation of values'. 'He possesses,' wrote the critic
Voytolovsky in 1905, 'a rare ability to devaluate all fetishes.'[4] But
he did not make the essential point that these 'fetishes' are merely
part of that superficial reality which is rejected by Andreyev, who
regarded no traditional belief as sacrosanct. A symbolic projection of
this whole part of his endeavour is the early story *The Tocsin* (1901),[5]

---

[1] Botsyanovsky, 'Leonid Andreyev i mirovaya garmoniya', p. 69.
[2] G. Chulkov, 'Leonid Andreyev. (Vospominaniya)', *PLA*, p. 36.
[3] Ibid., p. 10.
[4] L. Voytolovsky, 'Sotsial'no-psikhologicheskie tipy v rasskazakh Leonida
Andreyeva', *Pravda*, M., 1905, No. 8, p. 125.
[5] First published in *Kur'er*, 24 November 1901, No. 325. In May 1906 it was
published in a separate edition as No. 51 in the series *Deshovaya biblioteka
'Znaniya'* (*Znanie*'s Cheap Library').

i.e. if indeed it can be called a story. It is rather a symphonic fantasia, like Poe's poem *The Bells* which, together with Raskol'nikov's dream in the labour camp, it distinctly echoes. Like that of a piece of music, its effect is to evoke a mood rather than present a sequence of events issuing logically one out of another; and the mood created by the symbols of the fire and the tocsin is one of acute alarm. The work synthesizes and intensifies the mood which unites the seemingly disparate themes of many of Andreyev's early miniatures.

His onslaught on the Russian society of his day explains further why his name at the outset of his literary career was continually paired with that of Gorky. 'If they talked about Andreyev,' writes Chirikov, 'then without fail about Gorky also. And vice-versa.'[1] Gorky was similarly engaged in the task of exposure and indictment, but as soon as he perceived the implications of the positive content of Andreyev's philosophy, which became increasingly evident from 1905 onwards (by which time Gorky was lending his allegiance to the Bolshevik faction of the Social Democratic Party), the disruption of their 'alliance' inevitably ensued, and by 1909 they were being referred to as 'the two poles' of contemporary Russian literature, 'the two boundaries between which lie the most diverse movements with their diverse representatives'.[2] In Gorky's comments on Andreyev's successive works we will see the gradual widening of the gulf between them. Fully intelligible, therefore, are the remarks which Andreyev made to Kleynbort in 1914 when the latter pointed out to him that in one of his early feuilletons he had sung the praises of Gorky:

Yes, that happened—I was encouraging myself. But the fact of the matter is . . . what will one not write in a feuillton! When I came to speak as an artist, however, and not as a feuilletonist, I immediately showed my true face. My first stories are free from that which my friend fastened upon me. Society, of course, conceived during those years its own image of me. My stories also rang for it with the 'madness of the brave', and they linked Gorky and myself together. But even then our natures were no less dissimilar than they are now.[3]

The very scarcity of direct comment by Andreyev on Gorky's works

[1] E. Chirikov, 'Leonid Andreyev', *Russkie sborniki*, No. 2, Sofia, 1921, p. 65.

[2] V. Polonsky, 'O Leonide Andreyeve i Fyodore Sologube', *Vestnik znaniya*, 1909, No. 2, p. 113.

[3] L. Kleynbort, 'Vstrechi. Leonid Andreyev', *Byloe*, 1924, No. 24, p. 174.

suggests that he deliberately restrained himself lest he jeopardize their friendship or appear to be ungrateful; the only works of Gorky about which he spoke with undisguised enthusiasm were *The Lower Depths* (*Na dne*)[1] and *The Mother* (*Mat'*), though he regarded the second part of the latter as weak.[2] We have seen the debt to Gorky which Andreyev acknowledged, but it would be erroneous to take this acknowledgment as anything more than an expression of gratitude for the encouragement and counsel which he received at the outset of his literary career; there can be no question of any influence by Gorky on the development of his thought.

Considerable caution must also be exercised when considering the influence of Nietzsche on Andreyev. Whole works have been devoted to the quest for echoes of the German philosopher in his fiction, prominent amongst which are those of the Marxist M. A. Reysner[3] and the German critic Oswald Burghardt.[4] Much of Kaun's study of Andreyev treats of the same subject.[5] Nietzsche's ruthless attack on bourgeois values, on the great lies which condemn modern man to his slavish existence, on disparagement of the 'body' for the sake of the soul, on all that deforms life—this attack naturally awakened in Andreyev an intense interest and sympathy. But whereas for Nietzsche the human crisis had its source in the contradiction between the Christian philosophy and the world as it presents itself to man, for Andreyev it arose from man's detachment from the metaphysical entity. From 1876 onwards Nietzsche displayed nothing but scorn for metaphysics and Schopenhauer, and remained thereafter a positivist to the end of his life; all division of reality he pronounced 'a symptom of degenerating life'.[6] His disregard for the basic oneness of all men ran counter

---

[1] See Andreyev's letter to Mikhaylovsky of August 1902, *MAMK*, p. 55.

[2] See the extract from a letter of Andreyev to Chirikov of 10 January 1907 in: V. Afanas'ev, 'Neizvestnyy otzyv L. Andreyeva o romane Gor'kogo "Mat' " ', *Voprosy literatury*, 1960, No. 6, p. 163.

[3] M. A. Reysner, *L. Andreyev i ego sotsial'naya ideologiya. Opyt sotsiologicheskoy kritiki*, SPb., 1909, 151 pp. A *quondam* Professor of International Law at the University of Tomsk, Reysner became subsequently one of the authors of the constitution of the RSFSR.

[4] O. Burghardt, 'Gemeinsame Motive bei Leonid Andrejev und Nietzsche', *Zeitschrift für slavische Philologie*, Leipzig, 1941, vol. 17, pp. 353–72, and vol. 18, pp. 1–18.

[5] Kaun, op. cit., *passim*.

[6] F. Nietzsche, *The Twilight of the Idols* (translated from the German by A. M. Ludovici), London, 1911, p. 23.

to Andreyev's innermost convictions. Andreyev established an ideal for man's salvation which differed negligibly from Christianity in its ethical implications and which necessarily rejected the 'will-to-power' and 'synthetic man' or 'superman' who represented for Nietzsche at once the purpose and consummation of man's evolution.

While it is true, therefore, as Chirikov states,[1] that Andreyev was closer to Zarathustra than to the Marxists in his revision of values—a point which is most clearly evidenced by his attitude to the intellect—examination of the positive content of his philosophy at once illuminates the broad divergences between them. Criticism of Nietzsche is fully explicit in Andreyev's fiction as early as 1900— in *The Story of Sergey Petrovich*—and is encountered once more in his play *The Ocean (Okean)* (1911). Thus Voytolovsky's statement, made in 1905, that Nietzsche finds in Andreyev 'the most comprehensive and noble reflection' of his thought[2] must be drastically qualified by reference to the very different ideals which prompted their 'destructive' activity. Moreover, note should be taken of an entry in Andreyev's diary made when he was only seventeen to the effect that it was his intention, on acquiring the 'honourable status' of a 'famous writer', to harness his works to the task of mass destruction.[3] Even when discussing Andreyev's 'destructive phase', therefore, we would be wrong to exaggerate the incitement of Zarathustra.

Points of contact and similarity between Andreyev and other writers and thinkers will also be noted in the course of the analysis of his works, but our guiding principle throughout should be that which is indicated by Andreyev's friend, the writer Elpat'evsky: 'He responded when it harmonised with him, when it coincided with his mood.'[4] All the evidence points to the fact that in the works of the thinkers to whom he acknowledged some debt he sought primarily confirmation of his own independent understanding of life and the world.

[1] See Chirikov, loc. cit., p. 65.
[2] Voytolovsky, loc. cit., p. 125.
[3] See *BSN*, p. 55.
[4] S. Elpat'evsky, 'Leonid Nikolaevich Andreyev. Iz vospominaniy', *Byloe*, 1925, No. 27–8, p. 280.

# PART II

## Life and the 'Apostate': 1898–1905

### III

### 'DEPERSONIFICATION' AND SELF-WILL

'GOD, the devil, nature, eternity and infinity—these are my closest friends,' Andreyev declared to Skitalets in 1901.[1] Not surprising, therefore, is the predominantly serious tone of his early feuilletons, and the absence from them of that lightness of touch which is characteristic of the genre and which in the Russia of that time was displayed most conspicuously by Amfiteatrov and Doroshevich. This does not mean that he was devoid of a sense of humour. Gorky, for example, is one of many who testify to his skilful use of it in conversation,[2] and his letters to Goloushev contain ample evidence of this skill.[3] The theatre critic A. R. Kugel', who knew the writer well,[4] even pronounced humour 'the most powerful feature of his talent'.[5] The reason for its rarity in his feuilletons and articles is that from the beginning Andreyev made them the vehicle of his indictment of contemporary Russian life and, more particularly, of the Russian intellectual, which explains why half of what he wrote for *Kur'er* proved unacceptable to the censor.

[1] Skitalets, *Povesti i rasskazy. Vospominaniya*, M., 1960, p. 381.
[2] Cf. *KLA*, p. 13.
[3] Cf. 'Pis'ma L. N. Andreyeva k S. S. Goloushevu', *Zhar-ptitsa*, Berlin, 1921, No. 4–5, pp. 36–40.
[4] From 1897 until his death in 1928 Kugel' was editor of the journal *Teatr i iskusstvo* ('The Theatre and Art') and in 1908 founded the satirical theatre called *Krivoe zerkalo* ('The Crooked Mirror').
[5] A. R. Kugel', 'Literaturnye vstrechi i kharakteristiki', in his *List'ya s dereva*, L., 1926, p. 85.

Rarely in these early sketches does Andreyev descend below the middle rungs of the social scale. The object of his criticism and analysis is the type with whom he was most familiar—the *gimnazist*, the student, the intellectual, who is progressively welded by the educational process into a faceless, gregarious being in whom singularity and spontaneity of thought and action are systematically destroyed. 'All Andreyev's heroes,' writes the critic Arabzhin, 'are precisely heroes of our time, people of a determined social milieu, created by and possible only in the modern conditions of life of European society in general and Russian in particular.'[1] In his feuilletons Andreyev traces the formation of this 'depersonified' intellectual, the 'universities' through which he passes and which shape his character, and in this process he draws constantly on his own experience. A whole cycle of sketches is devoted, for instance, to the *gimnaziya*, that 'factory of stereotyped thought and mutilated souls' in Reysner's words.[2] From the outset of his conscious life the middle-class Russian is thrust on to a path of intellectual development which is frighteningly straight and narrow; on all sides it is fenced with rules and regulations which insulate it from the broad, healthy expanse of life. His inner world is deformed and rendered powerless to cope with life once he steps off the ordained path and he becomes, in consequence, a fugitive from life who seeks refuge either in the isolated 'underground' or in self-surrender to the directives of the 'common will'—that 'dense forest of rules,' as Andreyev puts it, 'in which the vagrant soul of the intellectual dashes itself everlastingly'.[3] Transgression of the norm brings on his head the whole weight of mass prejudice. 'Hitherto the hunchback has been only unfortunate,' we read; 'now he is gradually becoming a criminal. It is forbidden to be a hunchback where the majority have straight backs.'[4]

Thus the intellectual becomes a prisoner in a cell of his own construction, behind the walls of which his moral values, in detachment from life, become a reflection of his entire distorted being. Andreyev epitomizes the type in *The Sphinx of Modern Times* (*Sfinks sovremennosti*) (1901):

---

[1] K. I. Arabzhin, *Leonid Andreyev. Itogi tvorchestva. Literaturno-kriticheskiy etyud*, SPb., 1910, p. 84.

[2] M. A. Reysner, 'Introduction' to *Leonid Andreyev. Sobranie sochineniy*, 'Prosveshchenie', SPb., 1911–13, vol. i, p. xii.

[3] *Works* VI, p. 172.    [4] Ibid., p. 170.

Powerless both in sin and in virtue, eternally warring with a thousand enemies planted in his head and heart, offering bread with one hand and taking it away with the other, he weeps without sorrow and laughs without joy. His tongue is divided into a thousand tongues, and he himself does not know when it is lying and when it is telling the truth—this hapless sphinx of modern times vainly struggling to solve himself and perishing without succeeding.[1]

This inner chaos is the fruit of his attempt to suppress that which is insuppressable—the body or 'Self', to use Nietzsche's term, the subconscious instincts which are his heritage, the particle of cosmic life of which he is the momentary custodian. Andreyev is sharply opposed to the argument that this suppression is demanded by the need to superimpose harmony, law and order on the chaos which dwells in the soul of man, for the chaos, he maintains, is of man's own making; the superimposed harmony with which he seeks to suppress the demands of his instincts is the artificial harmony of a fleeting moment which runs counter to the natural harmony of universal life reflected in the inner equilibrium of the bold, free man. The instincts demand an outlet; they seek light and freedom, and in Chekhov's *The Three Sisters* (*Tri sestry*) Andreyev found a powerful expression of this seeking, this unabating demand. In the article of 1902 to which he gives the title of the play[2] he dwells on the perils of excessive suppression of life and beckons his readers to listen in Chekhov's play to life's 'boiling forces', its 'angrily protesting voice'.[3] The pessimism of the play is construed by Andreyev as an 'active pessimism', a pessimism which calls for action, and as a menacing warning. He writes: 'A. P. Chekhov crossed an imperceptible line—and life, the life which he once persecuted, began to shine with a victorious light.'[4]

Thus just as the articles and feuilletons which appear to exude the blackest gloom are, in reality, laments on man's corruption of life, so those which seem violently misanthropic are essentially analyses of the individual who is responsible for this corruption. Very different is the image of Shalyapin whom, in an eponymous

---

[1] Ibid., p. 177.

[2] It was first published in 1902 in a collection of articles and feuilletons by Andreyev and Goloushev (using their pseudonyms 'James Linch' and 'Sergey Glagol' ') entitled *Pod vpechatleniem Khudozhestvennogo teatra*, M., 1902, pp. 78–86. Brusyanin wrongly states that it was published in 1903 (see *BSN*, p. 92).

[3] *Works* VI, p. 324.

[4] Ibid., p. 323.

article of 1901, Andreyev presents as a living example of the
triumph of untutored genius, and in *Dissonance (Dissonans)* (1902)
he similarly applauds Ibsen's Dr. Stockmann and his rebellion
against the 'common will'; he asks:

Should not one cherish the experience of such a moment of spiritual
purification and the memory, lasting perhaps for the whole of one's life,
that if only for a few minutes one has succeeded in living, in feeling like
a man, instead of bleating and whirling an obsequious tail like one of the
great herd?[1]

In the plays of Ibsen—*An Enemy of the People, When We Dead
Awaken* and *The Wild Duck*—which were performed at the Moscow
Art Theatre in 1900 and 1901[2] Andreyev found ample material for
the continuation of his indictment and responded, as we have seen,
with an article on each. But it would be erroneous to speak of the
*influence* of Ibsen on Andreyev's thought. It is imperative that we
do not misinterpret his admiration of Ibsen's heroes, of the 'strong
individual' who tramples on mundane conventions in obedience to
his own impelling inner logic. The 'madness of the brave' held a
special significance for Andreyev which, as he pointed out to
Kleynbort, from the beginning differentiated him sharply from
Gorky. It did not in itself constitute the limit of his ideal. Significant, for instance, is the dénouement of *Dissonance*. The description of his reaction to the play is followed by that of his journey
home by carriage and of the peasant who drives him. He studies
this simple being so far removed from the cultured, bourgeois
intellectual, and suddenly he exclaims: '. . . there flared up in me
hatred for Dr. Stockmann and I wanted to emerge from my free
solitude and dissolve in this grey, obtuse mass of demi-people.'[3]
The strength of 'the brave' was necessary for the act of self-
liberation from the fetters of the 'common will', but at the same
time Andreyev perceived inherent dangers in this strength, and
many of his later works are devoted to the illumination of these
dangers. The act of self-liberation was important to him only as a
preliminary to the final act of self-immersion in the unsullied stream

---

[1] Ibid., p. 332.
[2] The title *An Enemy of the People* was changed to *Dr. Stockmann*. The
premières of the three plays took place respectively on 24 November 1900, 28
November 1900, and 19 September 1901.
[3] *Works* VI, p. 333.

of universal life which is objectivized in *Dissonance* in the person of the simple peasant.

It was his first concern, however, to unmask the monstrosity of bourgeois life, to display to his readers the chains with which they bound themselves, and to trace for them the consequences of their actions. 'Perhaps no other writer,' wrote Tsetlin in 1920, 'had so large a number of interesting and varied themes,'[1] but each new theme represents simply a different approach to the same distinctive feature of contemporary life—the state of detachment. Each story marks a new incision into the same wound, and there can be no doubt, despite Tolstoy's celebrated remark ('Andreyev wants to scare everybody, but I do not fear him'[2]), that he aroused genuine alarm among his public. 'Apart from a few elect,' writes Tsetlin, 'a whole generation of the Russian intelligentsia was afraid.'[3]

An entry in Andreyev's diary of 1898 paints the following picture of a family of his acquaintance:

Life for them is like a theatre in which they have occupied a quite comfortable box from which they gaze indifferently from side to side, criticising the public, slightly pitying those who are languishing in the heat of the gallery, slightly envying those who are sitting below them, but at peace, happy in the knowledge of their isolation, their facilities and the imminent performance.[4]

There is much in common between this portrait and Andreyev's first fictional delineation of the 'fugitive from life'—namely, the civil servant Andrey Nikolaevich, the protagonist of *By the Window* (1899),[5] who sits out his days by the window of his room, rarely trespassing beyond its threshold. The author's comments on his hero's reaction whenever he is asked about his life reveal that he has passed through the whole process of 'depersonification':

This question always caused Andrey Nikolaevich difficulty, because there is nothing to tell. He is thirty-four, but he remembers nothing of

---

[1] M. Tsetlin, 'O tvorchestve Leonida Andreyeva', *Gryadushchaya Rossiya*, Paris, 1920, No. 2, p. 244.

[2] See M. V. Nesterov, 'Pis'ma o Tolstom', in *L. N. Tolstoy v vospominaniyakh sovremennikov*, vol. 2, M., 1960, p. 287; and N. E. Fel'ten, 'Iz vospominaniy', ibid., p. 360. Boborykin subsequently gave his own version of this remark: 'He always wants to hypnotise us, but we do not succumb' (P. Boborykin, 'Na tragicheskom predstavlenii', *Teatr i iskusstvo*, 1909, No. 42, p. 721).

[3] Tsetlin, loc. cit., p. 249.        [4] *PNA*, p. 188.

[5] First published in *Kur'er*, 3, 5, and 7 August 1899, Nos. 212, 214, and 216.

these years—just a grey fog and that special fear which seizes a man in the fog when before his very eyes stands a grey, impenetrable wall.[1]

The self-incarceration of the hero signifies an attempt to escape from the element of 'accidentality' in life, from life as a multitude of unforeseeable combinations of events. Andrey Nikolaevich is not a rebel against the socialist 'ant-hill', like Dostoevsky's 'underground man', nor does he share the latter's gnawing consciousness of the sterility of the 'underground', his knowledge that there is 'something else, quite different, for which I thirst, but which I cannot find'.[2] They are related to one another simply by their common detachment from the 'living life' and by such consequences of this detachment as constant introspection and grotesque inflation of the ego. 'From loss of habit the "living life" oppressed me to such a degree that it even became difficult to breathe,' exclaims the 'underground man' after his humiliating second encounter with Liza.[3] Analogous sentiments are uttered by Andrey Nikolaevich whenever he breaks the routine of his existence.

In his work as a civil servant, which involves the mechanical repetition of identical functions, and in the stereotyped pattern of a life spent at his window Andrey Nikolaevich feels himself to be master of the situation. Every healthy impulse, every warm sentiment and pleasant sensation he meets, like Belikov, the hero of Chekhov's *The Man in a Case* (*Chelovek v futlyare*) (1898), with the destructive questions: Why? Whence? What will come of it? But though he succeeds in reducing his conscious life to a rigid circle of experience, his subconscious perpetually disturbs his peace with demands which find no gratification within this circle. 'Ah, thoughts . . . they are not so easily mastered'—these words of Ibsen's Hedda Gabler summarize his predicament. There is no escape from their infiltration; they 'come, thrust apart the walls, tear off the ceiling and fling Andrey Nikolaevich beneath the gloomy sky, into the endless square open on all sides, where he seems to be the centre of the universe and where he is so uncomfortable and terrified'.[4] His stifled instincts call for life and shatter his peace of mind with recollections of the one romance in his life, the fields, mown hay and the red disc of the moon. The work is punctuated

---

[1] *Works* I, p. 123.
[2] F. M. Dostoevsky, *Sobranie sochineniy*, vol. 4, M., 1956, p. 164.
[3] Ibid., p. 240.      [4] *Works* I, p. 117.

with notes of alarm denoting the author's hostility to his hero, his determination to allow him no rest. For Andreyev, as for Nietzsche, 'a sedentary life is the real sin against the Holy Spirit. Only those thoughts that come by walking have any real value'.[1] The story begins and ends, for example, with the detail of the flapping shutter on the other side of the street, which repeatedly breaks the silence. This simple detail is symbolic of the whole 'idea' of the work. Again, particularly disturbing for Andrey Nikolaevich is the time when the painters and carpenters proceed to transform the appearance of the aristocratic dwelling directly opposite his window, the centre-piece of his artificial cosmos, thus destroying momentarily his faith in the calculability of his vista. 'There are people who alarm and disturb,' writes Beklemisheva. 'To such people belonged Leonid Andreyev.'[2] In many of his early stories Andreyev, like Chekhov in *The Gooseberry Bush* (*Kryzhovnik*) (1898), made it his task precisely to instil this note of alarm into the world of the 'depersonified' fugitive from life.

The fulfilment of this task is continued in *The Grand Slam* (1899),[3] which Mikhaylovsky considered one of the best stories in *Znanie*'s collection of 1901.[4] The hero of Chekhov's *The Story of an Unknown Man* (*Rasskaz neizvestnogo cheloveka*) (1893) writes the following in his parting letter to the St. Petersburg bureaucrat Orlov:

With what tender, purely Asiatic, khan-like care you protect yourself against hunger, cold, physical exertion, against pain and worry. How early your soul has hidden itself in a dressing-gown. What a cowardly role you play before real life and nature with which every healthy and normal man wrestles. How soft, comfortable, warm, convenient everything is for you—and how tedious! Yes, it is fatally, desperately tedious, like solitary confinement, but you endeavour to hide even from this enemy; for eight hours a day you play cards.[5]

It is possible that Andreyev had these words in mind when he came to write *The Grand Slam*, though the idea of the work bears a

[1] F. Nietzsche, *The Twilight of the Idols* (translated from the German by A. M. Ludovici), Edinburgh and London, 1911, p. 6.

[2] *Rekviem*, p. 195.

[3] First published in *Kur'er*, 14 December 1899, No. 345, with the ironic subtitle *An Idyll* (*Idilliya*).

[4] Cf. N. K. Mikhaylovsky, 'Literatura i zhizn'. Rasskazy L. Andreyeva. Strakh smerti i strakh zhizni', *Russkoe bogatstvo*, 1901, No. 11, p. 66.

[5] A. Chekhov, *Sobranie sochineniy*, vol. 7, M., 1955, pp. 242-3.

certain resemblance to that of Tolstoy's *The Death of Ivan Il'ich*. The characters of the story are four card-players whose fortress or refuge is, in fact, their game. It is as though they have come to a tacit agreement to forget that they are living people, to limit their relationship to that of partners in the game, inhabitants not of this but of a less eventful and alarming world, and to admit to their discourse only the events of this artificial reality—the world of cards. Occasionally, the most vigorous member of the group, Nikolay Dmitrievich, brings with him snippets of news from the outside world, e.g. the latest developments in the Dreyfus case, but these innocent fragments are a source of terror to the others and they unanimously pronounce him a 'lightheaded and incorrigible man'.

In this work death is the counterpart of the importunate thoughts of Andrey Nikolaevich in *By the Window*. It is the one intruder into the smooth flow of their lives against which the card-players, like Ivan Il'ich, are powerless to insulate themselves. As Voytolovsky has indicated, death is much more than a melodramatic accessory in *The Grand Slam*.[1] Andreyev displays in this story his ability to create an illusion of naturalness while, in fact, forsaking all semblance of natural experience. Clearly abnormal is the speed with which the action hastens to its climax, its mechanical transitions from one stage to the next. A 'mysterious consciousness, mocking and malicious', as Korolenko puts it,[2] reveals itself in the fateful combination of cards which leads Nikolay Dmitrievich to his doom. The story presents the first of a number of instances in Andreyev's fiction of the 'living life' actively engaged, as a mystical, deterministic force, in conflict with those who ignore its dictates. The development of the action leaves no doubt that in Andreyev's seemingly paradoxical conception death in this work is the vengeance wrought by life on the apostate—one of those acts of vengeance on which he was to elaborate three years later in *The Wild Duck* and *When We Dead Awaken*.

Nikolay Dmitrievich knows that if the ace of spades is in the four bonus cards to which he, as declarer, is entitled according to the laws of the game, he will achieve his life's ambition—a grand

---

[1] See L. Voytolovsky, 'Sotsial'no-psikhologicheskie tipy v rasskazakh Leonida Andreyeva', *Pravda*, 1905, No. 8, p. 131.

[2] V. G. Korolenko (Zhurnalist), 'O sbornikakh tovarishchestva "Znanie" za 1903 g.', *Russkoe bogatstvo*, 1904, No. 8, p. 135.

slam in no-trumps, but at the precise moment when he is about to
take the bonus into his hands he is struck down by a heart-attack.
After the initial shock has passed the curiosity of his partner, the
cautious and methodical Yakov Ivanovich, is too much for him. He
turns up the bonus cards and there lies the ace of spades, and 'as
though the thought had come to him not of itself,' we read, 'but
had been whispered by someone in his ear, he said aloud: "But
that means that he will never know that the ace was in the bonus
and that in his hands he had his first grand slam. Never!" '.[1]

In this story Andreyev makes his point with a much greater
economy of means than in *By the Window*. No detail is superfluous.
Nevedomsky writes in reference to the characters of the work:

They are neither types nor characters, but merely statements. . . . These
players are not living people. . . . We do not know what kind of people
they are, what conditions of life have brought them to this state of
detachment and indifference to one another; there is nothing realistic in
the picture; it is exaggerated, invented.[2]

In Voytolovsky's opinion, they are social rather than psychological
types, 'social symbols, living reflections of that stifling atmosphere
in which their life passes'.[3] In reality they are abstractions of the
single type delineated in the feuilletons, and it is in the feuilletons
that Andreyev depicts the conditions of life responsible for their
detachment. They are abstractions in which only the most salient
features of the type receive emphasis, and the skeletal nature of the
entire work is a reflection of the dependence of all the elements of
the fiction on the author's pivotal idea. It is interesting that it was
this simplicity of its structure that was especially esteemed by
Mikhaylovsky.[4]

A less schematic, more psychological analysis of the 'depersonified man' is presented in *The Story of Sergey Petrovich*, which was
written the following year (1900).[5] It was his longest and most
important work to-date. No previous work had made such exacting
demands on him or dominated his thoughts to the same extent in
the course of composition. Complaining about the scarcity of free
time at his disposal in his letter to Mirolyubov of 23 March 1900,

[1] *Works* I, p. 29.
[2] M. Nevedomsky, 'O sovremennom khudozhestve', *Mir bozhiy*, 1903, No. 4,
p. 14.
[3] Voytolovsky, loc. cit., p. 130.        [4] Mikhaylovsky, loc. cit., p. 66.
[5] First published in *Zhizn'*, 1900, No. 10.

he wrote: 'My greatest trouble is that I cannot tear myself away from the story "Sergey Petrovich" (do you remember, about the Nietzschean?) which pursues me day and night and takes up every free minute.'[1] Brusyanin's statement that the story is based on a true incident[2] is confirmed by Pavel Andreyev who mentions a certain Aleksey Petrovich, a student friend of his brother, who committed suicide in circumstances similar to those presented in the story.[3] According to Fatov, however, Andreyev's hero differs considerably from his real-life prototype.[4]

The terms of reference of the work are considerably broader than those of the two which we have examined, for Sergey Petrovich is Andreyev's first rebel against the 'long, narrow, grey corridor'[5] of 'depersonification'. The work is important not only as a psychological study of an individual, but as a social document, for it reflects the entry into the Russian intellectual vacuum in the mid-nineties of the ideas of Nietzsche and the impact of these ideas on the mind of the average intellectual. Gekker writes in reference to this time:

We well remember this period of the mid-nineties when social thought, after its long hibernation, came to life again and in new feverish searchings for truth and justice fastened tenaciously and convulsively now on to the extremes of economic theories, now on to the illusory bliss of the individual satisfied in the consciousness of the omnipotence of his 'ego', his freedom and omniscience. The new generation, unfettered by traditions and obligations inherited from the past . . . and also unfettered within by moral principles, unadjusted to the fulfilment of any lofty aspiration—whether of a moral, social or religious, altruistic character—this young generation was left to itself and sacrificed to its doubts, vacillation and negation.[6]

Andreyev realized that this situation was fraught with danger. He foresaw the disastrous consequences of the entry of a violent cult of individualism into a society reared in the spirit of equally violent anti-individualism, and his vision of these consequences is conveyed through the experience of the student Sergey Petrovich.

The first chapter of the work has been neglected in previous discussions. The omission is serious, for it contains the key to the understanding of Andreyev's hero; it describes Sergey Petrovich

---

[1] *MAMR*, p. 75.  [2] *BSN*, p. 47.  [3] *PNA*, p. 161.
[4] *FTV*, pp. 88–9.  [5] *Works* I, p. 67.
[6] N. Gekker, *Leonid Andreyev i ego proizvedeniya*, Odessa, 1903, p. 30.

prior to his encounter with Zarathustra. The son of a poor civil
servant, he emerges as the quintessence of mediocrity. His physical
appearance is a reflection of his inner world: he is 'not ugly, but
unattractive, like hundreds and thousands of people. His flat nose,
thick lips and low forehead made him similar to others and erased
individuality from his face'.[1] His intellectual ability is similarly
devoid of distinction. That which others absorb instantaneously
requires of him tormenting efforts of will and concentration, and
even when fixed in his memory 'remained foreign, extraneous, as
though it were not living thought but a book which had fallen into
his head and pierced his brain with its corners'.[2] The consciousness
of his intellectual limitations is a constant source of pain to him.
He becomes a dreamer, 'naive and shallow',[3] picturing himself as
a handsome, intelligent and irresistibly attractive man-god worship-
ped by the masses and thus driving ever deeper the wedge between
himself and life. 'In reality,' we read, 'he was completely devoid of
the living ties with people which make their society pleasant and
indispensable.'[4] In this brief portrait, therefore, Andreyev illuminates the soil on which the seeds of Nietzsche's teaching are about
to fall. Four significant features are emphasized: firstly, the ideas
which succeed in entering the brain of Sergey Petrovich are not
born of life, but are taken from books; secondly, the effect of these
ideas is to detach him ever further from life; thirdly, rebellion
against his mediocrity is latent from the beginning; and fourthly,
this rebellion manifests itself in dreams of self-aggrandizement.

In Chapter II Sergey Petrovich is introduced by his gifted
friend, Novikov, to a new bookish image which immediately
assumes in his mind the proportions of an ideal—the 'superman' of
Nietzsche. The immediacy of the response has its explanation in
what Andreyev has already told us about his hero. The 'superman'
is the embodiment of those qualities with which in his dreams he
invests himself. But consciousness of the distance between himself
and this ideal gives birth to an outburst of bitter self-criticism. He
recognizes his natural kinship with the wretched hero of Gogol's
*The Overcoat (Shinel')*:

He saw a man named Sergey Petrovich from whom everything that makes
life happy or bitter but profoundly human was debarred. Religion and
morality, science and art existed not for him. Instead of a burning and

---

[1] *Works* I, p. 61.      [2] Ibid., p. 62.      [3] Ibid.      [4] Ibid., pp. 63–4.

active love, that which moves mountains, he felt in himself an ugly lump in which the habit of ritual was interwoven with cheap superstitions.[1]

This 'habit of ritual' and these 'cheap superstitions' constitute Andreyev's comment on the educational process and milieu which have deformed his hero's character.

The preoccupation of Sergey Petrovich with his ego now becomes more pronounced and his dreams of power increasingly persistent, but in his passage through the 'corridor' of 'depersonification' he has been shorn of whatever abilities he might once have possessed that would have enabled him to transform dream into reality. Like Raskol'nikov, he isolates himself from the world and subjects himself to a period of intense self-analysis: 'Day and night he lay on his bed or walked about, and the neighbours and landlady had already become accustomed to that monotonous sound of footsteps which is sometimes heard from prison-cells.'[2] In this airless cell Sergey Petrovich, convinced of his inability to display the strength and freedom of Nietzsche's hero in life, takes refuge in another of Zarathustra's precepts: 'Unto many life is a failure, a poisonous worm eating through unto their heart. These ought to see to it that they succeed better in dying.'[3]

Even in death, however, he fails to achieve his objective. Unquestionably the most powerful scene of the work is that which depicts the hero bracing himself to consume the phial of poison and the momentary victory of his instinctive desire to live over his intellectual desire to die. Significant is the apparently trivial episode which causes the postponement of his suicide attempt. As he is feverishly battling to overcome the resistance of his body and groping for the phial, the door of his room is suddenly opened by his landlady who puts the simple question: 'When shall I wake you?' Later works make it doubly evident that women occupy a special place in Andreyev's world. Probably under the influence of Hartmann[4] and Maeterlinck, he portrays woman as a creature of instinct whose sources of being, in the Belgian poet's words, 'lie far deeper than ours in all that is illimitable',[5] and for Andreyev the instincts

---

[1] Ibid., p. 69.     [2] Ibid., p. 78.

[3] F. Nietzsche, *Thus Spake Zarathustra* (translated from the German by A. Tille), London and Leipzig, 1898, pp. 95–6.

[4] Cf. Eduard von Hartmann, *Philosophy of the Unconscious* (translated by W. C. Coupland), vol. I, 2nd edn., London, 1893, p. 39.

[5] M. Maeterlinck, *Le Trésor des Humbles*, Paris, 1920, p. 89.

belong to that subconscious world of man which is a minute link in the chain of the 'higher reality'. In short, women in many of Andreyev's works appear as symbols of the life-force, and the intrusion of the landlady at this critical juncture represents the attempt of life to restrain this slave of books and lifeless ideas from his fateful intention.[1] The attempt is successful.

The next morning Sergey Petrovich wakes in the joyful consciousness of being alive, but the feeling is shortlived. It suddenly occurs to him that he has sent a letter to Novikov informing him of his intended suicide and his motives, and now, where his will had failed the day before, shame succeeds, restoring his contempt for life and man. 'That which Sergey Petrovich experienced,' we read, 'was like a proud and chaotic fever of megalomania.'[2] In this fever he swallows the poison, leaving for posterity only his torn jacket and, symbolically, his books. The general squalor in which the scene is enacted symbolizes, like that which surrounds Dostoevsky's Kirillov, the whole monstrosity and misguidedness of the act.

Even the suicide of Sergey Petrovich, therefore, falls short of the 'swift' death 'surrounded by hopeful ones and such as pledge themselves' preached by Zarathustra.[3] Both Voytolovsky[4] and Gekker speak of the beauty and nobility of the suicide and all that it signifies. Gekker writes, for instance: 'This death is one of the most beautiful in our literature and one of the most significant, for it triumphs over life . . . as a triumph of the individual "ego".'[5] From this statement it is but a step to the claim that Andreyev was advocating suicide, and indeed many of his readers made such a claim. Andreyev mentioned to Izmaylov a girl who sought his advice on the question of whether she should commit suicide because she belonged to the 'Sergey Petrovich type'.[6] But Teleshov recalls his frequent denials of the claim and his constant reassertion of his love of life.[7] The error of Gekker and Voytolovsky lies in their excessive identification of Andreyev with the German philosopher.

It has been stated that Andreyev's whole *Weltanschauung* pivots

---

[1] This episode in the story made a particularly strong impression on Tolstoy (cf. L. D. Opul'skaya, 'Tolstoy i russkie pisateli kontsa XIX—nachala XX v.', *Literaturnoe Nasledstvo*, 1961, No. 1, p. 122).

[2] *Works* I, p. 86.  [3] Nietzsche, *Thus Spake Zarathustra*, p. 94.

[4] Voytolovsky, loc. cit., p. 133.  [5] Gekker, op. cit., pp. 29–30.

[6] A. Izmaylov, *Literaturnyy Olimp*, M., 1911, p. 238, and 'Pis'ma L. N. Andreyeva k A. A. Izmaylovu', *Russkaya literatura*, 1962, No. 3, p. 195.

[7] Teleshov, 'Pro Leonida Andreyeva', p. 68.

on the principle of metaphysical impersonalism. It was this principle which prompted him to lay stress, while sympathizing with Sergey Petrovich, on the same defects in him as those indicated by Gekker in the generation of the nineties: 'He lacked all moral feeling and the emotions linked with it. He did not like people and was incapable of experiencing that great happiness, the equal of which has not yet been created on earth—to work for people and die for them.'[1] From the beginning, as we have seen, Andreyev emphasizes the egocentric nature of the student's thought, and it is this distortion of his hero that he deplores rather than his inability to elevate himself to a dominating height where his detachment from life would be even more pronounced. Self-will was the antithesis of Andreyev's conception of the way to happiness and freedom. He believed the path taken by certain elements of the Russian intelligentsia in its striving to extricate itself from the 'narrow corridor' inherited from the past to be false and deceptive, and it was his wish to expose Zarathustra as a false prophet. For Andreyev, contrary to Chirikov's contention,[2] the 'man-god' is not the inevitable result of the process of destruction and negation. 'A man has rebelled,' writes Chukovsky in connection with the hero of Andreyev's *Darkness* (*T'ma*) (1907), 'and a strange phenomenon, unprecedented in Russian literature—in his rebellion he has not asserted, but lost himself, his individuality. He has lost those concrete features which alone made him for us distinguishable, separate, individual, tangible, discernible and specially lovable.'[3] This was the only form of rebellion that Andreyev was prepared to sanction. He condemns one kind of 'depersonification' only to advocate another, the difference being that while the one is imposed from without and entails detachment from life, the other is a voluntary act prompted by the enlightenment which is born of contact with life.

Even in *The Story of Sergey Petrovich* there is a clear indication of the course to which the hero should have committed himself. We are told that the only genuine happiness which he discovered was in making wooden guns and arrows for his little brothers, mending the fences and benches in the garden and digging the soil

[1] *Works* I, pp. 69–70.
[2] E. Chirikov, 'Leonid Andreyev', *Russkie sborniki*, No. 2, Sofia, 1921, p. 71.
[3] K. Chukovsky, *Ot Chekhova do nashikh dney. Literaturnye portrety, kharakteristiki*, SPb.–M., 1908, p. 247.

during the summers in his native Smolensk—i.e. in selfless endeavour and re-established contact with the earth. 'But this was not the work,' writes Andreyev, 'to which he was predestined by his birth to a father who was a civil servant and by his education. Other people, suffering from the discord between their capabilities and their work, sometimes break the bonds and become what they wish—a worker, a ploughman, a tramp. But these are strong and bold men, of whom there are few on earth, while Sergey Petrovich felt weak, timid and guided by someone's alien will. . . .'[1] From the free and happy life which was within his reach he is guided by the 'alien will' of Zarathustra to a senseless and ignominious death.

The opposite of Sergey Petrovich is Nikolay, the central character of *Into the Dark Distance*, which was written later in the same year (1900)[2] and was well received by Gorky.[3] Nikolay possesses the strength which is lacking in Sergey Petrovich and succeeds in severing the ties which bind him to his family and its bourgeois *modus vivendi*. After a number of years he returns to see his parents and sister and the story begins at this point. Its interest lies in the fact that it is told from the point of view of the family. In this light Nikolay appears as an insoluble mystery and threat to all. 'There was something strange, indefinable in him,' writes the author,[4] and a little later: 'There was constantly an expression on his face which suggested that he was listening to something distant, important and audible to him alone.'[5] This vagueness soon becomes irritating to the reader, but it is explained by Andreyev's limited purpose in the work, by the angle from which he examines his hero, and by Nikolay's complete alienation from his environment. Andreyev seeks simply to confront the old with the new, bondage with freedom, and to demonstrate the incomprehensibility of freedom to those who have never known it.

The contrast between reality and the barely hinted ideal is present in one form or another in most of these early stories of Andreyev, receiving particularly poignant treatment in *The Little Angel* (1899),[6] *Pet'ka at the Dacha*—which distinctly echoes Chek-

[1] *Works*, I p. 74.

[2] First published in *Kur'er*, 25 December 1900, No. 357. Six years later (20 May 1906) it was published in a separate edition as No. 60 in the series *Deshovaya biblioteka 'Znaniya'*.

[3] Cf. *LN*, pp. 82–3.     [4] *Works* I, p. 101.     [5] Ibid., p. 105.

[6] First published in *Kur'er*, 25 December 1899, No. 356, with a dedication to A. M. Veligorskaya.

hov's *Van'ka—In the Basement* (1901)[1] and *Kusaka* (1901).[2] The transcendence of egoism usually reveals itself in one of two inseparably related forms: in simple altruism or in attachment to a large, abstract, supra-individualistic unit. Those works which pivot on simple acts of altruism—e.g. *Bargamot and Garas'ka, From the Life of Second Captain Kablukov* (*Iz zhizni shtabs-kapitana Kablukova*) (1898),[3] *Young Men* (*Molodyozh'*) (1898), *In Spring*, and *A Theft Was Imminent*—inevitably seem sentimental; there is a distinct artificiality, for instance, in the coincidence of the 'resurrections' of Garas'ka and Kacherin, the hero of *A Holiday* (*Prazdnik*) (1900), with the Easter festival. In the humanitarian attitude to the 'downtrodden man' which distinguishes a number of these works it is customary to see a reflection of the influence on Andreyev of Korolenko and, to some extent, Gorky;[4] but even if he did experience this influence, it should still be noted that altruism and respect for man were implicit in his whole philosophical conception of life. Like most of his contemporaries Andreyev held the author of *Makar's Dream* (*Son Makara*) in the highest regard and was one of the writers who appended their signatures to the congratulatory letter of 12 November 1903 which was sent to him on his completion of twenty-five years as a writer;[5] at the same time he was very conscious of a fundamental difference between himself and the older writer. Significant is Beklemisheva's remark that although he considered Korolenko honourable and necessary, he found him tedious,[6] and some years later he confided to Kleynbort: 'I find something lacking in Korolenko—a trifle perhaps, but without it the whole of Korolenko is unnecessary to me.'[7] There can be little doubt that this missing 'trifle' was the broad philosophical conception of supra-individualism or absolute self-transcendence and the eternal questions of life, death and immortality which it brought into focus.

[1] First published in *Kur'er*, 25 December 1901, No. 356.
[2] First published in *Zhurnal dlya vsekh*, 1901, No. 9.
[3] First published in *Kur'er*, 25 December 1898, No. 355.
[4] See, for instance, V. V. Vorovsky, *Literaturno-kriticheskie stat'i*, M., 1948, p. 163.
[5] The letter was actually written by Teleshov and was signed by Ivan Bunin, Veresaev, Zaytsev, Elpat'evsky, Serafimovich and Chirikov besides Andreyev and Teleshov himself. It was first published on 6 January 1962 in the newspaper *Vechernyaya Moskva* ('Evening Moscow') and was subsequently republished in *Voprosy literatury*, 1962, No. 4, p. 236.
[6] Cf. *Rekviem*, p. 257.
[7] L. Kleynbort, 'Vstrechi. Leonid Andreyev', *Byloe*, 1924, No. 24, p. 174.

In *On the River* (1900)—a story for which both Tolstoy and Gorky expressed their admiration[1]—the twin themes of altruism and self-transcendence, in the specific sense of immersion in life, are dovetailed. The protagonist, Aleksey Stepanovich, is roused from his apathy not simply by the opportunity, created by the flood, to assist those in distress, as Nevedomsky claims,[2] but rather by an instinctive sensation of the communion between himself and the awakening forces of nature. Though called upon to join battle with these forces, he is animated by the same 'cosmic energy'. A variation of the same theme is presented in *The Foreigner* (*Inostranets*) (1902)[3] in which the student Chistyakov is prised from his detachment and introspection by a reawakened consciousness of the mystical significance of the concept 'native land'.

Thus by 1902 Andreyev had described the entire arc which extends from the social-psychological *malaise* of 'depersonification' through individualistic rebellion to the transcendence of narrow individualism and resultant reconciliation with life. This arc is a prefiguration in miniature of the whole chronological development of his thought as expressed in his fiction. Conspicuous is the artistic inferiority of those works of this early period in which acts of altruism and self-transcendence constitute the philosophical and thematic nucleus; Andreyev was subsequently to refer to them with contempt.[4] Among the factors which prompted him to write them we should take into account the unexpected success of *Bargamot and Garas'ka*, the obligation, which he clearly felt constrained to meet and which was made more compelling by his close contact with Gorky, to respond to the change of social mood in the nineties, and also, perhaps, the wish to present, in simple terms, some intimation of the positive ideal which underlay his indictment of contemporary society. Whatever the cause, they do not show the true Andreyev of the period before the Revolution of 1905, and in this connection it is necessary to consider the subjective element in his works.

[1] Cf. *L. N. Tolstoy v vospominaniyakh sovremennikov*, vol. I, M., 1955, p. 358; and *LN*, p. 96. The story was first published in *Zhurnal dlya vsekh*, 1900, No. 5, pp. 525–40.
[2] Cf. M. Nevedomsky, 'Leonid Andreyev', in *Istoriya russkoy literatury XIX veka*, vol. V, edited by D. N. Ovsyaniko-Kulikovsky, M., 1910, p. 264.
[3] First published in *Russkoe bogatstvo*, 1902, No. 12, pp. 51–64.
[4] Cf. Kleynbort, loc. cit., p. 179.

# IV

## SUBJECTIVISM AND SOLITUDE

BLOK was tempted to combine Andreyev with Dostoevsky and Sologub and pronounce them a triumvirate of 'Russian satirists',[1] but Andreyev rarely displays the calm and detachment of the satirist; only on a very few occasions—notably in a number of his feuilletons and in his one-act plays—is he capable of contemplating the object of indictment from the required distance. He does not gaze upon his contemporaries from the pinnacle of his own virtue. There is no coldness in him; he never strikes an austere pose; the imprint of his own sufferings is clearly stamped on those of his protagonists—a fact which added considerably to the confusion of contemporary critics. 'L. Andreyev is a tremendous artist,' wrote Andrey Belyy in 1906, 'but he could exercise an even more sovereign hold over our souls if he could detach himself from his heroes, if he could contemplate from the heights of dispassionateness the chaos of life unfurled before him.'[2] The criticism reveals Belyy's failure to perceive that the fiction of Andreyev is not only an indictment of the world in which he lived; it is also a work of self-castigation.

Andreyev did not confine his self-analysis to his fiction and diaries. Many memoirists refer to his habit of constantly speaking about himself. But Chulkov adds that whereas with the majority of people the habit becomes irksome and objectionable, with Andreyev it was inevitable—a facet of his personality to be accepted or rejected, but not reformed; as a result, he states, it was not an imposition to listen to him: 'His conversations about himself were not egoism; they were his misfortune, sorrow, sickness, anguish.'[3]

The elements of social criticism and self-criticism are inseparably interwoven in Andreyev's works. The hyperbole and thickening of colours which characterize his portrayal of the social-psychological

[1] A. Blok, 'Ironiya', *Sobranie sochineniy v vos'mi tomakh*, vol. 5, M.–L., 1962, p. 348.
[2] A. Belyy, 'Vtoroy tom', in his *Arabeski*, M., 1911, pp. 489–90.
[3] G. Chulkov, 'Leonid Andreyev. (Vospominaniya)', *PLA*, p. 35.

*malaise*, as he diagnosed it, should be seen not simply as a literary device, but also as an indication, if not of the exaggerated proportions which this *malaise* assumed in Andreyev himself, then certainly of his extreme sensitivity to it. In this connection we might again quote Chukovsky: 'Andreyev magnified to grandiose proportions all the features of his contemporaries, and combined them all in himself. He is a synthesis of our era under a very powerful magnifying glass.'[1] Between Andreyev and his times there is this constant link; he spoke of the 'problems of the age', and uppermost among them was the problem of individual isolation.

The problems of solitude and communication haunted Andreyev from the beginning, as they did the symbolists, and he devoted to this subject a whole cycle of his early stories, to which belongs *Laughter*, written in January 1901.[2] In this work Andreyev breathes new life into the hackneyed theme of unreciprocated love, taking a small episode from his own life as his point of departure.[3]

Having waited for his girl-friend in vain for two and a half hours in the frost, the nameless hero, again a young student, is told by a friend that she has gone to a Christmas party. More students join them and the decision is made to don masks and force an entrance. When the others have taken their choice, however, the only one left for the hero is a Chinese mask, which he describes in the following terms:

It was, if one might put it thus, an abstract face. It had a nose, eyes and mouth, and everything was correct and in its place, but there was nothing human in it. It expressed neither sorrow, nor merriment, nor astonishment—it expressed absolutely nothing. It gazed at you straight and calm—and you were overpowered by irresistible laughter.[4]

In this expressionless mask he meets the girl and at once laughter convulses her. 'What's the matter with you?' he cries. 'It's shameful to laugh. Don't you feel behind my ridiculous mask a living human face—it was only to see you that I put it on.'[5] But the peals of laughter thwart his every attempt to express his feelings.

Unlike Andrey Nikolaevich and the card-players in *The Grand Slam*, the hero of *Laughter* does not consciously isolate himself

[1] K. Chukovsky, *Ot Chekhova do nashikh dney. Literaturnye portrety, kharakteristiki*, SPb.–M., 1908, p. 238.
[2] First published in *Kur'er*, 5 January 1901, No. 5.
[3] Cf. *FTV*, p. 70.  [4] *Works* I, p. 136.  [5] Ibid., p. 137.

from life; on the contrary, he actively seeks the romance which
Andrey Nikolaevich scorns. Nevertheless, the barrier, symbolized
by the expressionless mask, which makes communication between
himself and the girl impossible, is essentially the same as that
symbolized by the civil servant's window—the barrier of individual
personality—and at the same time it expresses the further idea of
the divorce between reality and appearance. 'There are only masks,'
says Tyukha, one of the characters in Andreyev's play *Savva* (1906).
'A multitude of masks. . . . Very amusing masks: I always laugh.'[1]
Moreover, Andreyev's distrust of appearance extended not only to
visible reality. Characteristic is the remark which he made in a
letter to Gorky in 1908: 'Thoughts lie, words lie, they all wear
masks.'[2] He shared in full measure that distrust of the word which
was integral to the aesthetics of the symbolists, believing it incapable of establishing genuine contact, of expressing the truth
which lies concealed beneath the surface of life. This conviction is
graphically represented in *Laughter*.

The overture to the cycle of works which hinge entirely on the
problem of communication is *The Lie* (1900).[3] It was the only work
in the 1901 *Znanie* collection of Andreyev's stories to which Mikhaylovsky took exception. He wrote: 'This strange story seems to
me to be a small dark cloud on the bright future of Mr. Andreyev
as an artist. The question is: will this little cloud grow into a sombre
storm-cloud covering the whole horizon or, having approached for
an instant, will it disperse in space?'[4] Tolstoy regarded the work
as 'the beginning of the false line' in Andreyev's development and
awarded it no marks in his system of evaluating the young writer's
stories.[5] In this work, however, Andreyev was giving one of the

---

[1] *Works* IV, p. 249.     [2] *LN*, p. 308.

[3] First published in *Kur'er*, 20 February 1900, No. 50.

[4] Mikhaylovsky, loc. cit., p. 73.

[5] It was Tolstoy's custom before 1907 to give Andreyev's works a mark out
of 5+ in his diary. Marks awarded to other stories are as follows: *Once upon a
Time There Lived, Silence, On the River, Into the Dark Distance* and *The Story of
Sergey Petrovich* ('with the exception of a number of weak parts'): 5 each;
*Bargamot and Garas'ka*: 2; *By the Window*: 'wholly unnecessary' (*vsyo ne nuzhno*);
*From the Life of Second Captain Kablukov*: 'false' (*fal'sh*): 1; *In Spring*: 5+;
*A Theft Was Imminent*: 'very bad' (p.o.—standing for *plokho ochen'*); *At the
Station*: 2; *The Little Angel*: 1; and *A Holiday*: 'it would be good, if there were
a sense of measure' (see V. I. Ulybyshev, 'Tvorchestvo L. Andreyeva v otsenke
Tolstogo', *Yasnopolyanskiy sbornik. Stat'i i materialy. God 1960–y*, Tula, 1960,
p. 153). This attentive attitude to each individual story is evidence of the powerful
impression which Andreyev made on his famous contemporary. 'He read the

first glimpses of his 'true face', to use the term he employed in his statement to Kleynbort,[1] and it is the progenitor of a number of his most characteristic and successful works.

As in *The Grand Slam* and *Laughter*, the characters are the tools of an intellect which has a point to make. Though written before *Laughter*, it reads almost like a sequel. The hero is convinced that by killing the girl who, he believes, has been unfaithful to him he will be killing the falsehood which torments him. Repeatedly she declares her love for him, but words are powerless to dispel his suspicions and he kills her. It then occurs to him, however, that he has made it impossible for himself ever to learn whether she was really unfaithful or not. He has killed not falsehood, but the truth which the girl has carried with her to the grave. And yet for a brief instant the truth had been revealed to him. 'I love you,' the girl says to him shortly before he kills her. Again he doubts her, but she suddenly embraces him and he states: 'The candle flame went out—darkness embraced us. I saw neither her face nor her eyes; her hands embraced my head, and no longer did I feel the lie. Closing my eyes I did not think. I did not live; I simply absorbed the feeling of her hand, and it seemed to me to be truthful.'[2] Sakhnovsky evidently overlooked the significance of this small episode when he wrote that 'life remains dumb for the hero of *The Lie*'.[3] In the 'night of the Unconscious', to use Hartmann's phrase,[4] that which is concealed from the intellect is at once revealed to the instincts. The dying flame of the candle and the ensuing darkness symbolize the transition to a different level of understanding. The face and eyes—the mask—are obliterated; there is only silence and an instinctive awareness born of the unerring sense of touch. But the moment passes; the bond is snapped and like Lermontov's Demon—a 'dark spirit of doubt'—the hero remains 'alone, alone in the whole universe'.

---

collections of Andreyev's stories from the first to the last page,' a Soviet scholar has written recently, 'marking them with numerous notes, underlinings and appraisals' (L. D. Opul'skaya, 'Tolstoy i russkie pisateli kontsa XIX—nachala XX v.', *Literaturnoe Nasledstvo*, M., 1961, No. 1, p. 121).

[1] Cf. *supra*, p. 39.     [2] *Works* I, p. 56.
[3] V. Sakhnovsky, 'Pisatel' bez dogmata. (Osnovnye motivy tvorchestva Leonida Andreyeva)', *Novaya zhizn'*, alm. I, M., 1916, p. 186.
[4] Hartmann, *Philosophy of the Unconscious*, vol. I, p. 285.

The most striking difference between this story and *The Grand Slam*—theme apart—lies in the conjunction of the skeletal plot with the hero's extreme sensitivity. Skitalets states that the work developed out of the failure of a girl to turn up for a meeting with Andreyev,[1] but this statement obviously requires qualification. Every extraneous impression was viewed by Andreyev in terms of the abstract problems which racked him. If the impression contained relevant material, immediately his creative fantasy began the work of feverish improvisation and adaptation. The real-life situation became the foundation on which he proceeded to analyse a problem of much broader significance. In some instances this superimposition of a problem foreign to the original involved simple adjustment of the real-life characters—well illustrated by *Once upon a Time There Lived* (1901),[2] in which he merely transformed the characters of the deacon and merchant whom he met in the Moscow University clinic for nervous disorders, where he spent six weeks early in 1901[3] 'after a "merry" trip to Nizhniy'.[4] In *The Lie* he goes further and transforms the original still more radically by the force of his emotional apprehension of the superimposed problem, creating a totally new reality in which all is refracted through the hero's exaggerated sensitivity.

The same creative process gave birth to *Silence*, which, as we have seen, was completed in August 1900.[5] According to Sof'ya Panova, the 'situation' of this work was furnished by the suicide of the daughter of the priest who conducted the services at the church which the Andreyevs attended in Oryol.[6] The events of the story can be briefly summarized. The priest, Father Ignatiy, receives no reply when he begs his daughter, Vera, to explain her silence after her return from St. Petersburg. Shortly afterwards she throws herself under a train without confiding the reason for her transformation. Her mother is struck with total paralysis on hearing the news and a wall of silence encloses the priest. In despair he visits his daughter's grave and puts his ear to it in the hope of hearing from beyond the explanation of her action, but again a chilling silence is the only response.

---

[1] Cf. Skitalets, op. cit., p. 380.

[2] First published in *Zhizn'*, 1901, No. 3, pp. 233–51.

[3] Andreyev entered the clinic on 25 January 1901. For descriptions of the 'original' deacon and merchant cf. I. A. Belousov, *Literaturnaya Sreda. Vospominaniya, 1880–1928*, M., 1928, p. 138; and *PNA*, p. 195.

[4] Skitalets, op. cit., p. 383.     [5] Cf. *supra*, p. 20.     [6] Cf. *FTV*, p. 203.

The story was written only four months before *Into the Dark Distance*[1] and Vera is clearly the precursor of Nikolay, while her conflict probably grew out of the potential conflict, which failed to materialize, between Sergey Petrovich and his father. Rebelling against her parents' values and way of life, she goes, against her father's wishes, to St. Petersburg and there she encounters ideas and a way of life which reinforce her antipathy. Like Sergey Petrovich, however, she lacks the strength to sever herself completely from the old life, and the ensuing inner conflict drives her to suicide. But Vera does not dominate the work in the way that the 'Nietzschean' dominates *The Story of Sergey Petrovich*. Her story is barely sketched and much is left to the inference of the reader. Its main function is rather to motivate the drama of her father and enable Andreyev to reiterate his thoughts on the absence of communication between people—once more with particular reference to the 'sacred unit' of the family and, perhaps implicitly, to that of the church.

Father Ignatiy is the voice of narrow, uncompromising dogma. His moral code is the cell which alienates him from life and it conceals a pernicious egoism. Small descriptive touches draw attention to his constant preoccupation with the maintenance of his dignity, and the suicide does not affect this basic trait of his character. His parishioners seek in vain an indication of suffering in his face; he feels their eyes gazing at him, but 'he endeavoured to straighten his broad, strong back and thought not about his dead daughter, but about how to avoid lowering himself'.[2] Nevertheless, a desperate battle has been joined in his mind between the nagging suspicion that he is in some way to blame for his daughter's death and the self-vindication in which his logical arguments invariably culminate when he puts this point to his wife. The latter, however, can only look at him in despair, and his arguments, like those of Dostoevsky's Grand Inquisitor, drown in the silence which engulfs them. Logic, like mathematics, shows us nothing more, states Schopenhauer, 'than mere connections, relations of one idea to another, form devoid of all content. . . .'[3] Logic is another kind of mask.

---

[1] *Into the Dark Distance* was written in December 1900.
[2] *Works* I, p. 90.
[3] A. Schopenhauer, *The World as Will and Idea* (translated from the German by R. B. Haldane and J. Kemp), vol. I, book 2, London, 1883, p. 157.

Whereas *The Lie*, therefore, contains a direct statement of the 'cure', in *Silence* it is stated obliquely through the characterization of the protagonist. Equally significant and meaningful is the characterization, if the term may be used, in *The Wall* (1901)[1]—a work which increased Mikhaylovsky's apprehension about Andreyev.[2] Here the scene is a leprosarium and the protagonists are its inmates. Facing the lepers is a wall which is described as follows: 'It rose straight and smooth, and seemed to cut the sky into two halves. And our half of the sky was brownish-black and towards the horizon dark blue, so that it was impossible to perceive where the black earth ended and the sky began.'[3] Repeatedly they dash themselves against it in an attempt to penetrate it and see what lies beyond, but their assaults are futile and the pile of victims mounts. The central character urges his fellow-sufferers to continue the struggle, but his appeal falls on deaf ears.

Various attempts have been made to decipher the symbolism of the work. Kaun, for instance, expresses the view that the wall is a symbol of the 'bureaucratic regime' of imperial Russia; he considers the story to be an incitement to rebellion against the oppressive power of the state.[4] Burghardt prefers to see it as a symbol of the innumerable rules and regulations with which man has curtailed his freedom.[5] Both interpretations are accurate as far as they go, but they fail to explain the whole symbolic complex. The wall cannot be considered in detachment from the lepers, for, like the majority of Andreyev's symbols, it is, in part, a visualization of a psychic condition. In a letter of 31 May 1902 to a Moscow doctor's assistant named Antonina Mikhaylovna Pitaleva[6] Andreyev

---

[1] First published in *Kur'er*, 4 September 1901, No. 244.

[2] Andreyev said to Izmaylov: 'Nikolay Konstantinovich (Mikhaylovsky) frankly told me what he did not like in me, and in the copy of his works that he gave to me he wrote: "To L. N. Andreyev from the admiring author, despite *The Lie* and *The Wall*" ' (Izmaylov, op. cit., p. 250).

[3] *Works* I, p. 139.

[4] Cf. A. Kaun, *Leonid Andreyev. A Critical Study*, New York, 1924, pp. 198–200.

[5] See O. Burghardt, 'Gemeinsame Motive bei Leonid Andrejev und Nietzsche', *Zeitschrift für slavische Philologie*, Leipzig, 1941, vol. 17, p. 360.

[6] Pitaleva had written a letter to Andreyev in which she asked him to explain the symbolism of the story. In October 1903 she was suspected of being implicated in the dissemination of propaganda among the workers in Kazan' and a search of her house resulted in the confiscation of Andreyev's reply. It was found in 1925 in the police files in Leningrad and published in the journal *Zvezda* (see A. Zhenevsky, 'Leonid Andreyev i ego "Stena". (Novyy material o Leonide Andreyeve)', *Zvezda*, L., 1925, No. 2, pp. 257–8).

interpreted the wall not only as 'the political and social oppression which exists both here in Russia and almost everywhere else in the West', but also as 'the imperfection of human nature with its sicknesses, its animal instincts, maliciousness, avarice, *etc.*'[1] He recommended to Pitaleva the interpretation of Gekker,[2] who wrote: 'The author wished to show . . . how contemptible, petty and often criminal are the relations between people, of *man*, and how necessary it is for man to change before he becomes worthy of that "new world" to which he aspires.'[3] The summons of the central character to continue the struggle is a call for battle primarily with the sickness or distortion of the modern mind. In short, *The Wall* is an allegorical representation of the pivotal thought of the works examined thus far.

[1] Ibid., p. 258.     [2] See ibid.

[3] N. Gekker, *Leonid Andreyev i ego proizvedeniya*, Odessa, 1903, p. 20. The article was first published in the newspaper *Odesskie novosti*, 1902, 21 May.

# V

## REALITY AND POTENTIALITY

DISCUSSING with Beklemisheva the autobiographical aspect of *Crime and Punishment* (*Prestuplenie i nakazanie*) and the possibility of whether Dostoevsky had himself committed a crime comparable to that of Raskol'nikov, Andreyev remarked: 'It is unimportant whether there was such an event in the life of Dostoevsky. Only one thing is important—that the act could potentially have been committed by him.'[1] With this same criterion of potentiality he surveyed the Russian scene of his day. He would have acknowledged that not every suspicion of infidelity results in murder, as it does in *The Lie*, and that not every clash between 'fathers' and 'children' culminates in suicide, as it does in *Silence*, but he firmly believed that the exaggerated form of these climaxes was justified if it served to highlight some underlying truth of human relations or human conduct in the context of prevailing conditions of life. He once remarked to Brusyanin: 'The artist takes from the life of society and the life of the individual only the inner essence in hidden form and it is his task to squeeze it from that which he has observed.'[2] In conversation with Sergeyev-Tsensky he compared himself in the execution of this task to a jeweller: 'You are a seeker of gold; you scour Russia for gold and find such nuggets as your Anton Antonych in "Movements" . . .; but I am a jeweller—out of the gold discovered by you and others I make jewels.'[3] The dramatic dénouements of certain of his works represent his conception of the potential consequences of certain attitudes and states of mind existing in society. This point is particularly

---

[1] *Rekviem*, pp. 265–6.

[2] *BSN*, p. 73.

[3] S. N. Sergeyev-Tsensky, 'Moya perepiska i znakomstvo s A. M. Gor'kim', *Sobranie sochineniy v desyati tomakh*, vol. 3, M., 1955, p. 602. Andreyev used the same metaphor when discussing this point with Brusyanin: 'There are two kinds of writers: seekers of gold, who rummage in the shafts and sands of life and quarry the ingots of human life, and jewellers who simply give the ready material its polish . . . I am a jeweller . . .' (*BSN*, p. 9).

germane to two stories written by Andreyev in 1902—*The Abyss*[1] and *In the Fog*.[2]

*The Abyss* begins on a deceptively idyllic note as the student Nemovetsky and his girl-friend Zinochka[3] stroll along gaily and converse idealistically about love. They recall the great loves of fiction and pledge that for love they would sacrifice their lives. Their visual images harmonize with the loftiness and purity of their conversation. Our attention is drawn to Nemovetsky's hand 'slender and white like a woman's'[4] and to the frailty, timidity and naïvety of Zinochka. It is not long, however, before discordant notes begin to enter the idyll. At first they are barely discernible, but the sense of foreboding is swiftly intensified by the rapidity with which they succeed one another. 'They did not see the shadows,' writes the author, 'for they were too absorbed in their talk;'[5] and again: 'They walked on, turning the bend of the unfamiliar road.'[6] The mood is sustained by the reference to the 'dark mass' of the wood which they approach and to which they seem to be irresistibly drawn. They both begin to experience unfamiliar sensations: Zinochka feels 'pleasure and shame' in contact with his hand, while Nemovetsky finds something 'acute and alarming' in the 'unfading image of the narrow hem of white skirts and the shapely foot'[7] which momentarily flits before his eyes, and with an effort of will he crushes the feeling. The transition from one world to another is indicated by Nemovetsky's reply when Zinochka asks him where they are: 'There, behind the hill, is the town.'[8] And at the entrance to the 'new world', the world of the wood and darkness, they encounter two prostitutes, who stand like heralds of doom.

From the moment they enter the wood events are enacted with gathering momentum. Set upon by a group of ruffians, Nemovetsky is concussed and Zinochka violently ravished. When he recovers his senses he goes in search of her and finds her unconscious and

---

[1] First published in *Kur'er*, 10 January 1902, No. 10.

[2] First published in *Zhurnal dlya vsekh*, 1902, No. 12. Mirolyubov took a considerable risk in publishing this story, for it had been stipulated by the censorship that *Zhurnal dlya vsekh* must confine itself to 'items suitable for family reading'; in the view of the censorship *In the Fog* was far from belonging to this category and from this time forth the journal was subjected to much closer surveillance (see *MAMR*, pp. 96–7).

[3] This name was not chosen at random by Andreyev. 'So far as "The Abyss" is concerned,' writes Sof'ya Dmitrievna Panova, 'it is undoubtedly pervaded by his infatuation with Zina Sib-va' (*FTV*, p. 204).

[4] *Works* I, p. 180.     [5] Ibid.     [6] Ibid.     [7] Ibid.     [8] Ibid.

naked. He bends over her body, and as he does so the air itself seems to him to be impregnated with lust: 'Here the revelry of beasts had taken place,' we read, 'and suddenly cast beyond simple, human, intelligible life, he smelt the burning lust which flooded the air and dilated his nostrils.'[1] His spiritual torment at this moment is wonderfully conveyed—the conflict between his efforts to associate this 'motionless and mute' body with the girl with whom he had so recently spoken about the immortality of love, and his efforts to suppress the images which he thought he had crushed, but which now rise again before his eyes: the white hem of the skirt, the black silhouette of the foot and of the shoe which so tenderly embraced it. His attempts at suppression are in vain. The gentle youth becomes a beast in a metamorphosis worthy of Ovid.

Thus Andreyev once more places his central character in an exceptionally dramatic situation, to the enhancement of which all elements of the fiction are subordinated. He illuminates the polar extremes of his hero's nature, and the transition from the one to the other is effected swiftly and with a kind of deterministic inevitability. At the same time the transition is convincingly motivated by the revealing 'lapses' of Nemovetsky prior to the dénouement. But even if the transformation of Nemovetsky is convincingly portrayed, the question arises of whether, in Andreyev's view, it had any special relevance to contemporary conditions of life.

The gentility and effeminacy of Nemovetsky are indications of the type of domestic and social environment which has produced him. He comes from the same kind of respectable family as Vera and Nikolay, and his education and upbringing have been based on the same 'respectable' principles of morality. Of love he knows only that with which poetry has acquainted him. Every attempt has been made to shield him from the darker aspects of life and human nature, and, unlike Vera and Nikolay, he does not question the standards of this life. The naked body of Zinochka represents for him, as does the dead body of Nikolay Dmitrievich for Yakov Ivanovich in *The Grand Slam*, a sudden confrontation with a truth for which he is totally unprepared. In the face of this body ideal notions of love are dissipated, and the 'explosion' predicted by Andreyev in *The Three Sisters* follows inevitably. For Andreyev it is the potentiality of this 'explosion' that expressed a fundamental truth about the society in which he lived, and in *The Abyss* he

[1] Ibid., p. 190.

translates potentiality into reality, just as Dostoevsky does in the crime of Raskol'nikov and the murder of Fyodor Pavlovich Kara-mazov. Before we consider society's reaction to this revelation, however, it is necessary to examine the related issues raised by Andreyev in *In the Fog*, which he completed by 25 August 1902.[1]

In *The Abyss*, as stated, the characterization of Nemovetsky is the only hint which the reader obtains of his background. The importance of the family scenes in *In the Fog* is indicative of the broader terms of reference of the work. Respectability is again the dominant feature of the family of the student Pavel Rybakov. His mother is attractive and naïve, his father—intelligent and seem-ingly enlightened. But Pavel, unlike Nemovetsky, rebels against this respectability and the moral principles to which his upbringing and education have accustomed him, and he approaches a prostitute. He finds in her two sources of gratification: a complete absence of moral pretentiousness, so blatantly in contrast with his father's 'lofty themes', and her body which his rebellious instincts crave. But the result of this gratification is a 'shameful disease', and now his torment enters its second phase.

His contamination appears to him as an irremediable disaster which has condemned him to a lingering death. Andreyev was criticized by a contemporary physician on the grounds that such a mental state was not justified by the nature of the disease, and he adduces clinical proof from the text of the story and statistical evidence of the prevalence of syphilis and gonorrhea in contem-porary Russia in an attempt to minimize the seriousness of Pavel's position.[2] The young student is plainly in no condition, however, to regard his plight with such commendable objectivity. He is con-scious only of the violent conflict which he has created between himself and his environment and of the fact that he has lost some-thing of inestimable value, and in despair he appeals for help.

But no aid is forthcoming. He feels all the futility of confessing to his 'lofty-minded' father, his naïve mother or the pure Katya Reymer, the friend of his sister who embodies that quality which he has lost and to which he hopelessly aspires. His total detachment from his family is symbolically represented by his abandonment of the house and his immersion in the fog. The fog, like the dark

---

[1] Cf. *MAMR*, pp. 96–7.
[2] M. P. Manasein, 'V meditsinskom tumane. ("V tumane", rasskaz Leonida Andreyeva)', *Novyy put'*, 1903, No. 8, p. 227.

wood in *The Abyss*, is a symbol of the world of deformed instinct, and its filth and dark yellow colour are a projection of this side of Pavel's nature, just as Katya Reymer is the symbol of his aspiration to purity. Katya and the fog are the symbols of his duality. As in *The Abyss*, once the scales have been tipped events hasten to a climax. As though led by fate, Pavel at once encounters the type of woman who is the immediate cause of his wretchedness and she becomes the victim of his vengeance; he murders her and then commits suicide.

With these two works Andreyev struck the most sensitive nerve in the body of Russian society. Their impact was tremendous, as Gorky had predicted it would be,[1] and it was by no means confined to the narrow literary circles of St. Petersburg and Moscow. If the fame which came to him with the publication of his first volume of stories was somewhat restricted, *The Abyss* and *In the Fog* quickly made his name known to the whole Russian reading public. 'Due to this "Abyss" noise, shrieking and hooting arose round the name of Andreyev,' writes Teleshov.[2] 'After the story "The Abyss",' notes another contemporary, 'they began to talk about Andreyev as they would about a man who had had the audacity to walk along the Nevsky Prospect in the costume of Adam.'[3] Tempting offers came in abundance from the leading journals and newspapers of the day. 'The pauper who had made a living with petty reportage and the painting of portraits,' comments Veresaev, 'became an established man.'[4] His works also began to be read abroad, particularly after Pyatnitsky came to an arrangement about their translation with the publishing-houses of K. and H. Steinitz and Ladyzhnikov in Berlin and Dietz and Markhlevsky in Stuttgart.[5] Heated controversy was conducted all over Russia and editors of newspapers and literary journals received letters from all quarters containing violent condemnations of Andreyev and equally fervent vindications. The papers *Novosti* ('News'), *Russkie vedomosti* ('The

[1] Cf. *LN*, p. 133.    [2] *KLA*, pp. 155–6.
[3] A. Dobrokhotov, *Kar'era Leonida Andreyeva. (Etyud o populyarnosti, arlekinakh i tolpe)*, M., 1909, p. 6.
[4] *VRSV*, p. 449.
[5] 'According to the contract with the German publisher,' Andreyev wrote to Mikhaylovsky in September or October 1902, 'I must publish the stories in Germany before they are published in Russia' (*MAMK*, p. 58). It was this arrangement which caused Kuprin to write to Chekhov from St. Petersburg in October 1902: 'The latest literary news is that L. Andreyev is no longer a Russian, but a German writer' (*Literaturnoe Nasledstvo*, vol. 68, M., 1960, p. 385).

Russian Gazette') and *Kur'er* published questionnaires and asked readers to send their opinions.[1] Botsyanovsky writes:

On the pages of these newspapers appeared a series of fervent letters from young people of both sexes and from people who had never taken a pen into their hands. These letters, however, were only a weak reflection of what was said about Leonid Andreyev in society, in private circles, wherever there gathered two or three people who were not foreign to social and literary interests.[2]

Much of the criticism was personal and abusive. Andreyev's rapid climb to success excited envy and hostility, and the less responsible elements in the press took advantage of his active social life and his theatrical dress—usually a *poddyovka*[3] and high boots—to ridicule him. 'Leonid Nikolaevich usually dismissed it with a joke,' writes Teleshov, 'but some jests hurt and offended him.'[4]

The campaign waged against him was initiated by the critic and editor of Suvorin's reactionary newspaper *Novoe vremya* ('New Times'), Burenin, who pronounced *In the Fog* a harmful, pornographic work.[5] With the aid of copious extracts from *The Abyss* and *The Wall* he tried to show that Andreyev was a writer whose success was achieved by pandering to vulgar tastes and perverted imaginations. He saw this success as testimony to the corrupt state of social morality and accused Andreyev of 'erotomania'.

Burenin's indictment was immediately taken up by Zinaida Gippius in *Novyy put'* ('The New Path'), the journal which she edited with her husband, Merezhkovsky; she wrote: 'The *gimnazist* from "The Fog" has helped more than one *gimnazist* to reveal in himself with pride the sources of secret, delectable horror.'[6] But the response which provoked society to open debate on a scale which had little precedent was that of Countess S. A. Tolstaya, the wife of Lev Nikolaevich, whose views, contained in a letter to Burenin, were printed in *Novoe vremya* a week after the appearance of

---

[1] See *FTV*, p. 185.

[2] V. F. Botsyanovsky, *Leonid Andreyev. Kritiko-biograficheskiy etyud s portretom i faksimile L. N. Andreyeva*, SPb., 1903, p. 3.

[3] A long, thickly lined coat fitted at the waist.

[4] Teleshov, 'Pro Leonida Andreyeva', p. 68.

[5] Cf. N. E. Burenin, 'Kriticheskie ocherki', *Novoe vremya*, 31 January 1903, No. 9666.

[6] Z. Gippius (Anton Krayniy), 'Poslednyaya belletristika', *Novyy put'*, 1903, No. 2, p. 187.

Burenin's article.[1] Reiterating the charge that Andreyev was guilty of appealing to the 'undeveloped, semi-intelligent reading public', she accused him of inviting them 'to see and examine the decomposed corpse of human degradation and to close their eyes to God's wonderful, spacious world, with the beauties of nature, with the majesty of art, with the lofty aspirations of the human soul, with religious and moral battles and the great ideals of goodness—even with the downfalls, misfortunes and weakness of such people as Dostoevsky portrayed.' The inference is that Dostoevsky's 'downfalls', unlike Andreyev's, are redeemed by the presence in his novels of those lofty themes which alone, the Countess claims, should form the subject of art.

There was an obvious irony, of course, in the fact that this attack on Andreyev was made by a translator of Maupassant[2] and the wife of the creator of *The Kreutzer Sonata* (*Kreytserova Sonata*), just as there was in the fact that it was initiated by Burenin, who since 1899 had admitted as a regular contributor to his paper 'that terrible revolutionary of sex', as Filosofov was to call him some years later,[3] Rozanov.[4] It was Tolstoy who had established in Russian literature that tradition of merciless frankness which Andreyev admired and followed. Indeed, *In the Fog* reads, in part, like an illustration to Pozdnyshev's story—to Chapters IV and V of Tolstoy's work. Yet Tolstoy himself echoed in private his wife's sentiments; A. B. Goldenveyzer recalls that he referred to *The Abyss* 'with disgust'.[5] There were few writers who agreed with him.

One of the first to express his scorn for the Countess's letter was Chekhov. In a letter to Ol'ga Knipper of 11 February 1903 he suggested that it was a forgery, somebody's idea of a joke.[6] A month previously (2 or 3 January) he had referred in a letter to the same addressee to the powerful impression that *In the Fog* had made on him,[7] and this is the reaction one would have expected

[1] See S. A. Tolstaya, 'Pis'mo v redaktsiyu', *Novoe vremya*, 7 February 1903, No. 9673, p. 4.
[2] See A. V. Amfiteatrov, 'Leonid Andreyev—Grafinya Tolstaya', in his *Literaturnyy al'bom*, 2nd edn., SPb., 1907, p. 100.
[3] See D. Filosofov, 'Vesenniy veter', *Russkaya mysl'*, 1907, No. 10, p. 107.
[4] Rozanov's *In the World of the Vague* (*V mire neyasnogo*) had appeared the previous year (1901).
[5] *Russkie pisateli o literaturnom trude*, vol. 3, L., 1955, p. 506.
[6] A. P. Chekhov, *Sobranie sochineniy*, vol. 12, M., 1957, p. 526.
[7] See ibid., p. 519.

from the author of *Volodya* (1887). Gorky was similarly appalled by the Countess's diatribe. In a letter to V. V. Kotlyarevskaya of 25 February 1903 Stanislavsky wrote: 'After Tolstaya's letter about Andreyev Gorky has no desire to know Suvorin. . . .'[1] Gorky regarded *In the Fog* as a major achievement, and the actress Mariya Fyodorovna Andreyeva, who was to become his common-law wife towards the end of the same year (1903), describes a reading which he gave of the story in a circle of friends: 'This work made a stunning impression on the whole audience, but it was necessary to see Aleksey Maksimovich himself; his whole being quivered and vibrated like a taut string.'[2]

But Andreyev's case was pleaded most eloquently in the letters sent to the press by members of the younger generation, and 'strange to say,' writes Herman Bernstein, the European correspondent of *The New York Times*, who subsequently managed Andreyev's affairs in America, 'the representatives of the fair sex were among the warmest defenders of the young author.'[3] The main argument advanced in his defence is summarized in the following comment of one young reader:

I have yet to meet anyone who would derive pleasure from reading the filthy scenes in the story 'In the Fog'. Everyone reads them with pain in his heart, with sympathy for the youth who is portrayed, and everyone carries away the desire to avoid the fate which fell to the lot of Pavel Rybakov. The importance of L. Andreyev's story lies in the *warning* which it gives, and one can be certain that reading the story will cause many young men to reflect on their lives and try to put a moral curb on their impulses. For the incentive to self-analysis and moral betterment we should express our gratitude to Leonid Andreyev.[4]

Andreyev's election in 1902 to regular membership of the *Obshchestvo lyubiteley rossiyskoy slovesnosti* ('The Society of Lovers of Russian Literature') seems to indicate a general acceptance of this view in more enlightened circles.

But Andreyev was not simply calling for a 'moral curb'; he was

---

[1] K. S. Stanislavsky, *Sobranie sochineniy v vos'mi tomakh*, vol. 7, M., 1960, p. 255.

[2] *Mariya Fyodorovna Andreyeva*, M., 1961, p. 48.

[3] H. Bernstein, *With Master Minds. Interviews*, New York, 1913, p. 158.

[4] Cf. N. Denisyuk, *Smuta obshchestvennoy sovesti. Po povodu proizvedeniy Leonida Andreyeva, polemiki nashey pechati i rasskaza 'Bezdna'*, M., 1904, p. 15. This work is largely compounded of extracts from the reactions of critics and correspondents.

beckoning society as a whole to undertake a radical revision of the moral bases of its life. It was duly recognized that the protagonists of his two stories were by no means villains. 'The student Nemovetsky is a very ordinary, average young man who has absorbed the passive practice of contemporary society,' wrote Gekker,[1] and a similar view of Pavel Rybakov was expressed by A. Bogdanovich, the editor of the journal *Mir bozhiy* ('God's World').[2] It was clear to these commentators that Andreyev's two students were the victims of a social disease, and the review sections of many of the 'stout journals' (*tolstye zhurnaly*) became one of the main platforms from which this disease was diagnosed. Bogdanovich and the professor of literature and critic Evgeniy Anichkov laid stress on the alienation of Pavel from his environment, on the abnormal conditions of family life in which a father, for all his intelligence and enlightened ideas, is incapable of winning his son's confidence.[3] The mother of Aleksey Tolstoy used *In the Fog* as her text for a scathing attack on the whole educational system,[4] while in 1908 another critic, in connection with the proliferation of literature dealing with sexual themes after the 1905–6 revolution, came perhaps closest of all to Andreyev's thought with her reference to 'the abyss in the modern intellectual' as 'the legacy of a long, refined but one-sided culture, the result of a narrow, rectilinear morality'.[5]

This survey of the reactions to the two stories conveys some idea of the sensitivity of society to the issues which they raised. Andreyev never again succeeded in moving society on quite so vast a scale to constructive discussion and self-criticism. Unfortunately, not a single critic pointed out that the two works were inseparably related to everything that he had written up to that time. To Andreyev, the experience of the two students was but one more manifestation of the 'sickness' to which he had devoted all his works thus far—man's loss of contact with the 'living life'. Andrey Belyy remarked that 'chaos is always behind the backs of L. Andreyev's

---

[1] Gekker, op. cit., p. 25.

[2] See A. Bogdanovich, 'Kriticheskie zametki', *Mir bozhiy*, 1903, No. 1, p. 11.

[3] See ibid., pp. 1–14; and E. Anichkov, *Literaturnye obrazy i mneniya 1903 g.*, SPb., 1904, pp. 61–73.

[4] See A. L. Tolstaya (A. Bostrom), 'Chto govorit roditel'skomu serdtsu rasskaz Andreyeva "V tumane" ', *Obrazovanie*, 1903, No. 12, pp. 62–83.

[5] E. Koltonovskaya, 'Problema pola i eyo osveshchenie u neo-realistov', *Obrazovanie*, 1908, No. 1, p. 117.

heroes',[1] but it must be emphasized that the chaos depicted by Andreyev is always the offshoot of ignorance—ignorance of the self, the penalty for which, he states, is disintegration of the personality once that which is unknown and neglected asserts itself. In an answer to critics of *The Abyss* which he published in *Kur'er* on 27 January 1902, he wrote:

It is possible to be an idealist, to believe in man and the final triumph of good, and to reject completely that modern two-footed creature devoid of plumage who has mastered only the external forms of culture, while remaining essentially an animal in many of his instincts and motives. . . . In the naïve complacency of cultured people, in their ignorance of the boundaries of their own 'I' (more precisely, in Nietzschean terminology, of the 'Self') I see a danger and obstacles to the further development and humanization of their imperfect nature.[2]

Here we have an explicit formulation of the problem which was coming increasingly to dominate Andreyev's thoughts and to provide the mainspring of his fiction.

[1] A. Belyy, 'Prizraki khaosa', in his *Arabeski*, M., 1911, p. 486.
[2] Quoted from *LN*, p. 136.

# VI

# CRIME AND PUNISHMENT

ANDREYEV'S preoccupation with the mind and with psychic condition soon began to attract more specialized comment. With his story *Thought* (*Mysl'*) (1902) he provoked animated discussion not only in society at large, but also in the contemporary psychiatric world; and the psychiatrists attached to the Academy of Medicine in St. Petersburg devoted an entire meeting to an analysis of the protagonist of the work. One result of this meeting was the publication by a certain Dr. I. N. Ivanov of a paper entitled *Leonid Andreyev as an Artist-Psychologist on the Basis of a Psychiatric Analysis of His Story 'Thought'* (*Leonid Andreyev kak khudozhnik-psikholog, na osnovanii psikhiatricheskogo analiza ego rasskaza 'Mysl'* '), in which he put forward obliquely the view that Andreyev was himself mentally sick. Since this conviction was shared by not a few of Andreyev's readers—testimony to which are the letters of his detractors to the newspapers after the publication of *The Abyss* and *In the Fog*—his letter of self-defence, addressed to the paper *Birzhevye vedomosti*, merits quotation in full:

A factual inaccuracy has crept into the paper of I. N. Ivanov which concerns me personally. Among other things it is said in the report: 'Evidently L. Andreyev has carried out a profound study of the question of which he treats, acquainting himself with it in primary sources, and in addition—this is no secret—he had himself the regrettable opportunity to make the practical acquaintance of psychiatry during his spell in a special clinic.'

This last remark, which infers that I have been psychically ill and in a clinic, is untrue and surprises me coming from the lips of so serious and honourable a writer as Dr. I. N. Ivanov. Never in my life have I suffered any psychic illness. Only once have I been in a hospital—to be precise, in Professor Cherinov's clinic for internal disorders. That was in February and March 1901, and the entry describing the nature of my affliction—palpitation caused by nervous and gastric disorders—is probably still in the clinic's books. It was there in the clinic that I began and finished my story 'Once upon a Time There Lived'.

While rumours alleging that I have been and still am insane were simply street-gossip, I did not consider it necessary to make any objection whatsoever. But now that they are cited in a strictly scientific paper, as fact, and are published as such by the newspapers, I request the publication of this explanation in order to establish the truth. The need for this is all the greater due to the tendency of a certain section of the public and criticism to connect the plots of works of literature with the personal life of their authors, and my silence in this case could lead to further errors which the writers themselves would not wish.[1]

Let us now examine the story which brought Ivanov to his conclusion.

According to Andreyev, the workings of the subconscious remain invisible to the hypertrophied intellect except at moments of crisis, when the circle of concept is broken by the invasion of new forms and the personality disintegrates. Such a crisis is created not only by simple suppression of the instincts, but also by certain types of conscious activity which conflict with their conditioned nature. In Andreyev's conception the subconscious passes from generation to generation undergoing a continuous process of conditioning which is dependent on the stimuli with which it is brought into contact. The result of a prolonged absence of certain stimuli is the alienation from them of that part of the subconscious which once reacted to them normally. In time this alienation will become so complete that a sudden confrontation with these same stimuli will plunge the personality into chaos. On the basis of this conviction Andreyev constructed the story of Dr. Kerzhentsev, the protagonist of *Thought*.

The work consists, for the most part, of the doctor's 'confession' addressed to a board of psychiatrists which has been convened to determine whether or not he is insane. Awaiting trial for the murder of Aleksey Konstantinovich Savelov, he records his state of mind comprehensively from the moment when he first conceived the idea of murder to the time of his arrest.

Significant are the points of similarity and dissimilarity between Kerzhentsev and Raskol'nikov. In the first instance, they are both guilty of the sin of self-detachment from the unity of mankind, conceived by Dostoevsky and Andreyev respectively as a spiritual and ontological entity, and *ipso facto* from the sphere of moral law;

[1] Quoted from N. Denisyuk, op. cit., pp. 53–4.

the name 'Raskol'nikov' epitomizes this sin.[1] The murders committed by the two heroes are objectifications of this mystical guilt. Three common features are born of their isolation: (1) an introverted nature which sees itself at war with its environment and seeks to impose its will on that environment which it reduces to a radically simplified abstract scheme; (2) monomania, or the concentration of the passions on a single goal fixed by the will; and (3) contempt for all moral frontiers 'both human and divine'. A further point of similarity is discernible in the complication of the initial motive for the murders which they commit by a second motive, which is the same in both cases. But the difference between their initial motives reveals a fundamental difference of character between them.

The initial motive of Raskol'nikov is primarily humanitarian. He convinces himself—and the conviction does not leave the reader entirely unsympathetic—that it is not wrong to kill one worthless being to bring happiness to a plurality of good beings. Only later is this humanitarian motive complicated by the 'idea of the superman', for whom no moral stipulations are sacrosanct. Kerzhentsev is totally devoid of the moral grandeur which sustains our commiseration with Raskol'nikov. The idea of murder first suggests itself to him as the direct result of two wounds inflicted on his vanity: the rejection of his proposal of marriage by Tat'yana Nikolaevna and, more important, her discovery of happiness in marriage to Savelov. The existence in Kerzhentsev from the beginning of this abnormally sensitive vanity at once distinguishes him from Raskol'nikov, giving him instead an affinity with the 'retort man' or 'intensely reasoning mouse' of whom the 'underground man' says: 'For forty successive years he will remember an insult down to the last, most shameful details.'[2] But in order to appreciate the nature of this vanity, it is necessary to determine more precisely what Savelov represents for Kerzhentsev.

The conflict between morality and amorality which plagues Raskol'nikov is foreign to Andreyev's hero. There is no moral drama in Kerzhentsev prior to the murder, nor from his childhood has his mind ever been afflicted by doubt as to the moral permissibility of his actions. From the beginning of his conscious life he

---

[1] The name is derived from the noun *raskol* which means 'split' or 'schism'. A *raskol'nik* is 'someone who has split off', i.e. an 'apostate' or 'sectarian'.

[2] F. M. Dostoevsky, *Sobranie sochineniy*, vol. 4, M., 1956, p. 141.

acknowledges a single god—his intellect, and views reality as a succession of challenges to its power. He severs every bond which links him to the outside world, loses consciousness of his dependence on its laws and, far from seeing his personality as the product of collective life, he makes it the fulcrum of reality and his intellect —the world's arbiter. 'Lord of myself,' he writes, 'I was also lord of the world.'[1] In short, Kerzhentsev achieves long before the murder the state to which Raskol'nikov comes to aspire. Significant, however, is his acknowledgment that in 'two categories of beings of a lower order'[2] he had always failed to inspire trust: women and dogs, i.e. creatures in whom reason, according to Andreyev's abstract scheme, is either non-existent or subservient to instinct or intuition. It was this instinctive distrust, we are led to assume, which prompted Tat'yana Nikolaevna to reject Kerzhentsev's proposal.

A preponderance of intuitive over intellectual activity is also a distinguishing characteristic of the artistic temperament, and it is in this type of temperament that Kerzhentsev recognizes his most bitter foe. When he informs us, therefore, that his father would certainly have become a famous artist or writer had he not turned to the legal profession, we see the reason for their bitter antipathy and for Kerzhentsev's perpetual quest during his childhood and youth for ways and means of asserting his superiority. Similarly, when it is learnt that Savelov is a writer, the true significance of the desire for vengeance which is the first motive for the murder becomes wholly clear. It is noteworthy that when Kerzhentsev endeavours to convince his judges of Savelov's insignificance, it is his illogical and erratic conduct that he stresses, comparing him to 'a child or a woman'.[3] But it must be emphasized that the vengeance is not wrought on Savelov himself; he is simply the instrument by means of which Kerzhentsev takes vengeance on Tat'yana Nikolaevna, whose preference of Savelov to himself and discovery of happiness with him represent an unforgivable distortion of his simplified, logical conception of reality. His 'second motive' is much less complex and issues directly from the first—namely, the desire to subject the intellect to the ultimate test of its powers— murder.

Both Raskol'nikov and Kerzhentsev, therefore, are ultimately impelled to commit murder by the 'idea of Napoleon', but their reactions to this idea are radically different. While for Kerzhentsev

[1] *Works* II, p. 134.　　[2] Ibid., p. 107.　　[3] Ibid., p. 99.

the act of murder represents merely the final link in a whole chain of acts of self-will, Raskol'nikov is totally unprepared by his past; hence his unabating doubts and fears, his conflicting emotions and the vacillation of his will and thought. Moments of passionate resolve alternate with moments of mental and physical paralysis. The theory of the 'right of the strong' is essentially foreign to his whole moral nature; hence the unsuppressable revulsion which the thought of murder arouses in him. Kerzhentsev also reacts with disgust, but its sources are aesthetic, not ethical. 'In a harmoniously working living organism,' he announces, 'there is a special kind of beauty; death, like illness and old age, is primarily ugliness.'[1] It is considerably easier for him to conquer his aesthetic prejudices than it is for Raskol'nikov to counteract the promptings of his conscience. It was on the basis of such observations that a contemporary psychiatrist pronounced Kerzhentsev a paranoid and Raskol'nikov a psychasthenic.[2]

Three results, states Kerzhentsev, must be ensured by the method of execution: avoidance of prison, the absence of protracted suffering in the victim, and the presence of Tat'yana at the fateful moment; she must witness in person the triumph of reason over the irrational which the murder is meant to symbolize. The moral sanction is forthcoming from his self-assertive moral code: 'For those who believe in God the crime is before God; for others the crime is before people; for such as I the crime is before me myself. It would have been a greater crime if, having acknowledged the necessity of killing Aleksey, I had not carried out this decision.'[3] But though he has no scruples, there are other antagonistic factors; they fall into two interrelated categories, of both of which he is dimly aware, but his simplified conception of reality prevents him from perceiving their full significance until it is too late. The factors of the first category are furnished by external reality in the form of the succession of 'accidents' which facilitate the execution of his scheme and create the impression that Savelov has been sentenced to death by someone else. They introduce a mystical element into the work akin to that of *The Grand Slam*. Firstly, the ruse of simulated insanity, by which he hopes to achieve the three

[1] Ibid., p. 102.
[2] Cf. D. A. Amenitsky, 'Analiz geroya "Mysli" L. Andreyeva. (K voprosu o paranoidnoy psikhopatii)', *Sovremennaya psikhiatriya*, 1915, No. 5, p. 235.
[3] *Works* II, p. 103.

results that have been stated, is suggested to him by a chance newspaper report about a cashier who simulated an epileptic attack to conceal a theft;[1] then Savelov foretells the manner of his own death; and finally, Tat'yana Nikolaevna, who is terrified by the potential dangers of Kerzhentsev's psychic state after his two successful rehearsals of insanity in public, asks him to visit them, and this act seems to Kerzhentsev to predetermine Savelov's fate independently of his own will. On a smaller scale, he perceives the working of this deterministic force in the fact that the murder is committed precisely at six o'clock in the evening—the very hour at which his proposal of marriage was rejected by Tat'yana Nikolaevna. The parallel with Raskol'nikov's experience is again striking, for chance also seems to favour Dostoevsky's hero; we sense more than coincidence when he happens to overhear in the Sennaya that the old usurer will be alone the following evening at seven o'clock[2]. Both writers create the illusion that life is conscious of the rebel in its midst and is hastening him to the climactic moment; Raskol'nikov survives at the cost of great spiritual suffering, but Kerzhentsev does not, owing to the factors of the second category that has been mentioned.

By the mere act of his failure to repent, Raskol'nikov places himself beyond the universal moral law and thus achieves his purpose. But from this point onward Andreyev develops his own thesis which has no counterpart in Dostoevsky's novel, and is more concerned with his hero's contravention of another law which, he holds, cannot be transgressed with impunity—the law of his subconscious. When assessing whether his parents and relatives will be useful in helping him to bolster up his hoax of insanity, Kerzhentsev's criterion for judgement is fatally defective. The murder is conceived by him in the firm belief that his intellect is the lord of his mind and that his subconscious world and body have been subjugated. He checks his body carefully, acknowledging that 'for a criminal the most terrible thing is not the police or the trial, but he himself, his nerves, the powerful protest of his body reared in

---

[1] It was believed by some people that a recent case in the courts had served Andreyev as a source of material in the story of Kerzhentsev—namely, the case of a Kievan student named Mishchenko who had simulated insanity with the same design of committing murder with impunity. Brusyanin states, however, that *Thought* had been completed by the time that Andreyev became acquainted with the case (see *BSN*, p. 76).

[2] See F. M. Dostoevsky, *Sobranie sochineniy*, vol. 5, M., 1957, pp. 67–8.

certain traditions';[1] and it is interesting that refusing to acknowledge the success of Raskol'nikov's act of self-will—presumably
because of the confession and exile to the labour-camp—he attributes the failure to Raskol'nikov's omission to take into account
the factor of his body. But even though Kerzhentsev, as a doctor,
has a specialized knowledge of the body, he is ignorant of its
innermost workings—of the 'body' in the Nietzschean sense of the
term, i.e. as a hierarchy of urges which determine character and
function for the most part unconsciously; as a result he is guilty of
the omission for which he criticizes Raskol'nikov. The story of
Raskol'nikov, as he interprets it, becomes a prediction of his own
experience and there can be little doubt that this is deliberate irony
on Andreyev's part. Unknown to Kerzhentsev, his subconscious is
genetically unprepared for the spilling of blood. In the long succession of generations which have conditioned its nature it has either
never known this stimulus or simply become alienated from it; and
now, when suddenly confronted with it by the intellect, which up
to this moment it has left unmolested, it rises to punish the impu-
dent pretender and reassert its supremacy. Kerzhentsev refers to
this phenomenon when he states that he himself is the only enemy
of his ego.[2]

The blow is dealt by the thought, which suddenly comes to him
after the murder, that perhaps he was not pretending at all, but
was, in fact, genuinely insane. His intellect disintegrates under its
weight: 'The single thought shattered into a thousand thoughts . . .,'
he writes. 'They whirled in a savage dance and their music was
a monstrous voice, sonorous as a trumpet, and it came from somewhere in the depths unknown to me.'[3] It is this ignorance of its
source which he cannot endure—the consciousness that his proud
intellect was always 'a slave, pitiful and powerless'[4] to an unknown
lord. He thought that he was deceiving others, but in reality he was
deceiving himself. 'O poor and useless reason,' Andreyev wrote in
his diary: 'You endeavour sometimes to free yourself from the
fetters laid upon you by the body—but in vain. You are either a serf,
humble and obliging, or an uninvited counsellor ignored from
above, or an enemy and tormentor poisoning the soul.'[5]

Of particular interest is Kerzhentsev's graphic presentation of
his psychic condition:

[1] *Works* II, p. 103.     [2] See ibid., p. 134.     [3] Ibid., p. 126.     [4] Ibid.
[5] *PNA*, p. 191.

Imagine that you were living in a house that had many rooms, that you occupied only one room and thought that you controlled the whole house. And suddenly you learnt that there was someone living in the other rooms. *Yes, living.* Some mysterious creatures were living there, perhaps people, perhaps something else, and the house belongs to them. You want to know who they are, but the door is locked and neither sound nor voice is audible behind it. And at the same time you know that it is there behind that silent door that your fate is being decided.[1]

The similarity of this allegory, both in its images and in that which they denote, to Poe's *The Fall of the House of Usher* is sufficiently close to suggest the possibility that Andreyev had the latter work in mind. Poe's obsession with the occult and fantastic was, as might be expected, a source of considerable interest for certain of the symbolists, especially Bryusov, whose stories were to reveal unmistakable signs of his study of the American writer, and it is noteworthy that the Moscow publishing-house *Skorpion* ('Scorpion') had begun a new edition of Poe's works in 1901. Evidence of Andreyev's admiration of Poe is forthcoming from Gorky's reminiscences,[2] and the parallels drawn by L'vov-Rogachevsky and Chulkov between certain of Andreyev's early stories and stories by Poe[3] are too numerous to enable us to accept Kugel's contention that Andreyev did not encounter the American writer till late in his life.[4] Very different is the testimony of Beklemisheva, who states that at the time she made Andreyev's acquaintance (1908) his infatuation with Poe was beginning to wane.[5] The common features of *Thought* and *The Fall of the House of Usher*, however, have not attracted attention.

In this story Poe treats of the same problem of personality as Andreyev in *Thought*, and since in both works the moral problem is secondary or, to be more precise, complementary to the philosophically interpreted problem of psychic disharmony, it can be said that they have more in common with one another than either

---

[1] *Works* II, p. 126.     [2] Cf. *KLA*, p. 37.

[3] Cf. V. L'vov-Rogachevsky, 'Myortvoe tsarstvo. (Po povodu rasskazov Leonida Andreyeva)', *Obrazovanie*, 1904, No. 11, pp. 73–130; and G. Chulkov, 'Tretiy "Sbornik" tovarishchestva "Znanie" za 1904 g., SPb., 1905', *Voprosy zhizni*, 1905, No. 1, pp. 303–4.

[4] Cf. A. R. Kugel', 'Literaturnye vstrechi i kharakteristiki', in his *List'ya s dereva*, L., 1926, p. 82.

[5] Cf. *Rekviem*, p. 257.

has with *Crime and Punishment*. In his essay on the nature and creation of the material and spiritual universe, *Eureka*, Poe postulates a unity of matter which he terms the Divine Being, of which man and his animate and inanimate environment are minute individualizations. The evolution of universal life, he states, pivots on the alternating processes of attraction and repulsion, which are manifestations of the alternating concentration and self-diffusion of the Divine Being; the universe as we know it is 'but his present expansive existence',[1] but, while it is in this cyclic phase of dispersion, the universe reveals in all spheres of its existence a desire for reintegration in the original unity. Equating dispersion with disharmony and, in conscious creatures, with frustration and aspiration, he makes unity synonymous with harmony and fulfilment. The same principles necessarily govern his conception of the human organism, in which he recognizes three separate but interacting faculties: the mind or intellect, the soul or spirit, and the body. No one of these faculties is self-sufficient and health is synonymous with the existence of a state of balance between them; but such a state is always most delicately poised and the slightest disturbance can lead to the hypertrophy or atrophy of one of the faculties at the expense of the others. In *The Fall of the House of Usher* Poe presents an allegory of this drama of the personality.

Poe's metaphysical theory of the essential unity of matter finds expression in the projection of the drama enacted by the characters, themselves symbols of the faculties, on to the inanimate environment—the house, which, like that of Kerzhentsev's allegory, symbolizes the total organism. On the second—or 'human'—level the source of the disharmony is revealed as the hypertrophy of the intellect, of which Roderick Usher is the symbol, at the expense of the body, symbolized by his sister Madeleine. Believing that he has finally destroyed the abhorrent physical aspect of his personality, Usher buries it—in its human incarnation—in the family vault far from his intellectual domain; but, though diseased, it still lives, and the distant knocking from the depths of his being is the exact counterpart, in its symbolic significance, of the 'monstrous voice' which strikes terror into Kerzhentsev. As in *Thought*, the direct confrontation of the intellect with an aspect of the personality from which it has become estranged, and which it has sought to subdue,

[1] J. A. Harrison (ed.), *The Complete Works of Edgar Allan Poe*, vol. 16, New York, 1902, p. 314.

results in the total disintegration which is objectivized in the collapse of the house.

In its essential meaning, therefore, Poe's story reads like an externalization of the drama of Kerzhentsev, and like an enlargement of Kerzhentsev's own allegory. But unlike Poe, whose interest lay primarily in the symbolic vision created by his fantasy, Andreyev was concerned above all with his intellectual thesis. In Poe the concrete form which the thought takes assumes complete command and engulfs the whole work; in Andreyev the allegory is briefly delineated and serves the single purpose of rendering more vivid the directly posed problem. The link between *Thought* and its antecedents in Andreyev's fiction is clear. In this work, described by Sakhnovsky as specifically a 'modern tragedy',[1] Andreyev continued his self-appointed task of undermining that misplaced confidence in the intellect which he held to be at once the most characteristic and deleterious manifestation of 'apostasy' in contemporary life by exposing its essential impotence. 'I was firmly on the ground,' writes Kerzhentsev, 'and my feet stood solidly on it, but now I am hurled into the void of infinite space.'[2]

No less than *The Abyss* and *In the Fog*, the work was conceived as a warning. The general is not only implicit in the particular throughout; at the end it becomes fully explicit in the challenge issued by Kerzhentsev to the board of psychiatrists. His principal motive for writing the 'confession' is his desperate desire to know whether or not he is genuinely insane, but how can the truth be expected from judges who are guided by the same treacherous, eternally lying intellect? 'You will think and speak,' he writes, 'and I will think and speak, and we shall all be right and not one of us will be right.'[3] The work ends logically with the problem unsolved. The psychiatrists are evenly divided in their opinion, and when asked whether he has anything to say, Kerzhentsev replies simply: 'Nothing!' On the advice of Gorky, Andreyev made this the last word of the story,[4] as Schopenhauer did in Book IV of *The World as Will and Idea*.

---

[1] Cf. Sakhnovsky, loc. cit., p. 173.    [2] *Works* II, p. 135.    [3] Ibid., p. 132.

[4] Gorky had written: 'Believe me, friend, that word should be the last word of the story, precisely that word. The jurors, the court audience, the questions—all is superfluous! They are trifles' (*LN*, p. 147). When first published the work ended with the additional sentence: 'The jurors withdrew to the consultation room' (*Mir bozhiy*, 1902, No. 7, p. 159).

# VII

## HUBRIS AND NEMESIS

IN April 1902 Andreyev informed Gorky that although he had already received an advance for *Thought* from *Mir bozhiy*, he had been influenced by Mirolyubov to send it to Mikhaylovsky for publication in *Russkoe bogatstvo*.[1] He expressed his intention of meeting his obligation to *Mir bozhiy* with another story 'about a priest' called *Arise and Walk* (*Vstan' i khodi*).[2] Mikhaylovsky did not accept *Thought*, however; Andreyev confided his response to Izmaylov:

He returned it to me with a letter in which he said that he did not understand such a story. What ideological meaning could there be in it? If it was simply a clinical picture of the spiritual disintegration of a man, he was not sufficiently competent to judge the accuracy of my portrayal of the sick man's psychology. He said that in this case a psychologist's judgement was necessary.[3]

Thus the work was published by *Mir bozhiy* after all (in the July issue). *Arise and Walk* was not completed until much later— 19 November 1903, and in the interim it underwent four changes of title: in a letter to Mikhaylovsky written in the same month as the letter to Gorky (April 1902) Andreyev stated that its title was *Father Vasiliy* (*O. Vasiliy*);[4] then, in other letters to him of 2 May and August or September 1902 respectively he refers to it as *The Priest* (*Pop*) and *Three Lives* (*Tri zhizni*), adding to the latter the note 'a story about a proud priest';[5] and subsequently it received its final title *The Life of Vasiliy Fiveysky*.[6] This vacillation in the choice of title is a reflection of the general difficulty which Andreyev experienced in writing the work. He wrote to Veresaev in August

---

[1] Cf. *LN*, p. 145.    [2] Cf. ibid., p. 146.    [3] Izmaylov, op. cit., p. 250.
[4] Cf. *MAMK*, p. 52.    [5] Cf. ibid., pp. 54 and 57.
[6] The name of the central character was taken by Andreyev from the senior sanitary inspector of Nizhniy-Novgorod, Vasiliy Mikhaylovich Fiveysky, whose tragic death from a disease of the brain at the age of 30 made a deep impression on the writer. Fiveysky's funeral coincided with a visit by Andreyev to Nizhniy-Novgorod in February 1903. Initially he had thought of calling his hero Vasiliy Chagin (cf. *LN*, p. 148).

1903: 'The idea of the work is important, but its execution is wretched; more work must be done on it,'[1] and as late as October he informed Mirolyubov that it was only half completed.[2] He managed to finish it in the following month, however, and it finally appeared, with a dedication to Shalyapin, in *Znanie*'s first literary miscellany dated 1903 and published in March 1904.

There is no evidence to confirm the suggestion of one critic that Andreyev may have been influenced to write the work by the discovery shortly before of the remains of the mystic saint Serafim Sarovsky (1759–1833).[3] Gorky believed that it was he who had provided Andreyev with his source of inspiration. He recalled the episode some years later:

Conversing with him about various seekers of firm faith, I related to him the substance of the manuscript 'Confession' of the priest Apollov,[4] and told him about one of the works of the unknown martyrs of thought —works which were brought back to life by Lev Tolstoy's 'Confession'. I told him about my personal observations on people of dogma—they are often voluntary prisoners of a blind, rigid faith and the more fanatically they defend its truth, the more painfully they doubt it.

Within a few minutes, he continues, Andreyev leaned towards him and said: 'I will write about a priest, you will see. . . . I even have the first sentence: "He was alone among people for he had made contact with a great secret." '[5] The first half of this sentence entered the third sentence of the final version of *The Life of Vasiliy Fiveysky*.[6]

This same episode has been briefly recalled by Mariya Fyodorovna Andreyeva in her memoirs: '. . . so far as I remember,' she writes, 'he (Gorky) told a story about a deeply devout priest who prayed for a miracle and believed in the possibility thereof. Subsequently Andreyev wrote "Vasiliy Fiveysky" on this theme.'[7]

The origins of many of Andreyev's major works can be traced to such chance conversations, and events and characters described by

---

[1] *VRSV*, p. 452.    [2] See *MAMR*, p. 105.

[3] See E. Zhurakovsky, 'Krakh dushi. Kriticheskiy ocherk o poslednikh proizvedeniyakh Leonida Andreyeva', *Vsemirnyy vestnik*, 1904, No. 12, p. 77.

[4] Aleksandr Ivanovich Apollov (1864–93), a priest in Simferopol' in the Caucasus, renounced the teaching of the Orthodox Church under the influence of the ideas of Tolstoy. Through Tolstoy his *Confession* (*Ispoved'*) achieved considerable renown.

[5] *KLA*, pp. 11–12.    [6] See *Works* III, p. 20.

[7] *Mariya Fyodorovna Andreyeva*, M., 1961, p. 48.

Gorky lie at the basis not only of *The Life of Vasiliy Fiveysky*, but
also of *Savva*, *Darkness* and *Sashka Zhegulyov* (1911). 'A single
phrase,' writes Gorky, 'and sometimes merely an accurate word,
was enough for him to seize the trifle that had been given to him
and develop it immediately into a picture, anecdote, character or
story.'[1] This willingness on Andreyev's part to accept material from
any source, which followed logically from his conception of himself
as a 'jeweller' as distinct from a 'seeker of gold', is responsible for
the variety of characters and situations in his works, but, as stated
earlier, the variety is superficial and veils an unusual uniformity.
In 1901 he wrote to Chukovsky: 'It is not important to me who
"he" is—the hero of my stories: a priest, a bureaucrat, a good soul
or a beast. Only one thing is important to me—that he is a man
and, as such, bears one and the same burdens of life.'[2] He expressed
similar sentiments to Brusyanin: 'I want to think about Russians,
Romans, Spaniards . . ., about man in general. . . . I attach
little importance to a man's material vestments; I take the spiritual
essence of man and seek the true nature of human life.'[3]

Herein lies the reason why the difference between his doctor of
medicine and his priest is not so great as their professions would
imply. Characteristic is a remark which he made to Kleynbort: 'I
assure you that I have seen the clergy only twice in my life: once
at a wedding, and again at a funeral.'[4] Factual knowledge of the
life of the clergy was not necessary to him for the creation of the
character of Vasiliy Fiveysky; he saw a man's station or profession
as yet another mask concealing his 'naked soul'.

The conflict portrayed by Andreyev in *Thought* is, in essence,
a conflict between the 'substance' of life and its form, of which
the intellect is a property. The collapse of Kerzhentsev is the consequence of his endeavour to effect the triumph of the form over
the substance. The same conflict is re-enacted in *The Life of
Vasiliy Fiveysky*, but in a somewhat different guise. Vasiliy
Fiveysky's self-assertion is founded not on faith in the omnipotence
of his intellect, but on a wholly egocentric and utilitarian faith in
God. The author writes in the first paragraph: 'When he became a
priest, he married a good girl and begot by her a son and daughter;

---

[1] *KLA*, p. 9.      [2] K. Chukovsky, *Lyudi i knigi*, M., 1958, p. 509.
[3] *BSN*, p. 12.
[4] Kleynbort, loc. cit., p. 179. Cf. 'Pis'ma Leonida Andreyeva k M. P. Nevedomskomu', *Iskusstvo*, 1925, No. 2, p. 266.

then he thought that everything had turned out well and long-lasting for him, as for people, and that it would remain so for ever. And he blessed God, because he believed in Him.'[1] The statement discloses the nature of the priest's attitude both to God and to his own life; it also provides the first hint of his mortal sin—pride. It will be seen that a feature of this rather long work (by Andreyev's standards) is the superimposition by the author of his own, as distinct from his hero's, responses to the events of the narrative, but this is clearly not the case in the quoted passage; here Andreyev is simply reproducing Vasiliy Fiveysky's own thoughts on his life. Considered in this light, the phrase 'as with people' is perhaps the most informative of all, for it indicates not simply the priest's self-detachment from people, but a tendency on his part to regard himself as something different from the average mortal, and this self-conceived difference is soon revealed to be the consequence of his belief in his own abnormal proximity to God, of his self-elevation to a 'privileged limbo' to which the ordinary man has no access. Vyacheslav Ivanov was the first to draw attention to the pride of Vasiliy Fiveysky,[2] but he omitted to stress the important point that from the beginning it is the most salient feature of Andreyev's hero; that Andreyev himself regarded it as such is shown by his adjunct in parentheses to the fourth of the five titles which the work received in the course of its composition.[3]

In this privileged position between life and God which Vasiliy Fiveysky creates for himself there is only one role which he can play—that of a passive recipient. His self-elevation above life renders him incapable of an active role and is tantamount to an abdication of responsibility for his earthly life; but his concern for his earthly welfare is far from diminished thereby, for it constitutes for him at once the evidence and condition of God's existence—a fact which signifies that from the outset he is potentially a doubter and a sceptic. For the first seven years of his married life he experiences nothing but 'divine beneficence' and it is unthinkable to him that this state of affairs should change, because his faith is firm; he believes, as the author ironically puts it, 'solemnly and simply'.[4]

---

[1] *Works* III, p. 20.

[2] See V. Ivanov, 'Novaya povest' Leonida Andreyeva. "Zhizn' Vasiliya Fiveyskogo" ', *Vesy*, 1904, No. 5, p. 46.

[3] Cf. *supra*, p. 87.      [4] *Works* III, p. 20.

But it does change. His son drowns 'in the seventh year of his well-being'[1] and his house is plunged into darkness. This is the first of a whole series of blows which swiftly transform his life and ultimately his attitude to God, and the rapidity with which they succeed one another creates the impression that a 'severe and mysterious fate'[2] is hovering over him, that he is surrounded by a 'special kind of air, pernicious and baneful'[3] and that they are the work of a 'sinister and mysterious predetermination'.[4] His parishioners sense this abnormality and consider any meeting with him a 'bad omen'.

These 'mystical' references all appear in the first paragraph of the work and condition the reader's mind at once for the accumulation of an abnormal order of events. In his examination of the relationship between the author and his hero the critic A. A. Smirnov came to the conclusion, in an attempt to explain the mystical element, that Andreyev immerses himself so deeply in the psychological world of his hero that it colours not only those parts of the work in which he describes his hero's experiences, but even the parts in which he speaks himself. The result, he maintains, is an 'inverted subjectivism', in which it is not the author imposing his attitude of mind on the hero, but vice-versa.[5] Closer investigation reveals, however, that there are, in fact, two separate and clearly distinct views of the events of the story, that the identity of attitude between author and hero claimed by Smirnov is non-existent. The mystical element suggests an interpretation of the events of which the hero himself is totally unconscious; it is only much later that he reads a mystical significance into his misfortunes, and even then it is a very different significance from that which they have for his creator.

The author's intermittent transitions from a purely narrative to an interpretative role were necessitated by the idea underlying the work, according to which the hero is blind to the true significance and the consequences of his 'apostasy'. In *Thought* the interpretative element posed few difficulties for the author due to his selection of the form of the *Ich-Erzählung*, which meant not only that the narrator could break off the narrative flow at any moment and comment on events, but also that everything was

[1] Ibid.   [2] Ibid.   [3] Ibid.   [4] Ibid.
[5] Cf. A. A. Smirnov (Treplyov), 'Razoryonnaya zhizn'. (Rasskazy L. Andreyeva s tochki zreniya zhiznennoy evolyutsii)', *Russkaya mysl'*, 1905, No. 9, p. 108.

described in retrospect and events could be judged and interpreted in the light of the known dénouement. Orthodox narration, in which the protagonist is referred to in the third person, is less flexible in this respect, and it may reasonably be assumed that it was partly the difficulties created by this problem which delayed so long the completion of *The Life of Vasiliy Fiveysky*, in which Andreyev reverts to this form. His solution is the two differing attitudes to the events described which are discernible in the work. The mystical element in the first two-thirds of the story is wholly the expression of the author's attitude and is integral to the philosophical scheme. It fulfils, in fact, three purposes: it conditions the reader's mind, introducing an ominous note of foreboding; it also evokes the mystical atmosphere which prepares the way for and renders more plausible the priest's subsequent mystical interpretation of his life; but most important of all, it denotes the presence in the management of events of a real force—that force which has been perceived in *The Grand Slam* and *Thought* and which appears in one form or another in Andreyev's every indictment of the 'apostate': namely, the force of 'avenging life'. Like the 'accidents' which lead Kerzhentsev to his shattering discovery and which appear to be in league with his stirring subconscious, the disasters which befall Vasiliy Fiveysky precipitate the moment of crisis. After the death of his son he cries to God: 'I believe!' but from his lungs bursts forth a 'devout wail, so madly similar to a challenge'.[1] After each successive misfortune he repeats this 'I believe!' and on each occasion the profession of faith is accompanied by a discordant note—a challenge, a forewarning, almost a threat until, in the end, he breaks out in open rebellion. The mask of faith is stripped from him and underneath is revealed the sceptic.

The work is dominated by the figure of the protagonist; the other characters exist only to project light on his inner world. The husband-wife relationship is but one of the means by which Andreyev exposes the degree of his detachment from life and normal human experience. The physical deterioration of Fiveysky's wife is a projection of her spiritual degeneration which, in its turn, is an indirect comment on her husband. In a desperate bid to rescue herself after the drowning of her son, she conceives the idea of bearing another child. After a momentary protest Fiveysky responds to her frenzied passion and she becomes pregnant. 'A peaceful and

[1] *Works* III, p. 23.

joyous calm,' we read, 'settled in the house of Father Vasiliy.'[1]

The pregnancy is primarily symbolic of a regained contact with life, and the trips of the priest's wife to collect mushrooms during the period of waiting represent an extension of the same motif: 'the thick forest,' writes the author, 'seemed to her alive, wise and caressing.'[2] The contrast between the world of nature and life in the Fiveysky household runs throughout the work. Like the priest's daughter, Nastya, as she gazes at the garden of the house, the family as a whole senses in nature something 'familiar, but eternally mysterious and luring'.[3] Repeatedly life seems to be striving to extricate them from their dark, secluded existence. In her alcoholic dreams, for instance, the priest's wife is possessed by the vision of phantoms clutching her hair and 'dragging her somewhere'.[4] This is only one of the numerous references in the work to this mysterious 'somewhere', and they drew from Vyacheslav Ivanov the criticism of 'incompleteness',[5] but the nature of this 'vague destination', which is 'the main thing in Andreyev's writings', as Sakhnovsky puts it,[6] is clearly expressed in the general symbolism of the work. Temporarily the Fiveyskys surrender to it and a new spirit enters their lives. The transition is symbolized by the lamp: the 'black, sooted glass' of former days is imperceptibly transformed into a light blue lampshade, and a bright light replaces the former 'blood-red glow'.[7]

But still the 'severe and mysterious fate' hovers above the priest's head. His second son turns out to be mentally and physically deformed. The two children of Vasiliy Fiveysky are symbolic projections of his psychic world, and the hostility of his daughter Nastya to the 'idiot' is symbolic of his psychic conflict. The 'idiot' represents Andreyev's first symbol of the deformed subconscious of the 'apostate':

The idiot wet his lips with his long, animal-like tongue and started to 'goo' with loud, monotonous, jumping sounds: goo-goo, goo-goo. . . . At times he fell into a state of heavy torpor, like a strange, nightmarish pensiveness. Propping up his head with his thin, long fingers and with the tip of his tongue slightly protruding he would look in front of him motionlessly from beneath narrow, beast-like eyelids. And then it would

---

[1] Ibid., p. 28.    [2] Ibid., p. 29.    [3] Ibid., p. 22.    [4] Ibid., p. 35.
[5] See V. Ivanov, 'Novaya povest' Leonida Andreyeva. "Zhizn' Vasiliya Fiveyskogo" ', *Vesy*, 1904, No. 5, p. 45.
[6] See Sakhnovsky, loc. cit., p. 172.    [7] Cf. *Works III*, pp. 27 and 29.

seem that he was not an idiot at all, that he was thinking something special, unlike the thoughts of anyone else, and that he knew something which was also special, simple and mysterious and which no one else knew. And one would think, on looking at his flattened nose with its broad, turned-out nostrils, the cleft back of his head which passed in an animal-like line right down to his back, that if he were given strong and speedy legs, he would run away into the forest and start to live there a mysterious forest life full of games, cruelty and dark forest wisdom.[1]

This deformed child—half-man, half-beast—is a projection of that which lives in the 'dark garret' of Vasiliy Fiveysky's being—that dark instinct, which in its normal, healthy form constitutes the soul of life, synthesizes and harmonizes the physical and spiritual powers of man, gives him a balanced understanding of life and the universe, and furnishes him with an essential store of productive energy. The subconscious in its healthy form is symbolically juxtaposed in the form of the churchwarden, Ivan Porfirych Koprov. 'In his judgments,' we read, 'Ivan Porfirych was quick and superficial and easily veered from them, often without noticing it himself, but his actions were firm, decisive and almost always unerring.'[2] With his firm, prominent cheeks, his huge black beard, the black hair which covers his entire body, his unquestioning faith in God, his self-confidence and joviality, he is clearly the exact opposite of the priest, and this explains their mutual hatred and apprehension. Fiveysky's timidity in the face of Koprov recalls another observation of Dostoevsky's 'underground man':

. . . if, for example, you take the antithesis of a normal man, that is, a powerfully reasoning man who has emerged, of course, not from the bosom of nature, but from a retort . . ., then this retort man becomes sometimes so passive in the face of his opposite that he conscientiously considers himself, with all his powerful reason, to be a mouse and not a man.[3]

Andreyev repeatedly captures his hero in his 'retort'—in meditative silence and solitude; he remarks: 'And whoever saw him would ask himself: what is this man thinking about?—so manifestly was profound thought inscribed on all his movements.'[4]

The answer to this question is revealed through Nastya, who is the embodied truth of his thought. This symbolic value is first

---

[1] Ibid., pp. 64–5.    [2] Ibid., p. 25.
[3] F. M. Dostoevsky, *Sobranie sochineniy*, vol. 4, M., 1956, p. 140.
[4] *Works* III, pp. 35–6.

suggested by physical similarity: she is described as 'thin and tall like her father, with large hands coarsened by work'.[1] No less than her father, she also seems to be surrounded by 'pernicious and baneful air': 'The dark shadow of the future,' we read, 'seemed already to lie on her six-year old heart also.'[2] Like her father she sits menacingly in the corner of the room: 'In the corner the wolf-like eyes of gloomy Nastya burned motionless and dry through her wiry, tangled hair.'[3] She says of her mother: 'I would kill her,' and shortly afterwards Father Vasiliy muses that 'if someone were to dig a grave, hurl this woman (his wife) into it with his own hands and bury her alive with earth, he would be doing a good deed'.[4] Nastya similarly expresses a desire to kill the 'idiot', and the deformity of the latter, as stated, is symbolic of the priest's efforts to realize this innermost desire. 'I love no one', she announces; 'Like me,' rejoins the priest.[5]

With each misfortune Father Vasiliy sinks deeper into thought. We read that the thought of Kerzhentsev was like a 'finely sharpened rapier', that it 'twisted, stung, bit, separated the tissues of events, crawled like a snake into unknown and gloomy depths'.[6] Into the same depths crawls the thought of Vasiliy Fiveysky: 'He thought about God and people and about the mysterious destinies of human life.'[7] But the thought of the priest is by no means so powerful or flexible a weapon: 'constant thought, heavy and dull, like a millstone . . . —it hung above his eyes like a heavy shroud.'[8] He turns his face from God to the world about him, spends his days at the confessional listening to the woes of his parishioners, and every man who confesses is described as 'his executioner'—the executioner of his faith. Closing his eyes to all but this suffering, he comes to see the life of the universe as a whole as simply an extension and reflection of his own experience. 'There existed a tiny earth,' writes the author, 'and on it lived one huge Father Vasiliy with his huge sorrow and huge doubts while other people seemed not to exist at all.'[9] The confession of Lermontov's Pechorin—'I look at the sufferings and joys of others only in relation to myself'[10]—is eminently true of Vasiliy Fiveysky. The usual

---

[1] Ibid., p. 34.    [2] Ibid., p. 21.    [3] Ibid., p. 26.    [4] Ibid., p. 47.
[5] Ibid., pp. 39–40.    [6] *Works* II, p. 108.    [7] *Works* III, p. 36.
[8] Ibid., p. 36.    [9] Ibid., p. 37.
[10] M. Yu. Lermontov, *Sobranie sochineniy v chetyryokh tomakh*, vol. 4, M.–L., 1962, p. 401.

complex of human sentiments is reduced in him to a single, monstrously inflated consciousness of uninterrupted pain and to a refined sensitivity to the negative aspects of life. Vyacheslav Ivanov saw him as a 'shadow of much-suffering Job',[1] but the shadow is distorted beyond recognition. Andreyev's hero questions the justice of divine dispensation and the last shred of his faith is rent by the confession of the peasant Semyon Mosyagin. He throws off his cassock, abandons his church and turns to the simple life of a farmer.

Again his life is transformed by restored contact with the earth. Once more his wife immerses herself in the life of the forest. The 'pernicious and baneful air' is replaced by the 'sharp and pleasant smell of grass and the fields'.[2] As during the pregnancy, however, the transformation in Vasiliy Fiveysky is superficial and illusory. The former sequence of events is re-enacted: firstly, the discovery of happiness; then the portrait of the priest sunk in thought with a look of 'proud anticipation' on his face; then the refrain: 'the same cruel and mysterious fate was hovering above his life';[3] and finally, the new disaster, the new vengeance of life: his house and wife are consumed by flames. The repeated progression confirms the mystical connection between the inner life of the priest and that which befalls him from without. This is not the blind, indiscriminate *Moira* of Greek tragedy or, as Kogan suggests, the implacable fate of Maeterlinck.[4]

But Vasiliy Fiveysky relishes this new misfortune, this new act of 'fate'; hence the reference to 'proud anticipation'. His suffering serves only to bolster the mystical idea which has been fermenting in his breast and which now, under the influence of this climactic misfortune and his reading of the gospel story about the healing of the blind man, takes possession of his whole being—the idea that his sufferings in this world are inflicted by a 'mighty hand' which is leading him to a 'great feat, a great sacrifice'.[5] He believes that he has been chosen to reveal to people the existence of God and of a purpose in their lives. At the beginning he saw the hand of God in the absence of misfortune from his life; now, deaf to the derisive

[1] V. Ivanov, 'Novaya povest' Leonida Andreyeva', p. 45.
[2] *Works* III, p. 56.    [3] Ibid.
[4] Cf. P. Kogan, 'Literaturnye napravleniya i kritika 80-kh i 90-kh godov', *Istoriya russkoy literatury XIX veka*, edited by D. N. Ovsyaniko-Kulikovsky, vol. 5, M., 1910, p. 100.
[5] *Works* III, p. 60.

gurglings of the 'idiot', he sees it in the abnormality of his suffering, and his faith returns with redoubled intensity. Once more he elevates himself to his 'privileged limbo' between man and God, symbolic of which is his abandonment of Nastya to the care of others. At the same time Nastya's departure from the town 'never to return'[1] foreshadows her father's impending doom. From the agent of this doom—the 'idiot'—he cannot detach himself.

The final scene, in which the priest calls on God to perform through him the revealing miracle—to resurrect the corpse of Mosyagin, killed in a landslide—is one of the most remarkable in Andreyev's fiction; it also confirms our interpretation of the symbolism of the work. The dénouement is essentially a variation of that of *Thought*. It is not the corpse which rises from the coffin, but the 'idiot'—the deformed subconscious rising to administer the final punishment—and the conclusion of *The Fall of the House of Usher* is repeated in the priest's vision of the church and the whole universe collapsing about him as his personality disintegrates in the face of this ultimate mockery.

Nevedomsky saw in *The Life of Vasiliy Fiveysky* the 'initial glow' of the 'light of undoubted idealism' in Andreyev's fiction.[2] It is clear, however, that so far as the basic principles of Andreyev's thought are concerned, it signifies no deviation at all from the line of development which can be traced from his earliest stories. The work issued logically from preceding works such as *The Lie*, *Silence* and *Thought*; indeed, Father Ignatiy is manifestly Father Vasiliy's fictional prototype. This succession of works reveals a process of increasing enrichment and complexity of artistic representation culminating in *The Life of Vasiliy Fiveysky* in what Asheshov termed a 'powerful, irresistible hypnosis'.[3] At the same time each new study of 'apostasy' embraces a different aspect of man's existence. The ideals, reason, love, morality and religion of modern man had all been unmasked as forces inimical to the 'living life'. Each work announced that man is his own executioner. In the war and revolution of the following three years Andreyev found further material to illustrate this truth.

---

[1] Ibid., p. 63.

[2] M. Nevedomsky, 'Ob iskusstve nashikh dney i iskusstve budushchego', *Sovremennyy mir*, 1909, No. 1, p. 169.

[3] N. Asheshov, 'Iz zhizni i literatury. "Zhizn' Vasiliya Fiveyskogo"—novoe proizvedenie g-na Leonida Andreyeva', *Obrazovanie*, 1904, No. 5, p. 81.

# VIII

## THE 'APOSTATE' AT WAR

ANDREYEV'S natural intellectual inclinations did not have the effect of curtailing the breadth and variety of his interests, of distracting his attention from more mundane and topical affairs. Indeed, the topicality of a whole succession of his works written between 1904 and 1908 incurred the disapproval of a number of critics, who saw in it the vulgarization of a rich and highly promising talent. Thus Chukovsky wrote: 'Such responsiveness is a very good thing, but it is the responsiveness of a reporter, not of a tragedian or symbolist,' and he compared Andreyev in this respect to Boborykin.[1] But Chukovsky displays here another lapse of judgement; the parallel is singularly inapt. Andreyev is never a chronicler. Life is never photographically reproduced in his works. Social-political events served him only as a general frame of reference for consideration of the more profound issues which they brought into focus.

*The Red Laugh* (*Krasnyy smekh*) is Andreyev's response to the Russo-Japanese War of 1904–5. Completed on 8 November 1904, it was first published in 1905 in *Znanie*'s third literary miscellany, which was dedicated to the memory of Chekhov. Sixty thousand copies of the work were sold—an enormous number for that time. Andreyev informed Veresaev that the work, which filled five printer's sheets (eighty pages), was written in nine days.[2] Such speed of execution was not unusual for him[3] and commentators were quick to draw attention to it. Criticism of this aspect of his works is implicit in the third of the four pieces of advice offered to him four years later by Tolstoy in his well-known letter of 2 September 1908, which may be regarded as the great novelist's testament to the younger generation of writers.[4] Signs of haste are

[1] Chukovsky, *Leonid Andreyev bol'shoy i malen'kiy*, p. 41.

[2] Cf. *VRSV*, p. 461.

[3] *In the Fog*, for instance, which filled two printer's sheets, was written in a week (cf. Andreyev's letter to Mikhaylovsky of August–September 1902, *MAMK*, p. 56).

[4] Cf. 'L. N. Tolstoy i L. N. Andreyev', in *L. N. Tolstoy. Perepiska s russkimi pisatelyami*, M., 1962, p. 667.

undoubtedly discernible in Andreyev's works and Gorky unceremoniously chastised him for it,[1] but hurried execution must not be taken to imply hasty preparation. Significant, for instance, are the remarks of Beklemisheva:

He did not write[2] in a hurry. But the process of creation was such that after bearing, contemplating and weighing it for months and sometimes even years, Andreyev would finish a large work in a few days. The theme would overpower him. It was like a sickness of many days' duration. And then, at a certain moment, everything would fall into place and become moulded in the author's creative fantasy.[3]

Nor was it only the theme to which he directed his attention during the 'preparatory' period; most of his major works, including *The Red Laugh*, testify to equally long deliberation on questions of structure and style.

Beklemisheva's comparison of the creative act in Andreyev to a 'sickness' is particularly relevant to *The Red Laugh*. 'Almost the whole of the time I was writing it I had palpitation,' he wrote to Nevedomsky, 'and once . . . I suddenly had a terrible feeling that my head would not bear it and that I would lose my sanity.'[4] Teleshov recalls that Andreyev found solitude unendurable during the writing of the work and that Aleksandra Mikhaylovna spent whole nights in his study wrapped in a shawl 'helping him with her presence and silence'.[5] The intensity of feeling which characterizes Andreyev's references to his creation is largely explained by this heavy toll which it took of him. 'I like "The Red Laugh",' he wrote to Veresaev in November 1906, 'perhaps because it was really written in the blood of my heart.'[6] Criticism of his former works, he stated in the letter to Nevedomsky, caused him little grief, but he found it difficult to forgive even indifference to *The Red Laugh*—'perhaps because,' he concludes, 'there is too little story here and too much pain, perhaps because those truly mad nights when it was written are still too alive in my memory.'[7] All the more grievous for him, therefore, must have been Gorky's criticism that the facts

[1] Cf., for example, *LN*, p. 278.
[2] Beklemisheva is clearly using the verb 'to write' here in the broad sense of to 'create' or 'compose'.
[3] *Rekviem*, p. 255.
[4] 'Pis'ma Leonida Andreyeva k M. P. Nevedomskomu', *Iskusstvo*, 1925, No. 2, p. 269.
[5] Teleshov, 'Pro Leonida Andreyeva', p. 68.      [6] *VRSV*, p. 464.
[7] 'Pis'ma Leonida Andreyeva k M. P. Nevedomskomu', p. 269.

were more terrible and significant than he appeared to have realized.[1]

Andreyev was himself conscious of the shortcomings of the work, however; he wrote to Tolstoy: 'For the first time in my life I am consciously experiencing war, and that which I have seen is so repulsive and so terrible that I cannot find words to express it. And this lack of real words is felt above all in my story, which is too artificial in its construction and details.'[2] In his immediate reply (written the following day—17 November 1904) Tolstoy not unexpectedly endorsed Andreyev's self-criticism; he wrote: 'There are many powerful pictures and details in the story; its defects lie in great artificiality and vagueness.'[3]

The opening sentence of the passage from Andreyev's letter to Tolstoy is particularly revealing, for it affords an insight into a fundamental characteristic of Andreyev the artist which sharply distinguishes him from the great realists of the nineteenth century. He described *The Red Laugh* to Veresaev as 'an audacious attempt to convey, while sitting in Gruziny,[4] the psychology of the present war'.[5] Thus personal experience or even observation of that which was to constitute the subject of a planned work was not considered by Andreyev to be an indispensable prerequisite for the artist. Psychological experience could be accurately reproduced, he maintained, without first-hand knowledge of the circumstances which created it. He remarked to Kleynbort in 1914: 'It is true that I do not worship reality; I like invention. But how often letters, facts and many other things convince me that I was right in my conjecture.'[6] Again, in connection with *The Story of Seven Who Were Hanged* (*Rasskaz o semi poveshennykh*) (1908), in which he studies the reactions of seven people to impending execution, he stated to Brusyanin:

I even had an opportunity to make use of the genuine notes of a political prisoner awaiting execution. . . . But to tell you the truth, they served me only as verifying material. They came into my hands when I had already completed the story, and I saw from them that many of the assumptions which I had made *a priori* coincided completely with the genuine psychological experiences of a living man awaiting death. . . .[7]

---

[1] Cf. *LN*, p. 243.     [2] *L. N. Tolstoy. Perepiska s russkimi pisatelyami*, p. 664.
[3] Ibid., p. 665.
[4] The reference is to Gruziny Street in Moscow where Andreyev was living at the time.
[5] *VRSV*, p. 461.     [6] Kleynbort, loc. cit., p. 168.     [7] *BSN*, p. 76.

While Turgenev and Tolstoy regarded intuitive insights as nothing more than clues towards a more profound understanding of life, which were liable to modification and correction in the light of observation, Andreyev advocated the substitution of the writer's own psychological or imaginative experience for real life.

Elpat'evsky's disclosures concerning the conception of *The Red Laugh* illustrate the measure of Andreyev's disregard for accuracy of detail. Andreyev was in the Crimea at the time, and Elpat'evsky, who had his permanent residence there, recalls that the writer once met him with the following exclamation: 'Well, yesterday I was at war. And I composed a story, a long story about war. . . . Yes, yes, don't laugh! You will see. Everything is already prepared in my head.'[1] It was discovered that the day before some Turks had been demolishing a rock near by. In the explosion one of the Turks was badly injured and was carried past Andreyev's house on a stretcher. From this episode to a panorama of war was but a step for Andreyev's agile fantasy. Three or four months later, when Elpat'evsky stopped off at Moscow on his way to St. Petersburg, *The Red Laugh* was already complete. 'L(eonid) N(ikolaevich) told me,' he writes, 'that apart from the wounded Turk, his knowledge of war was obtained from newspaper reports and the personal stories of a correspondent of his acquaintance who had returned from the war.'[2]

It would be vain, therefore, to seek in *The Red Laugh* a documentary account of war in all the multiplicity of its facets; the petty, humdrum details of life in the field are conspicuously absent. It would be equally vain to seek *normal* psychological experience. Veresaev, who fought in the war, declared its 'fundamental tone' to be untrue; he wrote: 'Omitted from view is the most terrible and most salutary attribute of man—his ability to accustom himself to everything. "The Red Laugh" is a work by a great neurasthenic artist who experienced war abnormally and passionately through the newspaper reports about it.'[3] The acuteness and rectilinearity of the psychological reactions to war presented in the work would seem to confirm Veresaev's statement. But it must be emphasized that Andreyev's attention was engaged by only two aspects of the subject of which he was treating—those aspects which are indicated

---

[1] S. Elpat'evsky, 'Leonid Nikolaevich Andreyev. Iz vospominaniy', *Byloe*, 1925, No. 27–8, p. 280.
[2] Ibid.   [3] *VRSV*, p. 452.

in the first two words of *The Red Laugh*: 'Madness and horror',[1] and he selects these two aspects because they enable him to make, at the cost of the psychological distortion which generalization and hyperbole necessarily imply, a point which he considered to be of incontestable validity. It has been seen that he experienced the events of his narrative with great intensity, but this should be taken as evidence not of the fact that *The Red Laugh* is in a sustained subjective mood, but of his ability to experience, as though they were his own, the emotions of his characters; more will be said on this subject later. Like all his major works, *The Red Laugh* is essentially a *pièce à thèse*, and Andreyev's answer to Veresaev would have been that the truth is to be sought in the thesis which determined the narrowness of his viewpoint and which underlies the entire narrative.

His purpose in the work cannot be understood without reference to its complex structure. It consists of nineteen 'Fragments', nine of which comprise Part I and the rest Part II. The first half consists of the reminiscences of a Russian officer who has returned from the war after having both his legs amputated and who finally dies from the more serious mental injuries which he has sustained. The narrator in the second half is the brother of the dead officer, who has not participated in the war, but who, under the influence of what has befallen his brother and the flow of reports from the front, relates his spiritual reaction to war and in the process likewise loses his sanity. It is important to note, however, that the reminiscences which constitute Part I are also recounted by the narrator of Part II. In Fragment 10 the latter remarks:

I believe that I have succeeded in reconstructing with sufficient accuracy the successive feelings which brought him [i.e. his brother—J.B.W.] to the end during that fatal night. In general, everything that I have noted down here about the war I took from my brother's words, which were often very confused and incoherent; only certain individual pictures had burned their way so inerasably and deeply into his brain that I can present them almost word for word, as he described them.[2]

The extremely fragmentary nature of Part I is explained, therefore, by two factors: firstly, it is a collection of 'certain individual

---

[1] 'My theme is *madness* and *horror*,' he wrote to Gorky in answer to the latter's criticisms (cf. *LN*, p. 244).

[2] *Works* IV, p. 123. Cf. also *LN*, p. 245.

pictures', specifically of those aspects of the war which tormented the officer and which led ultimately to the unhinging of his mind; and secondly, only those 'individual pictures' are presented which are remembered by the officer's brother. Thus the complexity of war is first reduced to specific aspects, which are then subjected themselves to a further process of selection, and the end result is those pictures which most graphically illustrate the 'madness and horror' of war. By such means Andreyev abstracts from war the two aspects which are relevant to his scheme.

Equally important is the question of whether Andreyev is writing about war in general or the war which was being fought in Manchuria. The question is legitimate, for the work contains no reference either to Russians or to Japanese. Though Andreyev informed Tolstoy that he regarded it as thematically akin to the latter's general anti-war polemic which had but recently found expression in the article *Come to Your Senses (Odumaytes')*,[1] there can be no doubt that he was more concerned with the particular war. In the letter to Veresaev, quoted above, he mentions specifically 'the present war', and the text supplies further evidence of this limitation of his terms of reference. It is clear that Andreyev felt this war to be essentially different from former wars. The officer, for instance, makes the following comment on the doctor who amputates his legs: 'He had taken part in the last European war almost a quarter of a century ago and often referred to it with pleasure. But the present war he did not understand and I noticed that he feared it. . . .'[2] Remarks of this type must have been in the forefront of Andreyev's mind when he expressed to Veresaev his astonishment that the censor allowed the work to be published;[3] he ascribed it to the 'magic' of Pyatnitsky. In *The Red Laugh* he wished to say that if war is senseless and criminal in general, the present war is even more senseless and criminal than usual. The main problem posed by the work is why he believed this to be so.

The picture of war painted by Andreyev differs radically from that of *War and Peace* and equally from that of Garshin's stories.

---

[1] Cf. Andreyev's letter of 15–16 November 1904 in *L. N. Tolstoy. Perepiska s russkimi pisatelyami*, p. 664.

[2] *Works* IV, p. 111.

[3] Cf. *VRSV*, p. 461. The censor did, however, object to a number of passages, the excision of which considerably reduced the size of the work (cf. 'Pis'ma Leonida Andreyeva k M.P. Nevedomskomu', *Iskusstvo*, 1925, No. 2, p. 268).

An overpowering sense of futility pervades the work. Here there is no 'higher purpose', no Providence, no reference to political or economic considerations. Andreyev depicts not a war of self-interest between two states, but a war between war and the mind of twentieth-century man. *The Red Laugh* is directly related to the works which precede it. The war served Andreyev as yet another means of illuminating the chaotic passions of the 'sphinx of modern times'. It emerges as a symbol of the unleashed power of deformed instinct. On entering this war the contemporary intellectual, as portrayed by Andreyev, undergoes one of two transformations: either his instincts, so long suppressed, assume absolute control of him, in which case he is transformed into a savage, like Nemovetsky, or his hypersensitive reason collapses before the spectacle of unparalleled horror. The words 'madness and horror' epitomize these two metamorphoses.

Dostoevsky's 'underground' hero makes the following comment on modern man:

At any rate man has become if not more bloodthirsty as a result of civilisation, then certainly more evilly, more disgustingly bloodthirsty than before. Formerly he saw justice in bloodshed and destroyed with a peaceful conscience whomsoever it was necessary to kill; now, though we consider bloodshed disgusting, we nevertheless engage in it even more than before.[1]

*The Red Laugh* throws this contradiction in the modern mind into unprecedented relief. It is most powerfully expressed in Fragment 18. The narrator receives a letter, addressed to his dead brother, from an officer who had belonged before the war to their intellectual circle. 'He liked books, flowers and music,' we are told, 'feared all that was coarse, and wrote poetry; my brother, as a critic, declared that he wrote very good poetry.'[2] The letter is an *exposé* of the beast lurking behind the cultured veneer; the officer writes: 'Only now do I understand the great joy of war, the ancient, primitive delight of killing men—clever, scheming, artful man, immeasurably more interesting than the most rapacious beasts. To take life constantly is as good as playing lawn-tennis with planets and stars.'[3] Overcome with rage and indignation, the narrator vents his curse on this poet and intellectual:

[1] F. M. Dostoevsky, *Sobranie sochineniy*, vol. 4, M., 1956, p. 151.
[2] *Works* IV, pp. 138–9.     [3]Ibid., p. 137.

Why did you kill my brother? If you had a face, I would strike it, but you have no face, you have the snout of a wild beast. You pretend that you are men, but I see claws under your gloves and the flat skull of an animal under your hat; I hear insanity rattling its rusty chains, hidden beneath your clever conversation. And with all the power of my grief, my anguished and dishonoured thought, I curse you, you wretched, imbecile animals![1]

This contrast between culture and bestiality lies at the basis of the whole work—the contrast between the 'flowers and songs', of which the narrator's brother dreams of writing on his return home, and the enormity of the deeds perpetrated by his own kind.

The two protagonists, however, illustrate the second of the two 'metamorphoses'—the insanity which results from confrontation of the hypertrophied intellect with the illogical. To them war appears in the form of a 'red laugh'[2]—a 'blood-coloured mockery' of their reason. They are mocked by war in the same way and with the same effect as Vasiliy Fiveysky is mocked by the 'idiot'. 'It is worse than the plague and its horrors,' cries the narrator. 'One can at least hide from the plague, take measures, but how can one hide from all-penetrating thought that knows neither distances nor obstacles?'[3] In *War and Peace* such obstacles are the moral concept of duty and instinctive awareness and acknowledgment of the wisdom of Providence. The Russo-Japanese War is employed by Andreyev to illustrate in the most emphatic form this gaping lacuna in the mind of the modern intellectual with his self-detachment from all extra-individualistic considerations and obligations. In *The Foreigner* Chistyakov had found salvation in the merging of his ego with the 'greater ego' of the nation; the heroes of *The Red Laugh* remain true to their 'apostasy'. The essential truth of Andreyev's verdict on his contemporary was confirmed by Vyacheslav Ivanov and Andrey Belyy; Ivanov wrote:

However exaggerated by the author is this fact of social psychology, one cannot but agree that a characteristic feature of what we are experiencing is noted in it. The roots of the phenomenon lie in the same antinomy, the

---

[1] Ibid., p. 139.
[2] The image was used by Blok in the penultimate quatrain of his poem *The Sated Ones* (*Sytye*), written in November 1905 (cf. Aleksandr Blok, *Sobranie sochineniy v vos'mi tomakh*, vol. 2, M.–L., 1960, p. 180).
[3] *Works* IV, p. 127.

same disharmony and conflict between the contemporary soul and its historical body, if the term may be used.[1]

Belyy, in turn, was moved to write:

Chaos within appears to us without in the form of madness—in the form of the atomisation of life into a countless number of separate channels. It is the same in the field of learning: clumsy specialisation produces a multitude of engineers and technicians with the mask of learning on their faces and with the chaotic madness of amorality in their hearts. The unprincipled application of learning is creating the horrors of the present war with Japan—a war in which we see before us the symbol of rising chaos.[2]

The motives underlying the narrowness of Andreyev's viewpoint, however, were not appreciated by the vast majority of critics, who approached the work with the traditional demands for objective realism. Typical were Mechnikova's criticism of the one-sidedness of the narrator, of his blindness to all but 'madness and horror',[3] and the complaint of A. E. Red'ko, the literary critic of *Russkoe bogatstvo*, that there were simply too many portraits of horror.[4] It is true that the concentration of horror fails to awaken a corresponding emotional response in the reader. Perhaps the most powerful instrument at the artist's disposal for the communication of such an emotion is contrast, and indeed Andreyev puts it to effective use in Fragment 1—in the criss-crossing of the planes of recollection and reality in the mind of the narrator's brother, which effectively evokes his incipient madness—and later in the contrast between his joy on seeing his home once more and the dismay of his wife and family at the sight of his legless body. But the episodes are brief and the device is rarely encountered. Moreover, the half-shades, the *chiaroscuri* of real life, which are alone capable of calling forth a genuine human response to the events described, are totally absent from the work. *The Red Laugh* is primarily a schematic representation of the horror of war, in which genuine horror is

---

[1] V. Ivanov, 'O "krasnom smekhe" i "pravom bezumii" ', *Vesy*, 1905, No. 3, p. 44.

[2] A. Belyy, 'Apokalipsis v russkoy poezii', *Vesy*, 1905, No. 4, p. 14.

[3] See E. Mechnikova, 'Psikhopatologiya v proizvedeniyakh Dostoevskogo i Andreyeva', *Vestnik vospitaniya*, 1910, No. 4, pp. 205–6.

[4] See A. E. Red'ko, 'M. Gor'kiy o vinovatykh i L. Andreyev o nepovinnykh. ("Dachniki" i "Krasnyy smekh")', *Russkoe bogatstvo*, 1905, No. 2, p. 57.

atomized by what Kaun has termed the 'verbal sledgehammer'.[1] Hence Bryusov's remark: 'There are some scenes which are even less alarming than simple newspaper reports.'[2]

The question we have raised, however, is whether it was really Andreyev's main objective to make a powerful emotional impact on the reader. If it was, then the criticisms of Mechnikova and Red'ko are, of course, perfectly valid. But we have attempted to show that his purpose was, in fact, quite different, and perhaps the most convincing proof of this is afforded by the work's structural peculiarities and Andreyev's employment once more of the form of the *Ich-Erzählung*. The defects of all previous analyses of the work have their source in the failure of the critics concerned to appreciate the fundamental fact that Andreyev is presenting not war, but a specific response to war. Once again he suffered from the critics' tendency to identify him completely with his heroes.

[1] See Kaun, op cit., p. 115.
[2] V. Ya. Bryusov (Pentaur), 'Sbornik tovarishchestva "Znanie" za 1904 god. Kniga pervaya', *Vesy*, 1905, No. 2, p. 61.

# IX

# THE 'GOD OF VENGEANCE'

IN a letter to Amfiteatrov of 20 March 1906 containing his reply to the latter's request for a contribution to the journal *Krasnoe znamya* ('The Red Banner'), which he was editing in Paris, Andreyev stated: 'Gorky himself is the Red Banner, while I am the Red Laugh—something devoid of all importance in the political sense. It is true that the nature of my literary activity makes me a revolutionary, but this is not the revolutionism which is required by the moment. . . .'[1] It was, of course, natural that the socialist parties should seek to enlist the support of the two writers whose every work 'shook, literally shook the whole of Russia',[2] and Gorky duly lent his support to the Social Democratic Party and, in 1904, to its Bolshevik faction. Early in 1903 he wrote to Andreyev: 'The situation is such that the Russian writer must be a political worker now, more than ever.'[3] But Andreyev steadfastly refused to heed this counsel, finding the restrictions which party discipline placed upon the individual quite intolerable. 'Like the departed Chekhov,' he said to Brusyanin, 'I say that party-spirit is death for an artist.'[4] According to Chirikov, he always felt more sympathy for the Socialist Revolutionaries, whose romantic heroism and self-sacrifice he considered to be a 'victory of the spirit over death itself',[5] but no political party succeeded in winning his active support.

The nearest that Andreyev came to actual involvement in the political struggle in Russia was his arrest on 9 February 1905—the day after he had permitted the Central Committee of the Social Democratic Party to hold an illegal meeting in his apartment. Skitalets, who happened to visit him at the time the arrest was made,[6] and nine members of the Committee were imprisoned

[1] 'A. M. Gor'kiy v perepiske sovremennikov (1895–1916)', *Voprosy literatury*, 1958, No. 3, p. 91.

[2] M. Tsetlin, 'O tvorchestve Leonida Andreyeva', *Gryadushchaya Rossiya*, Paris, 1920, No. 2, p. 255.

[3] *LN*, p. 170.    [4] *BSN*, p. 16.

[5] E. Chirikov, 'Leonid Andreyev', *Russkie sborniki*, No. 2, Sofia, 1921, p. 67.

[6] For an account of the arrest see: Skitalets, *Povesti i rasskazy. Vospominaniya*, M., 1960, pp. 389–90.

together with him. There are conflicting reports on the duration of his imprisonment; while Pavel Andreyev claims that it was six weeks,[1] the Soviet critic Rubtsov states categorically that he was released on 25 February[2] and Skitalets says that they were held for two weeks.[3] Since Pavel Andreyev is mistaken when he states that his brother was confined in Moscow's Lefortovskaya prison—for Leonid himself said that it was the Taganskaya[4] and this is confirmed by both Skitalets and Fatov[5]—and owing to the somewhat vague nature of Skitalets' description of the events, perhaps we should take the word of Rubtsov. Pavel Andreyev and Rubtsov agree, however, that he was bailed out for 10,000 roubles and, according to the former, the money was advanced by the wealthy Moscow merchant Savva Morozov,[6] the 'Maecenas' of the Moscow Art Theatre and owner of all its shares.[7]

After his release Andreyev spent the summer with his family in the Crimea and in the autumn returned to Moscow. But life in Moscow at that time was particularly unpleasant for those who had the misfortune to have their names on the lists of the Black Hundreds, and Andreyev was one of their number. His brother writes: 'These were alarming and gloomy days in his life, when every minute he expected to be mercilessly and senselessly beaten, when vengeance, animosity and hatred flowed over the whole city and oppressed the brain and heart. . . .'[8] After enduring three weeks of it he left with his family for Finland, where they stayed until November, and then travelled to Germany. In April 1906 he returned to Finland from Switzerland and was present at both the May demonstration in Helsingfors, at which he delivered a passionate speech against autocracy, and the assembly of the Helsingfors Red Guards early in July, summoned by the Social Democrats after the dissolution of the first State Duma. But threatened with

---

[1] See *PNA*, p. 203.

[2] See A. B. Rubtsov, *Iz istorii russkoy dramaturgii kontsa XIX—nachala XX veka*, Minsk, 1960, p. 154.

[3] See Skitalets, op. cit., p. 390.

[4] See L. Andreyev, 'Pamyati Vladimira Mazurina', *Kalendar' russkoy revolyutsii*, Petrograd, 1917, p. 227.

[5] See *FTV*, p. 333.      [6] See *PNA*, p. 203.

[7] Savva Timofeyevich Morozov (1862–1905) also supplied Gorky with funds for the revolutionary movement. Andreyev's cousin Zoya Nikolaevna Pockowska informed Fatov that Andreyev had himself received material assistance from Morozov as a youth and subsequently named one of his sons after him (see *FTV*, p. 215).

[8] *PNA*, p. 204.

possible arrest after the collapse of the revolutionary movement, he finally returned with his family via Stockholm to Germany.

No conclusions on Andreyev's political sympathies, however, i.e. so far as the various parties are concerned, can reasonably be drawn from any of these events. It is more than likely that he lent his apartment either as a favour to Gorky or simply because he wished to make some contact, however small, with the 'revolution-ism which was required by the moment'. The episode offers an instance of that discord between the man and the philosopher which showed itself on numerous occasions in the course of his life—an instance of the tendency of the man to regret at isolated moments his detachment from that world of social-political activity which the philosopher regarded as wholly superficial. But there is little evi-dence of these moments in his works, and in general he felt himself, as Skitalets put it, 'to be "above" all political parties, churches and religions'.[1] The philosopher is ever-present in his works which concern the revolution, to the profound regret of the realists and Social Democrats, and no work demonstrates this point more clearly than *The Governor (Gubernator)*.

Though it was written in August 1905, the work was not pub-lished until March 1906, when it appeared in the Social Democratic journal *Pravda* ('Truth').[2] The number of the journal was immedi-ately confiscated with the result that the story, to quote Lunachar-sky, 'did not become as well known as it deserved'.[3] *The Governor* is usually taken to be a response to the 'Bloody Sunday'—9 January 1905—when a procession of workers from the Vyborg quarter of St. Petersburg, carrying crosses and led by the priest (and *agent provocateur*) Gapon, marched to the Winter Palace to submit their grievances to the Tsar and were savagely mown down by the militia. The official estimate was 130 killed and several hundred wounded, though the number was probably much higher. Andre-

[1] Skitalets, op. cit., p. 405.
[2] Cf. *Pravda*, 1906, No. 3, pp. 1–58. This was the second work of Andreyev to be published in *Pravda*, the other being the story of 1904 *Ghosts (Prizraki)* which appeared in the November 1904 issue. It is difficult to reconcile his sub-mission of stories to this journal with the profound dislike which he professed for it in a letter to Nevedomsky of October 1904 (cf. 'Pis'ma Leonida Andreyeva k M. P. Nevedomskomu', *Iskusstvo*, 1925, No. 2, p. 265).

In 1928 *The Governor* was made into a film. Directed by Protazanov, it was called *The White Eagle (Belyy oryol)* and the leading role was played by Kachalov.

[3] A. Lunacharsky, 'Zametki filosofa. Sotsial'naya psikhologiya i sotsial'naya mistika', *Obrazovanie*, 1906, No. 6, p. 66.

yev's story begins with a similar episode, the only difference being that the action is transferred from the capital to the provinces. The workers of a provincial town have gone on strike for shorter hours and come in noisy procession to state their case to the Governor. Finding the vehemence of their appeal intimidating, however, the Governor in a moment of panic waves his handkerchief, which is the signal for the militia to open fire. The result of two short volleys is forty-eight dead, including nine women and three children, and many more wounded.

It has not been noted, however, that even the ensuing action of the story has a concrete, historical foundation. Chirikov states that the work was based on the murder of a governor in the provincial town of Ufa,[1] but there is stronger evidence that Andreyev had a more important event in mind. The immediate result of the 'Bloody Sunday' was an intensification of the campaign of terror conducted by the revolutionary parties, which in turn provoked violent measures of repression. The government was plainly unnerved. On 4 February 1905 the Grand Duke Sergey Aleksandrovich, who had been Governor of Moscow since 26 February 1891 and was held to be mainly responsible for the government's reactionary policy, was assassinated in the Kremlin by the Socialist Revolutionary Kalyaev (with Azef's assistance). Two days later, 6 February, i.e. the day after his arrest, Andreyev wrote to Veresaev:

The motive for the murder of the Grand Duke was the beating of demonstrators on the streets of Moscow on December 5th and 6th; it was then that the Socialist Revolutionaries 'sentenced' him and Trepov[2] to death, announcing the fact to everyone in proclamations. Everyone, even S(ergey) A(leksandrovich) himself, waited expectantly and the execution was duly carried out.[3]

The episode presented Andreyev with an opportunity to develop one of his cardinal theories of life.

Lavrin contends that *The Governor* is devoid of 'metaphysical' elements,[4] while the contemporary critic Kranikhfel'd wrote that it was 'one of the examples of publicistic literature which are so

---

[1] Cf. Chirikov, loc. cit., p. 59.

[2] Dmitriy Fyodorovich Trepov was Chief of Police in Moscow until 11 January 1905, when he was appointed Governor-General of St. Petersburg.

[3] *VRSV*, p. 460.

[4] See J. Lavrin, *Russian Writers. Their Lives and Literature*, New York, 1954, p. 260.

numerous in our day'.[1] Neither statement is defensible. The entire
work pivots on the mystical idea which was the sole reason for
writing it; hence the anger of Lunacharsky, who wrote: 'We have
before us a vivid example of the replacement of social psychology
with social mysticism.'[2] The structure of the work is itself proof
that actual events were not the immediate object of the author's
attention. The massacre and the events leading up to it are described in two short paragraphs at the beginning of the work,[3] and
the first sentence reads: 'Fifteen days had already passed since the
event, but it never left his thoughts—as though time itself had lost
its power over his memory and things had stopped altogether like
a damaged clock.'[4] Thus Andreyev is more interested in the effects
on the Governor of what happened than in the action itself and its
social implications. But this study of reactions does not trace the
development of such 'conventional' sentiments as remorse and fear;
psychological investigation, as Lunacharsky observed, yields to
metaphysical speculation.

An insight into the nature of Andreyev's conception is forthcoming from the initial title which he gave to the work. In early
October 1905 Gorky wrote to Pyatnitsky: 'Andreyev has written
his "Governor" and has entitled it "The God of Vengeance".'[5] The
title (*Bog otmshcheniya*) is reminiscent of the epigraph to *Anna
Karenina*: 'Vengeance is mine and I will repay' (*Mne otmshchenie i
az vozdam*), and it is possible that Andreyev was in some measure
influenced by the mystical idea of retribution which Tolstoy
develops in the novel. It is much more likely, however, that the
decisive influence came not solely from Tolstoy, but primarily from
the source from which Tolstoy probably derived his own idea—
Schopenhauer. There seems to be little doubt that Tolstoy's initial
conception was more philosophical than religious. It has been
ingeniously and convincingly argued by Eykhenbaum, on the basis
of the form of the epigraph in the early variant of the novel of 1873
(*Otmshchenie moyo* . . . ), that it was taken by Tolstoy not from
the Bible, in which this form does not appear, but from Chapter
62 of Book IV of *The World as Will and Idea*,[6] in which Schopenhauer comments on the Biblical statement:

[1] V. Kranikhfel'd, 'Zhurnal'nye otgoloski', *Mir bozhiy*, 1906, No. 4, p. 71.
[2] Lunacharsky, loc. cit., p. 72.     [3] See *Works* II, p. 23.     [4] Ibid., p. 22.
[5] M. Gorky, *Sobranie sochineniy*, vol. 28, M., 1954, p. 386.
[6] Cf. B. Eykhenbaum, *Lev Tolstoy. Semidesyatye gody*, L., 1960, pp. 201–3.

. . . no man has the right to set himself up as a purely moral judge and requiter, and punish the misdeeds of another with pains which he inflicts upon him, and so to impose penance upon him for his sins. Nay, this would rather be the most presumptuous arrogance; and therefore the Bible says, 'Vengeance is mine; I will repay, saith the Lord.'[1]

For Eykhenbaum this is an indication that the conception of the moral aspect of the novel formed under the influence of Schopenhauer's ethical theories, i.e. that Tolstoy regarded Anna and Vronsky as guilty not before society, but, in consequence of their slavery to their own egoistic desires, to the will, before life, 'eternal justice'. More significant is the fact that this was precisely Andreyev's interpretation of the novel; he wrote to Gorky on 6 August 1904:

. . . not for nothing did Tolstoy take a great interest in Schopenhauer: his 'Anna Karenina' . . . is an artistic embodiment of the world as will and idea. From this point of view the trivial consistorial moral 'vengeance is mine and I will repay' acquires a new, enormous significance which has nothing at all to do with theology.[2]

Thus it is quite conceivable that not only the idea which underlies *The Governor*, but also its original title were suggested to Andreyev by the utterance which became the epigraph to *Anna Karenina* and which he encountered in the same context of Schopenhauer's theories. Moreover, the fact that this title epitomized the 'metaphysical theme' confirms that it is the central theme of the work.

The crime of the Governor is presented not as a crime against forty-eight individuals, but as an infringement of a higher law of life, the penalty for which is death. 'Today I felt death here, in my head,' says the Governor to his son after seeing the dead lined up in a barn.[3] In Andreyev's conception, there is no essential difference between the Governor's crime and that committed by Kerzhentsev, but whereas in the latter instance he concentrates rather on the crime committed by the individual against the particle of eternal life which dwells within him and of which he is the transient objectification, in *The Governor* his attention is more specifically directed to the ties which bind the individual *ego* to its living environment. Thus facing the Governor is the mass of townsfolk, and their state of mind is similarly analysed as they argue for and against his execution. The work assumes, in part, the

[1] A. Schopenhauer, *The World as Will and Idea* (translated from the German by R. B. Haldane and J. Kemp), vol. I, book 4, London, 1883, p. 449.
[2] *LN*, pp. 218–19.     [3] *Works* II, p. 35.

form of a court-case with the difference that the sentence has already been passed by a judge who takes no account of individual sentiments and opinions—by life or the 'collective subconscious'. 'There were various thoughts,' writes the author, 'and there were various words, but there was a single feeling—a huge, dominating, all-penetrating, all-conquering feeling which, in its power and indifference to words, resembled death.'[1] Both the Governor and his contingent judges are transmuted into marionettes controlled by this higher will. At an advanced stage of the Governor's transformation the author remarks: 'If instead of him a doll had been propped up dressed in a governor's uniform and made to speak a few words, no one would have noticed the change.'[2]

The mystical element which pervades the entire work is revealed with particular clarity in the progressive detachment of the Governor towards the end from his human and inanimate environment. This clearly sensed determinism gives this work also a certain affinity with *The Death of Ivan Il'ich*, and it is perhaps no coincidence that Andreyev gave the Governor the name Pyotr Il'ich.[3] It is emphasized, for example, that the Governor begins to take his daily walks in the town unaccompanied. The streets are empty and the women, presented once more as the mouthpiece of primitive, supra-rational law, watch like vultures from behind their curtains. The proximity of the end is further indicated when Kozlov, one of the Governor's trusted officials, begins to take into his own hands the decoration and furnishing of the gubernatorial residence. 'In general,' we read, 'he arrogated to himself the rights of a domestic dictator, and everyone was content with this.'[4] Shortly afterwards it is noted that Sudak, the Chief-of-Police, allows himself for the first time the liberty of chastising the Governor's doorman and lackey: 'Before he would not have dared in any circumstances to scold a servant of the Governor, but now it somehow came about that it was possible to do so and even necessary.'[5] The alleged reason for the chastisement is their lack of circumspection and failure to take due precautions, but the rapidity with which the two incidents succeed one another suggests that they are both designed to mark

[1] Ibid., p. 46.    [2] Ibid., p. 53.

[3] For a study of affinities between the two works and Bunin's *The Gentleman from San-Francisco* (*Gospodin iz San-Frantsisco*) see: F. M. Borras, 'A Common Theme in Tolstoy, Andreyev and Bunin', *The Slavonic and East European Review*, vol. 32, University of London, 1953–4, pp. 230–5.

[4] *Works* II, p. 53.    [5] Ibid., pp. 59–60.

further stages in the detachment of the protagonist from his surroundings—in this instance, from his house.

The delivery to the Governor of a package containing an
amateurish, home-made bomb, which fails to explode, propels him
into a more advanced stage of 'de-individualisation'. Up to this
moment his hopes of escape were not completely extinguished; the
episode of the bomb reveals their futility. He sees the attempt to kill
him as the prelude: 'as though blind death were putting out tentacles
and groping in the darkness.'[1] Ties of blood are now meaningless;
his family feels itself to be 'abandoned, cast somewhere to the side,
and absolutely ignorant of his feelings and moods'.[2] His solitude is
complete; he stands alone before the law of life awaiting his punishment.

The assassination scene is a magnificent miniature not devoid of
an element of comedy. But the comic element, i.e. the struggling
of the assassin to extricate the revolver from the lining of his
pocket, is merely an episode inserted to reinforce the author's
central thought. It is noticeable that throughout the delay the
Governor makes no attempt to escape or offer resistance. The
episode was intended to underline the supernatural origin of this
act of justice. The story ends on the mystical note of the avenging
Law rising in symbolic guise from behind the tedious trifles which
make the lives of men and women a misery, as though to verify that
its will has been done. So ends Andreyev's response to the assassination of the Grand Prince Sergey Aleksandrovich.

*The Governor* is not the first instance in Andreyev's fiction,
however, of a mystical-philosophical interpretation of the antipathy
between the criminal and society. The direct antecedent of *The
Governor* in this respect is *The Thief* (*Vor*) (1904)—a work which
drew from Blok the comment: 'There is nothing here but wild
horror, for suddenly all masks are torn off.'[3] The attempt of the
thief Yurasov to disguise his appearance and identity with a coat of
English cloth and a German name succeeds in deceiving no one. At
every turn he encounters an unintelligible contempt and hostility.
Here Andreyev appears to be expressing the truth formulated thus

[1] Ibid., p. 64.    [2] Ibid.
[3] A. Blok, 'Sbornik tovarishchestva "Znanie" za 1904 god', *Voprosy zhizni*,
1905, No. 3, pp. 298–9. *The Thief* was published in *Znanie*'s fifth miscellany
(dated 1904, though issued on 7 March, 1905) after it had been turned down by
Mirolyubov, whom Gorky promptly pronounced 'a fool and a lout' (cf. *LN*,
p. 247).

by Maeterlinck: 'Though you assume the face of a saint, a hero or a martyr, the eye of the passing child will not greet you with the same unapproachable smile if there lurk within you an evil thought, an injustice or a brother's tears.'[1] But, as in *The Governor*, detachment from people is only part of a general process of detachment. The same antipathy exists between Yurasov and the landscape visible from the windows of the train in which he is travelling; '. . . from the beautiful, silently mysterious fields,' we read, 'there blew on him the same chill of alienation as from the people in the carriage.'[2] Andreyev's belief in the essential unity of the life-force emerges clearly from this picture of the combined repugnance of man and nature, of life as a whole, in the face of the 'apostate'. Yurasov's expulsion is complete: 'He is alone, and there are thousands of them, there are millions of them, they are the whole world; they are behind him and in front of him and on all sides, and nowhere is there salvation from them.'[3] His pursuers close in and, like the Governor, he is inexorably hounded to his doom.

Thus the theme of *The Governor* and that of *The Thief* are essentially one and the same—a fact which destroys the illusion, created by criticism, that the works in which Andreyev introduced events of the year 1905 form a separate and distinct group in the corpus of his fiction. *The Governor* was one of the few works of Andreyev of which Zinaida Gippius approved, but her praise is qualified by the observation that the story is 'spoilt simply by the same fault which invariably spoils all our recent fiction—by the fault that it is a "picture of the revolutionary period"; the revolution has not succeeded in literature'.[4] Like many other critics, Gippius failed to appreciate that Andreyev's theme existed long before the dawning of the 'revolutionary period' and was simply superimposed on the convenient situation which it afforded. In other words, he utilized the revolution, as he had previously utilized autobiographical events and episodes related by Gorky, as a means of expressing the ideas which lie at the basis of all his major works. From this time forth, however, the themes of punishment and retribution, which had dominated his works hitherto, were to be outweighed, though not completely eclipsed, by the themes of salvation and resurrection.

[1] M. Maeterlinck, *Le Trésor des Humbles*, Paris, 1920, p. 41.
[2] *Works* II, p. 10.     [3] Ibid., p. 20.
[4] Z. Gippius (Anton Krayniy), 'Bratskaya mogila', *Vesy*, 1907, No. 7, p. 58.

# PART III

*The Transcendence of Individuality: 1905–1911*

---

## X

## ANDREYEV AND THE RUSSIAN LITERARY WORLD

ANDREYEV'S defence of his freedom to express himself at will on political issues was paralleled by his steadfast resistance to every attempt to impose upon him a literary programme. 'I have always wished, and especially now,' he wrote to Chulkov on 6 December 1906, 'to stand outside all programmes. I wish to be free as an artist; a programme is binding and that is repugnant to me.'[1] The alloy of realism, symbolism and mysticism which his works present is the clearest reflection of his uncommitted position. It is further evidenced by the absence of any visible common feature among the contemporary writers for whom he professed a preference: Bunin, Sergeyev-Tsensky, Remizov, Sologub, Zaytsev and Grinevsky (Grin).[2] Inevitably this independence was bought at a price, for it meant that almost his every work was open to criticism from the 'purists' of the defined literary schools. He later summed up his position, in a letter to Gorky of 26 December 1912, in the following words: 'Who am I? For the nobly born decadents, a despised realist; for the congenital realists, a despised symbolist.'[3] Chulkov states in his reminiscences: 'He was everywhere a chance guest and was inwardly attached to no one.'[4]

The consciousness of his solitude continued to oppress Andreyev to the end of his days; it was no less the fundamental problem

---

[1] *PLA*, p. 14.    [2] See *Rekviem*, p. 37.    [3] *LN*, p. 351.    [4] *KLA*, p. 119.

of his life than of his thought. The desire to isolate himself from society and the mundane coexisted in him with the unabating need to unburden himself to a willing listener. At the same time there was something in his character which made it difficult for him to enter into a close relationship with new acquaintances. Pavel Andreyev records the following words from a letter which he wrote to Veresaev:

I have to cross a certain line, make a beginning, and then there is joy and pleasure and no difficulty. . . . I am even incapable of going visiting and have an absurd fear of other people's homes. I go nowhere. Yet on the occasions when I overcome this feeling and do go, I experience a very pleasant sensation, drink tea and think: 'I will always go visiting.' It is just the same with the theatre, exhibitions and thousands of other more or less important things. And certainly when I am visiting, no one who sees my ease and freedom from embarrassment would think or believe that in the cab I was in a cold sweat. I do not think that this is a kind of 'sickness'; it is rather an unpleasant and harmful peculiarity of my character. I have been sufficiently punished for it by the solitude in which I live.[1]

It was to this peculiarity of his character that Andreyev ascribed his inability to make people whom he liked believe in his sincerity. Typical is the following picture drawn by Blok of Andreyev in his house on the Kamennoostrovsky Prospect in St. Petersburg in autumn 1907:

There is a mass of people in the house; almost all of them are writers— some of them well-known, but I do not know what they are talking about; they are all detached from one another; dark gaps lie between them all, like those which are visible through the window, and the most distant from all, the most lonely is L. N. Andreyev; and the more pleasant and kind he is as a host, the greater is his solitude.[2]

Even Andreyev's undying affection for the 'Wednesday' group was inevitably tempered by the undoubted spiritual solitude which he felt in their midst. As both a thinker and an artist he had little in common with this society of 'realists'. The 1905–6 revolution served to bring their essential incompatibility into stark focus, for a sharp change took place in the nature of the group. Skitalets

[1] *PNA*, p. 189.
[2] A. Blok, 'Pamyati Leonida Andreyeva', *Sobranie sochineniy v vos'mi tomakh*, vol. 6, M.–L., 1962, p. 132. Blok dates this scene autumn 1906, which is impossible due to Andreyev's absence from Russia at that time.

pinpoints the 'Bloody Sunday' as the dividing line in its history; 'after this event,' he writes, 'an apolitical union of writers became impossible.'[1] *Thus It Was* (*Tak bylo*) (1905) was the last work for some years that Andreyev read to the group personally. It is true that the year and a half which he spent abroad thereafter made close relations impossible, but even if he had remained in Moscow the old relationship could not have been maintained. It should be added, however, that their differences did not create any personal hostility. Till the end of his life he remembered with joy and nostalgia his association with the group, and certain of its members, particularly Goloushev, remained his close personal friends. Indeed, it is only these personal relationships which offer a satisfactory explanation of why his association with the group lasted as long as it did.

Just as Veresaev was mystified by Andreyev's attachment to the 'Wednesday' group,[2] so Kleynbort found his long association with *Znanie* quite incomprehensible.[3] Again the most plausible explanation is to be sought in the sphere of personal relationships, particularly in his relationship with Gorky. It is significant, for instance, that Andreyev's break with *Znanie* came at the time when events and their divergent attitudes towards them were placing an increasing strain on their friendship. Although Gorky left for Capri after the failure of the revolution, he retained his editorial position. According to Chirikov, many Moscow writers disliked intensely this 'Bolshevik' control from Capri and they elected Andreyev editor of the miscellanies.[4] Gorky at first agreed, but then changed his mind, whereupon many regular contributors, including Andreyev, abandoned the enterprise. Thus the revolution severed Andreyev's external ties with the realist camp on its two major fronts; inner ties had been non-existent from the beginning.

The break with *Znanie* took place in the summer of 1907. Shortly afterwards Andreyev was offered the editorship of the literary section of the symbolist journal *Zolotoe runo* ('The Golden Fleece') by its publisher N. Ryabushinsky, but rejected it[5] and accepted instead, after some vacillation,[6] an editorial position with

---

[1] Skitalets, op. cit., p. 431.   [2] *VRSV*, p. 453.
[3] See Kleynbort, loc. cit., pp. 69–70.   [4] Cf. Chirikov, loc. cit., p. 67.
[5] Cf. V. N. Orlov, 'Istoriya odnoy "druzhby-vrazhdy"', *Letopisi gosudarst-vennogo literaturnogo muzeya. Kn. 7-aya. Aleksandr Blok i Andrey Belyy. Perepiska*, M., 1940, p. xxvii. The position was subsequently occupied by Blok.
[6] Cf. M. F. Andreyeva's letter of 4 February 1907 to I. P. Ladyzhnikov in *Mariya Fyodorovna Andreyeva*, M., 1961, p. 119.

the new St. Petersburg publishing-house *Shipovnik* ('The Wild Briar'). The editorial policy of this enterprise gave it a position among the organs of the time directly comparable to Andreyev's own literary position. It occupied a central position between *Znanie* on the one hand and *Vesy* ('The Scales') and *Zolotoe runo*, the principal organs of the symbolists, on the other. Among the writers who contributed to it, apart from Andreyev himself, were Blok, Belyy, Bryusov, Prishvin, Remizov, Sologub, Zaytsev, Sergeyev-Tsensky and Chapygin—in short, a cross-section of the contemporary literary world. Although it did display a slight leaning towards modernism, it was not loath to publish the works of Plekhanov, Chernyshevsky, Marx and Lunacharsky.

But even this freedom from a defined programme failed to bring Andreyev lasting satisfaction and he never felt any real attachment to *Shipovnik*; it served him simply, to quote Kleynbort, 'as a place where in the conditions of those years he could publish his stories and articles'.[1] He confided to Gorky that he cared for none of the modernists with whom he came into contact on the editorial board 'except perhaps for Blok',[2] and he withdrew from his editorial responsibilities barely a year after assuming them. Perhaps this is a further indication of the contradiction which tormented Andreyev between his desire for comradeship and his fear of compromising his independence. Since it was the comradely spirit of the 'Wednesday' group that he prized so highly, his disenchantment with *Shipovnik* was probably due to the absence from it of a comparable spirit. Interesting are Kugel' 's comments on the popularity of almanacs at this time:

In literature the vogue and easy success of almanacs completely ousted the old journal which, with all its faults, nevertheless represented a certain spiritual centre and had an editorial organisation where form and idea were elaborated and determined in spiritual communion with a circle of friends of the same views. In an almanac, however, a man was his own master.[3]

Nevertheless, as developments in the 'Wednesday' group had demonstrated, it required only an event of importance in the social-political sphere to transform comradely spirit into hardened doc-

---

[1] Kleynbort, loc. cit., p. 170.    [2] *LN*, p. 307.

[3] A. R. Kugel', 'Literaturnye vstrechi i kharakteristiki', in his *List'ya s dereva*, L., 1926, p. 93.

trine, and this experience must have instilled in Andreyev a lasting dread of such societies. In the final analysis, his attitude is best summed up in his own words in his letter to Chulkov of 6 December 1906: 'I can be a collaborator of any journal, apart, of course, from one that is reactionary and odious, but a close collaborator of none.'[1]

Somewhat more complex is the question of Andreyev's relations with the symbolists. It was obvious to most contemporary writers that he had far more in common with them than with the realists, and for Kleynbort and Veresaev the failure of any alliance to materialize was an insoluble mystery.[2] Brusyanin states that there was a marked tendency among the general public to associate him with the 'decadents'.[3] 'Leonid Nikolaevich himself understood,' writes Beklemisheva, 'that in the literary sphere he was closer to Blok, Belyy and Sologub than to Gusev-Orenburgsky and Chirikov.'[4] It has been seen that with few exceptions the comments of the symbolists, particularly those of the 'second generation', on the works written by Andreyev before 1905 were complimentary; they paid almost unanimous tribute to his talent. Reviewers of the *Znanie* miscellanies for *Vesy* invariably emphasized the fundamental differences between him and 'the various Teleshovs, Chirikovs, Gusev-Orenburgskys, Kuprins'.[5] 'Closer to him than most writers,' writes Blok, 'were certain symbolists, particularly Andrey Belyy and myself; he said this to me more than once.'[6] At the same time all the symbolists were conscious of the cultural gap between Andreyev and themselves, of his lack of 'refinement', of the fact that they belonged to different strata of the intelligentsia. This point was repeatedly emphasized by Zinaida Gippius, who, though acknowledging his talent, which she considered much greater than that of Gorky, pronounced him 'a Russian foreign to culture'.[7] The criticism became almost a *leitmotif* of symbolist reviews of Andreyev's works between 1906 and 1909 and was perhaps most forcefully expressed by Filosofov who stated that he was 'to a high degree illiterate'.[8] Gippius went so far as to declare him the principal

---

[1] *PLA*, p. 14.    [2] Cf. Kleynbort, loc. cit., p. 170; and *VRSV*, pp. 454–5.
[3] See *BSN*, p. 65.    [4] *Rekviem*, p. 259.
[5] I. Smirnov, 'Sbornik tovarishchestva "Znanie" za 1904 g. Kn. IV i V, SPb., 1905', *Vesy*, 1905, No. 4, p. 47.
[6] Blok, 'Pamyati Leonida Andreyeva', p. 130.
[7] Z. Gippius (Anton Krayniy), 'Chelovek i boloto', *Vesy*, 1907, No. 5, p. 54.
[8] D. Filosofov, 'Bez stilya', *Moskovskiy ezhenedel'nik*, 1908, 18 March, p. 42.

representative of a 'pseudo-decadence' guilty of a deliberate anti-cultural attitude, of barbarism, sacrilege and plagiarism.[1] A similar, though less extreme, view was expressed in 1908 by Bryusov, who wrote: 'The talent of L. Andreyev is an uncultured talent. As an artist, L. Andreyev is not linked with the higher spiritual life of his time.'[2]

The difference between Andreyev and the symbolists was revealed primarily in their divergent conceptions of literature. 'Our literature,' wrote Blok in his notebook for August 1909, 'is a *science* inaccessible to non-specialists. There are literary people, popular-isers, *etc.* (Boborykin, Potapenko, in part L. Andreyev), and there are *writers* (Val. Bryusov, A. Belyy).'[3] Ivanov-Razumnik was similarly inclined to see Andreyev as a 'populariser' and claimed that his huge success was to be explained in large measure by his ability to render symbolism intelligible to the broad reading public in the less esoteric form of 'allegorism'.[4] Between the 'symbol', as it was interpreted by the symbolists, and the 'allegory', as it was employed by Andreyev, there was indeed an immense difference. The allegory was used by Andreyev as a means of visualizing abstract ideas and the specific psychic conditions which he associated with them; it is always rationally translatable. He regarded art or form as basically a means of representing graphically and effectively a philosophical thesis. The attitude of the symbolists was quite different. Within Russian symbolism itself, of course, there was a division of opinion on the question of 'art for art's sake', but the definition of the symbol as an insight into the essence of things, as a rationally untranslatable link between the phenomenal and the noumenal, is one with which all the main Russian symbolists would have been in total agreement. For Belyy and Vyacheslav Ivanov symbolism was an integral conception of the world, knowledge of the irrational, of 'ideas' in the Platonic and Schopenhauerian sense of the term, and the communication of such knowledge demanded the extreme refinement of form into symbols. 'Form becomes con-tent, content becomes form,' wrote Ivanov,[5] thus formulating the

[1] See Gippius, loc. cit., pp. 56–8.

[2] V. Bryusov (Avreliy), '"Zhizn' Cheloveka" v Khudozhestvennom teatre', *Vesy*, 1908, No. 1, p. 144.

[3] Aleksandr Blok, *Zapisnye knizhki, 1901–1920*, M., 1965, p. 155.

[4] R. V. Ivanov-Razumnik, *Russkaya literatura ot semidesyatykh godov do nashikh dney*, 6th edn., Berlin, 1923, p. 378.

[5] V. Ivanov, *Borozdy i mezhi*, M., 1916, p. 212.

fundamental principle of Schopenhauer's aesthetics. This is what Blok meant when he called symbolist literature a 'science'. 'The knowledge of ideas,' wrote Belyy in 1904, echoing the thought of Baudelaire, 'reveals in transient phenomena their eternal and timeless significance. . . . To emphasize the idea in an image means to translate this image into a symbol and from this point of view the whole world is a *forest of symbols.* . . .'[1] In short, for the symbolists there was an essential link between philosophical and formal questions.

This 'philosophical' significance of form, which involved meticulous and painstaking linguistic and structural workmanship founded, in the case of Ivanov and Belyy in particular, on profound literary and philosophical erudition, was wholly foreign to Andreyev and, according to some memoirists, he suffered from a distinct feeling of inferiority in their presence. Chulkov believed that he even feared them.[2] Chukovsky saw him as a man who never really succeeded in shaking off his 'provincial' origins and regarded the fact that wherever he went he almost invariably took his family with him as a reflection of this attachment. He traces to the same 'provincialism' Andreyev's dislike of reading, his ignorance of languages and indifference to symphonic music, and adds: 'His "provincialism" was especially noticeable when he happened to meet such people as, for example, Serov, Aleksandr Benois or Blok, before whom he became strangely bashful; the difference between their "cultural levels" was too great.'[3]

Though Andreyev was not saturated with European culture as the symbolists were, we have seen that he was by no means unacquainted with the foreign sources of 'modernism'—in particular, idealistic philosophy. Not only his thought, but the formal aspect of his works also—especially that of his plays—bears clearly discernible traces of their influence. But the conception of the function of form with which he entered literature remained basically unaffected by these influences throughout his literary career. Though his works are rich in metaphor and evocative devices, the formal element never becomes one with the idea which it clothes in the sense in which such a fusion was understood by the symbolists. He never creates symbols in the narrow, specific, symbolistic sense of

[1] A. Belyy, 'Krititsizm i simvolizm', *Vesy*, 1904, No. 2, p. 11.
[2] See 'Predislovie Georgiya Chulkova', *PLA*, p. 10.
[3] K. Chukovsky, 'Leonid Andreyev', in his *Iz vospominaniy*, M., 1958, p. 254.

the term. Hence the remark of Kobylinsky (Ellis) on his works: '. . . in none of them is there a hint at a method of symbolisation, *i.e.* at a law of rhythmic transition from the real to the transcendental.'[1] Moreover, the concentration of the symbolists on formal perfection aroused in Andreyev, not without some justification, an instinctive distrust of their sincerity; he tended to regard it as pettiness and as indicative of a limited outlook. In a letter to Chulkov, written from Munich towards the end of 1906, he scoffs at their imitation of one another, describing them as 'artistic coiffeurs who curl the hair of the whole world like a poodle', and, a few lines later, as 'buzzing flies' who beat their wings a thousand times a second causing us to 'forget about the flight of the eagle'.[2] He believed that they were killing poetry, replacing its fire and power with the chill of rationalism and artificiality. 'I, Vikentiy Vikent'evich, am an honest writer!' he once declared to Veresaev. 'But Blok—he is a dishonest writer.'[3] He criticized the esoteric nature of the symbolist movement and its domination by a small number of talented people. He said to Herman Bernstein in 1908: 'Although I do not belong to that school, I do not consider it as worthless. The fault with it is that it has but few talented people in its ranks, and these few direct the criticism of the decadent school. They are the writers and also the critics.'[4]

His references to the symbolist movement are usually of such a general nature, and it is difficult to assess his opinion of individual figures. Kleynbort notes that he esteemed Merezhkovsky, but disliked him, while his references to Vyacheslav Ivanov were usually mocking.[5] Somewhat different, however, is the reference, in the letter to Chulkov of late 1906 in which he criticized the symbolists, to a certain 'I.': 'He has tremendous sincerity, but what sense can one make of this sincerity?'[6] It is difficult to think of any prominent symbolist apart from Ivanov whose name begins with this letter, and indeed no symbolist, with the possible exception of Belyy, surpassed the complexity of Ivanov's reasoning. In the same letter Andreyev also writes: 'B. is as cold as a sober-minded corpse in twenty degrees of frost.'[7] He could be referring here to Blok, Belyy or Bryusov, though one can only imagine that it was Bryusov.

[1] L. L. Kobylinsky (Ellis), 'Nashi epigony. O stile, L. Andreyeve, B. Zaytseve i mnogom drugom', *Vesy*, 1908, No. 2, pp. 63–4.

[2] *PLA*, pp. 20–1.    [3] *VRSV*, p. 474.

[4] H. Bernstein, *With Master Minds. Interviews*, New York, 1913, p. 165.

[5] Cf. Kleynbort, loc. cit., p. 178.    [6] *PLA*, p. 21.    [7] Ibid.

His opinion of Bryusov does not appear to have been too high; to Gorky, for instance, in March 1908 he expressed his intention of barring the poet's works from publication by *Shipovnik*.[1] By 1909, however, he appears to have revised his attitude somewhat, for Beklemisheva remarks that in that year he bought volume after volume of Bryusov's works and learnt many of his poems by heart.[2]

Despite his remarks to Veresaev on the question of honesty and dishonesty, there is no doubt that Andreyev felt a special regard for Blok. 'Of the younger men Aleksandr Blok is perhaps the most gifted,' he said to Bernstein;[3] Belousov and Chulkov confirm this esteem.[4] In Blok alone of the symbolists he perceived genuine inspiration and ability and an absence of the intellectual frigidity which he considered to be the blight of symbolist poetry. Both writers were conscious of a bond which united them independently of any personal relationship. 'The bond which linked me with L. Andreyev was established and determined immediately,' wrote Blok, 'long before my acquaintance with him; this acquaintance added nothing to it.'[5] Notwithstanding the entry in his diary of August 1909, it should be noted that Blok generally did not subscribe to the view of Andreyev as 'uncultured' and 'pessimistic'. 'These two charges,' he wrote in his article *On the Drama* (*O drame*) (1907), 'in which I sense the cloying and repulsive odour of a particular kind of party-spirit, cause me to love only more profoundly everything written by Andreyev. . . .'[6] In the works of Andreyev, particularly *The Life of Vasiliy Fiveysky*, *The Red Laugh* and *The Thief*, he seemed to find an echo and confirmation of that feeling which pervades his own poetry—the feeling of approaching universal catastrophe. But though 'they both divined something on one and the same transcendental plane', as Chulkov puts it,[7] it did not have the effect of bringing them together on earth. 'How many times I have been on the point of visiting you, how I have wanted to see you,' Andreyev wrote to Blok in 1908, 'but it never comes to pass, it never comes to pass. Why are you and I

[1] See *LN.*, p. 307.    [2] See *Rekviem*, p. 257.    [3] Bernstein, op. cit., p. 165.
[4] See I. A. Belousov, *Literaturnaya Sreda. Vospominaniya, 1880–1928*, M., 1928, p. 139; and *PLA*, pp. 41 and 44.
[5] Blok, 'Pamyati Leonida Andreyeva', p. 130.
[6] A. Blok, 'O drame', *Sobranie sochineniy v vos'mi tomakh*, vol. 5, M.–L., 1962, p. 187.
[7] G. Chulkov, 'Leonid Andreyev. (Vospominaniya)', *PLA*,, p. 41.

going against fate?'[1] Blok received another letter from him in 1911 concerning one of his poems, and it concludes with the words: 'Whether it is necessary to write this to you or not, I do not know—perhaps it is not necessary.'[2] These few words define their whole relationship.

All that has been said about Andreyev's attitude to 'literary schools' and to the symbolists *en bloc* and as individuals finds confirmation in the single instance of his collaboration with the latter. Up to 1906 Moscow was the centre of Russian symbolism; the publishing-house *Skorpion* was in Moscow and *Vesy* was its publication. By that year, however, symbolism had evolved from a school into a movement, within which sharp differences of opinion developed on fundamental philosophical issues. These differences manifested themselves in the germination of new organs. First there was a split in Moscow itself, which resulted in the founding of *Zolotoe runo*, and then a more basic schism revealed itself between Moscow and St. Petersburg with the appearance in the latter city of the *Fakely* ('Torches') miscellanies. It was a schism between the 'aesthetic' and 'mystical-philosophical' or evangelical trends of Russian symbolism which had always threatened to disrupt the unity of the movement. The three *Fakely* miscellanies, edited by Chulkov, were published between 1906 and 1908, but the idea behind them had arisen in 1905. On their pages appeared works by writers of diverse literary and philosophical views. Sologub, Vyacheslav Ivanov, Bryusov, Blok, Belyy, Gorodetsky, Remizov, Zinov'eva-Annibal, Meyer, Shestov and others appeared among the contributors. Chulkov stated that the miscellanies did not represent any particular school, but 'unite the zealous members of different schools in a single ideological theme'.[3] This 'single ideological theme' was given the name of 'mystical anarchism', which according to Vyacheslav Ivanov, expressed the symbolist 'tendency from isolation to community'.[4] It was based on the idea that mysticism, by virtue of the fact that it is the sphere of absolute inner freedom, is intrinsically anarchistic. Editorial policy called for a campaign against all impingement by 'external obligatory norms'[5] on this inner freedom, in the sphere of which alone could

[1] *Rekviem*, p. 86.     [2] Blok, 'Pamyati Leonida Andreyeva', p. 135.

[3] G. Chulkov, *O misticheskom anarkhizme*, SPb., 1906, p. 69.

[4] V. Ivanov, 'O fakel'shchikakh i drugikh imenakh sobiratel'nykh', *Vesy*, 1906, No. 6, p. 55.

[5] 'Predislovie Georgiya Chulkova' *PLA*, p. 8.

be realized the ideal of a genuine communion. While it is true that the philosophical basis of the miscellanies had been decided upon in 1905, that the idea of a 'mystical communion' (*sobornost'*) had always existed for the second generation of symbolists, and that the symbolists as a whole displayed negligible regard for social-political developments prior to 1907, there can be little doubt that an added acuteness was lent to the idea by the failure of the revolution. The collapse of hopes of external freedom accentuated the need for a more profound and durable freedom. Belyy wrote in reference to 'mystical anarchism' that it signified the 'ultimate limit of disillusionment with the positivist solution of questions concerning the meaning of life'.[1]

An invitation to contribute was duly extended to Andreyev, and *Thus It Was* appeared in the spring of 1906 in the first *Fakely* miscellany together with poems by Belyy, Bryusov, Sologub, Ivanov, Blok and Gorodetsky, stories by Sergeyev-Tsensky, Osip Dymov and Remizov, and Blok's play *The Puppet Show* (*Balaganchik*). With its attack on the inner slavery of man and its *exposé* of man's fear of freedom *Thus It Was* appeared to harmonize completely with editorial policy, and Andrey Belyy was moved to declare Andreyev 'the only mystical anarchist among contemporary Russian writers'.[2] Blok also identified Andreyev with the new trend in a letter to Belyy of August 1907.[3] Thus the anticipated alliance between Andreyev and a branch of the symbolist movement seemed at last to have been effected. Yet when the first miscellany appeared, writes Chulkov, 'Andreyev categorically disliked it. He felt himself to be in foreign company. Only Blok won his sympathy.'[4] The disenchantment was not immediate and he maintained contact with Chulkov from abroad. It was his intention to contribute to *Fakely* his second play *Savva*, dated 10 February 1906, which he termed a 'truly "torch-like" work',[5] but it appears that he owed a work to *Znanie* and he eventually gave it to Pyatnitsky. The break with *Fakely* came towards the end of 1906, when Andreyev was in Berlin. He wrote from there to Chulkov on 6 December: 'It is only here, having thought over everything in freedom, that I have come to understand the contradiction that I have

[1] A. Belyy, 'Vtoroy tom', in his *Arabeski*, M., 1911, pp. 488–9.
[2] Ibid., p. 489.
[3] Cf. *Letopisi gosudarstvennogo literaturnogo muzeya. Aleksandr Blok i Andrey Belyy. Perepiska*, M., 1940, p. 206.
[4] 'Predislovie Georgiya Chulkova', *PLA*, p. 9.     [5] *PLA*, p. 27.

entered into with myself by taking such a part in a journal with a *determined* social-philosophical colouring. Even the anarchistic programme is still a programme. . . .'[1] The thought of having to bear some part of the responsibility for what was said by writers like Ivanov and Bryusov[2] was abhorrent to him. The merest suggestion of a threat to his independence was sufficient to impel his withdrawal and bring his brief 'romance' with the symbolists to an end. Thereafter the vast majority of his works were published by *Shipovnik*.

[1] Ibid., p. 14.

[2] It should be pointed out that Bryusov had emphasized from the beginning the folly of gathering together under the banner of a single idea writers from diverse literary schools; he compared it with 'requesting the collaboration only of writers with yellow eyes or with surnames ending in vowels and sibilants' (V. Ya. Bryusov (Avreliy), 'Vekhi', *Vesy*, 1906, No. 5, p. 56).

# XI

# REVOLUTION AND EVOLUTION

T HE questions of freedom and revolution were the subjects of a protracted dialogue between Andreyev and Gorky during the period from early 1904 to early 1906. In February–March 1904 Andreyev wrote a story called *From the Depths of Ages* (*Iz glubiny vekov*) [with the variant titles *The Tsar* (*Tsar'*) and *Nebuchadnezzar* (*Navukhodonosor*)], to which Gorky refers several times in letters of that year.[1] Gorky was disappointed by the work because of what he considered a serious omission. His criticism infers that it consisted for the most part of a psychological study of an autocrat and his megalomania,[2] and he expressed his disapproval of the one-sidedness of the inquiry, i.e. of Andreyev's failure to extend it to the masses, to 'the tsar's experience of the depth of human slavery';[3] he wrote: 'The tsar becomes bored not because he seeks equality with the gods and loses faith in their existence . . . but because there are slaves everywhere and he, among them, is alone on earth.'[4] The theme of the slavishness of man rings out repeatedly in Gorky's letters of this period. He welcomed the repressive measures of the state as a spur to action and saw the assassination of 4 February 1905 as a vindication of his argument. 'Life is built on cruelty, horror, force,' he wrote shortly before that event; 'for reconstruction a cold, rational cruelty is necessary, that's all.'[5]

These salvoes from Gorky, in addition to personal dissatisfaction, prompted Andreyev's decision not to publish *From the Depths of Ages*.[6] He took his friend's advice to re-write it over the summer and the result was *Thus It Was*, dated 1 October 1905. Moreover, the work reflects his compliance with Gorky's wish that there should be a change of emphasis, for the state of mind of the autocrat is forsaken for that of the masses. Nevertheless, these mani-

---

[1] Cf. *LN*, pp. 210, 217, 219, 248, 253.    [2] Cf. ibid., p. 219.    [3] Ibid.
[4] Ibid.    [5] Ibid., p. 252.
[6] Only the short first chapter was published in the journal *Vesna* ('Spring'), edited by the writer and theatre critic N. G. Shebuev (1908, No. 1, p. 4).

festations of Gorky's influence coexist in the story with a clear indication of the fundamental difference between the attitudes of the two writers to the subjects of their epistolary dialogue.

The work is a simple statement of the fact that revolution is not necessarily the expression of an inner transformation in man, that revolution and freedom are not related to one another as cause and effect, and that the desire for vengeance is not to be confused with the desire for freedom. In a way which appears to be a deliberate and calculated refutation of Gorky's remarks about reconstruction through 'cold, rational cruelty' and which foreshadows with some accuracy the events of 1917–18, Andreyev portrays the mechanical transition from revolution motivated by the desire for vengeance to the establishment of a new tyranny. When the work was read before publication to the 'Wednesday' group, Gorky was one of many who took it to be a prediction of the forthcoming failure of the revolution and thought it premature and pessimistic. But Andreyev was less concerned with prognostication than with the affirmation of a truth of timeless validity which is directly relatable to his whole philosophical conception of life. His purpose in the work found expression four years later (1909) in the following declaration of Berdyaev in the collection of articles entitled *Vekhi* ('Signposts'): 'We will free ourselves from external oppression only when we have freed ourselves from inner slavery, *i.e.* take responsibility on ourselves and cease blaming external forces for everything.'[1]

Andreyev's conception of freedom was indubitably anarchistic; according to Beklemisheva, he acknowledged to Gorky in 1908: 'I do not know what I am. Probably an anarchist.'[2] But like that of Dostoevsky, this anarchism was not conceived in social terms; hence the difficulty which he experienced when endeavouring to define himself. It went beyond the social sphere and was tinged with that mysticism which gave him an affinity with the theoreticians of *Fakely*, though it will be seen that he differed from them on a fundamental point. He saw two paths open before him, on the subject of which he said to Brusyanin:

Russian life has turned out in such a way that every Russian citizen to

---

[1] *Vekhi. Sbornik statey o russkoy intelligentsii*, M., 1909, p. 22.
[2] *Rekviem*, p. 258. Gorky had himself written to Andreyev as early as 1902: 'I love you sincerely because you are an anarchist, you are a talented anarchist, you will never degenerate into a philistine' (*LN*, p. 150).

whom the future of his country is dear must be either a revolutionary or a man whose vision is restricted to 'petty deeds'. I could only be either a revolutionary writer or a writer striving to analyse and synthesize life and the human spirit. An impossible combination.[1]

Yet in the works in which he deals directly or indirectly with the revolution, especially in his play *To the Stars* (*K zvyozdam*), the attempt to achieve precisely this combination is visible. Throughout he remains true to his self-appointed task of effecting the stated synthesis between 'life and the human spirit' and views the revolution in the light of the same philosophical principles which determined his attitude towards the problem of 'apostasy'. In accordance with these principles he could not but conceive of social-political revolution as evasive of the main issue; this is the conviction which he expressed in *Thus It Was*. Moreover, he feared intensely the violence which revolution would unleash, not only as a man but also as a philosopher for whom everything antagonistic to and destructive of life was anathema; behind the vision of the good which revolution would bring there perpetually lurked the spectre of its potential evil, and in *Thus It Was* the evil asphyxiates the good at birth. There can be no doubt that he sincerely dreaded revolution. Always on the alert for its first rumblings, both in 1905 and a decade later he was one of the first to hear them. Skitalets describes the commotion at the meeting of the 'Wednesday' group on 9 January 1905 when the happenings of that day were reported: a brief silence followed which was suddenly broken by Andreyev's terse comment: 'This is revolution!'[2] Again, in 1914 he said to Beklemisheva: '"War" is written, but "revolution" should be read.'[3]

Yet these fears and 'philosophical' objections could not extinguish Andreyev's instinctive enthusiasm for the revolution. It has been noted that though he was 'almost the only writer who "fled the revolution"',[4] he lost little time in plunging into revolutionary activity in Helsingfors. The reason is to be sought partly in his wholly genuine protest against the maladministration of Russia and contempt for contemporary bourgeois society, and also, perhaps, as stated, in his wish not to appear reactionary. But perhaps the most important reason of all—and his works lend credence to this

---

[1] *BSN*, pp. 15–16.   [2] Skitalets, op. cit., p. 391.   [3] *Rekviem*, p. 229.
[4] Skitalets, op. cit., p. 392.

view—was his natural romanticism, that instinctive responsiveness to self-sacrifice in the name of the highest ideals which induced him to profess a certain sympathy with the Socialist Revolutionaries. In 1905 it became momentarily Andreyev's cherished dream to effect a reconciliation between his own philosophy of life and 'the revolutionism which is required by the moment', as he termed it to Amfiteatrov, and the only foundation on which he could realize this dream was that of an excessively idealized conception of revolution. Herein lies the explanation of the blatant artificiality of the picture of revolution which emerges from his works and also of its duality: on the one hand, its unrelieved horror and savagery; on the other, the sublime sacrifice of the idealists. Now the one, now the other is emphasized as the author's attention vacillates between them; there is perpetual tension. When assessing, therefore, on the basis of the vacillation in the early drafts of the work, the influence of Gorky on *To the Stars*, it would be well to remember the obvious difficulty, indeed the impossibility, of the task which the playwright had set himself.

Five years previously (1900) a considerable impact had been made on the Russian reading public by a work entitled *Astronomical Evenings* by the German astronomer and meteorologist Herman Klein. In a letter to Pyatnitsky of 26 October 1903 Gorky wrote: 'Leonid has been inspired by Klein and wants to portray a man living the life of the whole universe amid impoverished, grey, everyday life.'[1] No less interested in the theme, however, was Gorky himself, and in the same letter to Pyatnitsky he mentioned that he and Andreyev would be collaborating on the play. Six months later (April 1904) he asked Andreyev to let him take over the theme completely, but in his reply, written a few days later, Andreyev refused and reasserted the need for collaboration.[2] Not surprisingly, no joint composition ever materialized and each writer went his own way.

The first variant of the play which Andreyev wrote on the theme was entitled *The Astronomer* (*Astronom*). Though dated 20 October 1905, it seems to have been written in the spring of 1904, for Andreyev makes several remarks about it in his reply of early May to Gorky's request to take over the theme,[3] and it was almost certainly rumours about this play which prompted Chekhov's

---

[1] *Arkhiv A. M. Gor'kogo*, vol. 4, M., 1954, p. 143.
[2] Cf. *LN*, pp. 210 and 213.      [3] Cf. ibid., p. 213.

remark to E. P. Karpov at that time that Andreyev had already begun to write plays.[1] In this variant Andreyev selected as his setting an observatory in a small Russian provincial town. The appearance of a comet over the town is employed by the playwright as a means of contrasting the superstitions of the populace with the ecstatic reaction of a dedicated astronomer who, in this variant, bears the name of Verkhovtsev. The play ends with the destruction of the observatory by a fanatical mob during an eclipse of the sun and with the murder of the astronomer, who, even as he falls, endeavours to shield his telescope which is pointed to the stars.[2] The theme bears some resemblance to that of Knut Hamsun's *At the Gates of the Kingdom*, performed by the Moscow Art Theatre in February 1907 with the title *The Drama of Life* (*Drama zhizni*), in which genius similarly perishes for daring on earth to dream of the divine.

But as the social situation in Russia developed, Andreyev's scheme underwent a change, and he disclosed his new idea to Gorky early in 1905. His words are recorded by V. P. Troynov, an economist and the husband of Andreyev's youngest sister Zinaida:

Above in the mountains is an observatory, and a Russian scientist, the director of the observatory, lives there with his colleagues and family, while below a revolution is taking place. . . . 'Away with all trivial cares. Here the lowly earth is scorned; from here leads the path to the stars,' says the main character, the scientist Ternovsky. His son, Nikolay, is anxious to go below to the barricades, but he is held back by his love for his mother and the fear of bringing the anger of the government to bear on his father. His father is engaged in important scientific work. 'The more sun-spots are studied, the less spots there will remain in social life,' he says. Nikolay endeavours to lead the revolution from above. He is helped by his fiancée and a number of other characters. In the last Act the supporters of the government burst into the observatory to arrest Nikolay. But his father, in answer to the government commissar's threat to smash the observatory, stands before the reflector and proudly declares to the commissar: 'Don't you dare touch my instruments!'[3]

While applauding the choice of characters, Gorky characteristically deplored the absence from the play of violence: 'What kind of

---

[1] Cf. E. P. Karpov, 'Dve poslednie vstrechi s A. P. Chekhovym', in *A. P. Chekhov v vospominaniyakh sovremennikov*, M., 1954, p. 577.

[2] Cf. *Leonid Andreyev. P'esy*, M., 1959, p. 559; and A. B. Rubtsov, *Iz istorii russkoy dramaturgii kontsa XIX—nachala XX veka*, Minsk, 1960, p. 156.

[3] V. Troynov, 'M. Gor'kiy i L. Andreyev. Iz vospominaniy sovremennika', *Literaturnaya gazeta*, 1937, No. 42, 5 August, p. 4.

revolution can there be,' he said, 'without a punch on the head?'[1]
He proceeded to give his own idea of how the play should run: he
sent Nikolay to the barricades, disrupted the harmony of the
scientist's family and colleagues, banished the mystical element,
introduced two simple workers devoted to the proletarian cause,
and inserted numerous conflicts of opinion. He then revealed that
during his imprisonment in January and February of that year in
the Peter-and-Paul fortress he had written his *Children of the Sun*
(*Deti solntsa*), a play with a similar situation and set of characters,
and in the spirit of his own treatment of the theme he added:

Your people must be pitted against one another. Coarseness is necessary
here. This will come better from me. . . . This is the materialistic age.
Our home, my brother, is the earth, and we must arrange ourselves on
it well, joyously.[2]

Gorky's comments clearly made an impression on Andreyev and
he undertook a further revision of the work. He made some
significant concessions: he introduced the worker Treych; Nikolay
perished on the barricades; and his fiancée, Marusya, and the wife
of the astronomer received more positive roles. But the figure of
Ternovsky continued to dominate the play and it was certainly this
which Gorky could not accept. 'According to Andreyev,' writes
Troynov, 'he listened to it without excitement and said very little
about it.'[3] Andreyev also, however, was still not satisfied, though
his reservations were of a different character.

In his final variant, which he called not *The Astronomer* but *To
the Stars*, Andreyev partly reverted to the scheme of the second or
verbal variant related by Troynov; he diminished somewhat the
appeal of the proletarian cause by introducing the rather ridiculous
image of a second worker, Schmidt, and re-introduced the mystical
element. On the other hand, he also preserved some of the modifica-
tions prompted by Gorky: in addition to the retention of Treych,
Nikolay was still sent to the barricades and no substantial change
was made in the two main female roles of the third variant.
Andreyev clearly wished to effect a compromise without, however,
impairing his basic idea. Completed in November 1905, this final
version of the play was published the following year in the tenth
*Znanie* miscellany.

The plays of both writers depict the conflict between an indivi-

---

[1] Ibid.　　[2] Ibid.　　[3] Ibid.

dual dedicated to a life of abstract thought and the concrete demands of social life. In both cases the conflict is examined in the sphere of family relationships. But the action of the two plays takes place at different times. In Gorky's play there is no popular uprising. The unrest which follows an outbreak of cholera is merely a foretaste of a possible revolution in the future when the masses, awakened to the consciousness of their rights, will question the scientists and artists about the efforts they have made to relieve the ignorance, misery and inhuman cruelty of the people. In *To the Stars*, however, the revolution has begun. In addition, the play is broader in scope than Gorky's and presents a wider range of attitudes. Its burning topicality almost precluded from the start the possibility of production in Russia. While *Children of the Sun* was produced by Komissarzhevskaya's theatre and the Moscow Art Theatre in autumn 1905,[1] Andreyev's play was not performed in Russia until 10 June 1907, and even then in the distant outpost of Kharbin. The favourable response to the play of Nemirovich-Danchenko raised Andreyev's hopes of a Moscow production, but they were dashed by the censor. On 27 May 1907 it was performed at the theatre established by V. R. Gardin, with the aim of escaping the censor, at Terioki situated just inside the Finnish border—little more than an hour's ride from St. Petersburg.[2] Its main success, however, was in Vienna, where it was produced in October 1906 by the director and actor Richard Valentin for the *Freie Volksbühne*,[3] a theatre organization established a month previously by the Social Democratic newspaper *Die Arbeiter Zeitung*.

In an interview with a newspaper correspondent Andreyev stated that it was his purpose in the play to contrast the poetry of scientific achievement with vulgar reality,[4] but, in fact, it turned out to be somewhat more complex. Translated into the disposition of his characters his scheme becomes a contrast between Ternovsky, the astronomer, and the rest, who represent not so much 'vulgar reality' as a plurality of divergent, but not exclusively unsympathetic,

---

[1] The premières took place respectively on 25 October and 6 November, 1905. While the latter production was wholly realistic, the former was given a 'strong symbolist flavour' (see M. Slonim, *Russian Theater from the Empire to the Soviets*, Cleveland and New York, 1961, p. 144).

[2] The play was Gardin's first production at Terioki (see A. R. Kugel' (Homo Novus), 'Zametki', *Teatr i iskusstvo*, 1907, No. 22, p. 365).

[3] See *PLA*, p. 13; and *Leonid Andreyev. P'esy*, M., 1959, p. 560.

[4] See *Leonid Andreyev. P'esy*, p. 558.

attitudes to his philosophy. Ternovsky stands at the apex of the play's pyramidal character-alignment. He is Andreyev's first positive hero in the sense that through him the playwright gives the first direct verbal formulation of his *Weltanschauung*, as distinct from the simple indirect representations of it which he had given in such early stories as *On the River* and *The Foreigner*, and expresses, in a form which might be taken as a direct riposte to Gorky, his ideal conception of human advancement. The other characters are divided into two groups: the inhabitants of the observatory, and the revolutionaries who hasten there fresh from the battlefield and report, like the heralds of Greek tragedy, on the course of events 'down below'. The former group includes three subordinates of Ternovsky, in whom Andreyev appears to be presenting caricatures of three national types: the diligent, narrow-minded, 'teutonic' Pollak, the indolent Russian Zhitov, for whom life is little more than a kaleidoscopic mutation of visual impressions, and the excitable Jew, Lunts, through whom Andreyev expresses his abhorrence at the pogroms being conducted against the Jews by the Black Hundreds.[1] These three characters combine with Inna

---

[1] Antisemitism had reared its head again in Russia in 1903 after two decades of almost total peace. The wholesale massacre of Jews which took place on Easter Day (6 April) of that year at Kishinyov was followed by waves of pogroms in southern and western Russia in the autumn of 1904 and the spring and summer of 1905. This was not the only time that Andreyev expressed his sympathy for the Jews; he was to do so again a decade later—in 1914—in the pamphlet *About the Jews* (*O evreyakh*), published in Odessa, and, in 1915, in an article entitled *The First Step* (*Pervaya stupen'*) and a short story called *The Wounded Man* (*Ranenyy*), which were published in *Shchit* ('The Shield'), a miscellany edited by Andreyev himself, Gorky and Sologub which came out in Moscow and in the course of the following year went into two reprints. It should be noted, however, that the extreme importance attached to the 'theme of the Jew' in Andreyev's fiction by the American critics Ivar Spector (*The Golden Age of Russian Literature*, Idaho, 1952, pp. 259–70) and Joshua Kunitz (*Russian Literature and the Jew. A Sociological Inquiry into the Nature and Origin of Literary Patterns*, New York, 1929, pp. 140–4) is quite unwarranted. There is little basis, for instance, for the contention of the latter that Andreyev's Biblical figures—Lazarus (in the story of 1906 *Eleazar*), the characters of *Judas Iscariot* (*Iuda Iskariot*) (1907), and David Leyzer (in the play of 1909 *Anathema*)—are 'symbols' indicative of an 'unnatural psychological condition', common to all sensitive Russian liberals, which impelled them to circumvent the direct depiction of real, living Jews. This argument is blatantly confuted by *The Wounded Man*, in which the tragedy of the Jew is succinctly presented with great sympathy and power and without recourse to 'symbols'. There is no evidence that Andreyev's selection of Biblical figures in other works was in any way prompted by his meditations on the 'Jewish problem'; the selection was determined rather by the abstract problems which lie at the basis of the individual works concerned.

Aleksandrovna, the wife of Ternovsky, to form the human and philosophical background to the drama of ideas enacted between the astronomer and the revolutionaries, i.e. Marusya, Ternovsky's daughter Anna, her husband Verkhovtsev, who bears some resemblance to Chepurnoy in *Children of the Sun*, and the two workers, Treych and Schmidt.

On the front of the observatory are written in Latin the words spoken by Ternovsky in the second or verbal variant of the play: 'This is the shrine of Urania. Away with trivial cares! Here the lowly earth is scorned; from here leads the path to the stars.'[1] To the category of 'trivial cares' Ternovsky relegates 'death, injustice, misfortunes, all the dark shadows of the earth'.[2] The reality which monopolizes his attention is the 'spirit of music', the 'singing of the stars'. 'He who but once hears their voice coming from the depths of space,' he states, 'will become the son of eternity!'[3] His philosophy pivots on his glorification of the universality of life, which is echoed by Gorky's Protasov in *Children of the Sun*: 'Everything is alive. Life is everywhere. And everywhere are secrets. To revolve in the world of the wondrous, profound mysteries of being, to expend the energy of one's brain on their solution—this is the truly human life, here lies an inexhaustible source of happiness and vital, life-giving joy!'[4] But for Gorky the 'Cosmos' was 'deceptive and irrelevant',[5] a distraction from more urgent matters on earth, and Protasov is awakened to the error of his ways. Ternovsky, in contrast, is the mouthpiece of his creator.

Salvation from solitude and death, states the astronomer, lies in consciousness of participation in cosmic life, in transcendence of the individual ego. Mankind and matter are infinite objectifications of the life-force, distinguishable and subject to death only in their phenomenality, but essentially one and immortal. On this philosophical foundation he constructs his theory of evolution, in accordance with which the world-process is seen as a continuum of improvement, which is realized through the periodic creation by life of 'perfect forms', i.e. individuals who dedicate their transient existence on earth to the solution of the mysteries of the universe and the general enrichment of life: 'Like a gardener,' he declares, 'life cuts off its best blooms, but the earth is filled with their

---

[1] *Works* IV, p. 215.     [2] Ibid.     [3] Ibid., pp. 233–4.
[4] M. Gorky, *Deti solntsa*, Stuttgart, 1905, p. 53.
[5] See Troynov, loc. cit., p. 4.

fragrance.'[1] Andreyev stated in connection with the play: 'I am interested in that closeness which exists between the astronomer and his colleague who will not be born until a thousand years later, the touching trust with which he regards this comrade of the future, the link which exists between them.'[2] The designation 'son of eternity' is employed by Ternovsky to denote both the man who consciously participates in what might be called this 'relationship of evolution' and also the continuum itself which is activated through this relationship.

The external event which brings into focus the divergent attitudes to life of the protagonists is not so much the revolution as the cruel fate of Nikolay, who never appears on stage, but whose image pervades the entire play. Nikolay is the incarnation of the ideals not only of Ternovsky, but also of the astronomer's principal 'ideological' antagonist, Marusya, and this fact is in itself evidence that the difference between them is not so great as Marusya imagines. The objection of Marusya to aspirations 'to the stars' is their inefficacy as a means of improving life on earth; this argument is countered by Ternovsky with the claim that the one will flow automatically from the other—the erasure of 'social spots' from the study of 'sun-spots'. Marusya is conscious only of the physical suffering of Nikolay at the hands of his gaolers; Ternovsky derives comfort from the conviction that the destruction of the 'form' cannot affect the immortality of its achievement and from the knowledge that life, which is everywhere, will create another Nikolay, 'nay, better than he—in nature there are no repetitions'.[3] The present suffering momentarily eclipses for Marusya the positive achievement which results from it; Ternovsky, though far from insensitive to the agonies of his son, has the ability not only to perceive the positive achievement, but also to relate it to a continuous process of achievement which will ultimately triumph over the sources of evil and suffering. The difference between them lies only in the breadth of their respective visions—not in their conceptions of the task to which life should be devoted: the elimination of 'all the dark shadows of the earth'. To the realization of this task they are equally dedicated and herein Andreyev saw reason for hope of reconciliation.

It is clear that the philosophy of Ternovsky, while reiterating

---

[1] *Works* IV, p. 240.   [2] *Leonid Andreyev. P'esy*, p. 558.
[3] *Works* IV, p. 240.

the principles expressed indirectly by Andreyev in former works, includes a new dimension. Hitherto he had preached 'negatively' the transcendence of individualism as the essential prerequisite for a life of harmony, absolute freedom and happiness—in short, the philosophical premise of Ternovsky. In *To the Stars* he goes further and announces the existence among those who attain to this sublime knowledge of an 'aristocracy' whose immortality is not simply ontological, but also specifically of this world, of conscious life—the immortality of achievement. There are occasions in the play when it is difficult to disentangle these two different but integrally related conceptions. When informed by Marusya, for instance, of the mutilation of Nikolay in prison, Ternovsky cries: 'They have taken away my son! The madmen! In their blindness they have raised their hands against themselves!'[1] This statement is prompted by the conception of ontological immortality, of mankind as a single immortal entity, in accordance with which a crime committed by one individual against another is viewed as a crime against the eternal life which dwells within himself. But shortly afterwards Ternovsky rephrases his exclamation: 'They have taken away my son! They have taken away the light!'[2] Here Nikolay appears as the 'son of eternity', as one of the 'perfect forms' who activate the evolutionary process. Thus when one American student of Andreyev made the general observation that his conception of immortality 'had to do not with the after-life in the common acceptance of the term, but with actions that will live for ever',[3] he was expressing only half the truth, for his definition omits the underlying conception of ontological immortality.

The conception of evolution expounded in the play brings in its wake a new attitude to the intellect, which is at first confusing; it appears difficult to reconcile Ternovsky's worship of his intellect with Andreyev's dethronement of the intellect in *Thought*. The difference is perfectly obvious, however: it is the difference between thought divorced from life and thought devoted to the enrichment of life, between the self-assertive intellect, which brings about its own destruction, and the 'life-assertive' intellect, the conquests of which are immortal in so far as they constitute a link in the chain of evolutionary cognition. In Ternovsky intellectual inquiry is the

[1] Ibid., p. 239.    [2] Ibid.
[3] H. H. King, *Dostoevsky and Andreyev: Gazers upon the Abyss*, New York, 1936, p. 65.

means by which the subjective consciousness seeks to universalize itself. It is this type of thought that may be designated by Dostoevsky's term *proniknovenie*, of which Vyacheslav Ivanov writes: 'It is a transcension of the subject. In this state of mind we recognise the other Ego not as our object, but as another subject. It is therefore not a mere peripheral extension of the bounds of individual consciousness, but a complete inversion of its normal system of coordinates.'[1] There are clear affinities between Ternovsky's theory of evolution and Hartmann's ideal conception of the world-process as the progressive intellectualization of all aspects of nature, life and mind until mind becomes adequate to nature. Unlike Hartmann, however, Andreyev's astronomer postulates no ultimate conclusion. He believes simply in the progressive enrichment of conscious life through increasing knowledge of life and the universe, and this belief does not preclude sympathy for revolutionary idealism provided that it contributes to the realization of this 'higher process'; hence his sympathetic attitude to Marusya and his relationship of mutual respect with Treych. Andreyev's aim was to fuse the 'singing of the stars' and the 'music of revolution' into a single triumphant chord. The romantic conception of the revolution, on the basis of which he sought to effect this fusion, inevitably alienated him still further from Gorky and brought down on his head the thunderbolts of Lunacharsky.[2]

Andreyev himself expressed to Chulkov his own acute dissatisfaction with the form of the play: 'There is no power in it, no impact. . . . And the words are also petty—it is sickening. Every word should be like a millstone, and the soul of the reader should be ground between them into powder—that is how it is necessary to write.'[3] As on so many future occasions, he could not escape the blight of rhetoric when he came to expound his innermost convictions. But all the evidence indicates that he was fully content with the thought that he had endeavoured to express in the play. He was immensely gratified by the tumultuous reception given to it by the workers of Vienna. 'I am not fond of advertisements,' he wrote to his brother Pavel, 'but this time I feel like boasting, especially to the Social Democrats, *etc.* . . .'[4] He saw this reception

[1] V. Ivanov, *Freedom and the Tragic Life. A Study of Dostoevsky*, London, 1952, p. 26.
[2] Cf. A. V. Lunacharsky, *Kriticheskie etyudy*, L., 1925, pp. 205-61.
[3] *PLA*, p. 22.
[4] 'Leonid Andreyev. Pis'ma', *Russkiy sovremennik*, 1924, No. 4, p. 128.

as a vindication both of his 'poetic' portraits of the revolutionaries and of the synthesis which he had sought to effect.

Whatever criticisms are levelled against the play as a work of art, against the rhetoric and artificiality of the principal characters, the fact remains that Andreyev expressed in it some of his fundamental convictions on life—convictions which determined his attitude not to revolution alone, but to everything. He was repeating, in effect, his cardinal belief that the wretchedness of life will be banished only by the spiritual transformation of the individual. He sympathized with the revolutionary idealists in so far as they contributed to this transformation; but the violence preached by Gorky he could not accept and he disputed its efficacy. It was this attitude which prompted his statement to Chulkov on the conditions of social life: '. . . I do not accept life as it is and will never accept it, but I have no wish to hoist the standard of rebellion.'[1] His second play *Savva*, to which he gave the sub-title *Ignis sanat*, elucidates his thoughts on this question.

In a letter to Chulkov of 4 February 1906 he announced that he was working hard and that he had already written the play.[2] He added: 'It seems to have a certain force, but it is true that I will be abused for it until I die.'[3] Although *Znanie* was permitted to publish it in its eleventh miscellany, it was banned from the Russian stage. After its publication in Stuttgart it was finally performed in Vienna at the same time as *To the Stars*[4]—in October 1906—and on 12 April 1907 Meyerkhol'd directed a performance by V. R. Gardin's troupe at Terioki.

The plot and idea of the work had been devised by Andreyev as long ago as January 1902, when he outlined them in a letter to Gorky as an example of the type of story which he was constantly thinking up and then abandoning.[5] The external events of the work follow fairly closely those of a real-life episode—the attempt of a young inventor, Anatoliy Georgievich Ufimtsev,[6] to combat religious superstition by blowing up the supposedly miracle-working icon in the Znamenskiy monastery in the city of Kursk on 7 March 1898. The idea of blowing up the icon in the local monastery is

---

[1] *PLA*, p. 18.
[2] A few minor alterations were subsequently made and the play was finally completed on 10 February (see Rubtsov, op. cit., p. 164).
[3] *PLA*, p. 23.   [4] Cf. ibid., p. 13.   [5] Cf. *LN*, pp. 130–1.
[6] In the Soviet period Ufimtsev (1880–1936) became a well-known aircraft designer.

conceived by Andreyev's hero, Savva Tropinin, as the first and most important of a series of actions designed to liberate man from the burdens which he has laid upon his own existence. Against God, the greatest of human fetishes, he pits dynamite, the creation of man. The earth, he preaches, must be purged with fire and the old world obliterated. Yet his gospel of a new life encounters a wall of incomprehension. Almost his every tirade concludes with the question 'Do you understand?'—but no one does, and this silent response is clearly intended to denote life's rejection of this reformer. Andreyev's pronouncements on the inviolability of life in *The Wild Duck* constitute the perceptible 'sub-text' of the play and Savva suffers the fate of the lepers in *The Wall*. From the beginning the execution of his scheme is impeded by insurmountable obstacles, which appear with the weird inevitability of the 'accidents' which bear Kerzhentsev to his ruin. One such obstacle is the monk Kondratiy whom he selects to place the bomb; the selection is in itself symbolic of the bankruptcy of his utopianism. Kondratiy betrays the scheme to the abbot of the monastery, who orders the icon to be removed before the explosion and subsequently replaced. The masses proclaim a miracle and fall on Savva in one of the most horrific scenes in Andreyev's fiction. Understood by no one, Savva fades from the scene like a ripple on the surface of life.

There are two aspects of Savva which must be distinguished: on the one hand, the motives which prompt his action; and on the other, his conception of the means by which life should be reformed. The playwright is in complete sympathy with his hero's motives. Through Savva he gives expression to the same indictment of human stupidity and crassness and voices the same demand for the liberation of the spirit as he does through Ternovsky. But Savva proposes a solution directly opposed to that of the astronomer— eradication in lieu of conversion and transcendence, and it is on this question of solution that he runs counter to his creator.

Savva defines himself as an 'avenger'. 'Behind my back,' he cries to his principal antagonist, his sister Lipa, 'stands all that you have stifled.'[1] He announces that he is taking vengeance on man for his stupidity. 'But who gave you the right?' asks Lipa. 'Who gave you power over people? How dare you touch that which for them is a right, their life?' He replies: 'Who gave me the right? You did. Who gave me the power? You did. And I hold it firmly—try to

[1] *Works* IV, p. 290.

take it away!'[1] In Savva, this 'precursor of our Bolshevism' as Chirikov called him,[2] Andreyev shows the transition from a legitimate indictment of man's ignorance and slavishness to an obsessive extremism which goes far beyond the original objects of the indictment and encompasses the whole of life. Claiming to be a benefactor, Savva nevertheless wishes to destroy not only that which enslaves man, but all that man has achieved and constructed in the course of his long existence. Like the revolutionaries in Dostoevsky's *The Devils* (*Besy*), he knows no compassion in his fanatical desire to be a benefactor to people in spite of themselves, and his professed altruism cannot disguise a similar contempt and pernicious egoism. 'No, Savva, you love no one,' says Lipa; 'you love only yourself, your dreams. He who loves people would not take everything away from them and place his own desire higher than their life.'[3] Through Lipa Andreyev repeats Ternovsky's conception of life as an uninterrupted process of accumulative creation in which past, present and future are inseparably linked. Its symbol in the play is the throng which wends its way past the monastery in the final scene—solid, indestructible, endless, propelled and guided from within by infallible instinct. How pitiful by comparison, the playwright seems to say, is the figure of the lonely 'avenger' whom no one understands. The violent, rectilinear utopianism of Savva may be compared to the scheme of Kerzhentsev in so far as both signify attempts of the individual to reduce life to a simplified, abstract pattern. But the reality which they seek to adjust to their schemes is only the surface of life. Integrally related to the philosophical substructure of the play is the refrain spoken by Savva's brother Tyukha: 'There are only masks.'[4] Savva sees only the appearances of things and is blind to the underlying process; herein lies his tragedy.

Significant are the opening words of a letter of Gorky to Andreyev of March 1906: 'That Savva is like me—that's not important.'[5] The statement infers that Andreyev had directly compared him with his hero.[6] There seems to be little doubt, however, that the play was intended by the playwright as a repudiation not only of

---

[1] Ibid.    [2] Chirikov, loc. cit., p. 69.    [3] *Works* IV, p. 289.
[4] Ibid., p. 249.    [5] *LN*, p. 265.
[6] Yershov suggests that Gorky is referring to Savva Morozov (cf. P. Yershov (ed.), *Letters of Gorky and Andreyev, 1899–1912*, London, 1958, p. 175), but this makes no sense in the context of the letter which is wholly concerned with the change that had taken place in the relationship between the two writers.

the credo of Gorky and the Social Democrats, but equally of anarchism as a philosophy of destruction. 'In the midst of the unbearable conditions of our life,' wrote one contemporary critic, 'emotional anarchism has become a natural and even inevitable fact.'[1] The same social phenomenon was noted by Lunacharsky: 'The interest of the Russian public in anarchism at the present time is beyond doubt.'[2] The main apostle of this 'emotional anarchism' was, of course, Chulkov; hence Andreyev's remark in a letter to him written shortly after the completion of *Savva*: 'It is precisely your opinion that would be interesting.'[3] Chulkov's conception of a mystical, supra-individualistic communion, i.e. the positive or constructive aspect of his theory, was predicated on the destruction of the whole historical edifice. He declared:

Perhaps the socialists, of all those who have not crossed the boundary of mysticism, are closest to us insofar as they sincerely despise property. . . . The old bourgeois order must be annihilated in order to clear the field for the last battle: there, in a free socialist society, will rise the restless spirit of the great man-Messiah to lead mankind from mechanical construction to the wondrous embodiment of Eternal Wisdom.[4]

Andreyev reversed the order of Chulkov's priorities, claiming that external change would follow automatically from inner transformation. He shared Chulkov's contempt for bourgeois society, but could not tolerate the thought of its wholesale destruction; he could not renounce, together with the evil of the bourgeois order, the cultural heritage of man, the conquests of knowledge laboriously achieved by man in the course of history, and this attitude determined his sympathies no less in 1917 than it did in 1905–6.

The three works—*Thus It Was, To the Stars* and *Savva*—constitute a continuous and comprehensive exposition of Andreyev's attitude not simply to *the* revolution, but to politico-social revolu-

---

[1] A. Smirnov, 'Tragediya anarkhizma. ("Savva" L. Andreyeva. "Znanie" XI)', *Obrazovanie*, 1906, No. 11, p. 84.

[2] A. Lunacharsky, 'Zametki filosofa. O nastoyashchikh anarkhistakh', *Obrazovanie*, 1906, No. 10, p. 19.

[3] *PLA*, p. 24.

[4] Quoted from K. Mochul'sky, *Aleksandr Blok*, Paris, 1948, p. 139. Lunacharsky took violent exception to this comparison of the 'anarchist position' to that of the socialists. Regarding anarchism as a wholly individualistic cult—to use his own words, as 'enlightened bourgeois individualism'—he contrasted it with the socialist objective of communal solidarity (see Lunacharsky, 'Zametki filosofa. O nastoyashchikh anarkhistakh', pp. 37–8).

tion *per se*. In the first work he questions the motives which prompt it and criticizes its superficiality, its failure to correct the fundamental *malaise* of society. In *To the Stars* he contrasts the transient phenomenon of revolution with the eternal constructive process of evolution, and in the figures of Marusya and Treych accepts the former in so far as it contributes to the advancement of the latter. And finally, in *Savva* he specifies that which he rejects in revolution, exposing its inherent dangers and condemning its indiscriminate destruction. Eminently applicable to Andreyev are the words which Blok wrote to his father on 30 December 1905: '. . . I have absorbed everything that I can (from the "social sphere") and cast away that which my soul does not accept.'[1]

[1] Aleksandr Blok, *Sobranie sochineniy v vos'mi tomakh*, vol. 8, M.–L., 1963, p. 144.

# XII

# THE YEAR OF TRIALS

THE year from autumn 1905 to autumn 1906 marks the beginning of the painful three-year long transition from the first to the second of the two main phases of Andreyev's life during his literary career. It was a period of unbroken hardship and depressing experiences. The shadow of Vasiliy Fiveysky seemed to have darkened the path of his creator. Shortly after his return to Moscow from the Crimea in autumn 1905 his youngest sister Zinaida died of a brain haemorrhage at the age of 21. She died in the clinic in which almost five years previously he had written *Once upon a Time There Lived*. Pavel Andreyev recalls:

This death, the first in our family since our father's death, struck Leonid so forcibly that for a long time we feared for his sanity. Previously there had been thoughts of death; now they had received a concrete, real form—moreover, in the image of his youngest sister whom he loved so much and who, incidentally, was so like him. It was a long time before the oppressive and painful mood caused by her death eased and was replaced by a feeling of sadness induced by the irretrievable loss and the instability of everything on earth.[1]

The conditions under which he was living at the time served to intensify his gloom. We have seen that to protect himself he felt it advisable to leave the country, and he embarked on the travels which took him to Finland, Germany, Italy, Switzerland[2] and again to Finland before he finally made his way back once more to Germany. He wrote to Veresaev in April 1906 that so many new experiences had accumulated that he found it impossible to write.[3] During his absence from Russia he continued to follow events there keenly and experienced the final collapse of the revolution with a depth of feeling which no 'philosophical' consolation could completely

[1] *PNA*, pp. 203–4.
[2] Andreyev disliked Switzerland intensely; he gave vent to his contempt for the 'bourgeois Swiss' in a letter to Mirolyubov of 14 April 1906 (see *MAMR*, pp. 114–15).
[3] See *VRSV*, p. 462.

assuage. Particularly acute was his reaction to the violent suppression of the mutinies in the Baltic fleet at Sveaborg (Viipuri) instigated by the underground organization of the Socialist Revolutionary party after the dissolution of the first Duma on 9 July 1906 and the proclamation of the Vyborg Manifesto. According to his son, Vadim, Andreyev was himself actually involved in the uprising.[1] He arrived back in Germany, after two weeks of hiding in Norway, in the early days of August. He wrote to Chulkov on the 17th of that month: 'I have roamed for two weeks among the Norwegian fiords, am now sitting in Berlin with my family, and have been groaning for several days with the most excruciating neuralgia in the face.'[2]

The story *Lazarus*, which he wrote during that month, may be taken as a spiritual reaction to this succession of trials in general and, in particular, to the most painful of them—the death of his sister. Vorovsky's statement that the pessimism which affected the 'less stable elements of the intelligentsia' after the collapse of the revolution 'drove L. Andreyev also to the culmination of his philosophy of negation'[3] creates a false picture of Andreyev during the immediate post-revolutionary period. To ascribe his depression wholly to the failure of the revolution[4] is most implausible in the light not only of his complex attitude to the revolution, as described in the last chapter, but also of the facts of his personal life during the period under observation. His personal misfortunes unquestionably weighed more heavily upon him and it is they which are primarily reflected in the mood of his fiction. 'One way or another,' he wrote to Gorky some years later (February 1912), 'all that I write, think, and feel is the result of my personal experience.'[5] Moreover, caution is equally necessary when considering his 'philosophy of negation'. It must be repeated that in Andreyev's works negation is not an end in itself; it flows directly from his positive convictions; only in *Lazarus* is it born of despair. This work is a confirmation of the quoted words of Pavel Andreyev; it shows that the reality of death had momentarily assumed control

---

[1] *VLA*, May, p. 76.  [2] *PLA*, p. 11.

[3] V. V. Vorovsky, *Literaturno-kriticheskie stat'i*, M., 1948, p. 149.

[4] The same error is made by the critic Odnoblyudov (see V. Odnoblyudov, *Tragediya sovremennogo intelligentnogo obshchestva. Kritiko-publitsisticheskiy ocherk, po povodu proizvedeniya L. Andreyeva 'Mysl' '*, *v tesnoy svyazi s ego drugimi proizvedeniyami*, Elets, 1915, p. 49).

[5] *LN*, p. 324.

of his thoughts and that the weight of misfortune had dispelled his 'philosophical optimism'.

First published in *Zolotoe runo* in December 1906,[1] the work at once attracted superlative comments. Gorky pronounced it 'the best of all that has been written about death in all the world's literature',[2] while one American critic wrote: 'Nothing more pessimistic has ever been written than *Lazarus*.'[3] The contrast, on which all Andreyev's major works are founded, between the mystical collective principle, which was the source of his optimism, and the individualistic principle is presented in an unprecedented form. The emphasis is no longer on the perdition of the 'apostate', but on the threatening disintegration of the collective. The re-entry of Lazarus into the world of the living menaces the survival of life. The indifference of the infinite to life on earth, which is reflected in his eyes, severs the links which bind men together. In the opening scene the guests at the feast held to celebrate his resurrection continue to sit, but they are 'severed from one another like dim lights scattered over a field at night'.[4] There is no longer the same unity and cohesion of life in the face of an inimical force as there was in *Savva*.

The two principal episodes of the work are the clashes between Lazarus and Aurelius, a Roman sculptor, and Lazarus and Augustus, the Roman Emperor, which signify respectively the defeat and partial victory of life. Aurelius makes the long journey from Rome to see Lazarus in the hope of finding soul and life with which to animate his bronze. He seeks the opposite of what Lazarus has to give and is portrayed from the start as a figure contrasting with him in every conceivable way. The two of them are depicted sitting at night outside the house of Lazarus—the latter seeking the sun which is powerless to warm his frozen limbs and presenting to those who watch him the spectacle of a black silhouette, while Aurelius, his white chiton gleaming, seeks the moonlight which he aspires to reproduce in his marble sculptures. The sun has the symbolic value, as in Dostoevsky, of the source of life, while the moon is the symbol of death. Lazarus thirsts for life; Aurelius is doomed to a living death. It is noticeable that the resistance of

---

[1] *Zolotoe runo*, 1906, No. 11–12, pp. 59–68.     [2] *LN*, p. 280.
[3] Anonymous, 'Andreyev—a New Portent in Russian Literature', *Current Literature*, New York, 1908, vol. XLV, July–December, p. 285.
[4] *Works* III, p. 90.

Aurelius diminishes progressively as the sun retreats before the oncoming night. This is reflected, as was the mortification of the Governor, in his speech. Aurelius notes that his words are losing their meaning, 'as though they were rocking on shaky legs, as though they were slipping and falling, having feasted on the wine of anguish and despair. And dark gaps appeared between them— like distant hints of a great emptiness and darkness.'[1] Creation and destruction, night and day, black and white—such are the contrasts on which this scene is constructed. Aurelius breathes life into cold marble; Lazarus strikes death into living flesh.

But the morrow finds the contrasts erased; Aurelius has succumbed. He returns to Rome at once and declares simply: 'I have found it.'[2] Work begins immediately on the sculpture in which he seeks to embody the newly discovered truth. His spiritual oneness with Lazarus is symbolized by the clothes which he dons before meeting the experts who will assess the work. They are identical to the bizarre attire worn by Lazarus at the feast with which the story begins. The sculpture horrifies the experts. The butterfly vainly struggling to fly from the ledge on which it is perched was intended by its creator to symbolize the powerlessness of all things living to escape the fate of death. Andreyev perhaps had in mind here the symbolic sculpture of Rubek—'The Resurrection Day'—in Ibsen's *When We Dead Awaken*.[3] Aurelius's paralysing embodiment of hopelessness and despair is pronounced unfit to exist by the judges and is destroyed. Its creator is already destroyed; he can merely sit in his garden seeking vainly the life-giving warmth of the sun 'like a pale reflection of him who, in the far distance, at the very gates of the stony wilderness, sat just as still beneath the fiery sun'.[4]

Into the 'story of Aurelius' Andreyev breathes the accumulated gloom and pessimism of the passing moment in his life. In the clash between Lazarus and Augustus he struggles once more to elevate himself to the philosophical heights, but barely succeeds. Augustus is saved by his awareness of the responsibility which devolves upon him, as the head of the Empire, for the lives of the millions under his sway; the ties between himself and his subjects withstand the corroding influence of the gaze of Lazarus. But though Augustus can conceive of the victory of the collective principle in life, he

---

[1] Ibid., p. 95.    [2] Ibid., p. 96.
[3] See *The Collected Works of Henrik Ibsen*, vol. 11, London, 1910, pp. 417–18.
[4] *Works* III, p. 97.

knows that the ultimate victory belongs to death. As if to reaffirm this, Andreyev ends the work with the spectacle of Lazarus, now back in the wilderness after having been blinded by order of Augustus, walking into the distance in search of the sun, his black body with its outstretched arms forming 'a monstrous likeness to a cross';[1] the cross of Christ symbolizing eternal life is replaced by the cross of Lazarus symbolizing eternal death.

Notwithstanding this conclusion, however, the 'story of Augustus' represents the hesitant first stage in Andreyev's attempt to recapture his confidence in his former convictions after the total capitulation which is reflected in the 'story of Aurelius'. The succession of works written by Andreyev between October 1906 and May 1908, i.e. the works of the transitional period in his life, may be generically designated his 'Divine Comedy'. His play *The Life of Man* (*Zhizn' Cheloveka*) marks the next stage in the process of recovery. L'vov-Rogachevsky described the play and *Lazarus* as 'twins conceived and born in the terrible hours of anguish and despair'.[2] The statement is accurate only in so far as it indicates the similarity of the conditions under which they were written; the two works are by no means 'identical twins'.

*The Life of Man* was written in Berlin in October 1906; it took Andreyev only twelve days to write it. The play signified for him a new departure in dramatic form involving the use of stylized images and the reduction of life to a succession of fixed situations. While the five 'Pictures' (Acts) of the play present a scheme of human life, the Prologue presents a synoptic scheme of the whole— the 'theory' as distinct from the 'practice' which is enacted in the Pictures. The Prologue is spoken by the sinister symbolic figure of Someone-in-grey, who is present on stage throughout. He announces to the audience that before their eyes Man is about to complete the 'circle of iron predestination'.[3] The image is reminiscent of the words in Act III of *Savva* spoken by the hero to his sister: 'He, modern man, is intelligent; he is already prepared for freedom, but the past eats his soul and like a scab encloses his life in the iron circle of that which has happened. . . .'[4] The term 'iron circle' is

---

[1] Ibid., p. 104.
[2] V. L'vov-Rogachevsky, 'Shagi smerti. (Po povodu "predstavleniya" L. Andreyeva "Zhizn' Cheloveka" i rasskaza L. Andreyeva "Eleazar")', *Obrazovanie*, 1907, No. 3, p. 42.
[3] See *Works* I, p. 173.      [4] *Works* IV, p. 291.

used by Savva to denote the prejudices, misconceptions and illusions
which fetter the human spirit and thought and as such, though not
in the way that Savva advocates, the 'circle' is destructible.
Although Someone-in-grey speaks of the 'circle of iron predestination' as if it were the indestructible law of life itself, the fact that
the life of Man is compounded of the prejudices, etc., against which
Savva rails, leads to the conclusion that the two 'circles' denote one
and the same thing. This conclusion facilitates both understanding
of Someone-in-grey and the interpretation of Andreyev's purpose
in the work.

Many interpretations of Someone-in-grey are offered by contemporary critics. Arabzhin sees in him a personification of the
wall against which the lepers dash themselves in the allegorical story
of 1901.[1] Ganzhulevich believes him to be a symbol of eternity, of
the ghastly after-life unveiled by Andreyev in *Lazarus*.[2] Kranikhfel'd, on the other hand, interprets him as an unsuccessful objectification of the Nietzschean 'Self'.[3] The parallel with the 'wall' is
certainly the most plausible, though it remains undeveloped by
Arabzhin and requires qualification. The symbolic value of
Someone-in-grey is unquestionably narrower and more specific
than that of the 'wall'; it does not, for instance, embrace political
and social oppression. Yet Someone-in-grey is himself symbolically
'linked' with a wall. The stage-direction describing the room in
which Man is born—itself symbolic of the life which greets him—
contains the following remarks: 'Everything in it is grey, smoky, of
one colour: grey walls, a grey ceiling, a grey floor. From an unseen
source flows an even, weak light, and it also is grey, monotonous,
of uniform colour, ghostly, and it gives neither shadows nor bright
gleams of light. Noiselessly Someone-in-grey detaches himself from
the wall to which he is clinging.'[4] Thus Someone-in-grey is an
emanation or personification of *this* wall—the wall of the room
which symbolizes the life of Man, and since the life of Man is the
'circle of iron predestination', so Someone-in-grey may be viewed
as a symbolic interpreter of the law of this 'circle' which man, in

---

[1] See K. I. Arabzhin, *Leonid Andreyev. Itogi tvorchestva. Literaturno-
kriticheskiy etyud*, SPb., 1910, p. 68.

[2] See T. Ganzhulevich, *Russkaya zhizn' i eyo techeniya v tvorchestve Leonida
Andreyeva*, SPb., 1908, p. 81.

[3] See V. Kranikhfel'd, 'Literaturnye zametki', *Sovremennyy mir*, 1908, No. 5,
p. 95.

[4] *Works* I, p. 172.

his blindness, had made the law of his life, and which, as stated, is compounded of destructible prejudices and illusions. His greyness is symbolic of the greyness of such a life and the dimming flame of his candle, which recalls the ancient image of fire as the source of life, symbolizes its inexorable passing.[1]

The 'principle' or 'law' which for Andreyev was the fundamental cause of suffering and evil in life, of prejudice and misconceptions, was the 'principle of individuation', and Someone-in-grey emerges as the mouthpiece of this 'law' which controls the life of Man. Like the sinister Queen in Maeterlinck's *The Death of Tintagiles* (*La Mort de Tintagiles*) and the Sister-of-Mercy in Ibsen's *When We Dead Awaken*, he stands silently aloof throughout the action of the play and freezes the spectacle with his chilling gaze. But the similarity, it must be stressed, is wholly superficial. The 'fate' symbolized by Someone-in-grey is very different from that conceived by Maeterlinck in his early decadent period. It was not Andreyev's intention to conjure up an image of the classical conception of fate. The element of 'fate' in the play is not a 'mythological phenomenon', as Ovsyaniko-Kulikovsky termed it.[2] Just as the 'fate' which haunts Vasiliy Fiveysky is the offspring of the priest's own attitude to life and himself, so the 'circle of iron predestination' is Man's own creation. It is his own prosaic existence reduced to a rigid scheme; hence the prosaic appearance of Someone-in-grey by comparison with the majesty of Maeterlinck's Fate. 'Both Andreyev and Maeterlinck,' wrote Belyy, 'speak of the unknown, the fateful. But there are different kinds of "unknown": listen to the voice of silence in Maeterlinck and in Andreyev: is there really anything in common here?'[3]

Andreyev's purpose in the play was neither to probe into the 'mystery of life', as one critic put it,[4] nor to portray a 'universal man', to use Rubtsov's term,[5] although Man is indeed in his

---

[1] The conception of life as a 'candle which blazes up through some mysterious power and finally goes out' is also common in Russian folklore (see V. V. Brusyanin, 'The Symbolic Dramas of Andreyeff', *Plays by Leonid Andreyeff*, New York, 1915, p. xvi).

[2] D. N. Ovsyaniko-Kulikovsky, 'Zhizn' Cheloveka. (Zametki o tvorchestve Leonida Andreyeva)', *Sobranie sochineniy*, vol. 5, M., 1923–4, p. 160.

[3] A. Belyy, 'Smert'' ili vozrozhdenie?', in his *Arabeski*, M., 1911, p. 494.

[4] Cf. V. M. Khvostov, 'Zhizn' Cheloveka. (Po povodu dramy Leonida Andreyeva)', *Moskovskiy ezhenedel'nik*, 1908, No. 5, p. 33.

[5] Cf. A. B. Rubtsov, *Iz istorii russkoy dramaturgii kontsa XIX—nachala XX veka*, Minsk, 1960, p. 173.

creator's view representative of the overwhelming majority. The playwright had a specific type of man in mind—the man who describes the 'circle of iron predestination', the man who recognizes nothing higher than the dictates of his individual will and regards life as a war of individual wills, each seeking to subdue the other in the quest for personal well-being, i.e. once more the 'apostate'. The capital letter with which the name of the protagonist begins is an indication not so much of universality as of Andreyev's conviction of the prevalence of the pattern of life which he presents in schematic form and of the scope of his indictment. For the greater part of the play his Man emerges as a generalization of the outstanding type produced by contemporary Russian and European society. When the critic Rostislavov criticized the life of Andreyev's Man on the grounds that it was not 'a generalization of life, but only a crude carcase of its inevitable stages from birth to death',[1] he was closer to discerning Andreyev's purpose than he realized; what he should have said is that the life of Man is not a generalization of life, but a 'crude carcase' of true life or, to use once more Dostoevsky's term, the 'living life'.

Yet even this does not exhaust the complexity of Andreyev's scheme. Clearly pronounced are the features which Man has in common with his predecessors in Andreyev's fiction. Like Kerzhentsev and Vasiliy Fiveysky, he lives an intense inner life. Egocentricity characterizes his dreams of happiness and wealth. Like these heroes of former works, he has driven a wedge between himself and the rest of the world, and his detachment is symbolized by his dream of building his future home on a mountain in Norway. No less than Kerzhentsev he is imprisoned in the lonely castle of his thought. But Andreyev disrupts the bounds within which his protagonist may be considered a generalization. He does not completely divest him of individuality and transforms him at key moments in the play into an exception to the rule of which he is otherwise the personification. Throughout his life conforms externally to the pattern predicted by Someone-in-grey in the Prologue, but his unabating inner rebellion against this pattern is his vindication and in him glows the spark of genius which is immortality. The play becomes, to use the words of Blok, 'a vivid proof that Man is a man, not a doll, not a pitiful being doomed to decay,

[1] A. Rostislavov, 'O "Zhizni Cheloveka" ', *Teatr i iskusstvo*, 1907, No. 11, p. 191.

but a wondrous phoenix who overcomes the "icy wind of limitless space". The wax melts, but life does not wane.'[1]

'Awakened to life out of the night of unconsciousness, the will finds itself an individual, in an endless and boundless world, among innumerable individuals, all striving, suffering, erring; and as if through a troubled dream it hurries back to its old unconsciousness.' Thus Schopenhauer describes the life of man.[2] Born to the accompaniment of his mother's agonized shrieks into a world of vulgarity, epitomized in the birth-scene in the chatter of the Old Women and the Relatives who 'leave no stereotype commonplace unsaid',[3] Andreyev's Man begins his life—a life of bondage to the scheme delineated in the Prologue. The playwright selects for his hero, however, a man whose kick against the traces will be stronger than the average. He is talented and energetic, with a profession which is both artistic and socially indispensable: he is an architect. He enjoys with his wife during his years of poverty the happiness of mutual love, understanding and expectation of success. He firmly believes that he is the master of his life, that he holds the strings and that poverty is a passing phase, a temporary obstacle. He hurls at Someone-in-grey the gauntlet of challenge:

Against your sinister stagnation I set my living and courageous strength; against your gloom—my loud, ringing laughter! Ay, beat off the blows! You have a head of stone, devoid of reason—I hurl at it the red-hot shot of my scintillating thought; you have a heart of stone, devoid of pity— stand aside, I pour into it the burning poison of rebellious cries! . . . Covered with wounds, pouring forth scarlet blood, I gather my strength to cry: you have not conquered yet, evil enemy of Man![4]

The challenge is the expression of Man's rebellion against the life and values which he encounters at every turn; but his rebellion is vocal only. From this moment onward he proceeds to describe obediently the fated 'circle'. He attains wealth, respectability and 'happiness'. This summit of his mundane achievement is reduced to the fixed situation of a ball consisting of the succession of dull conventions which, in Andreyev's eyes, characterized the typical

---

[1] A. Blok, 'O drame', *Sobranie sochineniy v vos'mi tomakh*, vol. 5, M., 1962, p. 193.

[2] A. Schopenhauer, *The World as Will and Idea* (translated from the German by R. B. Haldane and J. Kemp), vol. III, London, 1883, p. 382.

[3] M. Baring, 'A Russian Mystery Play', in his *Russian Essays and Stories*, London, 1908, p. 144.

[4] *Works* I, pp. 190–1.

bourgeois conception of happiness and well-being. Dissatisfied with certain aspects of the production of the play by Komissarzhevskaya's company in February 1907, Andreyev wrote a long letter to Stanislavsky in which he disclosed the way in which he conceived this scene:

> In general, this whole 'ball' must depict openly the vanity of fame, wealth, *etc.*, happiness. . . . If I had succeeded in presenting what I wanted to, this picture of 'gaiety' should have been the most oppressive of all, hopelessly depressing. This is not satire, no. It is a representation of how sated people, whose souls are dead, enjoy themselves.[1]

With expressions of reconciliation and acquiescence on their faces the dancers move to the monotonous, mournful strains produced by three exhausted musicians, as though their movements are controlled by a more powerful will than their own. This regimented movement effectively evokes the emptiness and silence which surround Man in the hour of his triumph.

Even this triumph, however, is founded on an accident, for it is nothing more than an accident that his novel architectural ideas accord with a passing whim of society. This whim is the source of his happiness and prosperity; its passing signifies his ruin. When his son is accidentally killed by a stone thrown for no apparent reason by some nameless good-for-nothing, the 'ball' of his life is eclipsed by the humiliating awareness of the futility of his attempt to assert his own individuality and power. As his son lies unconscious, he turns in despair to Someone-in-grey with a prayer for justice. It is a noble prayer, bringing a brief gleam of hope, but the boy dies and his death sparks off the most powerful moment of the whole drama—Man's curse hurled at Someone-in-grey. To curse, according to Dostoevsky, is the only privilege which differentiates man from other animals and, perhaps, the only means whereby he can 'convince himself that he is a man and not a piano key'.[2] Such is the inner power of this curse that victory seems momentarily to lie with Man.

The impression of Man's triumph is sustained in the final Picture—the death-scene in the tavern—despite the playwright's inability to contemplate death with his former philosophical calm. His object here was manifestly to achieve a crescendo of horror. In

---

[1] *Leonid Andreyev. P'esy*, M., 1959, p. 567.
[2] F. M. Dostoevsky, *Sobranie sochineniy*, vol. 4, M., 1956, p. 158.

his letter to Stanislavsky he refers to the whole scene as a 'nightmare'.[1] Blok was one of many who disapproved of the excesses of the scene; he wrote: 'It is powerful, just as everything written by Andreyev is powerful, but there is a *hidden falsity* in it—that same falsity which always causes us pain when awaiting every new work by this writer and a secret fear for it.'[2] It will be seen, however, that the excesses were produced by an even more painful experience than that which Andreyev had undergone a year before.

Gorky was mystified by the choice of a tavern as the setting for this scene.[3] In February 1908 Andreyev was to rewrite it and he replaced the tavern with the crumbling house of Man in order to introduce a new set of characters at the expense of the Drunkards— the Heirs, i.e. a group directly related to the protagonist, like the Relatives in the first Picture and the Friends and Enemies in the third; the Drunkards stood in no such relationship and Andreyev was disturbed by this inconsistency. In reference to his selection of a tavern in the original version he stated in the Foreword to this new variant that he regarded it as nothing more than a setting which enabled him to portray effectively the solitude of Man in the closing moments of his life.[4] It also enabled him, however, to make a vital distinction.

The Drunkards, who inhabit the tavern-tomb, recoil at the sight of Man. To them he is a being from another world—the world of life and light. Though Man is himself no less an outcast than they are, he differs from them in one crucial respect. For the Drunkards life is unrelieved horror from which wine alone affords an outlet. Their fate is the fate of the average man devoid of self-awareness. In Man self-awareness is developed to a degree which makes submission impossible. His sole weapon is his curse but he wields it to the end, achieving thereby in the eyes of his creator a partial victory. This conclusion explains Andreyev's remark to Veresaev in connection with the play: '. . . everyone considers me a pessimist. This is a complete failure to understand me.'[5]

[1] See *Leonid Andreyev. P'esy*, p. 567.

[2] A. Blok, 'O drame', *Sobranie sochineniy v vos'mi tomakh*, vol. 5, M., 1962, p. 187.

[3] *LN*, p. 279.

[4] Cf. L. N. Andreyev, 'Smert' Cheloveka. Novyy variant pyatoy kartiny "Zhizni Cheloveka" ', *Literaturno-khudozhestvennye al'manakhi izdatel'stva 'Shipovnik'*, vol. 4, SPb., 1908, pp. 258–9.

[5] *VRSV*, p. 470.

When the contending forces in the lists are Someone-in-grey and Man with his life of misfortune armed only with a bold but lonely curse, it is difficult to see how the latter can, in any sense, be construed the victor. The explanation lies in the real import of the curse. Man's execration of life signifies his rejection of life, but not in its profounder meaning—only earthly desires which have no lasting life. Man's minimal self-awareness is sufficient to bring him to the rejection of life with this restricted meaning denoted by the 'circle of iron predestination', but it is unable to elevate him to that transcendental realm in which roams the thought of Sergey Nikolaevich Ternovsky. Man can be said to stand in Andreyev's hierarchy of cognition at an intermediate point between Ternovsky and the Drunkards. Combining in the life of Man those individual beliefs, values, convictions and illusions which he had rejected in former works, Andreyev now execrates them in their totality, and in this execration reveals the first stage of the liberation of man from the empirical world, of the inner ego from the outer, i.e. from the fetters which impede the free flight of the spirit towards the vision of the truth of life and immortality. This is clearly what Chukovsky perceived when he wrote: 'With his *The Life of Man* Leonid Andreyev endeavoured to reveal . . . the philistinism of mundane life, but not of being.'[1]

The play was published in 1907 in the first *Shipovnik* almanac, to the disgust of Gorky who wanted it for *Znanie*,[2] and was first performed at Komissarzhevskaya's theatre on 22 February of that year. It broke on the Russian literary world with an impact which can be compared only with that of *The Abyss* and *In the Fog*. Its formal and thematic novelty immediately provoked critical opinion from all quarters, and the mass of critical literature served to increase its popularity. One critic wrote two years later: 'There is no doubt that at the present time there could hardly be found two or three intelligent people who are not familiar with L. Andreyev's well-known play "The Life of Man".'[3] Symptomatic of the diversity of opinion that it aroused is the fact that while, on the one hand, it brought Andreyev in December 1907 the A. S. Griboedov prize

---

[1] K. Chukovsky, *Leonid Andreyev bol'shoy i malen'kiy*, SPb., 1908, p. 94.

[2] See Gorky's letter to Pyatnitsky in *Arkhiv A. M. Gor'kogo*, vol. 4, M., 1954, p. 218.

[3] O. Kube, *Koshmary zhizni. Kriticheski-psikhologicheskiy etyud o L. Andreyeve, Pshebyshevskom i dr. sovremennykh pisatelyakh*, SPb., 1909, p. 28.

from the *Obshchestvo russkikh dramaticheskikh pisateley i opernykh kompozitorov* ('The Society of Russian Dramatic Writers and Opera Composers')[1] and in 1908 the A. N. Ostrovsky prize, on the other it was forbidden performance in Odessa, where Duvan-Tortsov's production incited the Black Hundreds to action, Khar'kov, Kiev and the Volga cities. No action was taken against it by the censor who, in the official circular issued to provincial governors, appealed rather amusingly for 'conscientiousness' from producers and actors and forbade its performance only if local conditions made disturbances unavoidable.[2]

At first Andreyev had been sceptical about the fate of the play. He wrote to Pyatnitsky on 5 September 1906: 'Here is a play which interests me greatly: either a great failure, or a great success and a new form for the drama.'[3] Thereafter his scepticism appears to have increased. Veresaev writes:

Gorky and all the people around him (Andreyev) were of a very negative opinion of the play . . . and predicted its complete failure on the stage. Andreyev regarded with distrust the first telegrams from V. F. Komissarzhevskaya reporting the success of the play, thinking that they were deceiving him. Subsequently, when the success was clearly beyond doubt, he was seized by an ecstatic, purely hysterical joy.[4]

Gorky's criticism is expressed in a letter written to Andreyev from Capri in October 1906. The play had been brought to him at Andreyev's request by the publisher I. P. Ladyzhnikov. He displayed a complete inability to appreciate Andreyev's purpose. After applauding the play as his most successful attempt to date to create a new dramatic form and claiming the language to be 'the best that you have ever achieved',[5] he proceeds to criticize the artificiality and insignificance of life as Andreyev had presented it. He attacks the nature of the relationships depicted and concludes: 'All this has been written with too much stress on the form, and I can't avoid the natural desire to emphasize the insignificance, the incompleteness, the poverty of the life of your man.'[6] At the root of

---

[1] Andreyev was awarded this prize twice in his life—the second time in 1912 for his play *Gaudeamus*.

[2] See 'S.-Peterburg, 6-ogo maya 1907 goda', *Teatr i iskusstvo*, 1907, No. 18, p. 291.

[3] See *Russkaya literatura XX veka (dorevolyutsionnyy period). Khrestomatiya*, M., 1962, p. 580.

[4] *VRSV*, p. 468.    [5] *LN*, p. 278.    [6] Ibid.

Gorky's criticism clearly lies the misconception that Man is a generalization of man, rather than of a social-psychological type.

In the symbolist camp Belyy accepted the work as unequivocally as Blok; he wrote simply: 'It is impossible either to praise or condemn "The Life of Man". It can be rejected or accepted. And I accept it.'[1] Existing canons of art, he seems to be saying, cannot be applied to the work; acceptance or rejection is totally a matter of instinctive reaction, and both Blok and Belyy found in the play a response to their innermost thoughts on the nature of life and man. The attack on Andreyev from this quarter was spearheaded by Gippius and Bryusov, who both give expression to the same misconception as Gorky, which leads them to the conclusion that Andreyev had approached a theme which was simply too big for him.[2] 'A slander on man!'—such was the judgement of Bryusov.[3]

Not one of these critics, however, gave due emphasis to perhaps the most striking feature of all in the play—its autobiographical aspect. Blok called it 'a most autobiographical play',[4] but he was referring simply to the problems which the play raises. The scheme of Man's life is to a remarkable degree a scheme of the external pattern of the life of Andreyev himself. The poverty of Man in his youth, his achievement of success almost overnight, his subsequent renown and prosperity—all these experiences were experiences of his creator. Andreyev also invested him with certain of his own idiosyncrasies—for instance, that taste of his for the huge which made so striking an impression on Chukovsky.[5] An interesting episode in this connection is recounted by Beklemisheva. She recalls a party which was given in 1908 when the Moscow Art Theatre was showing its production of the play in St. Petersburg. Andreyev was the focal point of everyone's attention. When he saw him enter Z. I. Grzhebin—an artist, one of the publishers of *Shipovnik*, and the editor of the satirical periodicals *Adskaya pochta* ('Hell's Post'), *Zhupel* ('The Bogy') and *Otechestvo* ('The Fatherland')—remarked to her: 'Does it not seem to you that you and I are at the ball of Man? Don't you hear the chorus of voices reciting: "How wealthy! How sumptuous!"—a chorus which at this moment drowns the

---

[1] A. Belyy, 'Smert' ili vozrozhdenie?', in his *Arabeski*, M., 1911, p. 497.
[2] Cf. Z. Gippius (Anton Krayniy), 'Chelovek i boloto', *Vesy*, 1907, No. 5, p. 54; and V. Bryusov (Avreliy), ' "Zhizn' Cheloveka" v Khudozhestvennom teatre', *Vesy*, 1908, No. 1, p. 144.
[3] Ibid., p. 145.    [4] Blok, 'Pamyati Leonida Andreyeva', p. 133.
[5] See *KLA*, p. 75.

malicious hissing of his enemies? You and I are friends of Man, but there are enemies, you know.'[1] Grzhebin was right; that moment marked the pinnacle of Andreyev's fame.

It is not only Andreyev's life before 1906, however, which is reflected; the work is also astoundingly prophetic. There is no distortion when Vadim Andreyev employs the last three Pictures of the play as a schematic framework for the narration of the main events of his father's life from 1907 onward.[2] This will become evident in the following chapters of this study. In this respect the play may be regarded as confirmation of the point which we have emphasized throughout—namely, of the perpetual conflict between Andreyev the man and Andreyev the philosopher, of the failure of the man ever to measure up to his abstract ideal or to find the peace of mind which, he believed, that ideal afforded. Andreyev presents a unique spectacle of duality, though not the duality which has hitherto been ascribed to him, i.e. a duality or contradiction of ideals which renders his philosophy unintelligible. While his body proceeded obediently, like that of Man, to describe the 'circle of iron predestination', his mind returned again and again to preach the virtues of self-transcendence.

At the same time the special significance of the play lies in the evidence which it affords of his progressive recovery from the spiritual state which gave birth to the 'story of Aurelius'. The work was written, however, in the looming shadow of the greatest tragedy of his life—the death of Aleksandra Mikhaylovna, to whom the play was dedicated.

[1] *Rekviem*, p. 236.     [2] See *VLA*.

# XIII

## CAPRI

IN the note, addressed to his son Vadim, which Andreyev appended to the manuscript of *The Life of Man* he relates how, while writing the play, he searched aloud with Aleksandra Mikhaylovna for the words of Man before his death: '. . . I suddenly found them and looking at her I said: "Listen now: 'Where is my armour-bearer? Where is my sword? Where is my shield? I am disarmed. A curse on you!' " And I will remember for ever her face and her eyes as she looked at me. And for some reason it was pale.'[1] On recollection it seemed to him to be the pallor of foresight, for on 18 November 1906 she died from a postnatal blood-infection. Andreyev himself was now 'disarmed'.

Neither the influence of Aleksandra Mikhaylovna on him during his formative years as a writer nor the effect on him of her death should be underestimated. 'Much is written about us,' he remarked to Brusyanin in reference to her, 'but they rarely mention those who have such a decisive influence on our life and art.'[2] He wrote of her in a letter of 1908 to L'vov-Rogachevsky: 'The deceased was my active collaborator in my work—a sensitive, dispassionate critic who often changed both the form and trend of my work.'[3] That this was no exaggeration is confirmed by Gorky's tribute to her[4] and by the following comment of Veresaev: '. . . she had a vast intuitive understanding of what her artist-husband wanted and could give, and in this respect she was the living embodiment of his artistic conscience.'[5] It became Andreyev's habit to make it his first act on completing a work to read it to her, 'admitting no one else during this holy rite'.[6] He himself testifies to her contribution to *The Life of Man*. In the note mentioned above addressed to his

---

[1] *VLA*, May, p. 78.    [2] *BSN*, p. 65.

[3] V. L'vov-Rogachevsky, *Leonid Andreyev. Kriticheskiy ocherk s prilozheniem khronologicheskoy kanvy i bibliograficheskogo ukazatelya*, M., 1923, p. 21.

[4] See *KLA*, p. 26. 'Gorky had a great love for my mother,' writes Vadim Andreyev, 'and experienced her death as though it were the death of a member of his own family' (*VLA*, May, p. 81).

[5] *VRSV*, pp. 455–6.    [6] Skitalets, op. cit., p. 385.

son he wrote: 'In Berlin at night on the Auerbachstrasse . . ., when you were asleep, I would wake your mother after finishing my work, and read it to her, and we would discuss it together. It was on her insistence and with her direct help that I altered the "Ball" so many times.'[1] This same note also reveals that when he came to write the last Picture of the play his wife was just beginning her intense suffering;[2] it perhaps helps to explain, therefore, the concentration of horror in the Picture to which Blok took such exception.

Andreyev was enraged by the treatment which his wife had received from the German doctors. 'In such cases,' writes Veresaev, who was himself a doctor, 'the doctors are always blamed, but judging by his story the attitude of the doctors was truly shocking.'[3] This animosity served to reinforce Andreyev's contempt for Germany and the Germans in general. Even before his wife's death, in a letter to Veresaev of 7 November 1906, he had expressed his acute feeling of nostalgia for Russia,[4] and on 29 December he wrote to Teleshov from Berlin: 'You know, Mitrich, the best country in the end is Russia. I have come to love Russia here. . . . The German is spoilt to the marrow by his orderliness. Just as everything is in order in their language: subject, predicate . . ., so it is in their heads and in their lives.'[5]

Instead of returning to Russia, however, he accepted Gorky's invitation to join him in Capri and made his way there at the beginning of the new year (1907). 'For my father,' writes Vadim Andreyev, 'this period . . . was one of the most oppressive of his life.'[6] He stayed in the Villa Caracciolo, which had belonged in former days to the Marquis Caracciolo who had been put to death by Nelson. The house harmonized with his mood. 'The atmosphere of the dark rooms of this villa,' writes Gorky, 'was humid and depressing. Unfinished, dirty paintings hung on the walls like mildew stains.'[7] Andreyev was haunted by the idea of suicide and for a long time alarmed his friends with his state of mind. Death was the sole subject of his thoughts, and his letters make dismal reading. Even personal relationships suffered under the strain. He wrote to Veresaev in connection with Pyatnitsky: 'He is the only man in Capri with whom it is possible to have a heart-to-heart talk.'[8] He began to feel increasingly alienated from Gorky, to whom he

---

[1] *VLA*, May, p. 77.    [2] See ibid., p. 78.    [3] *VRSV*, p. 464.
[4] See ibid., p. 463.    [5] *Rekviem*, p. 57.    [6] *VLA*, May, p. 83.
[7] *KLA*, p. 29.    [8] *VRSV*, p. 466.

wrote in reference to this period some years later (February 1912): 'While I was living alongside you, I was waiting for the arrival of Veresaev to consult with him as to whether to end my relationship with you or not.'[1]

By degrees his depression was alleviated, however, by Capri itself—the scenery and the sea—and by the kindness of the people about him, and with this partial recovery came a remarkable transformation in his attitude to his work. His mind suddenly began to pour forth new schemes with unprecedented facility and he embarked on one of the most prolific periods of his literary career. Within the space of six months he conceived the scheme of *Tsar Hunger*, wrote *Judas Iscariot*, *Darkness* and the satirical one-act play *Love for One's Neighbour* (*Lyubov' k blizhnemu*), began *The Black Masks* (*Chornye maski*), drafted the preliminary sketches of *Sashka Zhegulyov* and *The Ocean*, and wrote three chapters of *My Notes* (*Moi zapiski*). Gorky writes in connection with this period:

I never saw Andreyev, before or later, work with such unusual industry and energy. He seemed to have overcome permanently his aversion for writing; he would sit at his desk night and day, half-dressed, dishevelled and happy, and his fantasy burned with a bright and inextinguishable flame. Almost every day he would tell me of a plan for some new story, exclaiming triumphantly: 'Now I am master of myself!'[2]

Andreyev could not possibly have made this statement, however, in the early days of his restored passion for writing; the evidence lies in his works themselves which, as after the death of his sister, reveal unmistakable traces of conflict between his perennial philosophical 'light' and the 'darkness' of the passing moment in his life. But again they are few and, for the most part, are confined to a single work, *Judas Iscariot*, which was the first work to issue from this 'creative explosion'; and even here there is no collapse of his fundamental philosophical convictions. There are good reasons, however, for momentarily postponing our examination of this work and considering the offspring of another scheme which was exercising his mind at this time.

[1] *LN*, p. 324. In his reminiscences of Andreyev Veresaev disputes his competence to have acted as his confidant in this matter due to his ignorance of the state of the relationship between him and Gorky at that time and suggests that the letter contains a misprint (see *VRSV*, p. 477).
[2] *KLA*, p. 32.

Soon after the completion of *The Life of Man* he conceived the idea of making it the introduction to a whole cycle of plays related to one another in both content and form. By May 1907 the project was clear in his mind and he wrote to Nemirovich-Danchenko on the 5th of that month: ' "The Life of Man" is the first in a cycle of plays linked by their oneness of form and the indissoluble unity of their basic idea. "The Life of Man" is followed by "human life" which will be depicted in four plays: "Tsar Hunger", "War", "Revolution" and "God, the Devil and Man".'[1] *Tsar Hunger* was the only one of the four plays to materialize. It was not completed until October 1907, i.e. after Andreyev's return to Russia, and it appeared in the seventh volume of *Shipovnik*. Since it is so closely connected with *The Life of Man*, however, it is fitting to examine it before the other works of the 'Capri period'. The severance of this link by critics is largely responsible for the prevailing view that it stands somewhat apart from Andreyev's habitual field of inquiry and represents an invasion of a sphere of interest which was intrinsically alien to him.

It is true that the play is also linked with the works devoted by Andreyev to the revolution. There is a strong possibility that it issued from the same unpublished story, *From the Depths of Ages*, as *Thus It Was*. This, at any rate, is the impression conveyed by Gorky's remark in a letter to Andreyev written in the autumn of 1906: 'I'm sorry that you want to reconstruct "The Tsar" into a play. . . .'[2] But *this* link must not be exaggerated. Andreyev went to considerable pains to emphasize that it was his intention to depict neither 'revolution in general' nor, contrary to Nevedomsky's contention,[3] the revolution of 1905–6, but 'rebellion'.[4] In the play itself he says specifically: 'Do not slander the revolution. This is rebellion.'[5] Revolution was to form the subject of the third in the cycle of plays. Hence his stinging reaction to Lunacharsky's remark that the play gave a picture of 'revolution as it is reflected in the mind

---

[1] *Leonid Andreyev. P'esy*, M., 1959, p. 563. See also: *VRSV*, pp. 468–9; and Andreyev's letter to Komissarzhevskaya of 1 March 1907 in 'V. F. Komissarzhevskaya i simvolisty', *Teatr*, 1940, No. 2, p. 113.

[2] *LN*, p. 282.

[3] Cf. M. Nevedomsky, 'Ob iskusstve nashikh dney i iskusstve budushchego', *Sovremennyy mir*, 1909, No. 1, p. 178. The same erroneous view is encountered in N. Bogomolov's article 'Sovremennyy individualizm i intelligentnoe meshchanstvo', *Vera i razum*, 1908, No. 19, p. 68.

[4] Cf., for example, Andreyev's emphasis of the point in *VRSV*, p. 468.

[5] *Works* V, p. 238.

of a petty bourgeois, an artist maybe but still a hopeless petty bourgeois'.[1] Andreyev wrote to Gorky: '. . . I can take it calmly. The time is near when I shall write "Revolution" . . ., and then even Lunacharsky will understand that by immortality I mean more than he does and that I fear death less than he. And I very likely even value the proletariat more highly than he does.'[2]

Examined from the point of view of the link indicated by Andreyev himself, i.e. with *The Life of Man*, the play assumes a somewhat different aspect from that which was seen by Lunacharsky or indeed any critic to date. In the former play, as we have seen, Andreyev had sought to reduce to the starkest contours the average empirical life of the individual, and his meditations on the theme had spurred him to create the symbolic image of Someone-in-grey and the 'circle of iron predestination', with which he equates the succession of the individual's contingent aspirations and misfortunes. In *Tsar Hunger* he approaches not the individual, but society with the same objective of capturing the quintessence of its empirical life; he could well have entitled the play 'The Life of Society'. He perceives the *perpetuum mobile* of social life to lie in 'hunger', interpreted in the broad sense of the term and synonymous with the Schopenhauerian 'will', and the same predilection for objectification of the abstract and impalpable prompts him to embody this force in the figure of Tsar Hunger.

Simplified by Andreyev no less than the 'categories' of people who surround Man (Relatives, Friends, Enemies, etc.), the units which describe the new 'circle of iron predestination' are larger. Perpetually goaded by their will individuals fall into classes, basically distinguishable into the successful and the unsuccessful or, in Andreyev's terminology, the 'sated' and the 'hungry'. The classes are wholly artificial units inasmuch as there is no real loyalty to them as such, only to the self, but when the self is powerless to realize its will it seeks support in the class and the united frustration of the class gives birth to rebellion. Though inflicting untold damage, however, the rebellion of the 'hungry' is doomed from the outset due to the possession by the 'sated' of the powerful weapons of culture and science—'books' and 'cannons'. Thus the *status quo* is momentarily restored and the farce begins once more. Such is the new 'circle' portrayed in *Tsar Hunger*, in which Andreyev views society from the height of the same philosophical principles as he

[1] A. Lunacharsky, *Kriticheskie etyudy*, L., 1925, p. 232.    [2] *LN*, p. 308.

did the life of the individual, diagnosing the same *malaise* and pointing the same moral.

Much that has troubled critics now becomes clear. The contradictory nature of Tsar Hunger, who appears to side now with the 'hungry', now with the 'sated', is explained by his symbolic value—the ubiquitous will which drives the exploiters no less than the exploited. The 'philosophical' detachment of the playwright also explains the schematic form of the work; it explains why he could reduce without qualms the working-class to three quintessential types: incarnations of brute strength, exhaustion resulting from exploitation, and struggling idealism. The intelligentsia is similarly reduced to the generic image of the 'Girl-in-black', who vacillates between the two halves of society, sympathetic to the lower but tragically bound to the higher.

Serafimovich wrote in reference to Andreyev's portraits of the workers:

He sincerely sympathised with the worker, and at the same time he was far-removed from him; he had never met him and was ignorant of his way of life, his culture and the social ideas which embraced the proletariat. He lived and breathed only in the milieu of writers, artists, professors, in the milieu of the intelligentsia. This is why he depicts the workers as monsters.[1]

All these remarks, apart from the last, are true, and it was quite as inevitable that Serafimovich should make them as it was that Lunacharsky should unleash his invective and Gorky his pent-up rage.[2] Only the third Picture of the play—'The Trial of the Hungry' —appears to have met with the qualified approval of the Marxist press, and on 23 March 1908 it was even published in Baku in the Bolshevik newspaper *Gudok* ('The Hooter'), which at the time was controlled by Stalin. Serafimovich correctly perceives Andreyev's sympathy for the working-class. It is evident both in his portraits of the workers and in his caustic depiction of the 'sated'. He is also careful to distinguish between the working-class and the dregs of society, the *lumpenproletariat*. Yet even in the portrayal of the latter the occasional sign of sympathy is discernible, e.g. in the cry of one unfortunate: 'We are hungry and, like dogs, are cast into the

[1] A. S. Serafimovich, *Sbornik neopublikovannykh proizvedeniy i materialov*, M., 1958, p. 408.
[2] See *Arkhiv A. M. Gor'kogo*, vol. 4, M., 1954, p. 236.

night. We have been robbed and deprived of everything: our strength, health, minds, beauty. . . .'[1] But here also the word 'hungry' is synonymous with 'subject to the dictates of the will'. It was unreasonable to demand of Andreyev that he view society as an economist would and quite ludicrous to identify him, as Vorovsky endeavoured to do, with a specific trend in current socio-economic thought.[2] From his exclusively philosophical, 'synthetic' viewpoint society as a whole appeared to him to be tarred with the same brush. His sympathy for one class and contempt for another are relatively unimportant. Working-class, *lumpenproletariat*, bourgeoisie—all are driven by the same force, and the destination to which they are driven is death. Hence the semblance of mutual agreement which seems to exist in the play between Death and Tsar Hunger: the latter feeds the former. The three symbolic figures in the play—Time, Tsar Hunger and Death, i.e. the three forces which dominate empirical existence—are proof of the wholly philosophical, abstract nature of Andreyev's conception.

There is one category, however, which stands apart from this turmoil of conflicting wills. It is represented by the 'second worker'—the idealist who proposes that 'the earth be burnt with dreams'.[3] While Tsar Hunger is treacherously inflaming the grievances of his comrades, he suddenly cries: 'Wait! There is another tsar, not Tsar Hunger. But I do not know his name.'[4] Andreyev goes no further than this; the name of the 'other tsar' was clearly to be revealed in the ensuing plays of the cycle. Here he draws the line between his idiosyncratic conceptions of rebellion and revolution, identifying the former with a society that is prey to the will and its inseparable concomitant, death, and the latter with an idealism synonymous with transcendence of these two forces. Viewed from a different angle it is also the line which Andreyev draws in *The Life of Man*; the 'second worker' may be taken as the counterpart of Man on the 'social' scale of ascending cognition. Strictly speaking, however, this distinction between individual and social 'scales' is an artificial one. The twin spheres of individual and social life are judged by the same philosophical criterion, the viability of which, as we have seen, had been imperilled by Andreyev's experiences in his personal life. It is for this reason that *Tsar Hunger* also has an

---

[1] *Works* V, p. 210.
[2] See V. V. Vorovsky, *Literaturno-kriticheskie stat'i*, M., 1948, p. 162.
[3] *Works* V, p. 203.    [4] Ibid.

autobiographical significance. It confirms the conclusions reached in our examination of *The Life of Man*—namely, that Andreyev had far from lost faith in his former convictions, and that his works of this period, in all their diversity, should be viewed as the record of the progressive restoration of his confidence in them. Testimony that this restoration was not easily achieved, however, is forthcoming from the first of the two works which he completed between *The Life of Man* and *Tsar Hunger*—*Judas Iscariot*.

Biblical stories, like the stories of Gorky, served Andreyev as a reservoir not of 'ideas', but of characters and situations—as a framework on which he could weave his philosophical patterns; *Lazarus* has already illustrated this point. His 'resurgence' at Capri was marked by an intense interest in the figure of Judas and he confided to Gorky his intention of writing a work about him. The 'idea' of the work, however, had been conceived by him before he left for Capri and he informed Chulkov about it in a letter of October 1906.[1] Gorky offered to lend him some studies of Judas which he had in his library, but he replied: 'I do not want them. I have my own idea and what is in those books might disturb it. Just tell me what they have written. . . . No—it isn't worth while; don't tell me anything!'[2]

Initially he found it impossible to concentrate. He told his son Vadim: 'I wrote the first forty pages without knowing what I was writing, without understanding or hearing a word. The image of your mother stood persistently before me. I threw away those first forty pages and only then was I able to write.'[3] Three days later he brought to Gorky the manuscript of *Judas Iscariot*, which is dated 24 February 1907; it was subsequently published in the sixteenth miscellany of *Znanie*. Although Gorky displayed enthusiasm for the work, Andreyev himself was very dissatisfied with it. 'I would continue to work further on it,' he said to Veresaev, 'for I have nothing else to do, but my head can't stand it.'[4] The explanation of this remark lies in the story itself, which is one of his most complex works. It was the product of a conflict in his mind, and his wish to return to the work was almost certainly prompted by his desire to eradicate it. But the conflict remains, and only a detailed examination can reveal the extent of it.

In the same letter to Veresaev he refers to the work as 'some-

---

[1] See *PLA*, p. 12.    [2] *KLA*, p. 31.    [3] *VLA*, May, p. 81.
[4] *VRSV*, p. 466.

thing on the psychology, ethics and practice of betrayal'.[1] Restricting themselves to the background to the betrayal, the betrayal itself and the death of Judas, the apostles—Matthew, John, Luke and Mark—are silent about the relationship between Judas and Christ. This relationship is moved by Andreyev on to the first plane. He invests the betrayal with a totally new significance and displays an understanding of Judas which has little in common with other attempts to see more in the motive for the betrayal than simple greed, e.g. those of Renan, Giovanni Papini and De Quincey.

The contrasting portraits which Andreyev painted of Judas are informative. It has been seen that externalization invariably accompanies, and frequently replaces, in Andreyev straightforward psychological data. Physical peculiarities always merit the closest attention, for they are often the key to the understanding of his works. A little more than a year after he wrote *Judas Iscariot*, during a sojourn in the Crimea, he persuaded Belousov to sit for him. At first the portrait went well, but one morning when, to Belousov's knowledge, it was still far from complete, he was met by Andreyev with the news that in his impatience he had completed it from memory. He was shown the finished version, and he writes:

Instead of my portrait I saw a strange figure; a head with reddish hair, a face distorted by a wicked smile, one eye half-closed, while the other gazed evilly and rapaciously from the canvas; the head was drawn into the shoulders and this gave the whole figure the appearance of a bird of prey. . . . 'What does this mean?' I asked in perplexity. 'Well, it's like this: last night I had a terrible desire to portray Judas, but there was no canvas ready and I decided to paint on your portrait.'[2]

This is the physical image of Judas which appears in the story. In acute contrast with it is the image described thus by Beklemisheva: 'One of the frequent subjects of his paintings is the faces of Christ and Judas alongside one another on the same canvas (or board), and the face of Judas, distorted by agony, is like the face of Christ. There is a common halo over their heads.'[3] In his description of the same picture Chukovsky compares Christ and Judas to 'twins'.[4]

[1] Ibid.
[2] I. A. Belousov, *Literaturnaya Sreda. Vospominaniya, 1880–1928*, M., 1928, p. 153.
[3] *Rekviem*, p. 264.
[4] See K. Chukovsky, 'Leonid Andreyev', in his *Iz vospominaniy*, M., 1958, p. 245.

This 'Christ-like' visage of Judas is seen only once in the course of the entire work—in the scene after the crucifixion in which Judas hurls back at the Chief Priest the thirty pieces of silver; Andreyev writes: 'That pretence which he had borne so easily all his life suddenly became an intolerable burden, and with a single movement of his lashes he cast it off. And when he looked again at Annas, his glance was simple and direct and terrible in its naked truthfulness.'[1] This 'second image' is also suggested in Andreyev's letter of 29 December 1906 to Teleshov, written from Berlin. Comparing the German newspapers to *Novoe vremya*, to betrayers of Christ, he adds unexpectedly: 'But they are not like Judas, who has a passion which vindicates him.'[2] A diametrically opposite attitude, however, is revealed in a letter of the preceding April to Veresaev, in which he wrote: 'One might think that people are derived not from Adam, but from Judas—with such refinement and grace do they execute the business of mass, wholesale selling of Christ.'[3] The conflict between the two portraits and between these two passing statements in his correspondence prefigures the conflict between the two images of Judas which emerge from the story. This confusion has given rise to violently conflicting interpretations of the story and its protagonist.[4]

It is clear that initially Andreyev had a determined philosophical scheme in view—the 'idea' mentioned to Gorky—which was intended to continue in a new guise his indictment of the self-assertive intellect. The portrait superimposed on the unfortunate Belousov was the visual expression of Judas regarded from this angle. In the story itself Andreyev devotes an inordinate amount of space, compared with previous works, to portraiture and maintains this physical image of Judas perpetually before the reader's eyes. Two facets of the image receive special emphasis: the skull and the eyes. The skull of Judas is described as giving the impression of being divided into four parts; 'beneath such a skull,' writes the author, 'there could be no calm or harmony; beneath such a skull

---

[1] *Works* III, p. 154.     [2] *Rekviem*, p. 58.     [3] *VRSV*, p. 463.

[4] A simple illustration of the existing diversity of opinion is the identification of Judas by Lyatsky with 'sophism' and 'rationalism' (cf. E. Lyatsky, 'Mezhdu bezdnoy i taynoy. ("Eleazar", "Iuda Iskariot" Leonida Andreyeva)', *Sovremennyy mir*, 1907, Nos. 7–8, pp. 65–7) and by Nevedomsky with the 'intuitive view of life' (cf. M. Nevedomsky, 'Leonid Nikolaevich Andreyev', in *Istoriya russkoy literatury XIX v.*, edited by D. N. Ovsyaniko-Kulikovsky, vol. 5, M., 1910, p. 271).

could always be heard the noise of bloody and merciless battles.'[1] His face is cleft into two halves: 'one always animated and creasing into countless wrinkles and armed with a black, sharply peering eye, the other deathly smooth and appearing larger than the other half because of its wide-open, blind eye.'[2] Andreyev represents in the physical image of Judas himself that psychic disharmony which in *The Life of Vasiliy Fiveysky* is projected on to the priest's children. The animated half with its keen eye is symbolic of the probing intellect, while the blind eye is the counterpart of the 'idiot'—the symbol of the atrophied 'subconscious'. This latter symbol is amplified by Judas's constant complaints of illness and fatigue, and the former by his references to the antipathy which exists between himself and animals, particularly dogs, which recall the similar lament of Kerzhentsev, and by the repeated comparisons of Judas to reptiles, which again recall Kerzhentsev and the similes with the aid of which he describes the penetrating power of his intellect. The names of reptiles are used repeatedly by Andreyev in similes and metaphors referring to thought and its sinuous workings, and they may be compared in this respect with the frequent mention, in reference to the limitations of the intellect, of 'walls' and 'stones' which play an analogous associative role; thus Judas is described as 'the red-haired, hideous Jew born amid stones'.[3] The 'battles' raging within his skull signify the attempts of the intellect to subdue the subconscious; it is noticeable that whenever Judas is taken unawares or suffers from a momentary lapse of self-confidence, his whole being appears to disintegrate and to be rent by struggling, chaotic forces, e.g.: 'Judas shuddered and even gave a slight cry of fear, and everything—his eyes, arms and legs—seemed to run in different directions. . . .'[4] Judas emerges, therefore, as the principle of unalloyed rationalism in a symbolic form which is wholly consistent with the form in which Andreyev was accustomed to clothe it.

In one important respect Judas is closer to Vasiliy Fiveysky than to Kerzhentsev. Before his downfall the latter recognizes no power outside his intellect, and though he suffers from the solitude which follows from his self-assertion, he finds complete gratification in the absolute freedom which he briefly acquires for himself. Judas, on the other hand, like Vasiliy Fiveysky, has not a self-sufficient nature; he acknowledges the existence of a higher truth beyond

[1] *Works* III, p. 107.  [2] Ibid.  [3] Ibid., p. 135.  [4] Ibid., p. 121.

himself and is consumed by the desire to unite himself with it. Among the rumours through which the past of Judas is hazily conveyed at the beginning of the story there is one to the effect that for many years he had been travelling constantly, as though seeking something with his 'thievish eye', and leaving a trail of unpleasantness behind him. It becomes clear that by 'unpleasantness'Andreyev means 'shattered illusions'—the destructive work of the sceptic. Constantly goaded onward by his avid desire for the truth which will resist his scepticism, he dissects the tissues of life like an anatomist, subjecting the souls of those he encounters to merciless scrutiny. But life does not yield the truth; it yields only falsehood and evil. Hence the profound contempt of Judas for man.

In the course of his quest Judas happens upon Jesus and the disciples, and the search is ended. In Jesus alone he finds the truth with which he seeks to replenish the void created by his scepticism. The image of Jesus is haloed with silence and mystery; as one critic put it, 'only a tender echo of His wondrous words is audible somewhere afar off'.[1] There are dissonant notes in his icon-like portrayal, e.g. his laughter at Peter's jokes,[2] but otherwise this is the Jesus of *The Legend of the Grand Inquisitor* (*Legenda o velikom inkvizitore*).

To the consternation of the disciples Jesus at once accepts Judas 'with that spirit of radiant contradiction which drew Him irresistibly to the outcast and unloved . . .',[3] and a puzzling spectacle reveals itself to Thomas: 'He examined Christ and Judas attentively as they sat alongside one another, and this strange closeness of divine beauty and monstrous deformity, a man with a kindly gaze and an octopus with huge, motionless, dull, avaricious eyes oppressed his mind like an insoluble enigma.'[4] The portrait is far removed from that described by Beklemisheva and Chukovsky. The symbolism of the striving of the intellect to apprehend and merge with the 'higher truth' is continued in the struggle of Judas to prove to Jesus his superiority to the disciples and to mankind as a whole. In all appearance he seems to achieve his goal. Andreyev embodies in the disciples, contemptuously referred to as 'the others', qualities for which he felt a particular aversion: the dogmatism and narrowmindedness of John and Matthew, the positivism of Thomas,

---

[1] A. J. Wolfe, 'Leonid Andreyev's "Judas Iscariot" ', in his *Aspects of Recent Russian Literature*, Sewanee, Tennessee, 1908, p. 20.
[2] See *Works* III, p. 134.      [3] Ibid., p. 106.      [4] Ibid.

Peter's weakness of will and character despite his great physical strength, and his attitude to them remains constant throughout. Notwithstanding his 'negative' role in the work, prompted by the scheme of ideas, Judas defeats the disciples on all points, but his triumph brings him no closer to Jesus; on the contrary, the gulf is broadened.

Judas preaches the sacrilegious lesson that man is naturally evil; this is the truth that he has apprehended in the course of his travels. Thus every village approached by the disciples becomes a test of the veracity of the conflicting attitudes to man: which will the reception confirm? Repeatedly Judas is proven wrong, and it is significant that he considers each warm greeting to be an act of deception: 'Again,' he laments, 'they have deceived Judas—poor, trusting Judas from Kerioth!'[1] This motif of 'deception' accompanies Judas throughout the work, and since it is undoubtedly meant to emphasize the instability of the truth perceived by the intellect, it may be taken as evidence that Andreyev does not at any stage detach his hero from his initially established symbolic role. But the 'truth of Judas' appears suddenly to be vindicated. In quick succession the disciples encounter two receptions of the kind predicted by Judas. After the first Judas swells with pride and seeks acknowledgment from 'the others' of his triumph; instead, he meets hostility and contempt, and from this day the attitude of Jesus changes towards him. Andreyev does not explain the transformation directly; he has recourse to a metaphor: 'For everyone He was a tender and beautiful flower, a fragrant rose of Lebanon, but for Judas he left only the sharp thorns, as though Judas was without a heart, nose and eyes and understood no better than anyone else the beauty of the tender and pure petals.'[2] This was not the first time that Andreyev had employed the metaphor of flowers and their fragrance to express the almost mystical power emanating from and diffused by the spirit of altruism and self-transcendence; it recalls Ternovsky's pronouncement on life, already cited: 'Life cuts off its best blooms, but the earth is filled with their fragrance.' The senses of Judas, however, are dead. The intellect is incapable of appreciating such intangible things; it can assess only the concrete and visible; it penetrates to the incrustations on the soul of man, but never reaches the soul itself; it judges man by these superficial layers, sees only the 'first reality', and though it knows that there

[1] Ibid., p. 113.    [2] Ibid., pp. 114–15.

is something beyond, it is powerless to penetrate further. The barrier between Jesus and Judas is the same barrier as that which exists between Judas and the soul of man. Alien to the life of the soul, Judas is *ipso facto* alien to Jesus. Andreyev affords material for no other interpretation up to this point.

After the second hostile reception, during which Judas lies shamelessly to save Jesus from the wrath of the villagers who believe the band guilty of stealing a goat, Jesus displays his anger. Again no explanation is furnished and the reader is forced to have recourse to hypothesis. The meaning of the episode seems to be that Judas has interposed himself between Jesus and the sacrifice which must be made. Significant is the conversation which follows between Thomas and Judas: 'Now I believe,' says Thomas, 'that your father is the devil. It is he who taught you.' Judas replies: 'So it was the devil who taught me? Yes, yes, Thomas. And did I not save Jesus? So the devil loves Jesus; does that not mean that the devil needs Jesus and the truth?'[1] It will become clear from our subsequent analysis of his play *Anathema* that Andreyev does, in fact, see Judas as 'the son of the devil', whom he interprets as the principle of reason passionately seeking the answer to the riddle of the universe. The great difference between Judas and Anathema, however, is that that which is condemned in the latter is pronounced in the former a 'vindicating passion'—namely, the desire to maintain truth, personified in *Judas Iscariot* by Jesus, on earth, to establish on earth the realm of eternal truth. Andreyev attempted an impossible task in seeking to combine this 'passion' with the role which Judas plays in the philosophical scheme up to this point in the story—the role of the intellect incarnate—for it is intelligible only as an expression of extreme altruism—a quality which is stridently incompatible with the egoism and *amour propre* of Judas, which are revealed in his efforts to establish his superiority in the eyes of Jesus, in his unabating vainglory, and in the repeatedly emphasized egocentric nature of his quest for truth epitomized in the cry '. . . the devil needs Jesus and the truth.'

The two attitudes to Judas are interwoven in the most bizarre way throughout the remainder of the story and both are discernible in the motive for the betrayal. The 'idea' comes to Judas during the rest period at the house of Lazarus at Bethany on the eve of the entry into Jerusalem, i.e. at a time when his triumphs over the

[1] Ibid., p. 116.

disciples, culminating in the vanquishment of Peter in a stone-throwing contest, have succeeded only in alienating him further from Jesus. He listens to Jesus addressing the disciples, and we read:

And peering at the swaying spectre, listening intently to the gentle melody of the distant and ghostly words, Judas gathered into his iron fingers the whole of his soul, and in its unfathomable darkness, silently, he began to build something huge. In the profound darkness he slowly constructed mighty edifices like mountains and smoothly piled them one on top of the other; . . . and something grew in the darkness, expanded noiselessly, thrust apart the boundaries. His head felt like a dome and in its impenetrable darkness the huge structure continued to grow, and someone was silently working.[1]

The description itself reads like an indictment, and in the pages immediately following the 'negative' attitude to Judas is sustained: the rational, egocentric motive for the betrayal is perceptible in his statement to Thomas a page later: 'But now He will perish, and Judas will perish together with Him;'[2] five pages later he is captured in silent meditation and the author writes: 'Falsehood itself spoken by a human tongue seemed like truth and light by comparison with this impenetrable and unresponsive silence;'[3] and on the following page his self-assertion culminates in his open announcement of his intention of occupying the first place at the side of Jesus. He remains the principle alien to Jesus and man, which Jesus, on Judas's own admission, compares to a 'dry fig-tree which should be cut down with an axe'.[4] Viewed from this standpoint, the betrayal is the last despairing means by which Judas seeks to realize his intention of occupying the first position, and this is the first motive of which Andreyev, in the vague, non-specific way which characterizes the entire work, provides any intimation. Judas knows from the beginning that the result of the betrayal will be the death of Jesus; he sees it as the supreme means of proving to Jesus the veracity of his conception of man as naturally evil. In life he has failed to win the favour of Jesus, but perhaps in death he will succeed in doing so. He plans to follow the crucifixion with his own suicide, as an expression both of his contempt for man and of the intensity of his desire to sit beside Jesus; he hopes to 'win' Jesus by the very power of his aspiration and by vindicating his misanthropy.

[1] Ibid., p. 121.  [2] Ibid., p. 122.  [3] Ibid., p. 127.  [4] Ibid., p. 122.

Here the Biblical account, according to which Judas commits suicide before the death of Jesus,[1] is wholly adjusted to the author's scheme.

At the same time the text affords material for a radically different interpretation of the betrayal which accords with what we have termed the 'second image' of Judas. Considered as an expression of altruism and noble sentiment, it appears rather as a challenge to man—to the moral integrity of man—than as the instrument of Judas's self-assertion. Seen from this angle Judas appears as a profound sufferer sacrificing his soul for the sake of man. This interpretation was placed on the betrayal by Botsyanovsky, who wrote:

Judas, who loves Christ more than the other apostles, betrays Him and subjects himself to a degree of spiritual suffering which is experienced by none of the disciples close to Christ and does so only in order to incite the disciples with his betrayal to a moral feat.[2]

The plausibility of this interpretation is enhanced by the sporadic references in the story to the silent entreaty of Judas that man will rise to the defence of the eternal truth which he, Judas, has placed in the shadow of death. This motif reaches its climax in the thoughts which pass through his mind as he witnesses the last moments of Jesus on the cross. As Botsyanovsky has indicated, it is repeated in Judas's constant incitement of the disciples to take up arms and protect Jesus, and the tone in which the pitiful performance of the disciples at Gethsemane is described leaves no doubt that the sympathy of Andreyev is with Judas. Yet this sympathy is totally at variance with the clearly perceptible basic idea of the work, according to which the self-sacrifice of Jesus is endowed with a significance not far removed from the Christian theological conception; it is employed by Andreyev as a further illustration of the truth contained in Ternovsky's 'flower metaphor'. *Judas Iscariot* is the first of a series of works of this period in which self-sacrifice is portrayed as a source of inextinguishable light radiating outwards and piercing the darkness which shrouds the minds of men.

Equally irreconcilable with the sympathy displayed for Judas and with the 'altruistic' motive for the betrayal is the burst of pride

---

[1] See *Matthew*, XXVII, 1–5.
[2] V. F. Botsyanovsky, 'Leonid Andreyev i mirovaya garmoniya', *Biblioteka teatra i iskusstva*, 1910, No. 10, p. 67.

which overcomes Judas after the death of Jesus. 'Limitlessly and joyously alone,' writes the author, 'he proudly felt the powerlessness of all the forces active in the world, and hurled them all into the abyss.'[1] All his life Judas has lived in terror of deception. As his scheme hastens to its fulfilment he is constantly plagued by doubt. He cries: 'Thomas! But what if He is right? What if He has stones under His feet and I have only sand? . . . Then I myself must strangle Him in order to establish the truth. Who is deceiving Judas—you or Judas himself?'[2] Here the 'egocentric motive'receives its most unequivocal expression and is directly comparable to the passion which drives on Kerzhentsev. His burst of pride after the death of Jesus confirms that any hope that he may have had for a moral transformation in man at the sight of Christ's suffering was very much secondary in his mind to the aspiration to elevate himself to the side of Jesus on the wings of his proven 'truth'. In the closing pages of the work the 'second image' of Judas is completely forgotten. The final scene shows him swaying from a tree on a mountain high above Jerusalem—the principle of reason, alien alike to man below and Christ above.

Thus *Judas Iscariot* appears to confirm Gippius's view of Andreyev as a writer who is 'unable to cope with the problems which he himself raises in his works'.[3] It has been our objective hitherto to disprove this view, to show that the problems which he raises are closely interrelated and centralized in an established *Weltanschauung*. It cannot be disputed, however, that in *Judas Iscariot* there are two distinct schemes which are not successfully dovetailed. In this respect it is a unique work in his fiction, and since it was written at a 'unique' time in his life—barely three months after the death of Anna Mikhaylovna—the explanation is most plausibly to be found in the disturbed condition of his mind when he wrote it, the clearest proof of which is its state of incompletion which he acknowledged to Veresaev. Perhaps this is what Blok meant when he wrote in connection with the work: 'Behind it is the soul of the author—a living wound.'[4] No hint of this 'wound', however, is forthcoming from his next story, *Darkness*—the second of the two works completed between *The Life of Man* and *Tsar Hunger*.

---

[1] Ibid., p. 153.  [2] Ibid., p. 138.
[3] Z. Gippius, 'Chelovek i boloto', *Vesy*, 1907, No. 5, p. 54.
[4] A. Blok, 'O realistakh', *Sobranie sochineniy v vos'mi tomakh*, vol. 5, M.–L., 1962, p. 107.

Completed on 20 September 1907, *Darkness* was published in November in the third volume of *Shipovnik*. While Andreyev was in Capri he made the acquaintance of a Socialist Revolutionary terrorist in hiding there named Pyotr Moyseyevich Rutenberg, whose party name was Vasiliy Petrov. It was he who organized the assassination of Gapon when it was discovered that the latter was an *agent provocateur*. Among the many stories which Gorky related to Andreyev was one involving Rutenberg and a prostitute; he recalled it some years later:

The episode was very simple. The girl in the brothel, sensing in her guest a revolutionary hunted by sleuths and forced to come to her, conducted herself towards him with the tender solicitude of a mother and the tact of a woman who was fully capable of feeling respect for a hero. But the hero, a tactless, bookish man, answered the impulses of the woman's heart with a sermon on morality, reminding her of that which she wished to forget at that time. Insulted she struck him on the cheek— a thoroughly deserved slap in my opinion. Then, understanding the whole coarseness of his error, he apologised to her and kissed her hand. . . . That is all.[1]

Gorky was never able to forgive Andreyev his adjustment of this episode to the point which he wished to make in *Darkness*.

The story is the second of the five works of the immediate post-revolutionary period—the others, besides *Judas Iscariot*, being *The Black Masks*, *Anathema* and *Sashka Zhegulyov*[2]—in which Andreyev presents variations of the thought expressed in Ternovsky's 'flower metaphor'. His point of departure is the conviction that in order to be an effective force for good idealism and virtue must be brought into direct collision with the deformity and evil of life. In *Judas Iscariot* the disciples are the butt of his irony precisely because they seek to keep their virtue pure and intact by avoiding all contact with the reality of life and man. Their every confrontation with this reality culminates in their flight—a motif which reaches its climactic point at Gethsemane: '. . . John fled, and Thomas and James fled, and all the disciples who were there left Jesus and fled.'[3] Refusal to flee might result, as it does in the case of Jesus and Nikolay, in the destruction of the individual form, but its feat and

---

[1] *KLA*, p. 34.
[2] This work, which is very close to *Darkness* in its basic idea, will not be subjected to detailed analysis in this study.
[3] *Works* III, p. 144.

example will live and exert influence for ever. In such an act Andreyev saw the highest expression of self-transcendence.

There are grounds for the hypothesis that it was not only Gorky's story about Rutenberg which led Andreyev to develop further his thoughts on this question through the character of a contemporary revolutionary. The questions of 'spiritual life' and 'moral integrity' were very much subjects of debate in certain circles of the Russian intelligentsia during the period from 1907 to 1909. The process of self-examination to which the intelligentsia subjected itself after the collapse of the revolution resulted in the defection from the ranks of the extremists of many who had been compelled by their integrity to revise their convictions. 'As the revolution ran its course,' writes one historian, 'this trend took on the character of a definite movement.'[1] There was a widespread feeling that in its social-political activity the intelligentsia had lost sight of basic ethical and philosophical principles. The most explicit formulation of this view appeared in 1909 in the collection of essays entitled *Vekhi*, and the premise which gave birth to the cycle of works written or begun by Andreyev at Capri can be directly related to the central point of the volume, expressed as follows by Mikhail Gershenzon in his introductory remarks:

The persons who have gathered here for a common cause differ, to some extent, both in the basic questions of 'belief' and in their practical aspirations; but in this common cause there is no disagreement among them. Their common platform is a recognition of the theoretical and practical primacy of spiritual life over the external forms of society, in the sense that the inner life of the personality is the only creative force in human life and that it, and not the self-sufficient principles of the political order, is the only solid foundation of any social structure. From this point of view, the ideology of the Russian intelligentsia, which rests on quite the opposite principle—on recognition of the absolute primacy of social forms,—is presented by the collaborators of the book as inherently false, i.e. as contradicting the nature of the Russian soul, and, in a practical sense, as futile, i.e. as incapable of leading to that end which the intelligentsia proposed for itself—the emancipation of the people.[2]

Manifest throughout the essays is the striving to destroy the illusion

---

[1] S. R. Tompkins, *The Russian Intelligentsia. Makers of the Revolutionary State*, University of Oklahoma Press, 1957, p. 213.
[2] *Vekhi. Sbornik statey o russkoy intelligentsii*, M., 1909, p. ii.

that a materialistic philosophy is inherently progressive, while idealism is by its nature reactionary. When *Vekhi* appeared Andreyev's reaction was negative.[1] He was incapable of lending his support to any body of opinion which condoned autocracy. The fact remains, however, that the thought expressed in *Darkness* anticipated the *leitmotif* of the volume. The trouble was that it was couched in a form which succeeded in antagonizing practically the whole world of criticism; in this respect it was a crucial work in his career. Taking the situation of the work from Gorky's story about Rutenberg—itself reminiscent of Kuprin's *Second Captain Rybnikov* (*Shtabs-kapitan Rybnikov*), which had appeared in *Mir bozhiy* in January 1906[2]—he fills it with the new content prompted by his 'idea'. The confusion which it created resulted primarily from his failure to expand beyond the given situation. Intending to portray a climactic spiritual experience, he presents the reader with the climax alone, isolated from the preparatory stages which would have made it plausible.

Andreyev's terrorist, who in his devotion to the revolutionary cause evokes the image of the ideal revolutionary painted by Bakunin and Nechaev, is forced, in order to escape the clutches of the police, to seek refuge in a brothel. The reader at once senses the author's hostility to his hero, illustrative of which is the irony with which he notes the terrorist's reaction to the prostitute Lyuba: 'And gazing at her standing there, he understood that she should be pitied; and as soon as he came to understand this, he immediately began to pity her.'[3] The tone is the same as that in which he refers to the disciples and expresses the same indictment. The 'sin' of the terrorist is not that he has dedicated his life to a cause which he considers higher than life, but that he has placed this cause between life and himself; he has isolated himself in a moral zone above life, and the defence of his self-conceived moral perfection becomes the

[1] See *LN*, p. 333.

[2] The only resemblance to *Second Captain Rybnikov* lies in the basic situation, and since this was undoubtedly taken by Andreyev from Gorky's story it is impossible to accept Dobrokhotov's contention that he was influenced by Kuprin's story (see A. Dobrokhotov, *Kar'era Leonida Andreyeva*. (*Etyud o populyarnosti, arlekinakh i tolpe*), M., 1909, p. 15). For the same reason it is impossible to agree with Clarence Manning, who alleges that Andreyev borrowed from Dostoevsky's *Notes from the Underground* (*Zapiski iz podpol'ya*) (see C. A. Manning, ' "T'ma" Andreyeva i "Zapiski iz podpol'ya" Dostoevskogo', *Slavia*, Prague, 1926–7, vol. 5, pp. 850–2).

[3] *Works* II, p. 150.

principal aim of his endeavour. His idealism, allegedly directed towards the elimination of social ills for the benefit of others, has evolved into an acute form of egoism.

His detachment from life is disclosed in its most innocuous manifestations—in his ignorance of women, his inability to smoke properly, his feminine way of holding a cigarette, his teetotalism. The ideal for which he risks his life has become an abstract devoid of living content. While he bases his claim to purity and nobility on his constant readiness to endanger his life 'for people', he nevertheless cries to Lyuba: 'So you think that I have kept myself for the likes of you? You rubbish, you need a beating!'[1] Such is his attitude to a woman behind whose words, writes Andreyev, 'were felt millions of crushed lives and seas of bitter tears and the fiery, constant revolt of enraged justice'.[2] But in the course of this night both the protagonists undergo a momentous awakening. The terrorist is roused to the reality of his 'virtue' when Lyuba asks him simply what right he has to be good when she is evil.

When he first enters the brothel and leads Lyuba away to her 'little nest', the terrorist catches a glimpse of their reflection in a mirror. Both are dressed in black and it occurs to him that they must present an ironic resemblance to a bride and groom. But then another parallel suggests itself to him: 'it's as though we were at a funeral.'[3] Thus at the outset Andreyev poses the question of whether the issue of this confrontation of social-political idealism with social injustice in its acutest form will be a marriage or a funeral, a source of light or a source of darkness. The answer is not given until some time later when Lyuba, endeavouring to persuade the terrorist to stay with her, says to him: '. . . if you love people and pity our joyless company, then take me. And I, my dearest, will take you!'[4] The proposal is made and his decision to stay denotes his acceptance.

But first he must give proof that he has completely severed himself in spirit from the false life which he has led hitherto. It is not enough for Lyuba that he should simply take her hand and remain with her; she demands of him the total sacrifice of his past and subjects him to the severest test of his sincerity. Surrounded by drunken, debauched women, he sits quietly on the bed with her and it seems to him that his whole life—conversations with his comrades, books, dangerous and fascinating work—has been

[1] Ibid., p. 160.   [2] Ibid.   [3] Ibid., p. 141.   [4] Ibid., p. 164.

irrevocably destroyed. And yet, we read, '. . . he himself was not destroyed by this, but somehow became strangely stronger and harder,'[1] and his spirit gleams with a 'white flame', the symbol here, as subsequently in *The Story of Seven Who Were Hanged*, *The Black Masks* and *Anathema*, of purification, of the pure subconscious stripped of its transient vestures—pride, complacency and egoism. In this transformation of the terrorist Andreyev once more contrasts the 'two realities', the superficial and the essential. He presents the reader with a gigantic paradox: the deformed life of the brothel serves to correct the deformity of the terrorist's personality, awakens him to his true self and, by virtue of having attained to this higher level of cognition, he becomes, in his creator's eyes, genuinely capable of affecting the lives of those about him, of conquering the evil in which they languish. Andreyev portrays not, as Gorky thought, a victory of 'the cattle and darkness over the human',[2] but precisely the opposite—a victory of the spirit over the 'darkness' which threatens to engulf it; such a victory he saw as an incomparably more effective ameliorative force in life than 'self-sufficient principles of the political order'. The expression of this conviction in the story is the 'resurrection' of Lyuba.

Andreyev appears to have had the story and feat of Jesus in mind throughout; even the external events of the work—the hunt, the betrayal, albeit unintentional, the arrest and the hero's calm submission to it—reinforce this impression. The feat of the terrorist is conceived as an act directly comparable to that of Christ, the evil of the brothel—as the cross which he takes on his back. It is true that he cries: 'This is not Christ; this is something else, this is more terrible,'[3] but this cry is rent from him by the sharp contrast between this unknown experience and his past, between the pain which attends genuine self-sacrifice and the moral complacency with which he embarked on his acts of terrorism. Before he is jolted by Lyuba's question, he boasts to her of his virtue, and she remarks with feigned surprise that he does not wear a cross round his neck. With a smile he replies: 'We carry our cross on our backs.'[4] At this stage of the work these words are a blasphemy in Andreyev's eyes; it is only much later that the terrorist can justifiably make this claim—when Lyuba has left him to take his revolver to the concierge, thereby unwittingly betraying him, and he sits alone feeling 'the whole weight of the burden which he has loaded

[1] Ibid., p. 171.    [2] *LN*, p. 318.    [3] *Works* II, p. 166.    [4] Ibid., p. 154.

on his shoulders'. Lyuba now boasts on his behalf: 'Your honour was taken from you,' she cries to the other women, 'but he has surrendered his himself. He went and surrendered: for my honour.'[1] She is resurrected by the immensity of his sacrifice, by the 'fragrance' of his moral feat, and at the end she is described as a girl 'in whose soul had been sown the seeds of moral achievement and self-renunciation'.[2]

This interpretation differs radically from that of the vast majority of critics, who put forward a view similar to that of Gorky. The great weakness of the story lies, as stated, in the excessively concentrated depiction of the hero's transition from the first to the second of his two positions, which drew from Kranikhfel'd and numerous other reviewers the criticism that there was no logical connection between them.[3] Indeed, the detail into which Andreyev goes when describing external scenes, e.g. the orgy and the arrest, seems at times to be almost deliberately designed to deflect the reader's attention from the inner world of his characters. His statement to Gorky in a letter of 11 February 1908 that the work had turned out 'unsuccessful' and 'confused'[4] may perhaps be taken as an acknowledgment of this defect. Criticisms such as that of Nevedomsky, however, who deplored the absence from the work of that 'light of idealism' which he cherished in *The Life of Man*,[5] are devoid of justification. Andreyev made it very plain that the work heralded no change of conviction on his part; he wrote to Gorky on 23 March 1908: 'I have not changed, so don't you change your attitude to me. In "Darkness" (apart from its weakness of form) and in "Tsar Hunger" I am still the same as I was in "Savva" and "Judas". And with *Shipovnik* I am the same as when I was with *Znanie*.'[6] His criticism of *Darkness*, like his criticism of *To the Stars*, concerned only the form in which he had expressed his thought; the thought itself, he believed, was beyond criticism. The importance which he attached to the story is conveyed by his reply to Kleynbort when the latter asked him in 1914 to which of his works he would give precedence; having recently re-read them

[1] Ibid., p. 172.    [2] Ibid., p. 181.
[3] Cf. V. Kranikhfel'd ,'Literaturnye otkliki. "T'ma"—rasskaz L. Andreyeva', *Sovremennyy mir*, 1908, No. 1, p. 98.
[4] *LN*, p. 302.
[5] Cf. M. Nevedomsky, 'O "nav'ikh" charakh i "nav'ikh" trupakh', *Sovremennyy mir*, 1908, No. 2, p. 229.
[6] *LN*, p. 307.

prior to their publication by A. F. Marks,[1] he replied: 'For me, if you are talking about satisfaction with one's offspring, in first place there has always been and will be "Darkness".'[2]

Gorky was capable of seeing the work only in the light of the reality which had provided the situation and characters—the story about Rutenberg. He wrote: 'This distortion of the truth made a very painful impression on me. I felt that Andreyev had perverted and destroyed a beautiful incident which I had hoped might be the theme of an inspiring tale. I know men too well not to value greatly the most insignificant manifestation of kind and honourable sentiment.'[3] Andreyev argued that it was his right as an artist to treat the facts as he chose. They discussed the subject calmly; 'but from that time on,' writes Gorky, 'something snapped between Andreyev and myself.'[4]

[1] He received from Marks for the right to publish the sum of 100,000 roubles.
[2] Kleynbort, loc. cit., p. 172.    [3] *KLA*, p. 34.    [4] Ibid.

# XIV

# ST. PETERSBURG AND FINLAND: THE 'TWO REALITIES'

ANDREYEV returned to Russia in the spring of 1907. He expected to be arrested at the frontier (at Verzhbolovo) for his part in the Sveaborg uprising, but encountered no difficulty. He travelled first to Moscow and then to St. Petersburg, where he took an apartment on the Kamennoostrovsky Prospect. He lived there for about a year before he finally settled in Finland. That he was still labouring under the weight of his sorrow is confirmed by Vadim Andreyev, who writes: 'A new period of life began for my father, a bustling period of social life in which he hurled himself from one side to another in attempts to break his grief.'[1] Most of his close friends were in Moscow and it was largely a period of making new acquaintances.

In his new apartment he began to organize 'Wednesdays' on the pattern of the gatherings in Moscow, but failed to recreate the atmosphere of the latter. Belousov visited one of them and was struck by the difference. Volynsky, Sergeyev-Tsensky, Yushkevich, Chirikov, Blok, Bogoraz,[2] Sergey Uspensky and the actor from the Aleksandrinsky Theatre Nikolay Khodotov were among the gathering. Andreyev was suffering from toothache and at his request Blok read *Darkness* which was then discussed. Belousov's comment recalls Blok's picture of Andreyev during this period:[3] 'Leonid Nikolaevich seemed to feel uneasy; he sat behind everybody and was silent, as though he was not in his own house.'[4] At the end of the evening Andreyev remarked to him: 'You see, it's not the same here as in Moscow; they praise a work aloud, and then go round the corner to tear it to pieces. It's not like Moscow. . . .'[5]

[1] *VLA*, May, p. 84. For a further portrait of Andreyev at this time cf. N. N. Khodotov, *Blizkoe—dalyokoe*, M.–L., 1932, p. 313.

[2] The critic Vasiliy Bogoraz was better known by his pseudonym 'Tan'.

[3] Cf. *supra*, p. 118.

[4] I. A. Belousov, *Literaturnaya Sreda. Vospominaniya, 1880–1928*, M., 1928, p. 139.

[5] Ibid.

In the course of the year his hatred of life in St. Petersburg became intense. He wrote some years later in his diary: 'After the noisy and senseless year of life in Petersburg my longing for the country was aggravated to such an extent that I was prepared to overcome all obstacles in order to escape from the capital where people positively prevented me from working.'[1] In his comments on his desire to escape we see a reflection of that special significance attached by him to the difference and antipathy between city and country which had already found expression in his fiction, particularly in *The Thief*. On the question of the place which 'nature' occupied in his thought he was to write in his diary towards the end of his life: 'I cannot write about nature. . . . The scarcity of landscape in my works and its secondary role invite the incorrect conclusion that in my world-philosophy 'nature' occupies the customary, semi-ancillary place as it does for all generally normal people.'[2] He made its precise significance for him clear in a conversation with Brusyanin during his life in Finland:

In order to write more freely about the 'extratemporal' and the 'extra-spatial', I myself must be outside time and space, and for this the solitude of the country is necessary. Here I have created for myself an atmosphere free from the influence of environment and have given my thought to space. . . . The city, as a manifestation of conscious life, would provide a bad foundation for my intellectualising; it would increase my tendentiousness. The country is nature, the bearer of the unconscious, the repository of the intuitive, whence I gather the strength which I need. Both the country and nearness to the country are necessary to me in order to counteract my intellectualising, my tendentiousness.[3]

Yet not for nothing did Chulkov refer to him as 'very much a man of the city'.[4] The city held a fatal attraction for him and urban motifs recur in his works as they do in Russian symbolist poetry— e.g. in Bryusov's *Urbi et Orbi* and Blok's cycle of poems *The City* (*Gorod*)[5]—where their appearance owed much to Baudelaire and Verhaeren. He continued to entertain the belief that the city meant people, company and freedom from solitude despite his early story

[1] *BSN*, p. 19.

[2] 'Stranitsy iz dnevnika L. N. Andreyeva', *Zhar-ptitsa*, Berlin, 1921, No. 3, p. 39.

[3] *BSN*, pp. 12, 18–19.    [4] *PLA*, p. 40.

[5] *The City* is the title which Blok gave in 1916, when his poems were about to be republished by *Musaget*, to the fourth section of the amended collection of 1906 *Accidental Joy* (*Nechayannaya radost'*).

*The City (Gorod)* (1902) in which he had shown that the very opposite was the case. The year in St. Petersburg, however, shattered this illusion once and for all.

The most complete record of his state of mind at this time is his story *The Curse of the Beast (Proklyatie zverya)*, which appeared in the autumn of 1907 in the first of the *Zemlya* ('The Earth') almanacs. It was written during the period of meditation on the approaching moment 'when once and for all,' as he put it in his letter to Gorky of 11 February 1908, 'I will leave this detestable city with its wretched bustle and once and for all come face to face with nature, with the sea, the sky, the snow, face to face with pure human thought.'[1] The contrast between city-life and life in the bosom of nature is developed in the story through the eyes of a schizophrenic, but his schizophrenia is not limited to this single empirical dichotomy. The work is not confined to the terms of reference of *The City*. The two poles of the contrast play an ulterior, symbolic role in two senses—psychological and metaphysical. Firstly, the images of nature and the city are developed respectively as symbols of solitude and corporate life. And secondly, while nature is identified with frigidity, eternity and mystery, the city, epitomized in the recurring epithet 'chocolate and cocoa', is the symbol of the calculable and predictable. These three interrelated contrasts are the constant foundation of the work.

The identification of nature in the initial part of the work with solitude and frigidity testifies that at the time of writing Andreyev had still not completely succeeded in exorcising the spirit of Lazarus from his mind. But in the course of the story the crisis in his beliefs is finally surmounted. *The Curse of the Beast* is an oblique commentary on his conflict with and final triumph over the dark thoughts which had plagued him since the autumn of 1905, and in this respect it is a key work in the transition from *Lazarus* and *The Life of Man* to the beatific vision of *The Story of Seven Who Were Hanged*. It may be viewed as an expression of the author's momentary vacillation and 'taking stock' before he found in himself the strength and faith to proceed.

His hero is the embodiment of his vacillation. Beginning with an outburst of love for the sea and forests, he then confides the fascination which the city holds for him. But joy at the intelligibility of city-life vies in his tormented mind with fear and hatred of its

[1] *LN*, pp. 302–3.

prison-like substance and of the people who live there with their 'small, compressed, cubic souls'.[1] Oppressed by his solitude, he yet comes to the discovery that surrender of it is tantamount to the surrender of his autonomy which is menaced by complete subservience to the corporate will. His complete disillusionment with the city in all its three connotations is expressed in the curse of the caged seal in the city zoo. While the zoo is patently a caricature of city-life, the curse is directly related to that hurled by Man at Someone-in-grey; it signifies the rejection of the slavish, mechanical existence which man has fashioned for himself, of the superimposed corporate life in which physical and spiritual solitude are paradoxically at their most acute, of the 'principle of individuation'. It has a symbolic and philosophical significance totally absent from Gorky's execration of Europe to which Zinaida Gippius compared it.[2]

Like *Darkness*, the story concludes with the theme of triumphant, resurrecting love. In the most lyrical episode of the work the hero and his beloved, manifestly the reincarnated spirit of Aleksandra Mikhaylovna to whom the work is dedicated, declare their love for one another and he exclaims:

And having said these holy words and heard this holy reply—I love you—I suddenly felt the majesty, the secret and menacing power of our human love. And I felt that even when no longer struggling, even when retreating and falling and weeping I had already conquered the unknown foe with that which I said loudly on this moonlit night: 'I love you.'[3]

The agonies of this lover were Andreyev's Inferno and Purgatory. Well chosen was his simile when, writing to Gorky from St. Petersburg early in 1908, he said that he felt as though he had spent a year 'travelling like Dante through hell'; but, he adds, 'my life is beginning to climb upward. . . .'[4] Now indeed he felt, to quote the last line of the second Cantica of *The Divine Comedy*, 'pure and disposed to climb to the stars', to climb the seven heavens of Paradise. Like Dante to his Beatrice, he cries at the end of *The Curse of the Beast*: 'I am coming to you, my beloved! Meet me tenderly. I am so tired! I am so tired!'[5] Such was the meaning for Andreyev of his retreat to Finland.

---

[1] *Works* VIII, p. 114.

[2] See Z. Gippius (Anton Krayniy), 'Repa', *Vesy*, 1908, No. 2, p. 73.

[3] *Works* VIII, p. 137.    [4] *LN*, p. 302.    [5] *Works* VIII, p. 144.

He had his 'enchanted castle', as Skitalets described it,[1] built in a completely desolate spot inside the Finnish border near the villages of Vammelsuu (Black River) and Rayvola (now Roshchino), which were situated about forty miles from St. Petersburg. He bought a small plot there towards the end of 1907 and increased it by buying up the land of neighbouring peasants. The house was designed, in co-operation with Andreyev himself, by the architect Andrey Andreyevich Ol' who shortly afterwards married Andreyev's sister Rimma. Andreyev called it the 'Villa Avance' since it was built on money advanced by the publishing-house *Niva* at a time when he was already two thousand roubles in debt to *Znanie*, and he was subsequently to refer to it as his 'ballerina'.[2] Vadim Andreyev describes it as

. . . ponderous, magnificent and beautiful. A tall square tower rose fifty feet above the ground. The vast slate roof with its many pitches, the gigantic square white chimneys—each the size of a watch-tower—the geometrical pattern of the beams, and the stout shingles—everything without exception was truly magnificent.[3]

It was his study which made the deepest impression on visitors; he remarked on it to Belousov: 'This has been my dream. Just think now! Having left a large Petersburg apartment, how could I shut myself up here in small rooms? When I am working I like to have interludes, to pace and think; here I have room to do so and no one disturbs me.'[4] Yet Bernstein's reference to the house as the 'House of Man'[5] seems to have been an accurate parallel. Brusyanin, for instance, notes the lofty ceiling and dark-grey walls of the study,[6] and Vadim Andreyev recalls that despite the light which flooded in from all sides through the numerous windows, it was still dark: '. . . even during the blossoming of our Finnish life, the spectre of the fourth Act of *The Life of Man* was already lurking in the corners.'[7] All agreed that the house was in a very marked way symbolic of its master.

By the spring of 1908 Andreyev was more or less permanently resident there. He finally left his apartment in St. Petersburg in

---

[1] See Skitalets, op. cit., p. 402.
[2] See F. N. Fal'kovsky, 'Predsmertnaya tragediya Leonida Andreyeva. (Iz vospominaniy)', *Prozhektor*, 1923, No. 16, p. 27.
[3] *VLA*, June, p. 94.    [4] Belousov, op. cit., pp. 144–5.
[5] See H. Bernstein, *With Master Minds. Interviews*, New York, 1913, p. 161.
[6] See *BSN*, p. 20.    [7] *VLA*, June, pp. 95–6.

May or June and when he visited the capital, mostly in connection
with his work for *Shipovnik*, he usually stayed with the Ol's. He
lacked only one thing to make his happiness complete—a wife. 'I
need a wife,' he wrote to Gorky on 11 February, 'not only a body
but a soul, that special type of woman's soul which cannot be
replaced by thousands of male souls. . . .'[1] He found such a 'soul'
in his secretary Anna Il'inichna Denisevich, whom he married
shortly after Easter 1908 at Yalta. She also had been married before
—to a St. Petersburg barrister named Karnitsky whom she had
divorced—and had a daughter by that marriage. Memoirists make
surprisingly few references to her, and the impression is given that
it was not quite the idyllic partnership of Andreyev's first marriage.
His cousin Zoya Nikolaevna Pockowska wrote to Fatov: 'His second
wife is very beautiful, but she was little suited to him. She also
loved him very much, but it was a more earthly love, whereas with
his first wife Leonid had very strong spiritual ties.'[2] Nevertheless,
Anna Il'inichna seems to have been a woman of singularly strong
character and this strength was of inestimable value to him during
his arduous last years.

Comparing this period of transition with the foregoing period
—the period of the 'story of Aurelius', *The Life of Man* and *Judas
Iscariot*—Andreyev wrote to Gorky in his letter of 11 February:
'. . . while I formerly thought that only death exists, now I am
beginning to suspect that there is only life.'[3] This spiritual transformation was marked by the appearance on 6 May 1908 in the
fifth *Shipovnik* almanac, of *The Story of Seven Who Were Hanged*,
which develops and brings to a radiant fulfilment the hope which
glimmers barely visibly in *The Life of Man*.

It is questionable, however, whether he realized, when he took
up his pen to write the story, where it would lead him. He confessed to Gorky in a letter of 23 March that he did not know what
would come of it all.[4] It is clear, for instance, that the philosophical
scheme was at first overshadowed in his thoughts by a more
immediate and topical objective. His original inspiration came
directly from the events of the times. *The Story of Seven Who Were
Hanged* was born initially of the bloodbath of governmental vengeance which followed the suppression of the revolution and more
particularly, as Persky has noted, the mass executions which took

---

[1] *LN*, p. 304.    [2] *FTV*, p. 215.    [3] *LN*, p. 304.    [4] Cf. ibid., p. 307.

place in 1908 at Kherson and Warsaw.[1] The work was initially dictated by the same desire to denounce the death penalty as animated Tolstoy when he wrote *I Cannot Be Silent!* (*Ne mogu molchat'!*), which was begun on 13 May 1908, i.e. after the appearance of Andreyev's story, though before Tolstoy had had a chance to read it. It is no coincidence that it carried a dedication to Tolstoy when it was published by *Shipovnik* in 1909 in the sixth volume of Andreyev's collected works.[2] 'I wrote the work with profound pain,' he stated to Tolstoy in the letter of 18 August 1908 in which he requested permission for the dedication, 'and it is not the story, which is bad, but my pain which I bring to you—a man who has stood over me all my life, from my earliest years, as the embodiment of conscience and truth.'[3] The income from the edition of the work, which was published in Moscow in 1909 with a portrait by Repin of the execution scene, was presented by Andreyev to prisoners of the notorious Schlüsselburg fortress.[4]

He expressed his sentiments on the contemporary state of affairs in Russia to Herman Bernstein during the latter's visit to Vammelsuu shortly after the completion of the work:

Russia today is a lunatic asylum. The people who are hanged are not the people who should be hanged. Everywhere else honest people are at large and only criminals are in prison. In Russia the honest people are in prison and the criminals are at large. The Russian government is composed of a band of criminals, and Nicholas II is not the greatest of them. There are still greater ones.[5]

These were the sentiments which Andreyev had carried with him in 1905 from the Taganskaya prison where he had met the well-known Socialist Revolutionary terrorist Vladimir Mazurin who was put to death while he was there. He gave voice to them in an article

[1] See S. Persky, *Contemporary Russian Novelists*, London, 1914, p. 236.

[2] The first four volumes of this collection of Andreyev's works had been published by *Znanie* between 1901 and 1907; in 1909 *Shipovnik* published volumes V–VII.

[3] 'L. N. Tolstoy i L. N. Andreyev', in *L. N. Tolstoy. Perepiska s russkimi pisatelyami*, M., 1962, p. 665. Though granting Andreyev's request, Tolstoy criticized the story severely in conversation with N. N. Gusev, taking exception to that which marred for him most of Andreyev's major works—its 'falsity' (see N. N. Gusev, 'Dva goda s L. N. Tolstym. (Dnevnik)', in *L. N. Tolstoy v vospominaniyakh sovremennikov*, vol. 2, M., 1960, p. 321).

[4] See P. Yakubovich, 'Leonid Andreyev. Rasskaz o semi poveshennykh', *Russkoe bogatstvo*, 1909, No. 1, p. 158.

[5] Bernstein, op. cit., p. 166.

which he wrote *in memoriam*:[1] 'Yes, he died peacefully. Poor
Russia! Bereaved mother! Your best sons are taken away from you,
your heart is torn to shreds. Blood colours the rising sun of your
freedom, but it will rise! And when you are free, do not forget those
who gave their lives for you.'[2]

The first chapter of *The Story of Seven Who Were Hanged*—'At
1 p.m., your Excellency'—was written while the author's mind was
largely preoccupied with these thoughts. The arguments against
the death penalty in this chapter are time-honoured and commonplace. A minister in the government is forewarned that an attempt
is to be made on his life the next day at 1 p.m. and that all precautions have been taken to thwart it. The rest of the chapter is devoted
to the illumination of the minister's changing reactions to this
announcement. With this type of theme, however, as *The Governor*
had illustrated, Andreyev can never be tedious. Stressing the contrast between the smile with which the minister greets the news
and the terror which surges within him when he is alone at night,
when all is silent, he shows that the ability, demonstrated in *Silence*,
to make silence almost audible and to probe incisively and alarm-
ingly into the effects of silence on the human mind had not forsaken him, and these are the qualities which prevent the first chapter
being banal. The arpeggio of horror, which culminates in the minister's heart-attack in a nightmarish scene of grotesque shadows
and ringing bells, is contrived with Andreyev's habitual sureness
of touch in this sector of human behaviour.

His claim is that life cannot be lived in the knowledge of when
and how one is to die. The same contention punctuates the early
part of the story proper, acting the role of philosophical premise
to the dénouement; and it is impossible, despite the vacillation of
the author's scheme at this point, to drive a wedge cleanly between
this first chapter and the rest of the work, as Kranikhfel'd endeavoured to do.[3] The minister's fear of death exists in varying degrees
of intensity in the figures of the seven who are awaiting execution,
and is used both as a yardstick to gauge more accurately the char-

[1] He wrote it in August 1906 and appealed to Chulkov in a letter of the following October from Berlin to ensure its publication (see *PLA*, p. 12); it was published in St. Petersburg before the end of the year.

[2] L. N. Andreyev, 'Pamyati Vladimira Mazurina', *Kalendar' russkoy revolyutsii*,
Petrograd, 1917, p. 228. This edition was a republication of the original of 1906.

[3] See V. Kranikhfel'd, 'Literaturnye zametki. (Rasskaz o semi poveshennykh)',
*Sovremennyy mir*, 1908, No. 5, p. 95.

acter of each in turn and as an intermediate state, a limbo between
life and death, from which the relationship between the two is seen
in a variety of ways leading up to the vision of Werner. As Andreyev
passes from one of his characters to another this limbo is gradually
transcended, and each transition marks a further step towards the
secret which lies beyond the 'wall'—the revelation of the higher
purpose and meaning of life. The social idealism of the sentenced
revolutionaries is forgotten in this upward surge, superimposed on
them by the author, towards a higher truth.[1] In his article *The
Destruction of the Individual (Razrushenie lichnosti)* Gorky naturally
took particular exception to this omission.[2]

Since Werner unifies and sublimates the experiences of the
other six—the bestial Yanson, the untamed, freedom-loving gypsy
and the other four revolutionaries—it is necessary that the other
images be viewed as rungs leading up to him, and some mention
must be made of the schematic way in which Andreyev aligns
them.

Significant are Werner's words near the end when he is telling
his comrades where to sit in the carriages which are about to convey
them on the first stage of their journey to the place of execution:
'. . . Tanya with Sergey, you (Musya) with Vasya . . ., I—alone.'[3]
In the works of a writer so enamoured of the schematic presentation of ideas as Andreyev one can never ignore pairings-off of images
of this nature. To do so means invariably to fall into the error of
Yuliy Aykhenval'd who sees *The Story of Seven Who Were Hanged*
as simply 'a multitude of details'.[4] These curt directions of Werner
throw light on the philosophical construction of the work.

Each in her own way, Musya and Tanya succeed in conquering,
or at any rate banishing, the presence of death. Musya, like one of
the great martyrs of old transposed into the modern world, perceives
in death by hanging—the death of martyrs—the surest path to
immortality. Her doubts about whether she merits this holy death
are dissolved in the thought that a man's value is gauged not only

[1] In his autographed manuscript of the work Andreyev carried this movement
even further in a chapter entitled 'I Write from the Grave', in which Werner
announces to the world the truth that he learns beyond. The chapter was omitted
from the final version, however, the result of which is the intensification of Werner's
spiritual experience shortly before his death.

[2] Cf. M. Gorky, *Stat'i 1905–16 gg.*, 2nd edn., Petrograd, 1918, p. 45.

[3] *Works* IV, p. 55.

[4] Yu. Aykhenval'd, *Siluety russkikh pisateley*, vol. 3, 4th edn., Berlin, 1923, p.
155.

by what he has done, but also by what he aspires to do. Her self-devised access to immortality is symbolized in her dream in which she challenges a whole regiment of soldiers to battle. The crucial point, she maintains, is not whether she kills any of them, but the single fact that they number thousands. 'When thousands kill one,' she proclaims, 'it means that the one has conquered.'[1] This conviction seems to elevate her above earthly life even before the execution and to deliver her from the nostalgia for this life momentarily roused in her by the sound of the guards' footsteps, the ringing of the prison clock, the rustle of the wind, the creaking of the lamp and the playing of the military band. In an early manuscript variant of the work the portrait of Musya had been more consonant with the 'masculine' nature of her scheme, but in the final version Andreyev succeeds in evoking from her an air of femininity, youth, grace and fragility, which was no small artistic feat.

But the achievement of Musya is only half of the formula which the author believed to be necessary for perception of the ultimate truth of life. Her inflowing philosophy had to be complemented by the outward-flowing philosophy of Tanya.[2] The individual, subjective vision of immortality, which rests on detachment from life, had to be reconciled and fused with a loving closeness and self-dedication to people. Tanya symbolizes in an absolute form this complementary half of the formula. She is the incarnation of altruism and self-effacement, the complete mother-image. In the court scene she is compared to a 'quiet pond at dawn reflecting every scurrying cloud'.[3] The emotions of the others find in her an unfailing and immediate response.

These two female images, in whom are embodied the final absolute qualities awaiting fusion in the person of Werner, represent a higher form of spiritual life than Sergey Golovin and Vasiliy Kashirin, just as these latter two are an advance on Yanson and the gypsy. The endowed superiority is perhaps a further indication of that veneration of woman which we have already encountered in Andreyev's fiction. From the point of view of characterization, however, the work undoubtedly reaches its highest level in the portraits of Yanson and especially the gypsy, for the simple reason

[1] *Works* IV, p. 38.
[2] This point was missed by Reysner who elevates Musya to the position of the 'purest and greatest' of this chosen band (see M. A. Reysner, *L. Andreyev i ego sotsial'naya ideologiya. Opyt sotsiologicheskoy kritiki*, SPb., 1909, p. 116).
[3] *Works* IV, p. 12.

that these images are the least schematic, the most alive. The only episodes which perhaps surpass them are those of Werner's vision and the final meeting of Sergey with his parents, this latter acquiring a tremendous emotional impact from the drastic economy of words employed.

The progression of increasing enlightenment brings the reader to Werner himself. From the moment of the appearance of the revolutionaries in court he is marked as a figure apart. The judges, for instance, address him with a certain respect, regarding him as the leader of the group even though there is no visible evidence of it. Well educated and gifted with a powerful will, he had at first loved life, we are told, and found the revolutionary struggle intoxicating. With time, however, he had begun to feel a coldness towards life and people, especially after a murder committed on the orders of the organization. It becomes quickly apparent that he belongs to the long line of Andreyev's super-intellectuals; that he lives by his intellect; that he deifies his intellect as Sergey Golovin does his body. His concentration in the death-cell on a difficult chess problem is the intellectual counterpart of Sergey's gymnastic exercises. The moment of supreme enlightenment comes, however, with the sudden suspicion that his intellect has failed him, that he has made a mistake in the game; and while he is striving vainly to discover where he has gone wrong, it occurs to him that perhaps his error is not the wrong positioning of bishops and rooks, but the very act of absorbing himself in a chess problem at a time when he is faced with the immeasurably greater problem of impending death.

In the light of a new waking consciousness he looks back over his life. Like Sergey and the others he sees life and death side by side, but now the coldness of the intellectual dissolves in the ecstasy of the visionary in a moment of profound insight which recalls the experience of Dostoevsky's Prince Myshkin during the few seconds before the onset of his epileptic attacks. As in *Darkness*, Andreyev has recourse to the image of fire: 'Tongues of fire seemed to flare up in his head; the fire sought to break out and illuminate afar the still dark, nocturnal distance. And now it broke out and lit up far on all sides the illuminated distance.'[1] In this dazzling light he sees the point at which life and death merge into one: 'It was as though he was walking along the highest mountain range, as narrow as the

[1] Ibid., p. 51.

blade of a knife, and on one side saw life and on the other saw death, like two shining, deep, beautiful seas merging on the horizon into one boundless, broad expanse.'[1]

The evolution of Werner's thought is the most complete record of Andreyev's spiritual and philosophical conquest of death and individuality. From the height to which Werner rises above the material universe death is seen as the continuation, not the end of life and, above all, the new life is not the chilling existence reflected in the eyes of Lazarus, but is as beautiful as the old. And with this revelation there is born in Werner a love of mankind which brings in its wake realization of the essential youth of the human race and of the manifold possibilities which lie ahead of it. He sees that it is too early to lose faith in its ability to build a new life. True love of man demands faith in him and his creative future.

It is this moment in Andreyev's art which gives his works their unity in the sense that it is the one to which his eye is constantly turned. We have seen that in his letter to Tolstoy of 18 August 1908 he referred to the work as 'bad', but one suspects that this was little more than a sop prompted by his clear awareness of the foreignness of his artistic method to the elder writer for whom he felt so profound a respect. The work is the clearest illustration of the truth of the words written about Andreyev by Chukovsky in 1908: 'He rejects one world in order to find immediately another. He is a poet of this other world . . .; here lies his strength and here lies his greatness.'[2] Here also lies the source of his optimism. The vast majority of critics have seen the story as a single beacon of light amid the prevailing gloom of Andreyev's fiction; in reality, its radiance is cast over all his works of the years of reaction and repression, including that which is alleged to be his most pessimistic work of all, *My Notes*.[3] The walls which collapse before Werner's eyes are the walls of the prison of his mind, the walls which symbolize the limitations of logic, the walls to which the odious hero of *My Notes* resigns himself as to the bounds of life itself. Beyond these walls, beyond the life supervised by Someone-in-grey lies the higher reality in which alone the individual can discover the meaning of

---

[1] Ibid., pp. 51-2.

[2] Chukovsky, *Leonid Andreyev bol'shoy i malen'kiy*, p. 62.

[3] It is noteworthy that *The Story of Seven Who Were Hanged* was dramatized after Andreyev's death. According to one account it 'was still playing in the provinces in the mid-twenties with great success and always made money' (S. Orlovsky, *Soviet Theaters, 1917-1941*, New York, 1954, p. 109).

his existence. In *My Notes* Andreyev returns to illustrate this truth in the 'negative' form characteristic of the works of the pre-1905 period.

Before he began work on *Judas Iscariot* he informed Gorky of his plan for another work; it is recalled by Gorky in his memoirs: 'The characters were two friends, one of them a visionary, the other a mathematician. One of them planned all his life to make a journey through the air, while the other kept destroying these fine dreams with practical calculations showing the engineering difficulties and the vast expense involved.'[1] The interest of the creator of Ternovsky in the latest developments in aviation is understandable, but he did not write his story on this subject until much later (1914) —a fact which offers further confirmation of Beklemisheva's insistence on the protracted digestive process which preceded the actual writing of his works.[2] Instead he concentrated his attention on the mathematician and built around him the story *My Notes*, which finally appeared on 13 September 1908. Even in this work, however, there is a reference to air travel in one of the footnotes to the 'confession' of the doctor of mathematics which may be regarded as a vestige of the original plan described by Gorky:

. . . I have come to understand that air flight within the bounds of our earth's atmosphere will change nothing in our aspiration to infinite flight and will make its futility even more painful. And instead of rejoicing at the successes of aviation, as my contemporaries do, I would suggest to them that they seriously consider whether complete immobility in its extreme form, firm and true crawling on the ground, is not better for man than deceptive fluttering in a cage.[3]

Like *Thought*, *My Notes* is a 'confession' written in the first person by a narrator who preaches a gospel directly opposed to that of Andreyev himself. The manner is the same as that employed by Poe in *William Wilson* and involved, of course, for the author the risk that the narrator may be interpreted as the mouthpiece of his own views. In *My Notes* Andreyev went to lengths to avert this misunderstanding which in some measure impaired the interest and value of the work. In order to underline his lack of sympathy with the doctrine enunciated he has recourse to a liberal use of italics in those parts of the text which most clearly bring out the negative qualities of the narrator. Yet despite this extreme measure he still

[1] *KLA*, p. 31.    [2] Cf. *supra*, p. 99.    [3] *Works* III, p. 199.

had the depressing experience of reading the following remark by
one critic on the story: 'After the works of Schopenhauer I do not
know of any that proves so mathematically the horror and useless-
ness of our whole lives.'[1] Gorky similarly criticized it on the grounds
that 'it preaches a passive attitude towards life, a doctrine which
I didn't expect and which is uncharacteristic of you'.[2]

The work offers little that is new in the way of insights either
into Andreyev's thought or into his artistic laboratory. His reason
for completing it so soon after *The Story of Seven Who Were Hanged*
was almost certainly the wish to juxtapose the doctor's philosophy
with the vision of Werner, just as in the original scheme outlined to
Gorky the mathematician was contrasted with the visionary. He
justifiably anticipated that this juxtaposition would suffice to
illustrate conclusively his own philosophical position. Thus, like the
revolutionaries, the doctor of mathematics is a prisoner; he is serving a life-sentence for the murder of his family. But whereas the
spiritual experience of the revolutionaries culminates in Werner's
transcendence of the prison, not only in the physical sense but also
in the philosophical sense of his individuality, the doctor makes the
prison the foundation of his philosophy; he becomes a 'magician of
self-incarceration', to use Vyacheslav Ivanov's description of
Raskol'nikov.[3] In both cases the prison is symbolic—as symbolic
as the 'wall' in the story of 1901, the image of which is re-evoked
in the doctor's remark on the walls of the prison in which he is
confined: 'The red bricks are reminiscent of blood and red pieces
of human flesh.'[4]

Though he is manifestly descended from Andrey Nikolaevich,
the hero of *By the Window*, the doctor has a much closer affinity to
Kerzhentsev in the sense that they are both creative, while the role
of Andrey Nikolaevich is wholly passive. Both Kerzhentsev and the
mathematician actually create reality in terms of the concepts
evolved by their intellects. Though there is no evidence which
suggests that Andreyev thought of the work in this way, *My Notes*
reads, in part, like the sequel to *Thought*. Both heroes are devotees
of the intellect and in both cases the intellect collapses after the
perpetration of an act of murder. The latter part of *Thought* de-

[1] A. Zakrzhevsky, *Podpol'e. Psikhologicheskie paralleli*, Kiev, 1911, p. 23.
[2] *LN*, p. 318.
[3] See V. Ivanov, *Freedom and the Tragic Life. A Study of Dostoevsky*, London,
1952, p. 79.
[4] *Works* III, p. 201.

scribes the attempts of Kerzhentsev to salvage his personality, to impose order on the chaos which has revealed itself. Noticeable throughout his 'confession' is his predilection for dwelling on the factual aspect of things, the avid way in which his mind seizes on physical reality as though he is afraid that it will slip away and elude his embrace. His accurate notification of dates and times is a further instance of the same thirst for the static. He struggles to weld the disintegrated parts into a synthesis. The philosophy of the doctor of mathematics is the embodiment of this synthesis. In the early part of his 'notes' he refers to a work which he had written some time previously during his imprisonment called 'The Diary of a Prisoner', in which he had described his state of mind on entering the prison and his struggle to overcome it; he recalls: 'Begun in distant youthful days of cruel disillusionments, the collapse of all beliefs and hopes, breathing limitless despair, it manifestly bears witness in places that it was written if not in a state of complete madness, then on the fateful border of it.'[1] The mental state which he describes is identical to that of Kerzhentsev after the murder of Savelov. Faith in the omnipotence of the intellect has been shattered and the personality is bereft of ties with the new reality which unfurls itself. Formerly the master, it is now a slave—a position which it finds intolerable. It attempts, therefore, to rebuild out of the remaining fragments a new artificial edifice, to recreate a reality with itself once more at the centre. Thus the mathematician cries: 'All the evil forces of life—solitude, prison, treachery, falsehood— all mustered against me, and I subjected them all to my will.'[2]

Whereas *The Story of Seven Who Were Hanged* portrays the transition from one plane of reality to the other, *My Notes* is the record of an attempt to perceive harmony on the 'first plane' alone. It is not inconceivable that it was partly Andreyev's intention to satirize here the 'socialist ant-hill' in much the same way as Dostoevsky did with the doctrine of Shigalyov in *The Devils*. The 'notes' have a dual purpose to perform. The doctor's first objective is to establish his innocence of the crime of which he is convicted, and the second—to preach his gospel of harmony. The two are closely interrelated. His premise is that the 'question of truth and untruth' is essentially irrelevant before the logical coherence of rational argumentation. He acknowledges that the jurors who sentenced him were right in their verdict, for 'as people who can

[1] Ibid., p. 191.   [2] Ibid., p. 213.

judge of things and events only by their appearance, they could not and should not have acted otherwise'.[1] Truth and falsehood do not exist; there is only plausibility, i.e. 'harmony between what is seen and what is thought on the basis of the strict laws of logic'.[2] Thus objective truth is relegated to a position subordinate to the combinations of the intellect, and it is on this foundation of 'logical harmony' that he pleads his innocence. So blatant is the self-indictment that it would be routine to enumerate the points against him. With every word in his defence he announces his guilt.

More significant is the realization of his second and main objective—the exposition of his world-philosophy. The replacement of the harmony of truth with the harmony of logic is an attempt to replace the harmony of the 'living life' with that of the intellect, which is synonymous with the substitution for flux of the static. In order that reality be reducible to a static formula, it must be taken in a strictly delimited manifestation; the implication is that the ability to see reality in the form of such a manifestation signifies the limit of the powers of the intellect. The symbolism of the work is hereby revealed. The doctor's cell is patently a symbol of the intellect, and the rectangle of the universe visible through the grill of its window symbolizes the total idea of the universe as it reveals itself to the intellect. The intellect constructs its world-philosophy on the foundation of this rectangular manifestation, thereby establishing harmony between what is seen and what is thought on the basis of the strict laws of logic. For the doctor the grill is 'a model of the profoundest harmony, beauty, nobility and power. Seizing the infinite in its iron squares it froze in cold and proud repose, frightening ignorant people, giving food for thought to the judicious and enrapturing the sage.'[3] Happiness, he states, lies in consciousness of subordination to this harmony and in the knowledge that freedom is superfluous; it becomes synonymous with slavery. He notes that the links of the chains which fetter him are shaped like the mathematical symbol of infinity. Slavery and infinity are thus merged. Like Shigalyov, he begins with absolute freedom and ends with absolute slavery.

'Free and profound thought which strives to understand life,' states Dr. Ragin in Chekhov's *Ward No. 6 (Palata No. 6)* (1892), 'and total contempt for the stupid vanity of the world—these are the two greatest blessings that man has ever known. And you can

---

[1] Ibid., p. 189.    [2] Ibid.    [3] Ibid., p. 200.

possess them even if you live behind three grills.'[1] Andreyev, like
Chekhov, was at pains to emphasize that thought detached from
life is by its nature shallow and blind. Like Ragin's philosophical
antagonist, Gromov, he juxtaposed the immeasurably profounder
truth of life. But the aspiration of Andreyev's mathematician is
different from that of Ragin; it is to create a world in which all is
calculable, and in this respect he bears a close similarity to the
heroes of Pirandello, particularly Henry IV. The conflict between
the flux of life and the static form which man seeks to impose upon
it as a refuge is the theme of many of Pirandello's plays, and the
form invariably crumbles to the playwright's bitter amusement.
There is not in Pirandello, however, the same stress as we encounter
in Andreyev on the moral distortion which for the latter, as for
Dostoevsky, is the inevitable concomitant of this self-extraction
from the 'living life'. Nor is there any counterpart to Andreyev's
'philosophy of the subconscious'. In Andreyev the attack on the
artificial form is conducted as much from within as from without—
by those 'other voices' which are 'acutely audible from the hidden
depths of the organism'.[2] From without the pure subconscious
weakens the doctor's self-confidence in the form of the artist, Mr.
K., who paints a portrait of him in which he captures that which
years of inner discipline, will-power and habitual falsehood on the
subject's part have been unable to conceal—the 'still, frozen look'
of the eyes, 'the madness gleaming somewhere in the depths, the
agonising eloquence of the soul, bottomless and infinitely alone
. . .'.[3] His whole being shudders. Just as Kerzhentsev is unable to
bear the sight of himself in the mirrors of his home after the murder
of Savelov, so the mathematician reels before his true portrait and
vainly protests. It was Andreyev's intention that his readers also
should reel before this portrait, before this powerful and awful
image of a creature whose conceit has been fatally wounded and
before the 'sacred formula of the iron grill' which he preaches.

[1] A. Chekhov, *Sobranie sochineniy*, vol. 6, M., 1955, p. 147.
[2] *Works* III, p. 219.    [3] Ibid., p. 216.

# XV

# ANDREYEV, CHRISTIANITY AND NIETZSCHE

I N the course of Andreyev's literary career few of his major works were written during the four-month period from May to August inclusive. 'In the summer I lead a lazy life, and do not write a line,' he informed Bernstein in 1908.[1] During the summer months he liked to absorb himself in his extra-literary interests—painting, photography, sailing, gardening, etc. Their value was wholly therapeutic and they undoubtedly played a part in his recovery from his experiences of the years 1905 and 1906. In Finland he gave himself to them with an abandon which astonished his numerous visitors and which has provoked the comment of most memoirists.

Equally astonishing was the abruptness with which he passed from one obsession to another. The most durable of them was painting which was in one sense an extension of his literary work inasmuch as characters from his works, as we have seen in the case of Judas and Jesus, were frequently the subjects of his canvases. It could well be that his artistic ability helped him to fix images before proceeding to their verbal portraits. Describing the paintings in Andreyev's house after a visit some years later, Kleynbort writes:

At the entrance to the study there was a full-length portrait of 'Someone-in-grey'; then followed scenes from 'The Life of Man' and black masks marching in a throng into the palace of Duke Lorenzo.[2] All these were works in a single colour by Andreyev himself, as were the self-portrait, the dying Tolstoy and the portrait of I. A. Belousov. Alongside these there gazed from the walls numerous faces by F. Goya.[3]

It was quite late in his literary career when Andreyev came to know Goya[4] and he immediately fell under his spell, filling the spaces between the cross-beams in his study with pencil and char-

---

[1] Bernstein, op. cit., p. 162.
[2] This was a scene from Andreyev's play *The Black Masks*.
[3] Kleynbort, loc. cit., p. 176.  [4] See *BSN*, p. 80.

coal copies of his paintings.[1] Perhaps some indirect influence of the
Spanish painter is to be observed in Andreyev's crowd-scenes,
particularly in *Anathema*.

In his literary work Andreyev's capacity for complete self-
abandonment revealed itself in the intensity with which he himself
experienced the emotions of his characters. 'He wept when writing
"The Story of Seven Who Were Hanged",' writes Beklemisheva,
'and he was ill when he was working on "The Black Masks".'[2] Most
of his writing was done at night. It was his custom, recalls Zaytsev,
to dine at 3 p.m., sleep till 8 o'clock, drink strong tea, smoke excessively, and then sit down to a night's work.[3] Anna Il'inichna
would man the typewriter. Chukovsky writes:

He would pace the carpet, drink black tea and recite clearly. The typewriter would hammer away madly, but would still hardly keep up with
him. The periods dictated by him would be controlled by a musical
rhythm which bore him along like a wave. He did not even write letters
without this rhythm, which was almost prosodic. He didn't simply write
his works; he was consumed by them as though by a fire. For a time he
became a maniac and saw nothing apart from them.[4]

No sooner was the work completed than the search for new material
began at once. His works were the issue of obsessions directly
analogous to his infatuations with photography, gramophones, etc.,
and the transitions from one to another were equally abrupt.

Tedium was something which rarely afflicted Andreyev during
the first years of his Finnish life. In addition to his 'interests', there
were his short but not infrequent trips to St. Petersburg and the
increasing flow of visitors to the 'Villa Avance', all impatient to see
his latest creation which had been widely publicized in the newspapers. In a letter of 19 January 1909 he was informed by Serafimovich that the 'Wednesdays' had been resumed in Moscow[5] and he
began again to send them his manuscripts. Just as he had in St.
Petersburg, he also endeavoured to form a similar group at Vammelsuu; he wrote to Belousov: '. . . I am arranging here a meeting
of Moscow and St. Petersburg writers to read reports and discuss
questions, and the meeting will be called "The Literary Week". I

---

[1] See *Rekviem*, p. 200.     [2] Ibid., p. 265.     [3] See *KLA*, p. 132.
[4] K. Chukovsky, 'Leonid Andreyev', in his *Iz vospominaniy*, M., 1958, pp.
249–50.
[5] See A. S. Serafimovich, *Sobranie sochineniy v semi tomakh*, vol. 7, M., 1960,
p. 433.

want to make such weeks regular occasions like the "Wednesdays".'[1]

Andreyev seemed during these years to be aflame with nervous energy and his health suffered seriously in consequence. To Teleshov, for instance, he complained early in 1909 of his constant headaches.[2] Having plagued him from the time of his suicide-attempts in his early youth, they became increasingly numerous and troublesome from 1909 onward, and his letters of his last years are full of references to them. His life was in many ways an unreal one, a perpetual search for distraction from worldly cares. Vadim Andreyev calls the period from 1908 to 1914 the third Act of *The Life of Man*.[3] The parallel is just. Andreyev had realized Man's dream of building a 'castle in Norway', but there was always 'an alarming and strange sensation of inconstancy and instability'.[4] Even in 1908 the transition to Act IV was clearly foreseeable and, indeed, had already begun.

'Not a single defender of this story do I remember,' wrote Kleynbort in 1914 in connection with *Darkness*. 'It was after this work that it became bad taste to praise Andreyev.'[5] His every work continued to be a literary event. Circulation figures gave the impression that his popularity was greater than it had ever been,[6] and Blok, writing in February 1909, refers to him as 'the most "read" and studied of contemporary writers'.[7] Eighteen thousand copies of *Tsar Hunger*, for instance, were sold in a single day.[8] The pressure of demands made upon him by the editors of almanacs, journals and newspapers became so great that he was compelled to write to the editorial board of the newspaper *Rech'* ('Speech') on 29 October 1909:

I consider it my duty to apologise to the readers and editorial boards of the almanacs, journals and newspapers to which I have undertaken to give my works in the near future ('Shipovnik', 'Sovremennyy mir', the miscellany of printers in Moscow edited by N. D. Teleshov, 'Russkoe slovo' and many others). For reasons which I find it inconvenient to discuss, I am not publishing my works in the present (academic) year.[9]

---

[1] Belousov, op. cit., p. 140.    [2] Teleshov, 'Pro Leonida Andreyeva', p. 71.
[3] See *VLA*, June, p. 106.    [4] Ibid., p. 96.    [5] Kleynbort, loc. cit., p. 172.
[6] See V. Kranikhfel'd, 'Literaturnye otkliki. "Anatema" i drugie', *Sovremennyy mir*, 1910, No. 1, p. 86.
[7] A. Blok, 'Dusha pisatelya. (Zametki sovremennika)', *Sobranie sochineniy v vos'mi tomakh*, vol. 5, M.–L., 1962, p. 367.
[8] See *BSN*, p. 66.
[9] 'Pis'mo Leonida Andreyeva v redaktsiyu gazety "Rech' " ', *Sovremennyy mir*, 1910, No. 4, p. 125.

A month previously he had reacted angrily to the persistent demands of *Sovremennyy mir* ('The Contemporary World') with a similar letter to the journal's editorial board.[1] Nevertheless, the period from 1907 onwards saw a gradual decline in the popularity of what he had to say and the manner in which he was wont to say it. He was never to recapture completely that position of 'dictator of thoughts' (*vlastitel' dum*) which he had occupied during the years of his protracted *critique*, and indeed in the closing years of his life there were occasions when he himself tended to look back on the works which he wrote after *The Life of Man* as a succession of acts of self-betrayal. He wrote in his diary on 22 April 1918: 'Yes, here lies the heart of the matter. I betrayed myself, treacherously betrayed myself. Born to curse, I spent my time distributing indulgences—a few curses, and then a whole barrel of honey and syrup.'[2] Not too much importance should be attached to this statement, however, for it conflicts violently with many of his comments on the works of the latter half of his creative life.

In many quarters of the world of criticism his rapid rise to fame had always been a source of disquiet. In his principal work on Andreyev Chukovsky presents a long list in alphabetical order of the abusive epithets applied to him by critics during the period from 1901 to 1908.[3] The personal nature of this abuse was intensified from 1907 onward. Critics and reporters became part of the Vammelsuu scene in their search for piquant snippets of news—so much so that Zaytsev could say that instead of Andreyev escaping from the capital, the capital had migrated to him.[4] The result was a flood of reports on the 'disorderly' life which he led there and mockery of his unorthodox daily programme. The truth was vindictively distorted. In reality, Andreyev was very strict in the allocation of his time and adhered rigidly to his regime during the months which he devoted to work. No guest could disturb his routine. The newspapers took little account of this and *Russkoe znamya* ('The Russian

[1] See 'Pis'mo Leonida Andreyeva, poluchennoe redaktsiey "Sovr. M." v kontse sentyabrya 1909 g.', *Sovremennyy mir*, 1910, No. 4, p. 124.

[2] V. L. Andreyev, *Detstvo*, M., 1963, p. 234. This work by Andreyev's son Vadim is essentially a reproduction in book form of the autobiography serialized in 1938 in *Russkie zapiski* ('Russian Notes') (*VLA*), though it contains a number of details and quotations from Andreyev's diaries, in addition to the postscript, which are not in the latter.

[3] Chukovsky, *Leonid Andreyev bol'shoy i malen'kiy*, pp. 72–6.

[4] Cf. *KLA*, p. 140.

Banner'), *Veche* ('The Popular Assembly') and *Novoe vremya* proceeded to besmirch his name in a manner which had little precedent. Always particularly hostile towards him were the Kievan critics, and it was the tone of their diatribes which provoked him on 5 September 1910 to write a letter to the editorial board of *Teatr i iskusstvo* raising the whole question of the standards of decency to be observed in criticism.[1]

Less abusive but equally persistent was the criticism which came from the main literary journals. He summed up the position in a letter to Gorky of March 1908: 'From top to bottom, on all floors of the Russian literary mansion, which sometimes closely resembles a house of pleasure, I am abused. . . . Yes, persecution. The Cadets, the mystics, the decadents, the Octobrists, the Black Hundreds—from all sides.'[2] He was particularly grieved by the sharp criticism to which his latest works, especially *Darkness* and *Tsar Hunger*, had been subjected by Lunacharsky in *Literaturnyy raspad* ('Literary Disintegration'),[3] a collection of articles published in 1908 and sponsored by Gorky which, according to Lunacharsky, 'appeared for the express purpose of giving a militant appraisal of the literature of that time'.[4] In reality, the contributors—among them Gorky himself, Lunacharsky, Kamenev and Friche—made it their task to reveal modernistic literature in its entirety as decadent and reactionary.[5]

Perhaps the most remarkable thing of all was Andreyev's extreme sensitivity to this criticism. There existed at the time a 'Bureau of Reviews' which supplied him with all the comments made on his works throughout the length and breadth of Russia. 'For the most part,' writes Skitalets, 'this was nonsense, gossip and often envious abuse, together with filth and slander. And for some reason Andre-

---

[1] Cf. L. N. Andreyev, 'Moyo ob'yasnenie. (Pis'mo v redaktsiyu)', *Teatr i iskusstvo*, 1910, No. 37, p. 679.

[2] *LN*, p. 307.

[3] Cf. A. Lunacharsky, 'T'ma', *Literaturnyy raspad*, vols. 1–2, SPb., 1908, pp. 148–72.

[4] 'Leonid Andreyev o Literaturnom raspade', *Literaturnoe Nasledstvo*, 1932, No. 2, p. 104. Andreyev's two letters to Gorky on this subject (dated 11 February and 23 March 1908) are presented in this article together with a rejoinder from Lunacharsky.

[5] Almost the only Marxist to profess any sympathy for Andreyev's works of the post-revolutionary period was Kirov (see 'Neopublikovannye i maloizvestnye stat'i i pis'ma S. M. Kirova. Mysli o literature i iskusstve', *Literaturnaya gazeta*, 1939, No. 66, 1 December, p. 3).

yev read this rubbish, every day poisoning his mood.'[1] Similar
testimony to this 'strange attentiveness' to the voice of criticism is
forthcoming from Blok,[2] and Veresaev describes the meticulous
way in which he collected all references to himself binding them in
massive volumes which occupied a prominent position on his bookshelves.[3] When Beklemisheva asked him why he devoted so much
time to critical comment, he replied tersely and angrily: 'If you
were in my position, you would read it.'[4] Beklemisheva herself
probably provides part of the answer with her reference to his repeated complaint that, even though he had read everything, he had
never found a critical appreciation 'which helped him to explain
his art, his achievements, his mistakes'.[5] The frustration which he
constantly experienced when reading reviews of his works found
expression in his comments on *The Red Laugh* in a letter of 11
March 1905 to S. V. Yablonovsky, one of the editors of *Russkoe
slovo*:

In general, the critics have not gladdened me excessively with their
attitude to this work: together with the abundance of quite unnecessary
and sometimes even offensive praise they have displayed little thought,
moderation and seriousness. Their reasoning, praise and abuse are
mechanical, tedious, cold, sluggish and uninteresting.[6]

He attached to the critic's role the very greatest importance and
expressed his ideal conception of constructive criticism to Kleynbort:

A work of criticism—God willing—is the same as a work of art. It
deepens our understanding of a work. After passing through the critic's
aesthetic soul, a work acquires in contact with it a new life. You are
present, as it were, in the laboratory in which the very devices and schemes
of the artist are analysed, but you should not praise one thing in order
to reject another; instead, you should enter into its very conception.
Every movement of the heart, every hint at a type should be traced with
inspiration in accordance with the artist's talent and philosophy of life.[7]

Andreyev's creative method was such that the merits and demerits
of much of what he wrote must have been unclear to him. It was
very rare for him to return to a work in order to study it once it had

---

[1] Skitalets, op. cit., p. 394.
[2] See Blok, 'Pamyati Leonida Andreyeva', p. 135.
[3] See *VRSV*, p. 468.    [4] *Rekviem*, p. 207.    [5] Ibid., p. 231.
[6] 'Arkhiv V. I. Semevskogo', *Literaturnoe Nasledstvo*, 1933, Nos. 7–8, p. 423.
[7] Kleynbort, loc. cit., p. 177.

been written. Behind his assiduous study of criticism there was the need which he felt for a constructive analysis of his art—a task of which he himself was temperamentally incapable.

Noteworthy is his emphasis on the need for a work of art to be evaluated in terms of the philosophy of life which it expresses. No one had more right to be sensitive to this point. He wrote to Gorky in late February 1912: 'Oh my Lord, . . . how many times has my soul been spat on and my words and meaning distorted.'[1] Misinterpretations of his thought caused his name to become inseparably associated with the pessimism of the immediate post-revolutionary years. When waves of suicides were sweeping the country, it became almost an act of ritual, writes Chukovsky, to write to Andreyev before taking one's life. But by 1908 the attitude of his public, as stated, was changing. On the evidence of the critic Kozlovsky, hardly any attempt was made to understand the symbolism of *The Black Masks*.[2] The play shared the same fate as *Darkness*, of which it might be termed an allegorical representation. Here, as in all his major works from 1906 onward, Andreyev sought to extract light from the gloom; his readers—those 'extremely nervous, mystically and gloomily minded beings with distended pupils', as Aleksey Tolstoy described them[3]—saw only the gloom and judged him accordingly.

We have seen that *The Black Masks* was begun at Capri. Conceived while he was working there on *My Notes* and, indeed, foreshadowed and largely explained in the latter work,[4] the play finally appeared in the seventh volume of *Shipovnik* in the autumn of 1908. Andreyev's subject once more is the conflict between the metaphysical and empirical personalities of the individual. The setting —the castle of Lorenzo,[5] Duke of Spadaro[6] and Knight of the Holy

---

[1] *LN*, p. 325.

[2] See L. S. Kozlovsky, 'L. Andreyev', in *Russkaya literatura XX veka, 1890–1910*, vol. II, part 2, edit. by S. A. Vengerov, M., 1915, pp. 252–3.

[3] A. N. Tolstoy, *Polnoe sobranie sochineniy*, vol. 13, M., 1949, p. 278.

[4] See *Works* III, p. 223.

[5] For certain of Andreyev's friends the name 'Duke Lorenzo' seemed to epitomize the writer himself and the life 'on the grand scale' which he was leading at Vammelsuu. It seemed to express his taste for hyperbole in real life as well as in art. According to Chukovsky, it was Repin who first applied the name to Andreyev himself (see *KLA*, p. 81).

[6] The name 'Spadaro' was taken by Andreyev from the name of a fisherman at Capri (see Gorky's reference in a letter to Andreyev of autumn 1906, *LN*, p. 280).

Spirit—is a projection of the protagonist's inner world, while the action is largely an externalization of his psychic conflict. It is possible that the symbolic framework was supplied by Poe's poem *The Haunted Palace*, but the content with which it is filled refutes Kugel's hardly disguised charge of plagiarism.[1]

The direct opposite of the mathematician in *My Notes*, Lorenzo opens his castle to the world; like the hero of *Darkness* he bares his soul to the test of reality. The guests who flock in are symbols in which he sees his diversity reflected—his heart, his thought, his lies. He is not aware of this, however, and merely expresses dismay at their ugliness. Equally dismayed are his wife, Francesca, his servants and his jester.

Andreyev's justification for this introduction of external characters into the projected subjective world of the protagonist was presumably that he was concerned not with these characters as objective figures but with the transformation which they undergo in Lorenzo's eyes in the course of the play. This transformation is employed as a means of illuminating the dichotomy of the hero's personality. The statement of the Cadet critic Gabrilovich (better known by his pseudonym 'Galich') that there are no contacts in the play with the 'non-ego'[2] should be replaced by the statement that the external exists but, as always in Andreyev, only for the purpose of casting light on the inner drama of the individual.

Andreyev's premise is that the personality of man is conditioned by his contacts with external reality, the potential result of which is the eclipse of the true personality. People disappear and are replaced by constantly changing masks. Even one's dearest are overcome by the same fate and the most powerful love becomes incapable of apprehending the essence of the eternally changing scene. Hence the increasing perplexity of Lorenzo as one after another women appear before him identical in appearance to Francesca; to each he responds as though she were his wife. His inability to see beyond the masks of empirical reality denotes the predominance of his empirical over his true personality. The black masks who throng into the castle—Poe's 'evil things in robes of sorrow'[3]—are symbolic

---

[1] See A. R. Kugel', 'Literaturnye vstrechi i kharakteristiki', in his *List'ya s dereva*, L., 1926, pp. 82–3.

[2] See L. Gabrilovich (L. Galich), 'O "Chornykh maskakh" ', *Teatr i iskusstvo*, 1908, No. 51, p. 914.

[3] J. A. Harrison (ed.), *The Complete Works of Edgar Allan Poe*, vol. 7, New York, 1902, p. 84.

of the false reality which has engulfed Lorenzo's soul. Extinguishing the lights, they plunge the castle of Act I into darkness.

In Act II the dichotomy of the hero's personality is externalized in the appearance of a 'second Lorenzo'. This is the first and only time in Andreyev's fiction that the individual sees his duality embodied in his own image. Before *The Black Masks* the only suggestions of the *Doppelgänger*-theme appear in the portrait of the mathematician in *My Notes* and in Kerzhentsev's terror before his own reflected image—the mirror-motif being one of the many variants of the theme used extensively by the German romantics, particularly Hoffmann[1] whose influence on Gogol' and Dostoevsky in this connection is well known.[2]

The two personalities confront one another in mortal combat in a scene which recalls the battle in Poe's *William Wilson* between the protagonist and his embodied conscience. The joust is resolved in the triumph of the true personality. The false Lorenzo is killed and is now subjected to the penance of being made to lie in his coffin and listen to the record of his sins from those whom he has wronged. The illusions have been swept away and the masks stripped off; only truth remains. The play concludes with a symbolic representation of the cleansing of the soul in the purifying flames of truth.

In *The Black Masks*, as in *Darkness*, the 'Divine Comedy' is re-enacted. Like Dante, the terrorist and Lorenzo are confronted with the corruption of their personalities and with the dark forces of the 'inferno' which is empirical life. They survive the test of both; the spirit of the terrorist 'gleams with a white flame' and Lorenzo ascends to paradise in a burst of radiance. One is tempted to suspect more than coincidence when Lorenzo cries to his servants

---

[1] That Andreyev was familiar with Hoffmann is confirmed by an unpublished letter to Nemirovich-Danchenko of 1914 or 1915 in which he recounts, albeit in distorted form, an episode from one of the German writer's stories—evidently *The Sandman* (*Der Sandmann*) and the part thereof which constitutes Act I of Offenbach's opera—in order to point out a parallel between it and his intentions in his play *Ekaterina Ivanovna* (1912). An extract from the letter is quoted in Herman Bernstein's Preface to his translation of *Ekaterina Ivanovna*, New York, 1923, pp. vii–viii.

In Andreyev's time the mirror-motif was perhaps most strikingly employed by Bryusov in the story *The Archive of a Psychiatrist* (*Arkhiv psikhiatra*) in his cycle *The Earth's Axis* (*Zemnaya os'*) (1907).

[2] For an interesting and provocative analysis of Dostoevsky's 'adaptations' of Hoffmann see: C. E. Passage, *Dostoevskij the Adapter. A Study in Dostoevskij's Use of the Tales of Hoffmann*, University of North Carolina Press, 1954, 203 pp

at the beginning of the play: 'The whole road must shine, blaze with lights like the road to paradise,'[1] and when he replies to the masks who complain of the cold in Act 1: 'Cold? Why to me it seems as hot here as hell itself.'[2] The 'presence' of the great Florentine is felt repeatedly. The importance which Andreyev attached to the theme has already been evidenced by his comments to Kleynbort on *Darkness*; these comments are echoed by the remark he made on *The Black Masks* in 1916 in a letter to A. Evlakhov: 'For me personally "The Black Masks" is the most important of my works; it is the closest to me and psychically the most cherished (despite its many formal defects).'[3]

Although it is to God that Lorenzo commends his soul, it should be noted that, as in *Savva*, Andreyev uses the term 'God' as little more than a designation of the 'second reality' or 'spirit of music', to use Blok's term. Conclusive proof that this is so is furnished by his next major play *Anathema*, which was published by *Shipovnik* in October 1909. At the same time we see in *Anathema*, as in former works, that the abnegation of individuality which is central to Andreyev's *Weltanschauung* produced an ethic which differed in no significant way from the Christian ideal. Indeed, the character in the play through whom he expresses his ethical ideal—the Jew, David Leyzer—is patently modelled on Christ. Many details confirm this: the rumour that he once healed a man blind from birth[4] recalls the act of Christ described in *John*, 9: 1–7; the people's wish to make him king recalls *John*, 6: 15; the entry into Jerusalem (*Mark*, 11: 8) clearly served as a model for the fourth Picture; and the words of Leyzer to the mob which stones him at the end of the play—'Why do you persecute me like a thief and frighten me with cries as though I were a robber?'[5]—are manifestly a paraphrase of the words of Jesus at Gethsemane (*Mark*, 14: 48). Andreyev's introduction of these 'Biblical elements' into the allegorical exposition of his wholly secular philosophy predetermined the fate of the play. Inevitably there had been critics who had pronounced *Judas Iscariot* an 'arch-blasphemous composition',[6] but the criticism cannot be compared either in quantity or savagery with that

---

[1] *Works* I, p. 234.     [2] Ibid., p. 239.
[3] Quoted from A. Linin, 'Neuere Forschungen über Leonid Andrejev', *Zeitschrift für slavische Philologie*, Leipzig, 1930, vol. 8, pp. 214–15.
[4] See *Works* III, p. 293.     [5] Ibid., p. 320.
[6] Ya. Bogorodsky, 'Strannaya apologiya', *Pravoslavnyy sobesednik*, Kazan', 1909, No. 2, p. 234.

provoked by *Anathema*. The explanation is to be sought primarily in misunderstanding of *Anathema*, which was taken by certain circles of the clergy to be a *critique* and mockery of Christianity, and also, perhaps, in the desire of the forces of reaction to make their presence felt on the stage.

In February 1909 the play had passed the censorship without incident after Andreyev had made a few insignificant changes— mainly in the stage-directions. Even after its first performances at the Moscow Art Theatre the following October[1] the governor of Moscow, A. A. Adrianov, informed Stolypin that the play could have no harmful effect on society. But Nemirovich-Danchenko soon displayed signs of anxiety. It was estimated that forced cancellation of the play would mean for the Art Theatre a loss of thirty thousand roubles in Moscow alone and, *in toto*, a sum at least ten times as great.[2] Nemirovich-Danchenko travelled to St. Petersburg to see Stolypin on 22 October, but the Prime Minister had left for the south. When he discovered, however, that the matter had been turned over to the press department, Nemirovich-Danchenko took this as a good sign and returned to Moscow.

After the play had twice been checked, the press department issued a directive to local authorities containing the following stipulations: 'The production of "Anathema" is not to be prevented, . . . unless the production of this play presents difficulties due to purely local conditions or unless deliberate blasphemy is seen in the production itself.'[3] Taking advantage of the ruling the clergy, in close alliance with the Black Hundreds press, prevailed on local authorities to forbid performance of the play in Mogilyov, Grodno, Khar'kov, Samara, Poltava, Yaroslavl', Vladivostok, Zhitomir and Astrakhan'. The editorial of *Teatr i iskusstvo* in which the directive was printed also contained a telegram received from Saratov: 'Bishop Germogen spoke for the second time about the works of Leonid Andreyev and anathematised him.'[4]

The Black Hundreds press—mainly the newspapers *Russkoe znamya* and *Kolokol* ('The Bell')—and the clergy proceeded to deliver a scathing attack on the play, and the voice of Germogen (Hermogenes), Bishop of Saratov, rang out piercingly. He published his indictment in a pamphlet entitled *Modern Followers of Anathema*

---

[1] The première took place on 2 October 1909.
[2] See Editorial, *Teatr i iskusstvo*, 1910, No. 3, p. 51.
[3] Editorial, *Teatr i iskusstvo*, 1909, No. 47, p. 3.      [4] Ibid.

*and His Dissension* (*Nyneshnie posledovateli anatemy i ego kramoly*),
in which he wrote: 'The aim of the work "Anathema" is to mock in
the most blasphemous way our Lord Jesus Christ and also all His
deeds, *i.e.* Christianity.'[1] With this object in mind, he maintained,
Andreyev had (1) made Anathema triumph over David, i.e. Jesus;
and (2) shown that all the acts of goodness performed by Leyzer
are powerless to relieve sorrow and misfortune, in consequence of
which God appears as a 'deceiver'.[2]

In sharp contrast to this onslaught was the defence of the play
by the Exarch of Georgia, Bishop Innokentiy, who saw in it nothing
less than the 'apotheosis of Christianity'.[3] It is also significant that
Germogen won little support for his case when he addressed the
Holy Synod. The subsequent investigations of the newspaper
*Birzhevye vedomosti* revealed that no steps had been taken by the
Synod, not even by the Metropolitan Vladimir, to have the play
removed.[4] Germogen turned, therefore, to the Rector of the St.
Petersburg Spiritual Academy, Bishop Feofan, who of all ecclesias-
tical figures at that time enjoyed the greatest influence in court
circles. Towards the end of November the latter authorized the
dispatch to all eparchies of a circular forbidding the clergy, on pain
of the strictest penalties, to read the play. He then proceeded to
make use of his influence in the higher circles of society and
confided his wishes to an influential aristocrat, Shirinsky-Shikhmatov. The latter in turn reported to Pobedonostsev that Christ
was being shown on the stage at the Moscow Art Theatre, whereupon A. V. Bel'gardt, the head of the government's censorship
department, was asked to check a performance.

Bel'gardt saw the play from beginning to end and found that
with the exception of a single word, which was quickly removed,
the censored text was being strictly adhered to and that the play
contained 'nothing offensive to religious feeling'.[5] He also talked
with Kachalov and Vishnevsky, who played Anathema and Leyzer
respectively, and questioned Nemirovich-Danchenko as to whether
Vishnevsky had changed his make-up since the early performances.[6]

---

[1] 'Ep. Germogen ob "Anateme" i "Anfise"', *Teatr i iskusstvo*, 1910, No. 2, p. 36.
[2] Ibid.
[3] Quoted from *Russkoe slovo*, 1910, No. 9, 13 January, in Rubtsov, op. cit.,
p. 216.
[4] See Editorial, *Teatr i iskusstvo*, 1910, No. 3, p. 51.    [5] Ibid.
[6] See V. Nemirovich-Danchenko, *My Life in the Russian Theatre*, London,
1937, p. 179.

'It turned out,' writes *Teatr i iskusstvo*, 'that reference had been made to the make-up as one of the proofs of the blasphemous nature of the production. . . .'[1] When photographs confirmed that no change had been made, Bel'gardt left for St. Petersburg perfectly satisfied and 'with the gratifying feeling, not without spite, that he would expose Shirinsky-Shikhmatov and avenge the undeserved reprimand he had received from Pobedonostsev'.[2] Three days later (9 January 1910), however, Stolypin yielded to the demands of the provincial governors and issued a directive prohibiting further performances. The Art Theatre was ordered to remove it from its repertory. It was performed thirty-seven times in all and the projected film of the play, which was to have been made by A. O. Drankov and for which Andreyev had already written the scenario, never materialized.

It is necessary to establish first of all what is represented by the two main characters of *Anathema*. Persky observed that the play was 'born of a philosophical conception which relates it to Goethe's "Faust" '.[3] Similarities to the *Faust* legend are indeed discernible, but Andreyev's conception differs fundamentally from that of Goethe. For example, two very different conceptions of the 'power of darkness' are presented. There is nothing glorious or heroic in Anathema as there is in Mephistopheles or Milton's Satan, and it is noteworthy that his knowledge is as limited as that of man. He does not converse with the Almighty for his path is barred by the Guardian, who personifies the line of demarcation between the intellect and the truth which lies beyond its grasp, and it is with the Guardian that he makes his wager. In fact, Anathema stands somewhere between Mephistopheles and Faust. As distinct from the former, he is not subject in his actions to the hidden purpose of Providence; he is an autonomous being who demands knowledge of ultimate truth, and herein lies the Faustian aspect of his nature. But whereas Goethe's Faust, unlike the Faust of the *Volksbuch* and Marlowe's Faust, is redeemed by his refusal to acquiesce, by that unabating striving for the unattainable which brings him progressively nearer to the idea of moral perfection, Anathema dashes himself in vain against the 'wall', and anguished by the contrast between his own view of the world and the 'essential harmony'

[1] Editorial, *Teatr i iskusstvo*, 1910, No. 3, p. 51.
[2] Nemirovich-Danchenko, op. cit., pp. 180–1.
[3] S. Persky, *Contemporary Russian Novelists*, London, 1914, p. 243.

which he suspects but to which he, like the vast majority of men, is blind, he makes it his purpose to reveal to the world that life is fundamentally unjust. He selects David Leyzer as the instrument for the realization of this design.

To Andreyev, therefore, belongs the interpretation of Satan's sin not as pride, but as the refusal to accept life without logical explanation. He is both Pushkin's 'spirit of negation, spirit of doubt', and at the same time a fanatical seeker of truth who cries to the Guardian: 'The name! Give the name! Illuminate the way for the Devil and Man!'[1] But like the hero of *My Notes* he is the prisoner of his logic and the way remains barred. An Italian critic defined him as 'the incarnation of that evil principle which constitutes in the dark vision of Andreyev the substratum, the essence of reality';[2] in fact, he represents the precise opposite: a principle which is not so much evil as limited and shallow; hence the name 'Nullus' by which Leyzer addresses him and his association with the colour grey—Andreyev's recurring colour-symbol of empirical reality and the 'principle of individuation'. Andreyev seems to have had in mind, rather than Mephistopheles, the Satan of *Genesis*, with whom Anathema's quest for knowledge gives him an obvious affinity, and noticeable is Andreyev's attempt to recreate in Anathema the image of the serpent—even to the extent of making him, like Judas, crawl on his stomach in mock servility. The play is a variation of the eternal myth of the Tempter. Moreover, Anathema is far more subtle than Mephistopheles. He brings to Leyzer wealth, which he knows the latter will distribute. He also knows that no permanent good will result from this beneficence. Yet even though all is enacted as he foresees, it is Leyzer who, by virtue of his self-renunciation, triumphs and attains to the truth which Anathema is incapable of apprehending. In a letter of 1913 to Amfiteatrov Andreyev defined his Jew as an 'assertion of a moral feat, of self-abnegation, a protest against the individual in the name of the general . . .'.[3] He sought in the play to give consummate expression to the interrelated ideas which underlie *Judas Iscariot*, *Darkness* and *The Black Masks*. A lengthy analysis would involve unnecessary repetition.

[1] *Works* III, p. 262.
[2] A. Capri, 'Leonida Andreyeff', in his *Letteratura Moderna*, Firenze, 1928, p. 81.
[3] *Rekviem*, p. 261.

While *Anathema* is essentially a synopsis of Andreyev's fundamental convictions, his next important play, *The Ocean*, which appeared early in 1911,[1] may be regarded as an appendix to this synopsis. Attempting to clarify still further the ethical implications of his philosophy, he again employed the method of contrast, making use on this occasion, as he had in *The Story of Sergey Petrovich*, of the philosophy of Nietzsche.

The basic points of divergence between Andreyev and Nietzsche have their source in the German philosopher's rejection and Andreyev's acceptance of the metaphysical entity as an eternal and indivisible unity. Nietzsche's rejection of absolute Being necessarily precluded belief in absolute knowledge; knowledge, he maintained, like reality, is in a state of constant flux. It was his belief, therefore, that man can never attain to the complete self-knowledge which Andreyev, like Schopenhauer, believed both possible and necessary for man's deliverance from anguish and frustration. He consequently replaced Schopenhauer's ideal of self-abnegation with the ideal of unimpeded activity, the unfettered 'will to power', the release of all 'urges'. This emphasis on the primacy of intrinsic power necessarily presupposed the belief that the ultimately self-justifying ends can only be individual lives, and this conviction is fundamental to all Nietzsche's philosophical constructions. Though equally devoted, therefore, to the affirmation of life and to the rejection of reason, Nietzsche and Andreyev came to diametrically opposed conclusions on the nature and purpose of life. The ethical implications of their disagreement form the subject of *The Ocean*.

On a different level the play was, in part, a product of Andreyev's intense love of the sea. This love can be traced back to his childhood; he was to write in his diary in 1918: 'Even as a boy, in desperately arid and dusty Oryol . . ., I felt a great longing for the sea.'[2] The proximity of the sea was certainly one of the main reasons for his choice of Vammelsuu as the place for his permanent home. At the same time he found it as difficult to write about the sea as he did about other aspects of nature. He wrote: 'Why am I unable to write about the sea? I want to, and cannot. . . . Of course, I have tried, but the result is cheap, obnoxious rhetoric—rhetoric produced

---

[1] It was first published in a separate edition by the publishing-house *Prometey* ('Prometheus').

[2] Entry of 28 April 1918, 'Stranitsy iz dnevnika L. N. Andreyeva', *Zhar-ptitsa*, Berlin, 1921, No. 3, p. 38.

by ecstasy, because all words are too small and insignificant. . . .'[1]
*The Ocean* is the attempt to which he refers and this may be taken
as his comment on the work. He is abiding by his habitual practice
of criticizing the formal aspect of his works (in this case with more
than usual justification) without reference to their philosophical
content; indeed, when commenting on the play from the standpoint of the thought which it expresses, he pronounced it one of his
favourite works.[2]

There is a possibility, suggested by Yershov,[3] that the play grew
out of an early story, *Mutiny on Shipboard* (*Bunt na korable*), which
Andreyev did not complete or publish; he refers to it in a letter to
Gorky of December 1901.[4] The first draft, however, was made at
Capri. We have seen that his strolls by the sea at Capri played a
part in alleviating his sorrow, and his selection of the sea as the
'main character', as he described it to Beklemisheva,[5] may have
been a response to that expanse of water which for Gorky was 'more
beautiful and deeper than love and woman'.[6] It is also possible that
his contact with Gorky at Capri had a direct influence on the play.
Our basis for this hypothesis is the similarity between the scheme
or symbolic framework of *The Ocean* and the verbal picture painted
for Elena's benefit by the artist Vagin in Act II of Gorky's *Children
of the Sun*: 'On the prow of a ship someone will stand alone. . . .
He has the face of a man who has buried all his hopes behind him
on the shore . . ., but his eyes burn with the fire of a great
stubbornness . . . and he sails in order to create new ones . . .
lonely among lonely people.' The scientist Protasov then takes up
the theme: 'There is no need for a storm, gentlemen! Or—no!—
let there be a storm, but ahead, on the ship's course, let the sun
burn! Call your picture "To the sun!"—to the source of life!'[7]
Gorky could well have drawn Andreyev's attention to this moment
in his play when the latter confided to him his plan for *The Ocean*.
Yet another possibility suggests itself, however, owing to the
distinct similarity to Vagin's picture of that part of Zarathustra's
song, *The Seven Seals*, in which the sage announces his love of the

---

[1] Ibid., pp. 38–9.
[2] Cf. *Teatr i iskusstvo*, 1910, No. 37, p. 679.
[3] Cf. P. Yershov (ed.), *Letters of Gorky and Andreev, 1899–1912*, London,
1958, p. 159.
[4] Cf. *LN*, pp. 118 and 121.
[5] Cf. *Rekviem*, p. 237.     [6] *LN*, p. 280.
[7] M. Gorky, *Deti solntsa*, Stuttgart, 1905, pp. 90–1.

sea and 'all that is of the sea's kin'.[1] Perhaps Andreyev's meditations on the 'superman' in connection with the intellectual content of the play called to mind this part of *Thus Spake Zarathustra*—a work, as stated, with which he was very familiar. Alternatively, he could have been reminded of it by the episode in Gorky's play.

Whatever the source of influence, however, the first variant dissatisfied Andreyev and he continued to work on the play in Finland. Informative is Brusyanin's recollection of the time when Andreyev took him and Chukovsky for a trip on the Black River in his motor-launch, presumably in 1909 or 1910, and proceeded to describe to them his conception: 'In his verbal rendering of that which was still in the process of being written, Andreyev appeared before us as an astonishing narrator. He was creating before our eyes and, as it subsequently turned out, it was during this trip in the boat that he developed many of the details of the work.'[2] Thus the impression is given that Andreyev was almost starting afresh. Unfortunately, Brusyanin does not mention the points of divergence between this verbal variant and the final version, but from Chukovsky's reference to the same episode it appears that the difference of 'idea' was negligible; when discussing the difference he mentions only the rhetorical nature of the final version; he writes: 'In his exposition I liked "The Ocean", but when the play appeared in print, it turned out that it was unrelieved rhetoric and, in addition, extremely trite.'[3]

Not a few of Andreyev's contemporaries have recorded similar discrepancies between his verbal improvisations on the schemes that momentarily absorbed him and the literary end-products in which they crystallized. Tolstoy, for instance, after criticizing severely the Prologue of *Anathema*, remarked to Chertkov: 'And yet when he described the content to me, something good emerged.'[4]

---

[1] See F. Nietzsche, *Thus Spake Zarathustra* (translated from the German by A. Tille), London and Leipzig, 1908, p. 315.

[2] *BSN*, p. 23.

[3] K. Chukovsky, 'Leonid Andreyev', in his *Iz vospominaniy*, M., 1958, p. 263.

[4] V. G. Chertkov, 'Zapisi', *L. N. Tolstoy v vospominaniyakh sovremennikov*, vol. 2, M., 1960, p. 48. Though Tolstoy was bitterly critical of the form of *Anathema* and indeed of Andreyev's whole conception (see V. Bulgakov, *L. N. Tolstoy v posledniy god ego zhizni*, M., 1957, p. 245), it occupied, according to Beklemisheva, a place on the shelf at Yasnaya Polyana which was kept for 'special' books (see *Rekviem*, p. 243). It is necessary to add, however, that most of the pages of the volume containing the work, which can still be seen at Yasnaya Polyana, are uncut (see V. I. Ulybyshev, 'Tvorchestvo L. Andreyeva

Similar is Veresaev's comment on Andreyev's description to him of his plan for *Tsar Hunger*: 'In its original rendering it seemed more vivid and magnificent to me than in its realised form.'[1] In the majority of cases no one was more conscious of this failing than Andreyev himself; this is particularly true, as we have seen, so far as *The Ocean* is concerned.

The final version of the play was written feverishly by Andreyev in the space of two weeks. 'He hurried about his study as though raving, his hair on end, his eyes burning,' writes Skitalets, recording the words of Anna Il'inichna.[2] He laid considerable hopes on its production, but again he suffered at the hands of the censor and had to be satisfied with a few performances in the south. Once more he paid the penalty for introducing a 'religious' element into his works.

In the figure of Khaggart, the pirate-captain piloting his ship with its black sails over the ocean, Andreyev embodies his grossly simplified conception of the 'superman', of the 'will to power' incarnate, unfettered by dogma and rational considerations. The guiding principle of Khaggart's life is an undeviating adherence to the elemental truth of life. He is a transfiguration of nature, and his roving over the ocean 'in quest of the sun' is the roving or flux of existence itself in its cyclic evolution.

For no apparent reason, however, he suddenly interrupts his quest and settles with his boatswain, Khorre, in a derelict castle on the shore. The explanation is furnished some time later in the play—in Khaggart's account of his execution of a group of prisoners and of the reaction of one of them. 'I saw a man burning,' he says, 'tied to the mast. Just think! His hair was crackling, but he sang and laughed as though he were at a wedding.'[3] Andreyev says nothing more about the prisoner, but one can assume that this episode is intended to represent a head-on clash between his own ideal and that of Nietzsche, between the 'son of eternity' and the 'superman'. This disregard for life in its immediacy has a disquieting effect on Khaggart and he retires to the shore to contemplate it. Now his

---

v otsenke Tolstogo', *Yasnopolyanskiy sbornik. Stat'i i materialy. God 60–y*, Tula, 1960, p. 152). There is no reference by memoirists to any discussion of the work by the two writers when Andreyev stayed at Yasnaya Polyana on 21 and 22 April 1910.

[1] *VRSV*, p. 468.    [2] Skitalets, op. cit., p. 404.    [3] *Works* II, p. 207.

'oceanic truth' clashes with a new truth, the 'truth of the shore', and at this point the attitudes of Andreyev and Nietzsche momentarily coincide. The shore is the habitat of the 'herd' presented in the form of fishermen, who also roam the ocean, i.e. life, but only in order to catch fish, i.e. to exist. The vulgar chatter of the women in Act I is strongly reminiscent of the first Picture of *The Life of Man*. The striving of the organist Dan—the counterpart of the organ-grinder in *Anathema*—to drown with his chords the powerful music of the ocean, epitomizes the philistinism, narrowness and slavery of life in this land of petty passions and superstitions.

Yet another attitude to life is introduced in the person of the Abbot, who represents the Christian ethic as distinct from the Christian dogma. His contemptuous attitude to the latter is marked by the 'curse in Latin' with which he replies to his excommunication by the Pope for begetting a daughter. Though his scorn for the fishermen is no less than that of Khaggart, he appoints himself their protector and shuns no means of fulfilling his task. At the same time he admires Khaggart's strength and is unable to reconcile in himself these conflicting sympathies. His life is an agony of contradiction which wrings from his lips the cry: 'O Lord! Why have you given me a heart which can pity both the murdered and the murderer?'[1] In the figure of the Abbot Andreyev does not reject the Christian ethic, but exposes it as ineffective. The altruism of the Abbot achieves the sole end of preserving the fishermen in their philistine *modus vivendi*. He is incapable of bridging the gulf between the fishermen and life, the shore and the ocean, and stands between them inclining now towards the one, now towards the other.

Between Khaggart and the Abbot stands the latter's daughter Mariet, through whom the playwright pronounces his judgement on both. Mariet, not Khaggart, is for this reason the central character of the play. The demands which she makes of life and the truth which she seeks are the yardstick by which the other 'truths' are assessed. Appalled by the cowardice with which the fishermen react to the arrival of the pirates, she rebels against the shore. No longer can she sympathize with the aims and beliefs of her father. In Khaggart she encounters the strength and resolve, the lack of which she bewails in the fishermen, and she announces her readiness to sail with him beneath the black sails in search of another god.

[1] Ibid., p. 244.

'He who makes people cowards is not God,' she proclaims.[1] She marries Khaggart, with her father's blessing, and bears his son, Noni.

Although she severs herself from the fishermen, however, she cannot cut the bond which ties her to her father, and the values of the latter are refined in her into an acute sensitivity to injustice. Her marriage to Khaggart signifies a momentary harmony between two philosophies of life founded on the points which they have in common, but these points in common are outweighed by their points of divergence, which have their source in radically different attitudes to man. While for Khaggart justice is a human concept, a concept of 'the shore', for Mariet and her creator it is a basic law of life which exists independently of the individual, and infraction of this law is a crime against life which must be avenged. When the Abbot is murdered by Khorre, therefore, and Khaggart makes only a feeble pretence of punishing the culprit, Mariet rejects him as uncompromisingly as she does the fishermen. As he puts out to sea, she stands on the shore cursing him and threatening him with the vengeance of her son, in whom the ideal qualities of strength and justice will coexist in harmony. On this optimistic note of belief in the possibility of synthesis ends what we might term Andreyev's 'second period'.

[1] Ibid., p. 248.

# PART IV

## *The Tragedy of the Idealist: 1912–1919*

---

### XVI

### THE IDEALIST AND SOCIETY

OST of the major works of Andreyev's last years have certain features in common which give them a unity within the general unity of his fiction. Though they constantly remind the reader of works of both the preceding periods, this does not fully justify the statement of Kaun that during these years 'Andreyev created nothing that was new in form or in motive'. Sakhnovsky wrote aptly in his highly contradictory article: 'Remaining within one unchanging category of world-philosophy from the first day of his life as a writer, he makes ever more complex the form in which he expresses his thoughts and feelings, his disclosure of the unchanging and mysterious content of life which he divines as an artist, and herein lies his power, complexity and interest as a master of his art.'[1] These words were written in 1916 and their truth will be seen in our examination of the main works written by Andreyev from 1912 onward. The spring of Andreyev's talent was far from exhausted, and the facility with which he devised new schemes weakened only towards the end of his life under the burden of failing health and the pressure of deeply experienced events.

Even in the years 1912–13 his health was on the verge of total collapse. At first the Salamandra insurance company of St. Petersburg refused to insure his life, and did so in the end only because of the advertising value.[2] He wrote to Belousov in 1913: 'I have

[1] V. Sakhnovsky, 'Pisatel' bez dogmata. (Osnovnye motivy tvorchestva Leonida Andreyeva)', *Novaya zhizn'*, alm. I, M., 1916, p. 186.

[2] See F. N. Fal'kovsky, 'Predsmertnaya tragediya Leonida Andreyeva. (Iz vospominaniy)', *Prozhektor*, 1923, No. 16, p. 27.

tired fantastically over the last six years—as though I have spent six years running without interruption on a rope.'[1] He took care to point out, however, that no change had taken place in his fundamental beliefs; he wrote to Gorky in a letter of 12 August 1911— his first letter to him since 23 March 1908:[2]

Of course, bitterness has been added with the years; I've become sadder, darker, as if I had donned mourning, but this relates more to my personal life, my character, than to my views. I think, however, that even in my personal life, under somewhat more favourable conditions, I could return to my former gaiety, my insatiable and gay longing to live. Recent years have tormented me, and very frequent headaches make me unbearably gloomy.[3]

In similar vein he wrote to Goloushev: 'It needs only completely healthy, red blood to run through my body for every little part of my brain and heart to start radiating thoughts, images, a universal hallelujah.'[4]

During these moments of 'radiation' his thoughts with few exceptions found expression in this last period in dramatic form. Since 1908 all his most important works had been plays, and this trend continues. He wrote to Goloushev in 1914: 'I am totally preoccupied with dramatic images; neither psychologically nor even physically have I been able to devote a single thought to anything else.'[5] Indicative of this preoccupation are his *Letters on the Theatre* (*Pis'ma o teatre*), unique productions on Andreyev's part inasmuch as they are entirely theoretical. The first letter appeared in the March 1912 number of the journal *Maski* ('Masks'), edited by Fyodor Komissarzhevsky, and was republished together with a second 'letter' in 1914 in the twenty-second volume of *Shipovnik*. It will suffice to mention here that the first letter, which was written before his next three plays—*Professor Storitsyn*, *Ekaterina Ivanovna* and *Thou Shalt Not Kill* (*Ne ubiy*)—contains his call for a more psychological drama. 'Life has gone inward,' he states, 'but the stage

---

[1] *Rekviem*, p. 69.
[2] Not counting a one-line telegram of 11 November 1910.
[3] *LN*, p. 313.
[4] *Rekviem*, p. 95.
[5] Ibid., pp. 95–6. This statement was not strictly true, for he was also devoting much time to painting and in 1913 some of his canvases were displayed at an exhibition in St. Petersburg (cf. Belousov, op. cit., p. 151; Kleynbort, loc. cit., p. 169; and *LN*, p. 76).

has remained on the threshold.'[1] Life itself has evolved a new protagonist—the mind, and if the stage is to be a mirror of life, it must renounce the antiquated 'drama of spectacle' and elevate the mind 'in its joys, sufferings and struggle'[2] to its rightful position of primacy. External action must be supplanted by subtle psychological movement, noise by the silence of the study. A reflection of the development of Andreyev's thoughts on this question is his resurrection and dramatization of *Thought* in 1914.

A feature of the three plays of the years 1912–13 which distinguishes them from their immediate predecessors is their more obvious topicality. The particular and concrete are no longer completely submerged by the general and abstract, but rather coexist with them, the result of which is that the element of social criticism is much more overt than in the works of the pre-1905 period. This development in his art is marked by a complete reversal of the basic formula of the works of the early period. Now it is the individual who embodies and gives voice to the author's ideals, while the 'apostate' is society.

Andreyev's increased preoccupation with topical issues also manifests itself in the number of satirical trifles which flowed from his pen during these years, most of which are thinly disguised political or social indictments, e.g. *The Death of Gulliver (Smert' Gullivera)* (1911), *The Pretty Sabine Women (Prekrasnye sabinyanki)* (1911), *A Horse in the Senate (Kon' v senate)* (1915) and *The Monument (Monument)* (1916). The greater prominence of the social element explains in particular the anger which, on the evidence of Ivanov-Razumnik, *Professor Storitsyn* aroused when it was performed in the south,[3] and, in general, the keen public reaction to the major plays of these immediate pre-war years. His every work continued to be an event. 'As yet there is no evidence of a decline in his popularity,' wrote one American critic in February 1914, 'though it was predicted years ago by competent and favourable critics.'[4] Nevertheless, this same critic errs when he states that in these plays 'the larger problems are either altogether wanting or

[1] L. N. Andreyev, 'Pis'ma o teatre', *Literaturno-khudozhestvennye al'manakhi izdatel'stva 'Shipovnik'*, vol. 22, SPb., 1914, p. 232.

[2] Ibid.

[3] See R. V. Ivanov-Razumnik (Skif), 'Tlennoe i netlennoe. (O "Professore Storitsyne")', *Zavety*, 1913, No. 1, p. 155.

[4] T. Seltzer, 'Leonid Andreyev', *The Drama*, 1914, No. 13, February, p. 7.

occupy a secondary position'.[1] The public certainly lost sight of them behind the screen of social comment, but the problems raised by Andreyev continue to overlap purely topical terms of reference, and there is no doubt that his overriding interest lay, as in the past, in this extension. This is particularly manifest in *Professor Storitsyn*, in which the topical theme and the 'larger problem' are developed through two separate relationships.

Andreyev wrote to Gouloushev in 1912: 'In general, if you wish to distinguish Russia and things Russian from Europe, which it has come to resemble so closely that they are like two peas, then add to every word: boorish.'[2] On all sides he saw evidence of a coarsening of social manners and of the intrusion of a contagious vulgarity into Russian social life during the years immediately preceding the outbreak of the Great War. In *Professor Storitsyn*, which, written in 1912, was ultimately published in 1913 in the eleventh *Zemlya* almanac, he portrays this social disease in the figure of Savvich, and the conflict between Savvich and the protagonist is a conflict between the prevailing coarseness of life and idealism. It is the conflict of Chekhov's *The Three Sisters*. Nor does the resemblance rest there. Andreyev takes, for instance, the same symbolic battlefield as his predecessor—the house of the idealist. The conquest of the house of the sisters by Natasha and her unseen ally Protopopov has its counterpart in the hounding of Storitsyn from his house by Savvich; the expulsion in both cases denotes the triumph of ugliness and vulgarity over beauty and idealism, although Andreyev invests the dénouement with a significance which is not encountered in Chekhov's play. The most obvious difference lies in the methods of conquest. That of Natasha is a victory of serpent-like infiltration; Savvich, on the other hand, conquers with the fist. K. Narodin, the critic who reviewed the play for *Sovremennyy mir*, made the following comments on the significance of Savvich:

The fist of Savvich has become the nightmare of our life. In what sphere has he not shown himself to be conqueror and master? Is it not Savvich who has turned himself into a deputy of the Russian parliament and hurled dirt at the Russian woman and Russian youth? Is it not Savvich who has trampled on whole nationalities, stamping with the heels of his boots on religion, culture and language? Is it not Savvich who has armed himself with a truncheon and beaten defenceless citizens on the streets of the cities? Is it not Savvich who has thirsted for blood and called for

[1] Ibid., p. 10.   [2] *Rekviem*, p. 92.

pogroms against the Jews? . . . Slowly but surely he has poisoned all our life, crawled into all its corners and made this life coarse, ugly and ignoble.[1]

These words convey the power of Andreyev's symbol and the impact which it made; the play was invariably performed to a full house both at the Aleksandrinsky Theatre in St. Petersburg and the Malyy Theatre in Moscow.[2] The true source of alarm was not so much Savvich himself, for he is at least open in his vulgarity, but the ubiquitousness of 'savvichism', which is represented in the play by the varying measure in which the *malaise* exists in the other characters.

The broader, philosophical problem debated in the play emerges directly from this topical theme and is developed primarily through the clash between Storitsyn and his life-long friend Telemakhov, a military man and, like Kerzhentsev, a doctor of medicine. The issues involved are basically the same as those which underlie the antagonism between Judas and Jesus, and the philosophical theme of *Darkness* is plainly discernible. In his youth Telemakhov, we are told, was an idealist like Storitsyn, but a series of misfortunes breaks his faith in life. His wife betrays him, they part, and he is left with the onus of supplying her with a regular monthly allowance. Like his marriage, his scholarship is also unrewarded with success. His ideals collapse and he emerges in the play as the voice of the sober, positivist view of life, though his addiction to wine remains as both a sign of his disillusionment and a symbol of the unsound basis of the view of life to which he gives expression. He makes it his task to open Storitsyn's eyes to life as it really is, i.e. as it presents itself to the realist. Storitsyn is the complete opposite of his friend. He lives in a world of ideal essences, and his cult of beauty and the 'imperishable' has made him a European celebrity. Loss of contact with the reality of life, however, renders his idealism sterile, as it does that of the terrorist in *Darkness*. While he contemplates the 'imperishable', Savvich gains control of his house and wife. It is to Savvich, therefore, that Telemakhov aims to open his eyes. In this way the topical and philosophical levels of the play are dovetailed.

[1] K. Narodin, 'Krasota i kham. (L. Andreyev. "Professor Storitsyn" i "Ekaterina Ivanovna")', *Sovremennyy mir*, 1914, No. 5, pp. 40–1.
[2] See E. Beskin, 'Moskovskie pis'ma', *Teatr i iskusstvo*, 1913, No. 1, p. 11.

So far as the playwright's attitude to Storitsyn is concerned, Act I is strongly reminiscent of the early part of *Darkness*. The Professor's detachment from life and the ineffectiveness of his idealism are the pivotal themes. In Act II, however, Andreyev's attitude changes with the addition of a new dimension to the character of his hero. Though continuing to preach his beliefs, the Professor is portrayed as slowly succumbing to the disillusionment which has transformed the character of Telemakhov. 'I do not know where the graves of my hopes and joys are,' he announces to his 'disciple', Princess Lyudmila Pavlovna; 'they are scattered over the whole world. Sometimes the whole world is only a cemetery for me, while I am the dumb watchman of the graves.'[1] But immediately he returns to his favourite theme: "Today a curtain has fallen away from the world, and I see the imperishable in everything.'[2] He struggles to maintain his faith; rhetoric yields to conviction, profound feeling, inner drama. The gulf between the Professor and the reality of life is progressively narrowed; it is a gradual process, not a sudden collision such as that presented in *Darkness*, with the result that his psychological reaction is more clearly motivated than that of the terrorist. His momentary capitulation to despair in Act III is precipitated by the news brought by Telemakhov at the conclusion of Act II that Elena Petrovna, Storitsyn's wife, has frittered away their meagre capital on the stock-exchange and plunged him into debt. Telemakhov takes advantage of the situation to reproach his whole way of life, but Andreyev's sympathy is now wholly with Storitsyn, and when Telemakhov remarks, 'Even every cat on the staircase knows that you have fallen as though from heaven,' the playwright makes him add: 'But I am a biologist and realist—I apologise.'[3] From the beginning Storitsyn voices the ideals of his creator, but ideals must be fought for if they are to have any real value for life, and the Professor is redeemed by his suffering.

The house of Storitsyn is now wholly in the power of Savvich, who alone can pay the debt. The degree of Elena Petrovna's subservience to the will of Savvich is conveyed by the conversation between them with which Act III opens. This is the first of the four conversations in this Act which finally close the gap between Storitsyn and the reality of the situation and bring him to that state of utter despair which is experienced by the terrorist in the

[1] *Works* VIII, p. 266.     [2] Ibid.     [3] Ibid., p. 273.

wake of Lyuba's crucial question. The *coup de grâce* is the Professor's confrontation with his son Sergey, who with his low, flat forehead and bestial jaws—reminiscent of the workers in *Tsar Hunger* —is both a symbol of the young generation growing up under the influence of 'savvichism' and a living indictment of his father's past. This confrontation is the counterpart of the reproaches to which the 'false' Lorenzo in *The Black Masks* is compelled to listen as he lies in his coffin.

Even in this final scene of Act III, however, in which Storitsyn surrenders to self-degradation, he does not completely forsake his dignity and nobility and, according to Batyushkov, Apollonsky, in his generally applauded rendering of the role in the Aleksandrinsky Theatre's 1912 production, took care to observe this point;[1] it foreshadows the dénouement of the play and the 'philosophical' conclusion in Act IV. Storitsyn abandons his house and seeks refuge in the apartment of Telemakhov. The latter naturally sees this event as the most blatant vindication of his positivism and misanthropy. Once more the realist and the idealist clash on the point of man's essential nature. Telemakhov makes his position clear: '. . . you simply do not want to lower your gaze to the earth, but I am a realist, I am a biologist and realist! I have no wish to know your unreal values. Fly in the heavens, but I hold firmly on to the earth and will not release it, and I know that we, all the Professors Telemakhov and Storitsyn, are alone on this night among a pack of wolves.'[2] The misanthropic view of man is again juxtaposed as an expression of self-assertion with the principle of self-transcendence. 'You yourself are alone and unfortunate,' replies Storitsyn. 'I pity you. . . . It is a lie, Telemakhov! There is no Storitsyn; he is a phantom and illusion.'[3] The spirit of Storitsyn has survived the encounter with empirical reality, the 'perishable', and rises above it to merge with the life of the universe. Herein lies the philosophical, as distinct from the social, significance of his abandonment of his house. 'Our house, yours and mine,' he says to the Princess, 'is the whole world.'[4] On the 'physical' plane rules the spirit of 'savvichism', with which positivism itself, in the person of Telemakhov, now becomes synonymous—such is the import of the scene in this

---

[1] See F. Batyushkov, 'Okolo pravdy. (Po povodu dramy Leonida Andreyeva "Professor Storitsyn")', *Ezhegodnik Imperatorskikh Teatrov*, 1913, No. 1, p. 130.
[2] *Works* VIII, p. 296.　　[3] Ibid.　　[4] Ibid., p. 299.

final Act in which Telemakhov arranges the thrashing of Savvich by his batman and Volodya, Storitsyn's elder son. Storitsyn listens to the scene in anguish and moves to leave this house which has fallen prey to the same spirit of darkness as his own. He steps forth 'blind to his surroundings, terrible with his expression of concentration and complete renunciation of the visible',[1] but he reaches no further than the door before he falls and dies. The burden of the body is shed and the spirit emerges free to blend with the storm raging without. Behind him remains the Princess—the counterpart of the resurrected Lyuba and the unborn child of Lorenzo—as the living assurance of the immortality of his ideals and achievement. The play ends, like *Anathema*, with the positivist gazing on incredulous and pitiful.

Hitherto this work has remained unappreciated as a typical expression of Andreyev's 'transcendent optimism'. It was the 'social theme' which claimed the public's attention, and the philosophical debate between Storitsyn and Telemakhov was eclipsed by the massive presence of Savvich. Moreover, the 'social' fate of Storitsyn was viewed by many as symbolic of the fate of Andreyev himself; the play seemed to symbolize his forced descent from the clouds, from the abstraction of *Anathema* and *The Ocean*, and the writer Aleksandr Kipen records that the actor who played Storitsyn at Odessa was made up to look exactly like Andreyev—an improvisation, he adds, which 'the main local newspaper regarded with complete approval'.[2] Once more the source of misunderstanding was failure to determine the precise nature of Andreyev's understanding of life. In his next play, *Ekaterina Ivanovna*, which made an even greater impact on the public, he again gave the appearance of 'stepping somewhat aside', to use Beklemisheva's expression,[3] in the sense that abstract problems seemed to be forsaken for social comment; once more, however, appearances are deceptive.

---

[1] Ibid., p. 304.   [2] *Rekviem*, p. 191.   [3] Ibid., p. 253.

# XVII

## CONFLICT BETWEEN THE SEXES

WE have seen that in *The Abyss* and *In the Fog* the problem of sex is presented by Andreyev as a particularly expressive focal point of a broader social-psychological problem which is appraised in the light of fixed philosophical convictions. Radically different was the treatment which it received in the literature of the years following the first revolution. The wave of disillusionment with civic or public ideals which swept the intelligentsia after the débâcle of 1906 served to undermine further the dykes erected by despairing defenders of the traditional principles of morality, and the principle of civic responsibility gave way to that of anti-political individualism and a desire for freedom from all moral restrictions. A superficial Nietzscheanism exalting the qualities of naturalness and obedience to the instincts acquired sway over the minds of contemporary youth and rapidly engendered an almost pathological preoccupation with sex. Literature naturally responded to this social mood and writers looked back for inspiration to Andreyev's two stories of 1902, the clearest evidence of which is Potapenko's *A Story of One Youth* (*Istoriya odnoy molodosti*), a pastiche of *In the Fog*, which appeared in serialized form in the August, September and October 1907 numbers of *Sovremennyy mir*. 'In no other period has there been such general pilfering of methods and devices, plots and themes, epithets and characters as there is now,' wrote one critic in 1909.[1] One loses sight of any 'technical' debt, however, in the difference of spirit and 'philosophy' which characterizes these works. Artsybashev's *Sanin*, Sologub's *Fairy Magic* (*Nav'i chary*), Verbitskaya's *The Keys of Happiness* (*Klyuchi schast'ya*), Nagrodskaya's *The Wrath of Dionysus* (*Gnev Dionisa*), Kamensky's *Leda*, Kuzmin's *Wings* (*Kryl'ya*), and Chirikov's *Exile* (*Izgnanie*) and *Return* (*Vozvrashchenie*)—all served to confirm the prevailing conviction that sexual desire is the only reality.

In view of Andreyev's sensitivity to significant changes in the social mood, it would seem natural to see his play *Anfisa* (1909) as

[1] P. Pilsky, *Problema pola, polovye avtory i polovoy geroy*, SPb., 1909, p. 22.

a response to this trend. Bishop Germogen pronounced him guilty in the play of 'conscious preaching of perversion and abominable sins'.[1] In moments of frankness Andreyev confessed, according to Beklemisheva, that he wrote his 'realistic' plays, of which *Anfisa*, in addition to *Days of Our Life* (1908) and *Gaudeamus* (1910), was considered an example despite the isolated symbolic image of the grandmother, 'for the broad public to whom his tragedies were foreign and incomprehensible'.[2] But his attitude towards the problem of sex was much too serious to admit of frivolous treatment of it in his fiction, and there is ample evidence of this seriousness in *Anfisa*. For most of the authors named above he had nothing but contempt. 'Artsybashev,' he said to Brusyanin, 'will begin at the hips, describe everything in detail and stop at the neck. All his heroes in "Sanin" are headless.'[3] Again, in a letter to Belousov of 1914 we find him reproaching Aleksey Tolstoy for abusing the theme of sex in his works,[4] and a year later, in a letter to the actress E. A. Polevitskaya in connection with his play *He Who Gets Slapped* (*Tot, kto poluchaet poshchochiny*), he states that it is polemically directed against the vulgarization of the 'very concept of love' by Artsybashev and Surguchov in their dramas *Jealousy* (*Revnost'*) and *Autumn Violins* (*Osennie skripki*).[5]

Like Bryusov's story *The Sisters* (*Syostry*) in his cycle *The Earth's Axis*, *Anfisa* tells of the love of three sisters for one man. The latter, Kostomarov, bears a resemblance both to Bryusov's Nikolay and to Artsybashev's Sanin; he is a rebel against conventional morality and his rebellion manifests itself |in gross licentiousness. While Sanin emerges as a positive hero, however, Kostomarov is devoid of redeeming features. The first variant of the play, entitled *The Master* (*Gospodin*), was dominated by the figure of Kostomarov and was probably, in consequence, entirely polemical. But once again Andreyev superimposed an abstract philosophical idea on the social-psychological theme and the result was the growth

---

[1] 'Ep. Germogen ob "Anateme" i "Anfise"', *Teatr i iskusstvo*, 1910, No. 2, p. 36.
[2] *Rekviem*, p. 239. Andreyev himself remarked in connection with *Days of Our Life* in an undated letter to Kugel' written shortly after the completion of the play (most probably in October 1908): 'I am very pleased that you like the play, though I myself regard it as a trifle' ('Pis'ma Leonida Andreyeva A. R. Kugelyu', *Rabochiy i teatr*, 1934, No. 27, p. 18). In a letter of 3 October 1908 to Komissarzhevskaya he referred to it as 'unsophisticated, realistic, extremely simple' (see 'V. F. Komissarzhevskaya i simvolisty', *Teatr*, 1940, No. 2, p. 115).
[3] *BSN*, p. 78.    [4] See *Rekviem*, p. 71.
[5] See *Leonid Andreyev. P'esy*, M., 1959, p. 581.

in importance of the figure of Anfisa, the sister who stands between Kostomarov's wife Aleksandra and the youngest sister Ninochka. A variation of this idea was subsequently to be presented in *Ekaterina Ivanovna* which, written in 1912, was published in 1913 in the nineteenth volume of *Shipovnik*. Since it was Andreyev's unrealized intention to follow *Anfisa* with a sequel entitled *The Judgement on Anfisa* (*Sud nad Anfisoy*), it is possible that *Ekaterina Ivanovna* grew, in part, out of this conception.

In both plays the conflict between the sexes is the form in which Andreyev presents the conflict between life and the 'apostate'. The contrast, hinted in former works, between the 'feminine' principle of instinct and intuitive knowledge and the 'masculine' principle of self-assertion, self-gratification and amoral reason forms in both cases the philosophical and thematic basis. The action of *Anfisa*[1] can be briefly summarized. The heroine comes to Kostomarov already defiled by her marriage to an officer in Smolensk, which leaves her overcome with shame and disgust. In Kostomarov she finds a man who, she believes, values her 'feminine truth' and she gives herself to him unreservedly. But once more she is deceived by the corrupt 'masculine' principle which is ever seeking to spread the contagion of its influence. It espies its next victim in Ninochka, who, like her sisters, succumbs to the deception and is on the point of total submission when life or the subconscious, in the symbolic guise of the mute grandmother, rises to defend itself and decrees the destruction of the profaner through the agency of instinct incarnated in Anfisa. While Bryusov's Mara kills her two sisters in order to enjoy alone the caresses of Nikolay, Anfisa strikes at the source of the perversion, and the poisoning of Kostomarov has the same philosophical significance as the assassination of the Governor. In *Ekaterina Ivanovna* this same conflict between the sexes becomes a powerful instrument of social indictment.

'The judgements pronounced by the public on the principal characters of his plays ("Anfisa", "Ekaterina Ivanovna"),' writes Beklemisheva, 'both amused and delighted him as evidence that his readers and audience were agitated by the themes on which he touched.'[2] Nevertheless, Andreyev expressed to Gorky his dis-

---

[1] The play was produced in 1909 at the Dramatic Theatre in St. Petersburg, with Samoylov as Kostomarov and Golubyova as Anfisa, and in 1910 at Nezlobin's Theatre in Moscow.

[2] *Rekviem*, p. 242.

satisfaction with *Anfisa*. '. . . I just didn't succeed with it,' he wrote in a letter of December 1912.[1] His attitude to *Ekaterina Ivanovna* was quite different, for in this play he felt that he had successfully realized the ideal of an intensely psychological drama which he had established for himself in the first of his *Letters on the Theatre*; he wrote in the second 'letter': 'I cannot but say, wishing to be sincere, that I consider my drama "Katerina Ivanovna", despite its vicissitudes of fortune, to be a new drama.'[2]

The play presents the tragedy of woman in a masculine world. Andreyev conceived of his heroine as the elevating spirit of 'dance', as the bearer of a specific 'rhythm' which is disrupted by the forces of the life which she enters. He wrote to Nemirovich-Danchenko, who produced the play at the Moscow Art Theatre: 'She had come to *dance* in life where others did not dance. Instead of dancing, they jostled and elbowed one another. . . . She lost her rhythm and she commenced to whirl ever more rapidly.'[3] As in *Professor Storitsyn*, the twin elements of social criticism and philosophical idea are fused into an indissoluble whole. The former is realized in a way which distinguishes it from the corresponding element in the earlier play. We have seen that in the figure of Savvich Andreyev presents in exaggerated form a social *malaise* which reveals itself in other characters in the play also; there is both Savvich and 'savvichism'. There is no centrifugal force, however, radiating outward from Mentikov, in whom the social indictment is centralized in *Ekaterina Ivanovna*. He is presented as a being who simply by virtue of his existence condemns the society which tolerates him. 'Like a parasite, he exists only as a result of our uncleanliness,' says Georgiy Dmitrievich Stibelev, the husband of the heroine. 'If he is allowed to crawl he will crawl, and if he is forbidden, he will crawl in another direction. And he is always there, always seeking, always at the ready.'[4] At the opposite end of the moral scale stands Ekaterina Ivanovna, femininity incarnate with all its symbolic connotations. Between the two of them Andreyev places a cross-section of the intelligentsia—Stibelev, a deputy in the Duma, his brother Alyosha, Koromyslov, a society artist, and a host of students and other artists. The significance of this character-alignment is clear.

---

[1] *LN*, p. 351.    [2] 'Pis'ma o teatre', p. 261.
[3] Quoted from H. Bernstein's Preface to his translation of *Ekaterina Ivanovna*, New York, 1923, p. vii.
[4] Works VIII, p. 208.

Mentikov and Ekaterina represent incompatible principles; the existence of the one necessarily entails the extinction of the other; a society which tolerates Mentikov thereby sentences Ekaterina to spiritual death. Her fall symbolizes the rejection of the higher 'feminine' truth of life by the rational, egoistic 'masculine' principle. Only by reference to these ideas can her actions and fate be plausibly explained.

The divorce between external and inner action is established at once. The three shots which Stibelev fires at his wife at the very beginning of the play miss her physically, but inflict a fatal wound on her soul. The motive is his unsubstantiated suspicion that she has committed adultery with Mentikov. The suspicion itself denotes the incompatibility of the heroine and her environment, and this disharmony is externalized in the 'unpleasant asymmetry' of the setting to which reference is made in the opening stage-remark.[1]

The action of Act II takes place six months later and the setting is the estate of Ekaterina's mother, to which the heroine fled with her children on the fateful night of the shooting. She is pursued there by Mentikov, with whom, we learn, she has since committed adultery, the result of which was pregnancy and an abortion. Thus the sin with which she is charged by her husband becomes reality after the charge is made. Her submission to Mentikov is not so much a reaction to the accusation and the shooting, however, as a reflection of their consequences. The spirit of Ekaterina is dying, and only her body remains at the mercy of the 'masculine' world in which she lives. The act of adultery is the symbol of Mentikov's triumph over her. Repeatedly in this Act she refers to her death. 'I am dead, I am in the grave,' she says to Mentikov,[2] and to Alyosha she says of herself: 'She no longer exists, Alesha; she was killed before your eyes.'[3] Her lament is interrrupted by the appearance of a contrite Stibelev who implores her to return to him. For a brief moment she beguiles herself with the hope of a possible resurrection, especially when he informs her that he has come not 'for that'. The rest of the Act, however, belies these words and reveals his contrition to be a mask of desire. Towards the end of the Act the dichotomy of the heroine is magnificently portrayed—between her avid desire for resurrection and her progressive loss of control over her body. A stage-direction reads: 'She stands before him, erect and with her arms thrown back, as if she is about to fly or fall into

---

[1] See ibid., p. 180.     [2] Ibid., p. 200.     [3] Ibid., p. 203.

an abyss.'[1] In a last despairing attempt to convey to him her inner drama she has recourse to the 'higher language' of music. But it is too late; the incipient spell is broken by the entry of Mentikov and hope is extinguished.

Two years elapse between Acts II and III. In Acts III and IV we see only the body of Ekaterina in the 'abyss' into which it has fallen. Again and again her body is defiled, for this is all that is demanded of her in this masculine world. The masculine-feminine antithesis on which the whole work pivots is clearly formulated in Koromyslov's remarks to Stibelev towards the end of Act III:

In Katerina Ivanovna there is too much of this—how might I put it to you without distorting my meaning?—female, feminine element, that which belongs solely to them, in brief. . . . She lies to me also, though, it seems, for no reason. And you and I, Georgiy Dmitrievich, think that they are lies, but they mean simply that she does not believe in logic, just as you do not believe in the devil; she does not believe in your external world, your facts, because she has her own world. Understand her, if you wish to![2]

But no one wishes to, and in vain she cries out for the head of a prophet in Act IV when forced in a grotesque scene to perform Salome's dance—a symbolic vilification of the principle of 'dance' with which she sought to enrich life—by the corrupt gathering of artists and musicians assembled in Koromyslov's studio. Her husband stands meekly by, and when she is finally dragged away by one of this debauched company, it is he who kneels to put on her shoes. The play ends logically with the remark of Mentikov: 'Our Ekaterina Ivanovna has gone.'[3] His triumph is complete.

The play gave rise to abundant and varied critical comment. Its defenders were heavily outnumbered. Especially severe, as usual, were the Kievan critics.[4] An animated debate was conducted on the pages of *Teatr i iskusstvo*. One of the first to rise to its defence was Sologub, with whom Andreyev had developed a close friendship during their period of collaboration on the editorial board of *Shipovnik*, but he does little more than discuss general questions of theatre 'ethics', disputing the very legitimacy of discussing the merits and demerits of the protagonists of drama, whose effusions on the stage in complete spiritual nakedness he sees almost as

---

[1] Ibid., p. 209.  [2] Ibid., pp. 227–8.  [3] Ibid., p. 243.
[4] See *Rekviem*, p. 69.

religious acts of contrition not to be blasphemed by mundane judgement.[1] His article was followed shortly afterwards by a broadside from Kugel', according to whom Andreyev, like Tolstoy, reveals a conception of adultery as transgression of a 'mystical limit', beyond which lies the downward path to inevitable destruction; he then echoes Lunacharsky's comments on *The Governor* with his criticism of the psychological motivation of the heroine's actions.[2] The defect of this interpretation is that it lays the guilt on Ekaterina and takes into account neither the element of social criticism nor Andreyev's explicit statement of the symbolic-philosophical significance of the conflict between the sexes. This misplacement of guilt was rectified by Prince N. M. Volkonsky in his defence of the work and its heroine,[3] yet even here no explanation is offered to satisfy the critics of the psychological aspect of the work, as was correctly pointed out by another reviewer.[4] The debate presents another example of the dilemma to which criticism was inevitably brought when ignoring the fact that Andreyev's characters, however realistically they are depicted, are almost always symbols of abstract entities, while their drama is invariably a philosophical allegory. It may be argued, of course, that Andreyev himself claimed to have created specifically a *psychological* drama, but he was mistaken in his claim. As always, the motivation of the action is to be sought wholly in the substratum of ideas, and as on numerous other occasions, Andreyev fails to reconcile this motivation with plausible human experience.

For Andreyev's final word on his heroine, which seems to be a direct riposte to the view put forward by Kugel', we must turn to the question she puts in the speech of self-defence which he prepared for her and which was discovered among his posthumous papers by Bernstein: 'Has the human conscience been blunted to such an extent, or are the conceptions of justice, of good and evil, so confused, that the innocent victim is on trial, while the murderers and hangmen are pitied, praised, and permitted to remain undis-

[1] F. Sologub, 'Prizyomistye sudyat', *Teatr i iskusstvo*, 1913, No. 7, pp. 162–4.
[2] See A. R. Kugel' (Homo Novus), 'Zametki', *Teatr i iskusstvo*, 1913, No. 14, p. 324.
[3] See N. M. Volkonsky, 'V zashchitu Ekateriny Ivanovny', *Teatr i iskusstvo*, 1913, No. 18, pp. 402–5.
[4] See N. Nikolaev, 'Opyt blagozhelatel'noy kritiki', *Teatr i iskusstvo*, 1913, No. 24, p. 501.

turbed in their comfortable homes?'[1] This same question is implicit
in his next play *Thou Shalt Not Kill* which, written in 1913, was
published in 1914 in volume XXII of *Shipovnik*. Here Andreyev
adopts the same formula for the expression of his social *critique*:
the portrayal of another 'innocent victim'. At the same time the
drama of abstract ideas is still in evidence, though not so obviously.
Andreyev himself emphasized this point in the long letter of 1913
to Amfiteatrov to which reference has already been made:[2] 'It is
true that "Thou Shalt Not Kill" is a work of a realistic character,
at least in its external form. But it signifies neither a turn in the
direction of true realism nor a rejection on my part of my former
mystical-symbolic searchings.'[3] The abandonment of the intellectual
milieu is the first thing which strikes the reader. Andreyev portrays,
in fact, a variety of social types, but at the centre alike of the
dramatic action and the scheme of ideas stand characters from the
lowest rung of the social scale—the janitor Yakov and the maid
Margarita. Andreyev passes here from one mystical-symbolic incarnation of the primitive moral bases of life—woman—to another:
the people (*narod*), conceived no longer, as it was by Dostoevsky,
as a God-bearing force, but, like woman, as a victim of the moral
vacuum of the age. The physical might of Yakov, like the body of
Ekaterina, is a tool used by others for the gratification of their own
individual desires. The idea developed in the play is essentially a
variation of that of the earlier play, and the destruction of Yakov
expresses the same indictment as the fall of Ekaterina—society's
rejection of a potential power for good. Since Andreyev does not
introduce, however, the symbolic-philosophical 'conflict' which we
are investigating in this chapter, we will not undertake a detailed
examination and will pass on to his next play *Thought*, in which it
plays a significant, if not dominant, role.

Andreyev spent the first half of 1914 in Italy with Anna Il'inichna and the children and missed both the rehearsals and the
nineteen performances of *Thought* by the Moscow Art Theatre, the
first of which took place on 17 March. Nevertheless, he was in
constant touch both with Nemirovich-Danchenko, at whose insistence the Theatre undertook to produce the play, and with
Leonidov who played Kerzhentsev. A point which he was at pains to

---

[1] Quoted from H. Bernstein's Preface to his translation of *Ekaterina Ivanovna*,
New York, 1923, p. vi.
[2] Cf. *supra*, pp. 29–30.    [3] *Rekviem*, pp. 259.

emphasize in his letters was that the play was completely self-sufficient, i.e. that it was fully intelligible without reference to the story.[1] Though it may be true, as one commentator lamented, that the play affords insufficient material for a psychiatric analysis of Kerzhentsev,[2] the scheme of ideas is presented quite as clearly as it is in the story. The differences between the two works are largely explained by the change of genre—by the need for dialogue and visual projection of the inner drama. The first Picture of the play, which has no counterpart in the story, seems to have been Andreyev's attempt to meet this latter need.

The setting is the study of Kerzhentsev, in the corner of which stands a large cage containing a dying orang-outang. The significance which Kerzhentsev reads into the moribund state of the ape predicts the whole development of the ensuing action and his own fate. 'He is yearning,' he says to his interlocutor, the 'very pale young man' Kraft, 'he is dreaming dimly of the time when he was a man, a king, a higher form. Do you understand, Kraft: was!' But then he modifies his statement:

Either he has already been a king, or . . . listen, Kraft! . . . or he could have become a king, but something prevented him. He is not recalling the past, no!—he is yearning and hopelessly dreaming of the future which has been taken away from him. He is filled with aspiration towards the higher form, with yearning for the higher form, for before him . . . before him, Kraft, stands a wall![3]

The dying ape is a prefiguration of the Kerzhentsev of the final three Pictures of the play—the Kerzhentsev whose aspiration towards the 'higher form' of amoral superhumanity through the agency of the autonomous intellect brings him into fatal collision with the natural law of life in the form of his own subconscious. The harmony of the personality is shattered and he reverts to the primal form of man: 'And again he became covered with hair,' the doctor says of the ape, 'again he stood on all fours. . . .'[4] But the memory of the aspiration remains as a source of unabating torment.

[1] See, for instance, his letter to Leonidov of 13 February 1914, *Rekviem*, pp. 79–80.

[2] See D. A. Amenitsky, 'Analiz geroya "Mysli" L. Andreyeva. (K voprosu o paranoidnoy psikhopatii)', *Sovremennaya psikhiatriya*, 1915, No. 5, p. 225.

[3] L. N. Andreyev, *Mysl'. Drama v shesti kartinakh*, Berlin, J. Ladyschnikow, n.d., pp. 7–8.

[4] Ibid., p. 8.

As in the story, the murder of Savelov is the experiment which Kerzhentsev conducts on himself to test the power of his intellect. He sets out to succeed where the orang-outang failed. The second Picture transports the reader to the study of Savelov. Andreyev presents a much rounder portrait of the writer in the play than in the story and introduces through him a motif which is barely hinted in the latter; though seemingly irrelevant, it fits integrally into the scheme of ideas. Savelov is portrayed as a writer bitterly dissatisfied with his work, as the enemy of all pretence, of superficiality both in life and particularly in art. He is weary of playing the role of a mirror merely reflecting the deceptive external appearance of things and aspires to penetrate into their inner substance. Like the words of Tyukha in *Savva*, the self-criticism of Savelov is meant to offset the superficiality of the intellect's understanding of reality. When Kerzhentsev repeats the claim that he makes in the story—that man will some day be a god and his throne will be a book, Savelov replies: 'Your worship of books seems to me simply . . . ludicrous and unintelligent. Yes! There is also life!'[1] Thus Savelov, a writer, denounces books as a basis for understanding life, while Kerzhentsev, a doctor of medicine, acclaims them. Kerzhentsev calls for bookishness, invention in real life, while Savelov calls for real life in books.

The murder in the third Picture is followed in the fourth and fifth by Kerzhentsev's encounters with the two other female characters of the story (besides Tat'yana Nikolaevna)—his housekeeper Dar'ya Vasil'evna and Masha, the nurse in the mental hospital. Both encounters receive greater prominence in the play than in the story, and the symbolic-philosophical overtones of the 'conflict' between the sexes are unmistakably in evidence. While Dar'ya Vasil'evna, like a herald of doom, precipitates, with her request that he see a doctor, the disintegration of his personality, Masha emerges as the embodiment of simple, untutored faith before which he recoils in perplexity. The play ends with him flanked on the one side by Masha, on the other by Tat'yana Nikolaevna—powerless before the 'secret' which they represent.

Thus whereas in *Ekaterina Ivanovna* the drama of abstract ideas and the element of social criticism are in a state of equipoise, in *Thought* it is the philosophical element which predominates. Even the latter work, however, like the story *Thought*, is not devoid of

[1] Ibid., p. 41.

social implications. One suspects that in the dying orang-outang Andreyev is presenting not only a symbol of the Kerzhentsev of the last Pictures of the play, but also a caricature of contemporary society, of that contemporary man whom he was to describe in the first months of the war as a 'savage in a top-hat, as a barbarian in a laboratory'.[1]

Finally, both plays testify that his poor health, his solitude at Vammelsuu and his contempt for society had failed to undermine the premises of his thought. As if to reaffirm this, he published in January 1914 in *Sovremennyy mir* his short story *Above Death* (*Nadsmertnoe*), which carried the alternative title *The Flight* (*Polyot*)[2]—a work which, to his astonishment, won the plaudits even of Zinaida Gippius.[3] In the figure of Yuriy Mikhaylovich, the pilot in the story, he resurrects the visionary of the preliminary sketch out of which developed *My Notes*.[4] In brief, the story relates how even the best that earthly life has to offer—the love of his beautiful wife—cannot bind the pilot to the earth. His attachment cannot withstand the sensation of limitless freedom and self-immersion in the infinite which he experiences during flight. The work ends with him flying ever onward having abandoned all thought of return. In the collection of articles entitled *At This Menacing Hour* (*V sey groznyy chas*) which he produced soon after the beginning of the war Andreyev wrote: 'Life is like a mountain on which every new upward step reveals new distances, radiant horizons, the transparent firmament. And there is a high zone, a wondrous zone high above the lowly earth in which the difference between suffering and joy is lost and they merge harmoniously to form a single powerful feeling of flight, of sublime altitude.'[5] In the flight of Yuriy Mikhaylovich into this 'wondrous zone' Andreyev re-acclaims the spiritual conquest of Werner. Regarding the story as definitive of the philosophical content of the entire corpus of his fiction, he wrote to Goloushev on 15 December 1916: '. . . just as the earth is round and to all human creations there is a gate on which is written "Enfin", so there is a gate to me also whence it is most fitting to carry out a survey. This is my story "The Flight" or "Above Death".'[6]

[1] L. N. Andreyev, *V sey groznyy chas*, Petrograd, n.d., p. 7.

[2] L. N. Andreyev, 'Nadsmertnoe', *Sovremennyy mir*, 1914, No. 1, pp. 1–18.

[3] See Andreyev's reference to this fact in a letter to Goloushev of 9 January, 1915, *Rekviem*, p. 99.

[4] See *supra*, p. 197    [5] *V sey groznyy chas*, p. 82.    [6] *Rekviem*, p. 133.

# XVIII

# WAR

**M**ORE than twenty years previously—in 1893, when he had found life particularly oppressive—Andreyev had written in his diary: 'Oh if only there was war! . . . Life has become so stifling! . . .'[1] This attitude to war as a 'release' from the tedium and stagnation of life characterizes his reaction to the events of August 1914. He greeted the war not with the 'mystical alarm' of Blok, but with the passion of an idealist who saw it as a purgatory in which the petty, bourgeois interests of society would be consumed and the way cleared for the restoration of heroic aspirations and noble questions of principle. He said to Beklemisheva: 'If I were to be asked what is the matter with me, I would say: this is a resurrection from the dead. It is not only my personal resurrection, but above all the resurrection of Russia.'[2] In a letter of 11 August to his brother Andrey he compared himself to Lazarus and described the 'immense, sublime and unprecedented enthusiasm' which he saw about him, adding: 'Everyone is proud that he is Russian; just think of it—I am also!'[3]

Like the majority of the intelligentsia and his fellow writers in Europe he gave voice to an ardent patriotism, which he continued to profess throughout Russia's 'terrible years'. Vadim Andreyev calls it a veritable 'sickness with Russia'.[4] It was not, of course, a spontaneous chauvinism. His criticism of Russian society does not obscure the love of Russia which is reflected in such diverse works as *The Foreigner* and *Sashka Zhegulyov*. According to his son, the reason for its scant emergence in his fiction was his fear of rhetoric: 'Throughout his life love of Russia was in his blood . . ., but it was hidden and suppressed; he did not dare confess to it.'[5] Gorky recalls his astonishment when on one occasion in Finland shortly before the outbreak of war he did 'confess' to it:

. . . he started to speak about the Russian people in words that he was

[1] *BSN*, p. 17.     [2] *Rekviem*, p. 268.
[3] 'Pis'ma k bratu', *Zalp*, 1933, No. 1, p. 68.
[4] *VLA*, August–September, p. 89.     [5] Ibid., p. 99.

not wont to use; he expressed himself in broken, incoherent sentences, but with a tone of profound conviction which was undoubtedly sincere. . . . The force of his arguments did not consist in their logic or in their appeal, but wholly in the deep feeling they betrayed—a sentiment of suffering compassion for his people, a sentiment so strong and so vividly disclosed that I could not have believed it of Leonid Nikolaevich. His whole body trembled; his nerves were taut.[1]

It was this same sentiment which moved Andreyev to write in 1914 the pamphlet entitled *There Is No Death for the Man Who Loves His Native Land* (*Net smerti dlya togo, kto lyubit Rodinu*).

At Vammelsuu he lived for the postman's visits and his mood fluctuated with the fortunes of the Russian armies. Guests came rarely, and when they did they were subjected to his long disquisitions on the true significance of events. It has been indicated that from the beginning he regarded the war as the prelude to revolution. Germany's declaration served to deflect the attention of the public from the fact that there had been barricades on the streets of Petrograd in July, and inner dissension and class antagonism were momentarily forgotten. But Andreyev did not forget, and convinced that only a victorious war could bring a victorious revolution, he demanded that everyone he met share his beliefs and pray for a Russian victory. Apart from the small group of exiles gathered round Lenin and Trotsky there were few who did not.

During the first two years of the war he found all criticism of Russia intolerable, and when Gorky, who returned to Russia towards the end of 1913, published in December 1915, in the new journal *Letopis'* ('The Chronicle'), his article *The Two Souls* (*Dve dushi*), in which he called on Russia to eradicate its 'Asiaticism' and emulate the West, Andreyev publicly rebuked him on the pages of *Sovremennyy mir*.[2] Although he collaborated with Gorky (and Sologub) in 1914 to form the *Russkoe obshchestvo dlya izucheniya zhizni evreyev* ('The Russian Society for the Study of the Life of the Jews') and in 1915 to publish the *Shchit* almanac,[3] he had, in general, few words of praise for his former friend during these years.

According to Beklemisheva, there were some who were dismayed

---

[1] *KLA*, p. 37.
[2] Cf. L. N. Andreyev, 'O "Dvukh dushakh" M. Gor'kogo', *Sovremennyy mir*, 1916, No. 1, pp. 108–12.
[3] Cf. *supra*, p. 136.

by Andreyev's failure to participate in the war which he welcomed so openly.[1] These people were unaware of the gravity of his physical condition. Three times during the war he was compelled to enter a clinic. Returning from a stay in Moscow in November 1914, Vadim Andreyev found his father in the Gerzoni clinic in Petrograd suffering from acute neuralgia in his right hand. 'My father', he writes, 'felt absolutely shattered and sick.'[2] Andreyev wrote to his brother Andrey on 13 November 1914: 'I tell you truthfully that once cured of my affliction (I am useless in my present state) I would endeavour to fight were it not for mother—I speak seriously and consciously.'[3] His fighting, however, was done exclusively with the pen.

His thoughts on the war find expression in his publicistic articles and two works of a semi-publicistic nature which he wrote in 1914 and 1915 respectively—the play *King, Law and Liberty* (*Korol', zakon i svoboda*) and a story in diary form *The Burden of War* (*Igo voyny*). His interest in the war literally drove him to publicism; he felt no natural inclination towards it. To Nikolay Iordansky, the editor of *Sovremennyy mir*, he wrote on 29 December 1915: 'I am of a very modest opinion of my publicistic works and find it essential for myself that my articles be subjected to editorial discussion.'[4] He gives in these articles full rein to the passions which he hesitated to introduce into his fiction and they reveal his fears of rhetoric to have been fully justified. He appears in them to have lost all sense of that physical reality of war which had haunted him during the years 1904–5. Only once in the early days of the war does the full horror of the events taking place in East Prussia seem to have struck him forcibly—on the night of 15 August 1914, when his brother Andrey left Finland with his regiment for the front. The entry which he made in his diary after the parting sounds a very different note from that of his articles of the ensuing months.[5] In the latter his pronouncements seem to emanate, to use Chukovsky's words, from 'a world of the fantasy which has nothing in common with real life'.[6] Declaring the war to be above all a 'war of the

---

[1] Cf. *Rekviem*, p. 269.

[2] *VLA*, August–September, p. 95. Andreyev left the clinic on 20 November after a two-month confinement only to return in May 1915 for a further three weeks (cf. 'Pis'ma k bratu', pp. 70–1).

[3] 'Pis'ma k bratu', p. 70.  [4] *Rekviem*, p. 139.

[5] Cf. L. N. Andreyev, 'Ot'ezd. (Iz dnevnika)', *Literaturnyy al'manakh 'Grani'*, vol. 1, Berlin, 1922, pp. 5–7.

[6] K. Chukovsky, 'Leonid Andreyev', in his *Iz vospominaniy*, M., 1958, p. 269.

spirit',[1] he viewed the life-and-death struggle of the individual Russian soldier in terms of the antipodal Russian and German cultures, which are identified respectively with faith and reason. He announced his agreement with the opinion of the philosopher Vladimir Frantsevich Ern, expressed at a public meeting of the Moscow *Religiozno-filosofskoe obshchestvo* ('Religious-Philosophical Society') in October 1914, that it was impossible to dissociate the bestiality displayed by the German army from German culture, and maintained the view, which was often heard in discussions of the time, that a straight line could be drawn from Kant to Krupp.[2] The war appeared to him as a great symbol of the philosophical antithesis which lies at the basis of his fiction.

He wrote in the opening article of *At This Menacing Hour*:

Not for empirical and contingent Russia, but for a conceivable, desirable and possible Russia has the Russian people taken up arms. . . . When Germany beckoned to culture, it strangled true culture. When it beckoned to freedom, it strangled freedom also in the vice of mechanism, in the categorical imperatives of dogma, in its worship of discipline—its only love which was sincere and genuinely ardent.[3]

He calls on his readers to oppose the force of 'mechanism' with the might of the Spirit, to feed themselves on culture and the words of great men of the past. He describes his emotion on hearing the singing of a column of troops departing for the front, and then turns abruptly on the Bulgarians, in the article *To the Merchants in the Temple* (*Torguyushchim v khrame*), for allowing the Germans to transport arms to Turkey through their country: 'The Slavonic world is ashamed,' he writes, 'and lowers its eyes when it hears the name "Bulgarian".'[4] He summons Russia to the aid of the Serbs before the Austrians wreak vengeance on them, and in a series of three articles extends his plea to Britain and France to rise to the defence of Belgium. Germany and Belgium represented for him the two poles of the conflict; he writes: 'The war has two faces: the dim and gloomy face of the German rejected by God, and the radiant countenance of the Belgian. In contrast to the gloom and flatness of the German soul stand the mountainous heights of the

---

[1] *V sey groznyy chas*, p. 6.     [2] Ibid., p. 108.     [3] Ibid., pp. 6–7.

[4] Ibid., p. 27. In connection with this article he wrote to his brother Andrey on 20 November 1914: 'According to telegrams, the article about the Bulgarians has provoked a storm of indignation in Sofia; Bulgarian writers are composing a protest at special meetings' ('Pis'ma k bratu', *Zalp*, 1933, No. 1, p. 70).

Belgian spirit.'[1] He was deeply moved by the news that Maeterlinck had joined the Belgian army as a volunteer and been wounded
in battle.[2]

The fate of Belgium constitutes the theme of *King, Law and
Liberty*, which was completed in October 1914. Though he received
for it a formal expression of gratitude from the Belgian Prime
Minister,[3] he was later to refer to it in his diary with considerable
contempt, and Vadim Andreyev rightly pronounced it 'my father's
weakest play'.[4] It is little more than an extension of his publicistic
articles and many of the dominant motifs of the latter find their way
into it. They are expressed mainly through the central character,
the poet Émile Grelieu, an obvious symbol of Maeterlinck. All the
characters are singularly lacking in depth. Francois, the aged
gardener of the Grelieus and intended symbol of the masses, has
all the features of a caricature, and Andreyev fails to move us with
the character of the girl in the black dress trying to find her way to
Longwy, through whom he seeks to convey the suffering inflicted
by war on the civilian population. The stoicism of Grelieu's wife
Jeanna when her husband and two sons depart for the front introduces a moment of genuine drama, but it is in vain that we seek
inner drama in Grelieu himself. The inner conflicts which produce
his decisions are sacrificed in the interests of extreme idealization.

Most successful of all are the fourth and fifth Pictures, in which
the playwright develops his 'philosophical' conception of the
significance of the war. In the former, Grelieu, home again and
confined to his bed after having been wounded, is visited by Count
Clermont and the Prime Minister Lagarde, who stand respectively
for King Albert and Vandervelde. They come to him for the final
sanction of the measure which, they fear, alone remains to them if
they are to halt the German advance—the breaching of the dykes
and the flooding of the lowlands. The symbolic meaning with
which Andreyev invests this measure emerges clearly from the
speech in which Clermont contrasts the purgative element of fire
with the cold, dark chaos of water: water is the chaos which will
extinguish the flame of the German reason. After elaborating on the

---

[1] *V sey groznyy chas*, p. 51.

[2] See his letter of 11 August 1914 to his brother Andrey, 'Pis'ma k bratu',
p. 69.

[3] He received a similar honour for his publicistic articles from the Serbian
Prime Minister (see 'Pis'ma k bratu', p. 70).

[4] *VLA*, August–September, p. 99.

thesis of Ern, Andreyev proceeds in the fifth Picture to portray the panic and confusion of the Germans when the rumbling of the approaching tide reaches their ears. It is on this note that the play should have ended, but here, as in the greater part of it, the publicist holds sway over the artist, and another Picture is appended to complete the apotheosis of the hero and give consummate expression to the patriotism and optimism which the play was intended to inspire.

*The Burden of War*, which was published in 1916 in volume XXV of *Shipovnik* with the subtitle 'The Confessions of a Little Man about Great Days' (*Priznaniya malen'kogo cheloveka o velikikh dnyakh*) and with a dedication to Repin, presents further evidence of Andreyev's tendency to view the war through the prism of the ideas and ideals which had formed the intellectual substructure of his fiction from the beginning. In the 'confessions' of the average, bourgeois family-man Il'ya Petrovich Dement'ev he traces the transition in the popular consciousness from rebellion against the dehumanization inflicted by war, the reduction of the individual to a 'cell' in the social organism, to joyous acclamation of the resurrecting unity and brotherhood which this 'organism' implies. The central theme even of this essentially documentary work is the transcendence of individuality. The diarist asks:

Is there a difference between the living and the dead? Where do the dead go? Whence come the living? And again, after long thought, I saw them all, the living and the dead and the people of the future, all their extraordinary mass fleeting before me like a vision and flying together with the clouds beneath the moon, together with the rays of the sun, the rain, together with the wind and the river. And I came to understand that I am completely, even ludicrously immortal: Petersburg can fall a thousand times, but I will still be alive.[1]

Such was the message which Andreyev brought to the Russian people from the silence of his study in the Finnish wastes. Shortly afterwards he duplicated it in the dialogue entitled *A Nocturnal Conversation* (*Nochnoy razgovor*), but never published the work.[2]

In the final analysis, his attitude to the war is directly comparable to his attitude to the revolution of 1905–6. In both cases he

[1] L. N. Andreyev, 'Igo voyny', *Metel' literaturnye al'manakhi izd. 'Shipovnik'*, vol. 25, Petrograd, 1916, pp. 221–2.

[2] It was published posthumously (1921) in Helsingfors by the publishing-house *Biblion*.

cherished the hope that man would be prised both by the sheer magnitude of events and above all by the principles at stake, as he interpreted them, from the narrow rut of his individualism and materialism. By the spring of 1916, however, his hopes had all but collapsed under the weight of the news of repeated defeats at the front and before the spectacle of the wretchedness of life in Petrograd. Even the late months of 1914 found him tormented by the contrast between his ideals and reality. During sober moments of reflection he was forced to concede that no significant change had transpired in man or society, and this is the bitter conclusion which finds expression in his other works of the first two years of the war. His mood is reflected in the doleful play *The Waltz of the Dogs* (*Sobachiy val's*) with its subtitle 'A Poem of Solitude' (*Poema odinochestva*),[1] his mystical-philosophical interpretation of events— in the plays which we will now examine.

[1] The first variant of the play, a study of dashed hopes and frustrated ambition, was written in 1914, but Andreyev later subjected it to radical alteration—without, however, changing the theme—and it was not completed until the autumn of 1916. It was neither performed nor published during his lifetime. Found among his papers by his wife after his death (see C. Poupeye, *Les Dramaturges Exotiques*, Brussels, 1926, p. 158), it was produced by I. N. Pevtsov and Vasiliy Sakhnovsky at the Moscow Show Theatre (*Pokazatel'nyy teatr*) in 1920 and published in 1922 in the Paris journal *Sovremennye zapiski* ('Contemporary Notes') (28 April, pp. 1–66).

# XIX

## THE MYTH OF THE 'CAPTIVE SOUL'

ANDREYEV began to write *He Who Gets Slapped* in mid-August 1915 and completed it a month later.[1] It was first published in 1916 in volume XXIV of *Shipovnik* with a dedication to Goloushev. The opportunities which the play afforded for colourful spectacle induced Drankov to make a film of it in April 1916 under the direction of V. P. Kas'yanov and I. F. Schmidt, who also produced the play at the Moscow Dramatic Theatre, and with Pevtsov in the main role,[2] and as late as 1956 the American composer Robert Varda made the plot the framework of his opera *Pantaloon*. The productions of the play at the Moscow Dramatic Theatre in October 1915 and at the Aleksandrinsky Theatre in Petrograd in February 1916 enjoyed considerable, though shortlived, success. At the première of the latter Andreyev received as many as fourteen curtain-calls.[3]

At the same time there were many who were puzzled by the play. 'I remember the perplexity and questions in the intervals . . .,' writes Beklemisheva in reference to a performance at the Aleksandrinsky Theatre.[4] Few of his plays are so pregnant with hidden meaning. In his review of the work Goloushev called it a 'masquerade' and saw the characters as 'Chinese silhouettes reflected on a screen'. He continues: 'They live their illusory life, but their real life is there, behind the screen, and it can only be sensed, not seen.'[5] There are, in fact, two distinct levels of meaning or planes of action

---

[1] See his reference to it as complete in a letter to Goloushev of 10 September 1915, *Rekviem*, p. 117.

[2] The scenario was written by A. Ivanov-Gay. Most of the shots were taken in the Salamonsky Circus, and its director, G. Radunsky, and leading performers took part. Every opportunity to expand the action of the play was utilized, and 'He's' break with the outside world, Mancini's nocturnal 'adventures', and activity in the circus-arena were all visually presented. In 1915 Andreyev had also come to an agreement with Drankov concerning the filming of *Thou Shalt Not Kill*, but the plan appears to have collapsed (see 'Kino-teatr', *Teatr i iskusstvo*, 1915, No. 48, p. 906).

[3] See *VLA*, August–September, p. 102.     [4] *Rekviem*, pp. 240–1.

[5] Quoted from *Leonid Andreyev. P'esy*, M., 1959, p. 582.

behind the screen of the purely external: the first expresses the social polemic of the work, while the second is metaphysical and its action is presented in the form of myth. We will consider them in this order.

Andreyev's setting is a circus in a French city—more precisely, the office of Papa Brike, the manager of the circus. The dominant motif of Act I of the play is the contrast and antipathy between 'here' and 'there', the circus and the world without, which are identified respectively with talent and culture. Throughout the work the antithesis has distinct moral implications, talent being associated with innocence and culture with corruption. Within the circus company itself Andreyev distinguishes between varying degrees of spiritual proximity to 'here', just as he distinguishes between varying degrees of 'savvichism' in *Professor Storitsyn*. The happiest are those who live in ignorance of the existence of the outside world, those whose minds are uninfected by the 'contagion' of books—the horseman Bezano and his partner Consuella. Brike is 'nearer' to the circus, but on his own confession he has read 'their books',[1] and the living evidence of his contamination is his common-law wife, Zinida, the beautiful and passionate lion-tamer, whose closeness to 'there' reveals itself in her attempted seduction of Bezano.

From 'there' suddenly appears 'He' with the plea that he be accepted in the circus as a clown. Greeted as a being from an alien and hostile world, as a 'phantom', he eventually gains his wish by the sheer force of his enthusiasm and is allotted the role of the clown whom the other clowns slap. His real identity is never disclosed, though we learn that he is an intellectual of renown. The significance of and motives for his action do not become completely clear until mid-way through the play, when he is confronted by 'The Man', the embodiment of the quintessence of 'there'. 'He', we discover, comes to the circus robbed by 'The Man' not only of his wife, but also of his ideas, which have been vulgarized for popular consumption. Culture is branded as the vulgarization of talent. Moreover, the mere existence of talent is a source of profound embarrassment to the purveyors of culture, and 'The Man' implores 'He' to vow that he will never return 'there'. 'He's' agreement to this request carries the same force as the curse of Man.

[1] See L. N. Andreyev, 'Tot, kto poluchaet poshchochiny', *Al'manakhi izdatel'stva 'Shipovnik'*, vol. 24, Petrograd, 1916, p. 20.

Various attempts have been made to understand the symbolic significance of the role which 'He' performs as a clown. Sologub took it to be symbolic of the act of Christ: 'He who gets slapped,' he writes, 'has taken on himself . . . the sinfulness of the world.'[1] Alternatively, Andreyev might have had in mind the 'underground man's' words on the particular kind of pleasure to be derived from humiliation:

It is so subtle, so inaccessible sometimes to rational understanding that slightly limited people or even simply people with strong nerves will find it totally incomprehensible. 'Perhaps those who have never received slaps will also fail to understand,' you add with a smirk, and thereby you politely hint to me that during my life perhaps I also have experienced a slap and therefore speak as an expert.[2]

Andreyev, however, does not appear to be plumbing these psychological depths; he seems to interpret the role of his hero as a form of vengeance. One of 'He's' early performances, for instance, draws the following comment from Jackson, the chief clown of the circus: 'Today he received so many slaps that there were enough for the whole stalls.'[3] On the same occasion Brike remarks to 'He': 'In your slaps there is a certain savour . . . do you understand, a certain odour!'[4] 'He' protests that the audience laughs, but Brike replies: 'But without pleasure, without pleasure, He! You pay, but you immediately transfer the account to their name; this is bad acting; they will not like you.'[5] The submission of 'He' to the slaps of his fellow clowns is a parody of his fate in the external world, a parody of the profanation of his ideas. Society's rejection of his ideas signifies its rejection of those principles which could ennoble and enrich its life; thus, in essence, he is presenting his audience with the spectacle of their profanation of their own lives.

Andreyev regarded 'He' as directly related to his heroes of former works. When the critic A. Evlakhov drew a parallel between 'He' and Lorenzo,[6] he responded in a letter to him with the following comments:

---

[1] F. Sologub, 'Mechtatel' v teatre', *Teatr i iskusstvo*, 1916, No. 1, p. 15.

[2] F. M. Dostoevsky, *Sobranie sochineniy*, vol. 4, M., 1956, p. 141.

[3] 'Tot, kto poluchaet poshchochiny', p. 40.     [4] Ibid.     [5] Ibid., p. 41.

[6] Evlakhov's study of the play (*Kto poluchaet poshchochiny v novoy drame L. Andreyeva?*, Rostov, 1916, 29 pp.) is unobtainable, but a synopsis of the views which he puts forward is given by A. Linin in 'Neuere Forschungen über Leonid Andrejev', *Zeitschrift für slavische Philologie*, Leipzig, 1930, vol. 8, pp. 214–15.

While you have understood Lorenzo correctly, you have boldly and with equally profound understanding linked him with the distant and seemingly dissimilar 'He'. They are, of course, related to one another. . . . Lorenzo is higher, more innocent and pure than the earth-burdened, earth-bound 'He'; Lorenzo is suspended there, while 'He' crawls on the earth—but their paths run parallel and their objective is the same.[1]

'He's' abandonment of the outside world is not accompanied at once by his complete liberation from its influence. Significant at the end of Act II are his words in reference to 'The Man': 'This is the shadow which I cannot lose!'[2] It is not until 'He's' second encounter with 'The Man'—at the beginning of Act III—that he finally severs all ties with the clinging past. He says simply: 'Listen: you are not my shadow; I made a mistake. You are the mob.'[3] This point in the play is directly comparable with that at which the terrorist resolves to remain with Lyuba in *Darkness* and with the moment when Lorenzo emerges triumphant from his duel with his 'false' personality.

At the same time it should be noted that Andreyev considered neither 'He' nor, as Kugel' claimed,[4] Brike to be the central character of the play. 'The true pivot of the drama lies not in "He", but in Consuella,' he wrote to Polevitskaya, for whom he created the latter role.[5] Consuella is the antithesis of 'The Man'. These two figures mark the two poles between which the other characters are grouped, and we might say that the path followed by 'He' runs from 'The Man' to Consuella. He arrives at the circus, however, to find her on the point of being sacrificed to the world which he has abandoned. She has fallen into the power of the degenerate Mancini, who adopts her as his daughter and seeks to marry her to the Baron, evil incarnate. 'He' rises to her defence, and it is at this stage in the play that we enter the realm of myth.

In the same letter to Polevitskaya Andreyev wrote: 'This myth-play tells the story of beautiful gods who are tormented by earthly oppression and have gone astray in the labyrinths of the petty and oppressive passions of man.'[6] The 'recognition scene' of the 'gods', in which the whole mythical substructure of the play is disclosed,

---

[1] Ibid., p. 215.     [2] 'Tot, kto poluchaet poshchochiny', p. 57.
[3] Ibid., p. 65.
[4] See A. R. Kugel', *Russkie dramaturgi. Ocherki teatral'nogo kritika*, M., 1934, p. 158.
[5] *Leonid Andreyev. P'esy*, M., 1959, p. 581.     [6] Ibid., pp. 581–2.

takes place in Act II. Here Consuella emerges as the incarnation of Psyche, the human soul in its primitive, untarnished purity languishing in captivity to the earth, 'He'—as an 'old god in changed garb'[1] who has descended to earth to rescue her. The mystical relationship between them is intensified as the play progresses. Even so, there is an absence of true harmony between them, just as there is between Prince Myshkin and Nastasiya Filippovna in *The Idiot* (*Idiot*), in which Dostoevsky presents a variation of the same archetypal myth. The ornate, passionate rhetoric of 'He' leaves her breathless, but she is already yielding to temptation. Unable to elevate her above the evil which is about to take possession of her, 'He' poisons her. To the toast of 'To your happiness, to your freedom, Consuella!' he snatches her soul, still innocent, from her yielding body and consumes the remainder of the draught himself. But the conflict is not ended. Before the poison begins its work, a shot is heard. The Baron sheds his earthly mask and speeds above in pursuit of his quarry. The battle for the purity, innocence and beauty of the soul is transposed from the world of contingent experience to the plane of the world-process. 'I am coming,' cries 'He' to the Baron. 'There also you and I will dispute eternal possession of her.'[2]

Andreyev presents in the play a 'pagan' or secular version of the myth which had been invested by Vladimir Solov'yov and Dostoevsky with a deeply religious significance. Beneath the 'masculine-feminine antithesis' of *Ekaterina Ivanovna* we see the contours of the same myth, in which Andreyev displays that mystical conception of woman which gave him an affinity with Blok. In both plays the myth represents an extension of the social polemic, the transference of the issues involved in the latter on to the broader screen of metaphysical entities. Though the most complex, *He Who Gets Slapped* is one of Andreyev's most successful attempts, from the artistic or structural point of view, to achieve this characteristic fusion. Enjoyable both as a plain drama and as an intellectual exercise, it was popular with all sections of the theatre-going public. Andreyev attached much greater importance, however, to his play *Samson Enchained* (*Samson v okovakh*).

The history of the creation of this play reads like a love-story. Complete infatuation, disenchantment, hatred and the possessiveness of a jealous lover—all these emotions were experienced by the

[1] 'Tot, kto poluchaet poshchochiny', p. 53.    [2] Ibid., p. 105.

playwright in the course of its composition. The preliminary sketches of the play appear to have been made in Rome in March 1914,[1] but Andreyev does not seem to have begun work on it in earnest until his return to Vammelsuu from Petrograd in December 1914. Shortly before putting pen to paper he wrote to Goloushev: '. . . the day after tomorrow I am beginning a large work which has very great importance for me.'[2] Vadim Andreyev describes his condition:

Overcoming the pain in his hand and a sudden nervous blindness which hindered his work—black, blinding spots sometimes obscured his vision and the room and environment appeared to him as though through a torn curtain—my father continued to write, agitated and almost happy.[3]

Two months later the work was complete. In a letter to Goloushev of February 1915 he wrote:

I am worn out by my work. Only after two months of constant toil have I finished 'Samson Enchained', a tragedy. . . . A good work, and my head is full of it; it is difficult for me to speak of anything else. Soon I will read it in Petrograd, send it to Nemirovich and will be despondent if the Art Theatre does not take it and if Kachalov does not accept the part.[4]

It was over a year later, however, before he read the play in public. Though he informed his brother, Andrey, in a letter of 26 June 1915, that it was complete,[5] a letter of 7 December to the same addressee contains the note: 'I am working so much that smoke is pouring from my eyes: I am altering "Samson" for the third time; I want to please Lyubov' Gurevich.'[6] The reading of the play took place in Moscow at the house of Teleshov on the Pokrovsky Boulevard in a scene reminiscent of the old 'Wednesday' meetings. Many of the old members of the society were present relishing their memories of the past, but the past was not re-enacted. Veresaev recalls the evening:

Andreyev read the play. Immediately afterwards we went to supper. Not a word about the play. Andreyev did not ask for comments and spoke all the time about unrelated matters. No one considered it possible to express

---

[1] Cf. the extract from Andreyev's letter of 18 March 1914, to his brother-in-law A. P. Alekseyevsky, *LN*, p. 359.

[2] *Rekviem*, p. 97.  [3] *VLA*, August–September, p. 98.  [4] *Rekviem*, p. 100.

[5] Cf. 'Leonid Andreyev. Pis'ma', *Russkiy sovremennik*, 1924, No. 4, p. 143.

[6] Ibid., p. 145. Lyubov' Gurevich was at that time theatre-critic of *Russkaya mysl'* and *Rech'*.

his opinion without his permission, but seemingly he did not need it and it would have been unpleasant for him. Looking at him it was strange to recall the old Andreyev who used to listen so avidly at those same 'Wednesdays' to the severest criticism.[1]

Embittered by abuse and misinterpretation of his works, worn out by ill health, overwork and constant disillusionment, he would have suffered unendurable pain had a word been spoken against the 'masterpiece' which had demanded so much of him. When Teleshov, who was editing the publications of the new *Knigoizdatel'stvo pisateley* ('The Publishing-House of Writers') in Moscow, requested a contribution from him,[2] he declined abruptly to give him an excerpt from the play. In a letter of 26 January 1916 he stated: 'In no circumstances can I give you "Samson". I even conceal its content from interviewers.'[3] In fact, he never published the work. His dream of having it staged by the Moscow Art Theatre was not realized, partly due to Kachalov's inability to see himself in the role or to develop any enthusiasm for it,[4] until four years after his death (1923) when it was performed in Berlin, and it was published in 1925 in the Paris *émigré* monthly *Sovremennye zapiski*.[5]

The fruit of his toil was a succession of scenes of unsurpassed grandeur, in which the historical period is evoked in all its exotic colour and magnificence, and a 'Biblical' language which may be compared in its wealth of imagery to the most colourful pages of *The Life of Vasiliy Fiveysky* and *Judas Iscariot*. So far as its 'idea' is concerned, the play is directly related to its immediate antecedents. Andreyev takes only the last part of the Biblical story, and when the curtain rises Samson is already blinded and a prisoner in a Philistine dungeon. In terms of the underlying scheme the play begins at the point at which *Ekaterina Ivanovna* and *Thou Shalt Not Kill* end. Like Yakov, Samson is a symbol of the mystical 'soul' of the people and his blindness and chains denote his vassalage to the powers of evil. He has lost contact with the people and God and, like Yakov, he wanders in a moral void. He is another 'god' who has 'gone astray'. He abandons himself to the temptations of Philistine life. Though he is aware that he is needed by Delilah and her brothers, Galial and Adoram, who believe in his divine power, in the war

---

[1] *VRSV*, p. 476.     [2] See *Rekviem*, p. 61.     [3] Ibid., p. 62.
[4] See *EMKT*, p. 300.
[5] L. N. Andreyev, 'Samson v okovakh', *Sovremennye zapiski*, 1925, No. 24, pp. 41–142.

which they are waging against Egypt, he succumbs to the prospect of riches and comfort with which they lure him. His dungeon is exchanged for the palace of Delilah.

The dramatic action of Acts II, III and IV resides in the attempts of the people to win back from its captors the divine power which alone can liberate them. It is significant that the 'woman of Judaea', the symbol of the people, is herself blind; her blindness is symbolic of the helplessness of the people while its 'soul' is in captivity. The metamorphosis of Samson takes place during the lion-hunt on which he is conducted by the Philistine princes. The false glitter of Philistia, its corrupting sirens, its depravity and earthly delights are replaced by the whining of the wind and the roar of the lion, and in these primitive sounds Samson hears the voice of God. He is roused from his sleep and casts off his fetters. He turns on the oppressors of the people, and the temple of Dagon, where he is led in the final Act to swear an oath of allegiance to the pagan god, crumbles before his might. Philistia is destroyed and with it the corruption of the soul in the form of the blind Samson.

The most serious criticism came from Gorky, whose painstaking study of the play is evidenced by his carefully composed list of factual inaccuracies, e.g. Andreyev's confusion of Judaea with Israel.[1] The main weakness, as Gorky pointed out, lies in the vagueness of Delilah. Her transformation from the princess of Philistia into the martyr who shares the fate of Samson in the temple of Dagon is wholly unmotivated. It seems that Andreyev saw her as a kind of counterpart to Lyuba in *Darkness*; it is noteworthy that the terrorist and Lyuba are compared specifically to Samson and Delilah at the end of the latter work.[2] But she remains a sketchily drawn figure and it is impossible to divine Andreyev's thought here with assurance. Notwithstanding these defects, however, *Samson Enchained* ranks among Andreyev's most notable achievements. It may be looked upon as the last major flowering of his talent, after which comes a sharp decline in his creative ability. His total exhaustion on completing the work is well conveyed in his letter of 7 February 1916 to Beklemisheva, in which he wrote:

[1] Cf. *LN*, pp. 358–9. Andreyev does not appear to have paid much attention to Gorky's letter, which is dated November–December 1915, for the same inaccuracies are found in the final version of the play on which he was working in early December (cf. the letter to his brother Andrey of 7 December, *supra*, p. 253).

[2] Cf. *Works* II, p. 180.

'Samson' has completely exhausted me, sucked from me all will for work, all ability to be inspired by some other theme. Whatever I begin, it all seems insipid and uninteresting; within half-an-hour I am bored and yawning. I have gone through all my old, prepared themes and yawned over each of them. I have begun works and abandoned them, and even now I am still beginning and abandoning. My head refuses. Nor do I feel like reading. I wander restlessly through the house. You will not believe this, but I have no desire even to speak.[1]

His remaining works can be divided into two groups: those in which he seeks distraction from the present and its problems, and those in which he gives vent to his bitterness and disillusionment. To the first group belong the plays *Youth* (*Mladost'*) (1915), a purely autobiographical work in which he recalls his life during his last years at the *gimnaziya*, and *Dear Phantoms* (*Milye prizraki*) (1916), a psychological study of the young Dostoevsky which was written in one week;[2] the one-act play *Requiem* (*Rekviem*) (1916)[3] and the novel *Satan's Diary* (*Dnevnik Satany*) (1919) comprise the second. The feature that is common to them all is that they bear witness to the ebbing powers of their creator. He no longer derived satisfaction from his work. He was tired of isolation and silent absorption in his thoughts, and thirsted for activity and contact with affairs. 'My father was no longer able to remain aside,' writes Vadim Andreyev, 'to sit in Finland and take part in current political life simply as an incidental collaborator on an incidental newspaper.'[4] In this mood lies the partial explanation of Andreyev's subsequent activity and, in particular, of his association with the new Petrograd daily *Russkaya volya* ('The Russian Will').

[1] *Rekviem*, p. 234.
[2] 'From the biography of Dostoevsky is taken only his image—as I understand it—and one episode,' Andreyev confided to Leonid Grossman: 'the nocturnal call on Dostoevsky by the renowned critic and poet* who were impressed by his first novel . . . Through the creations of Dostoevsky to his life and spirit—such is my path. I do not know whether the Dostoevsky of my play is historical, but I think that on some very important plane he is profoundly genuine . . .' (L. Grossman, *Bor'ba za stil'. Opyty po kritike i poetike*, M., 1927, p. 278).
* In Andreyev's play it is Nekrasov and Belinsky who call to congratulate Dostoevsky after reading *Poor Folk* (*Bednye lyudi*); in reality, Nekrasov was accompanied by Grigorovich.
[3] It was in 1916 that the play was submitted to the censor, but it is possible that it was written somewhat earlier. Reference to a 'first variant' is encountered in Beklemisheva's memoirs (see *Rekviem*, p. 248), but she makes no mention of when it was written.
[4] *VLA*, October, p. 93.

# XX

# *RUSSKAYA VOLYA* AND REVOLUTION

DURING the first two years of the war Andreyev identified himself with no particular journal or publishing organization, though he maintained close ties with *Shipovnik* until it closed in 1916. Of his major works, apart from those published by the latter and those which appeared posthumously, no two were published by the same concern. His contributions were still in great demand, but he always turned down offers of prolonged collaboration. When Belousov remarked with surprise on his failure to join the group of Moscow writers who had formed *Knigoizdatel'stvo pisateley*, he replied: 'Now my relations with them are good, but if I join them there will surely be some kind of conflict and row on a question of principle. . . .'[1] And when Iordansky invited him to work for *Sovremennyy mir*, he wrote in a letter to him of 29 December 1915: 'The only condition on which I can enter any journal is that my role be not restricted to simple collaboration and that I be given a certain influence on the whole course of affairs. And what influence can I have in "S.M." where even now Asheshov is writing against me?'[2] Disagreement with editorial policy and the fear of being unable to make his disagreement felt and effective—these were the factors which deterred him at this time from committing himself to collaboration with any single organization. A year later, however, *Russkaya volya* came into existence.

Few people had any factual knowledge of the background to the establishment of the paper. Korolenko testifies to the existence of many conflicting reports at the time.[3] But the unprecedented wealth of the paper was for many sufficient cause for suspicion in itself. On 26 April 1916 the newspaper *Rech'* announced the organization of an important paper designed to serve the interests of heavy

---

[1] *Rekviem*, pp. 70–1.

[2] Ibid., p. 138. With his article *Literature, Silence and Drums* (*Literatura, molchanie i barabany*), published in the February 1915 issue of *Sovremennyy mir* (pp. 132–8), Asheshov began a sustained attack on Andreyev's attitude to the war.

[3] See V. G. Korolenko, 'Starye traditsii i novyy organ', *Russkie zapiski*, 1916, No. 8, p. 249.

industry. Some months before this V. P. Litvinov-Falinsky, an influential official in the Ministry of Trade and Industry, had acquainted the chiefs of the police department with the plan to establish a paper which would be progressive in appearance with large financial backing and the collaboration of the biggest 'names' in literature and journalism.[1] It would act in the interests of heavy industry and commerce in their conflict with the revolutionary movement among the workers. The principal organizing figure behind the scenes in the ensuing months was A. D. Protopopov, Vice-President of the fourth State Duma, who was present at the meeting of representatives of the Petrograd banks on 15 July 1916 at which it was agreed to devote five million roubles to the new enterprise—a sum which doubled the outlay on any previous paper or journal. This initial agreement was signed by ten large banking concerns. In August 1916, however, rumours arose in the press of a secret meeting in Hamburg between Protopopov and a well-known Hamburg banker and adviser of the German embassy in Sweden, Dr. Warburg, the result of which was that those industrial circles which had ties with Anglo-French capital cooled towards the plan, and the money was eventually advanced, the following autumn, by only three banks, all of which had ties with German capital.

At the meeting of 15 July Protopopov emphasized the need to attract to the paper the most eminent writers of the time, and among those who had agreed to collaborate he mentioned Gorky, Andreyev and Korolenko. This announcement was very premature and neither Gorky nor Korolenko accepted the invitation; they were both aware of the source of the capital, as Korolenko made clear in the article in which he stated his reasons for refusing,[2] though the mere involvement of Protopopov was in itself reason enough. Andreyev had shortly before (late May–early June, 1916) turned down 'through lack of time and strength'[3] an offer of the editorship of *Birzhevye vedomosti*, assuming instead a position on the editorial board 'in order to influence the trend'.[4] But he immediately accepted the invitation to become editor of the literary, critical and theatre sections of *Russkaya volya*.

---

[1] See Yu. Oksman, '"Russkaya volya", banki i burzhuaznaya literatura', *Literaturnoe Nasledstvo*, 1932, No. 2, p. 168. Our account of the main stages in the establishment of the paper is largely based on this article.

[2] See Korolenko, loc. cit., pp. 249–67.

[3] 'Pis'ma k bratu', *Zalp*, 1933, No. 1, p. 73.     [4] Ibid.

There were three main reasons for his acceptance: (1) his mood at the time, that eagerness for activity which has already been indicated; (2) the opportunity which, he believed, the position afforded of exercising a real and effective influence on the editorial policy of an important publication; and (3) the increasing gravity of his material situation, the combined result of lavish spending and the gradual decline in his productivity. Moreover, though he was aware of the source of the capital which financed the paper, he sincerely believed at first that its claims to be progressive were genuine. He had no idea of the real purpose of the enterprise. His sentiments are clearly expressed in a letter to his brother Andrey of 24 June 1916:

I have become a member of the editorial board of a large, new and very rich Petrograd newspaper founded by a whole association of capitalists and banks. I joined only after I had become convinced that the paper would be of a broadly progressive orientation, and in my agreement with the publishers I defended in every way my independence and influence on the form which the paper will take. My special assignment: I control three sections: literature, criticism and the theatre. I have as many assistants as I want and invite whomsoever I please irrespective of the editorial board. In other words, while having an influence on the general state of affairs, I have within the paper my own journal, so to speak, on the questions which are closest and most important to me. . . . The agreement: on a five-year contract my salary for management and articles is 36,000 a year and 1,500 for literature. In addition, they are obliged to print whatever I give them. In short, I can earn on the paper without effort up to 40–50 thousand—such financial splendour as I have not even dreamed of.[1]

Thus he believed not only that his financial worries were momentarily at an end, but also that he had at last obtained the position of power which he craved and from which he could hit back at those who placed on events an interpretation which differed from his own. He wrote to Skitalets: 'At last I have made up my mind—all or nothing: either the destruction of my enemies or my own ruin! I have finally taken command of a warship and am taking to the open sea in full sail.'[2] There is no doubt that he sincerely believed that his cherished independence would be in no way compromised.

His first task was to invite other writers to contribute. His offer

[1] 'Leonid Andreyev. Pis'ma', *Russkiy sovremennik*, 1924, No. 4, pp. 148–9.
[2] Skitalets, op. cit., p. 406.

was accepted at once and unequivocally by Ivan Bunin and Kuprin, while Aleksey Tolstoy promised to contribute 'not very often, but not too infrequently'.[1] Sologub, who with his novel *The Tip of the Sword* (*Ostriyo mecha*) and his articles for Suvorin's journal *Lukomor'e* ('The Curved Sea-Shore') rivalled Andreyev's output of patriotic literature, also accepted and wished to be a regular contributor, but he expressed to Andreyev his concern that so little importance was attached to his participation by the chief editor of the paper, M. M. Gakkebush-Gorelov.[2] That Andreyev himself was at times disturbed by doubts as to the political motives of the bankers who controlled the publication is revealed by the letter of acceptance, dated 26 August 1916, in which Sergeyev-Tsensky endeavoured to banish them[3]—successfully, it seems.

Gorky and Korolenko, as stated, flatly refused to participate. Gorky displayed a sincere concern for Andreyev; he wrote to Korolenko in a letter dated 21 and 22 October 1916:

L. Andreyev torments me greatly. I love him and consider him a very talented man, but our relations are shattered and I am unable to point out to him that he should not dally with Protopopov's paper. Should I write to him? He is as conceited as a poodle and he says that he 'fears my influence'. This is nonsense; I have never attempted to influence him and I know that I could not influence him; he is too sharply defined an individual. I have a tremendous desire to extricate him from this mess, but I don't know how to. The newspaper will devour him.[4]

Gorky and Korolenko were joined in their opposition to the paper by Serafimovich, Shmelyov and Chirikov. Particularly galling for Andreyev was the refusal of Blok. The letter of 6 October 1916 in which he invited the poet to contribute discloses both the extent of his ignorance of the purpose behind the organization of the paper and the hopes which he laid on it; he wrote: '. . . it is called a bank, Germanophil, ministerial paper, and all this is a lie. . . . It is a pity that there is no opportunity to speak with you and tell you

---

[1] Quoted from Oksman, loc. cit., p. 182.

[2] See Sologub's letter to Andreyev of 5 November 1916, ibid., p. 184. Gakkebush-Gorelov had left the editorship of *Birzhevye vedomosti* to assume the position at the head of *Russkaya volya* (see 'Pis'ma k bratu', *Zalp*, 1933, No. 1, p. 73); he was a close associate of the State Counsellor S. M. Propper, the publisher and actual controller of *Birzhevye vedomosti*.

[3] See Oksman, loc. cit., p. 185.

[4] *A. M. Gorkiy i V. G. Korolenko. Perepiska, stat'i, vyskazyvaniya*, M., 1957, pp. 81–2.

all my plans. Probably they are very naive and journalistic work will soon clip my wings, but in the meantime there is much that I want and much that I am seeking.'[1] Blok had spent a long time at the front and was unaware of the issues involved in the controversy to which the paper had given rise, so that he was guided in his decision not to contribute mainly by information and advice offered by friends. 'My ears buzzed with the news that it was a paper which belonged to Protopopov, and I refused,' he wrote subsequently in his reminiscences of Andreyev.[2] In his letter of reply, dated 29 October 1916, however, he preferred to plead a complete absence of inspiration: 'Everything literary in me is silent.'[3] A week later (4 November) Andreyev responded bitterly with the remark: 'Since I am not one of your friends or associates, Aleksandr Aleksandrovich, I naturally cannot count on the trust and respect which you show them.'[4] Blok attempted to heal the wound with profuse apologies in another letter of 21 November,[5] but Andreyev did not reply, and it was on this note of bitterness that their enigmatic relationship ended.

'Indeed, I have heard much that is dark about this newspaper,' wrote Aleksey Tolstoy to Andreyev in his letter of acceptance, 'but your name paralyses all evil rumours.'[6] This is the attitude which Andreyev expected of everyone. The refusals of the writers mentioned above and the campaign waged against the paper, even before it appeared, by other newspapers which feared the competition were all taken by him as personal insults. 'It seemed to him,' writes Vadim Andreyev, 'that his name should have been a sufficient guarantee of the honour of the paper.'[7] But he adds: 'Perhaps his irritation was partly explained by the fact that he himself, in his soul, felt that he was covering with his name something which it should not have covered, that "Russkaya volya" was by no means so free as he wished to think. . . .'[8]

For the moment, however, Andreyev succeeded in suppressing whatever doubts he may have had and the first edition of the paper came out in December 1916. He abandoned the 'Villa Avance' for semi-permanent residence in Petrograd. His self-immersion in the

---

[1] *Rekviem*, p. 87.    [2] Blok, 'Pamyati Leonida Andreyeva', p. 135.
[3] Aleksandr Blok, *Sobranie sochineniy v vos'mi tomakh*, vol. 8, M.–L., 1963, p. 475.
[4] *Rekviem*, p. 88.    [5] Blok, *Sobranie sochineniy . . .*, vol. 8, p. 476.
[6] Quoted from Oksman, loc. cit., p. 183.    [7] *VLA*, October, p. 93.
[8] Ibid.

new role of editor was reminiscent of his former obsessions with photography, gramophones, etc.; with the same ardour he plunged into the technicalities of printing. But his infatuation with the paper was as short-lived as Blok had prophesied it would be.[1] The work took a heavy toll both of his health and of his creative ability. He sought in his articles to convince the Russian public of the rightness of his view of the war, but his position was constantly undermined by the repeated defeats of Russian arms and the increasing chaos at the front. His exhortations of the people and army to greater efforts are punctuated with increasingly preponderant notes of alarm and warning. 'There is no joy for the defeated in anything,' he wrote in his article *Woe to the Conquered (Gore pobezhdyonnym)*, 'and those popular movements to which defeat has served as a stimulus are for the most part joyless and bloody.'[2]

His fears were momentarily allayed by the revolution of February 1917 which, he hoped, by bringing internal disorder to an end would result in a more united and determined campaign against the Central Powers. He saw it as a step towards the eventual eradication of militarism and the realization of his dream of a 'United States of Europe'.[3] 'Gay and excited, he seemed several years younger,' recalls Vadim Andreyev. 'His face was covered with fine wrinkles of laughter, his grey eyes were young and full of life; it was a long time since I had seen them like that.'[4] But again his high spirits were short-lived and masked his dark presentiments of disaster. In his typewriter a sheet of paper was discovered by his son on which were written the significant words: 'The holiday of the soul, which has lasted three days, is at an end. A new character has entered the revolution—the machine-gun.'[5]

On 28 April 1917 he was enlisted by the Provisional Government as a writer of propaganda,[6] but his article *Ruin (Gibel')*, which appeared two days later in an edition of *Russkaya volya* which went into a million copies, may hardly be considered a response to this

---

[1] Blok wrote in his reply to Andreyev's invitation to contribute: 'It is likely that when you have reached the end of the ordained path of disillusionments, pain and anger, you will leave the paper; everything else apart, you are completely unsuited for newspapers' (Blok, *Sobranie sochineniy* . . ., vol. 8, p. 475).

[2] L. N. Andreyev, 'Gore pobezhdyonnym', *Russkaya volya*, 1916, 15 December, pp. 6–7.

[3] See L. N. Andreyev, 'Put' krasnykh znamyon', *Russkaya volya*, 1917, 8 March, p. 2.

[4] *VLA*, October, p. 105.     [5] Ibid.

[6] See *The New York Times*, 1917, 28 April, p. 1.

appointment despite its consonance with the government's aims. It was written with a sincerity and anguish born of shattered illusions. He opened the article with the words: 'Yes, Russia is in mortal danger. She is close to death and I do not know whether she will be alive in a month's time or whether she will perish.'[1] He was compelled to admit to the vanity of the hopes which he had laid on the revolution and to acknowledge the Provisional Government's failure to fire the nation with a new enthusiasm. The whole fabric of Russian life appeared to him rent by distrust and disunity and seemed to be subject to a 'strange centrifugal force'.[2] He referred with anger to the 'dark, ignorant, distrustful' peasants, who had lost faith in the cause for which they were fighting, cut off the supplies of grain and created famine, and bewailed the attempts to undermine the united will of the army by dishonourable talk of a 'separate peace', which he saw as a betrayal of the Allies. Knowing that his words would bring on him a storm of abuse from all sides, he paid no heed: 'That does not trouble me. Let them beat me from the right and from the left. Russia has long been beaten from the right, and now she has been turned over and is being beaten from the left. If I also merit a beating, it will only bring me closer to Russia and that is the only thing I wish.'[3]

When he returned to Vammelsuu in the spring of 1917, all traces of his excitement and enthusiasm had disappeared. He aged almost perceptibly. His shoulders began to droop and his animated monologues of former days rarely disturbed the silence. The children and his sailing afforded him his only respite from the ominous reports in the mass of newspapers which he received of defeats and the collapse of the military organization. By September 1917 all his hopes had been extinguished and in his article published in *Russkaya volya* on the fifteenth of that month, *Veni Creator*, dedicated to Lenin and replete with the bitterest irony, he plumbs the lowest depths of despair. His election by the Petrograd editors to the 'Pre-Parliament' convoked by Kerensky on the eve of the October Revolution and his presence at its few meetings did little to dispel it. Kugel', who saw him there, describes him as 'pale, alarmed and pensive'.[4]

[1] L. N. Andreyev, *Gibel'*. (*Chto zhdyot Rossiyu*), Petrograd, 1917, p. 2.
[2] Ibid., p. 13.    [3] Ibid., p. 16.
[4] A. R. Kugel', 'Literaturnye vstrechi i kharakteristiki', in his *List'ya s dereva*, L., 1926, p. 87.

With the departure of Amfiteatrov at this time from the editorial board of *Russkaya volya* his volume of work increased considerably. Nevertheless, he found time to visit the theatre and numerous meetings, both literary and political, and his mood seems to have improved somewhat. It is noteworthy that his letters of 1917 to his brother Andrey, which are the best record of his sentiments while he was working for the paper, contain no evidence that he laboured under pressure. The most critical remark appeared in a letter of 30 September in which he complained about arguments with the publishers and about 'the slowness of some, the lack of talent in others'.[1] But the days of *Russkaya volya* were already numbered. The objections of the shareholders to the profuse expenditure on the paper became increasingly persistent, and it was decided either to sell or to give up some of the shares. Up to the last minute the employees, Andreyev included, received no concrete information about the progress of the negotiations that were taking place in the background. 'No one knows anything definitely,' Andreyev wrote to his brother in mid-October, 'and they are all asking whether we have been sold or not. Even I do not know.'[2] According to I. V. Gessen, a prominent journalist and important figure in the Constitutional Democratic (Cadet) party, the paper was sold on the very eve of the October Revolution and the new proprietors appointed the erstwhile Socialist Revolutionary terrorist Boris Savinkov to Andreyev's position.[3] Immediately afterwards, however, the paper's offices and equipment were taken over by the Bolshevik *Izvestiya* ('News'). Broken in body and spirit, Andreyev sadly wended his way back to Vammelsuu.

His return to Finland found him in the position of his hero in the fourth Picture of *The Life of Man*. His literary reputation in Russia was dwindling to nought and his material situation deteriorated rapidly with the confiscation, after the closing of the border by the Bolsheviks, of the royalties from the sale of his books and the productions of his plays. The decay of the 'Villa Avance' is vividly described by Vadim Andreyev:

There was little money and it was impossible not only to replace broken things with new, but even to heat all the fifteen rooms. . . . Already

[1] 'Leonid Andreyev. Pis'ma', *Russkiy sovremennik*, 1924, No. 4, p. 153.
[2] Ibid., p. 156.
[3] See I. V. Gessen, 'Poslednie dni Leonida Andreyeva', *Arkhiv russkoy revolyutsii*, vol. I, 2nd edn., Berlin, 1922, p. 309.

the walls in the dining-room were disfigured by large patches of damp where they were covered with grey material. The frosts brought so fierce a cold into the house that accidentally spilt soup froze in the hall in a matter of minutes and the children skated on the large oval puddle which formed in the middle of the room as though on a rink. After the dining-room the other rooms also quickly lost their inhabited appearance: mildew covered the beams of the wooden ceilings, black pieces of cob-web hung in the corners, the floor-boards parted with a creak. It became necessary to abandon the study which lasted longer than the other rooms; the November blizzards swept piles of snow on to the floor through the cracks in the rickety window-frames. The ice age of our house had begun.[1]

So far as literature was concerned, the autumn and winter were completely unproductive. The tapping of his typewriter was heard only on the rare occasions when he made an entry in his diary. Cut off from his friends, he languished in what his brother Pavel could only compare to 'the strictest solitary confinement'.[2] Dumas and the newspapers were his only reading. He also found relief in skiing and riding, though his weak heart and asthma forced him in the end to forgo the latter. Symbolic of his condition was the alteration which he made to the vast portrait of Someone-in-grey which hung in the hall: the candle was replaced by a stump with a barely flickering flame. When his son asked him the reason for it, he replied simply: 'It is time. It has long been time.'[3]

With the arrival of the first warm days of spring, however, new life temporarily filtered into the house. His study was 'resurrected' and he began to write his last work *Satan's Diary*, which remained uncompleted and was published posthumously in Helsingfors.[4] The novel conveys the impression that he was aware of the proximity of his death. It might be described as a hurriedly compiled 'encyclopaedia' of the major themes of his fiction. It is the final chapter of his polemic against modern man. Satan, bored with life in hell, comes to earth in the form of a wealthy American, Henry Wandergood, and his ingenuous philanthropy is contrasted with the ruthless egoism of the man, Thomas Magnus, whom Voronsky saw, with little justification, as a personified indictment of Bolshevism.[5]

[1] *VLA*, November, pp. 101–2.
[2] *PNA*, p. 206.
[3] *VLA*, November, p. 112.
[4] L. N. Andreyev, *Dnevnik Satany*, 'Biblion', Helsingfors, 1921, 279 pp. In 1922 it was converted in Petrograd into a play of five Acts and ten Pictures.
[5] Cf. A. K. Voronsky (Nurmin), 'Leonid Andreyev. "Dnevnik Satany"', *Krasnaya nov'*, 1921, No. 1, p. 295.

Selecting Satan as the mouthpiece of his innermost convictions, Andreyev makes Magnus the direct heir of Kerzhentsev. The central theme of his works rings out in the following address of Satan to the reader:

Your reason is like a beggar's sack containing only crusts of stale bread, but here you need more than bread. You have only two conceptions of existence: life and death; how can I explain to you the third? The whole of your existence is nonsense simply because you do not have this third conception, and where can I acquire it for you? Now I am human like you. I have your brain in my head. Your cubic words jostle one another sluggishly and prick one another with their sharp corners in my mouth, and they cannot tell you about the Extraordinary.[1]

Throughout the novel Satan acts in conformity with this 'third conception' which words are powerless to express. His love of man, his disparagement of the human intellect, his mockery of Church and State, of all human institutions and values—all spring from his awareness of the higher truth of life which he endeavours, with increasing disillusionment, to communicate. 'Love thy neighbour!' he cries, in a scene which is an obvious parody of *The Legend of the Grand Inquisitor*, but the Roman Cardinal claims that love in excess is perilous because it blinds one to the defects in people. He worships the daughter of Magnus, who reminds him of the Madonna, only to learn that she is not his daughter but his mistress. All manifestations on earth of the 'third conception' are revealed to be illusory, and in the end Satan is exposed by Magnus to the mockery of all, thus sharing the fate of Storitsyn, Ekaterina, 'He' and Samson. Fascinating and provocative in conception, like all his works, undistinguished, except for certain portraits, e.g. the Cardinal, in its execution, scathing in its diatribes against man, *Satan's Diary* was in every sense of the term Andreyev's 'last word'—the 'word' of an exhausted artist and of a thinker who had nothing more to say.

<hr>

[1] *Dnevnik Satany*, p. 10.

# XXI

## EXILE AND DEATH

'WE live like complete Robinson Crusoes,' Andreyev wrote in his diary on 12 May 1918, 'and it would be unbearable if it were not for the children.'[1] The counter-revolution had begun the previous February and the front which developed between the Reds and the Whites passed directly through Andreyev's villa with the result that for a time the family was almost entirely isolated from the world. In the spring it became increasingly difficult to obtain food even with money, and by May Andreyev was all but penniless. Hunger continued to plague the family throughout the spring and summer. The situation in Finland deteriorated rapidly as large numbers of refugees crossed the border at the risk of their lives, presenting the Finnish government with an impossible task. In a letter of 25 August 1918 to an unknown addressee, who was about to visit the Ukraine with an appeal for supplies, Andreyev wrote:

In present conditions . . . Finland is unable to feed a large number of people, and every new mouth, every Russian refugee who crosses the border at his own peril, every Russian child who is brought here by his parents from hungry and terrible Petrograd is an involuntary burden for the Finnish people who are themselves living from hand to mouth and are in need of the most basic necessities.[2]

For the Andreyevs the position did not improve until the winter when they succeeded in mortgaging the house.

Andreyev made his last visit to Petrograd in February 1918 on receiving news that his mother, who was staying with his sister Rimma, had contracted pneumonia. He knew that he faced possible arrest. To Mariya Iordanskaya, who had been co-editor with her husband of *Sovremennyy mir*, and who travelled back with him to Finland, he described his experiences:

[1] 'Stranitsy iz dnevnika L. N. Andreyeva', *Zhar-ptitsa*, Berlin, 1921, No. 3, p. 39.

[2] 'Neizdannye pis'ma Leonida Andreyeva', *Zveno*, Paris, 1926, No. 164, p. 12.

My apartment was searched several times during this period and every-thing was rifled—my luggage, books, papers and letters. They were looking for me. They tried to force my servant with threats to tell them where I was. Very rarely, at dusk, I would go out for a while and take a breath of air. I could have been arrested even on the street if I had been recognized.[1]

He returned only when he was sure that his mother was out of danger—towards the end of February.[2] What he saw in Petrograd during this visit greatly increased his despondency and in a letter to Sologub he lamented that he saw no force powerful enough to halt Russia's impetuous course towards destruction.[3]

He did not condemn the revolution at once, however. In a letter of March 1918 to L. A. Alekseyevsky, the son of his sister Rimma by her first marriage, he looked ahead to the 'new majestic struc-ture, spacious and radiant' which would replace the 'old house of Russia, fusty, fetid, infested with bugs'.[4] Once more the word 'revolution' fired his romantic dreams. At the outset of the counter-revolution, when the Whites were executing their opponents with a complete lack of discrimination, he remarked to his son: 'I am repelled when they abuse the Reds in my presence. In Finland the Reds have conducted themselves excellently. . . . It is a pity that the Whites have triumphed. For this is the end of the revolution. The end of the revolution—do you understand what that means?'[5] Mannerheim halted, however, at Beloostrov; in Russia the revolu-tion continued to survive, but it was very far removed from the revolution of which Andreyev dreamt, and his initially tolerant attitude towards the Finnish Bolsheviks soon gave way to an uncompromising hatred of their Russian comrades. Taking no account of the state of the Russian army, he regarded the Bolshe-viks' conclusion of a separate peace with Germany as an act of

[1] M. K. Iordanskaya, 'Emigratsiya i smert' Leonida Andreyeva. (Vospomin-aniya)', *Rodnaya zemlya*, vol. i, New York, 1920, p. 45.

[2] The full force of Andreyev's concern for his moth erreceived expression in a letter which he wrote to her from Vammelsuu nearly two weeks later (10–11 March) (cf. 'Pis'mo Leonida Andreyeva', *Obshcheye delo*, Paris, 1920, No. 89, 2 September, p. 3).

[3] Cf. V. Desnitsky, *A. M. Gor'kiy. Ocherk zhizni i tvorchestva*, M., 1959, p. 234.

[4] Cf. V. Desnitsky, 'M. Gor'kiy i L. Andreyev v ikh perepiske', in *M. Gor'kiy. Materialy i issledovaniya*, vol. i, L., 1934, p. 133.

[5] *VLA*, November, p. 111.

treachery. He branded the leaders of the revolution as immoral and devoted his final energies to hastening their overthrow, propagandizing the counter-revolution as a crusade in which all civilised nations were honour-bound to participate. In a letter written shortly before his death to V. L. Burtsev, once a rabid revolutionary and now an equally rabid mouthpiece of the interventionists in his newspaper *Obshcheye delo* ('The Common Cause') which he was publishing in Paris, he announced himself ready to devote his talent to the struggle against the 'Savva' who had won control of Russia and to the rescue of those who were perishing and of the cultural heritage of mankind.[1]

At first the force of his hatred made it difficult for him to regiment his thoughts and express himself coherently. 'The revolution sometimes tormented him like an unwritten story,' writes Vadim Andreyev.[2] On 6 February 1919, however, appeared his *S.O.S.*, his hysterical response to Woodrow Wilson's idea of the Prinkipo Conference in which he called on the Allies, as he had in conversation with Herman Bernstein in the dark days of 1908,[3] to intervene and save Russia from the 'barbarians'. The call for negotiation addressed by the powers of the Entente to the Bolsheviks is compared by him to the act of Pilate, and the fate of Russia—to the fate of Jesus. Refusing to accept the upheaval in Russia as revolution, he declares it to be the 'Chaos and Darkness which have been summoned by the war from their black nether regions and armed by the same war for the destruction of peace'.[4] It was not the physical suffering inflicted on the Russian people that he saw as the Bolsheviks' greatest crime; he writes:

The loss of all faith in human and divine justice, unpunished trampling on all the highest attributes of the human soul is an incomparably greater and more bitter torment than all the physical agonies in the Bolshevik torture-chambers. This is why we are all almost insane; this is why even the most steadfast of us are separated by only a thin line from ultimate despair and suicide. It is difficult to keep alive; deliverance from life seems almost a happiness.[5]

[1] See E. Chirikov, 'Leonid Andreyev', *Russkie sborniki*, No. 2, Sofia, 1921, p. 74.
[2] *VLA*, November, p. 115.
[3] See H. Bernstein, *With Master Minds. Interviews*, New York, 1913, pp. 166–7.
[4] L. N. Andreyev, *S.O.S.*, Helsingfors, 1919, p. 15.      [5] Ibid., p. 13.

Passing over the heads of governments, he addressed his appeal directly to the free peoples of the earth.[1]

He considered himself to be quite irreplaceable in his role as a 'verbal crusader'. He wrote to a friend in July 1918:

Very responsible work awaits me in Petersburg. I will say without false modesty: if I leave the ranks completely, it will be difficult to find another person who could replace me. This knowledge is far from cheering; it lays a heavy responsibility on me and compels me to take the same care of myself as I would of a horse. Hence my concern for my health which I *must* have.[2]

In the same letter he distinguishes his work from that of other journalists:

Whereas they must write every day in order to make up for their lack of power with frequent repetition, I have only rarely to give an article, but an article of such a kind that its influence will be prolonged and durable. Thus Kartashov[3] writes to me, on the basis of information received from London, that even now 'S.O.S.' is acquiring a special importance. There is a daily service in church with a priest and archpriest and with the ringing of bells. What can I do?—I'm an archpriest![4]

*S.O.S.* was telegraphed to London and Paris for publication in the newspapers, and according to one commentator it was broadcast from Finland direct to America with the financial assistance of refugee bankers.[5] It was published in London in 1920 by the Russian Liberation Committee with an introduction by the leader of the Cadet party, Pavel Milyukov. This latter fact pleased Andreyev immensely; he wrote to Gessen on 9 June 1919: 'I have heard about

---

[1] The mocking Bolshevik response to the pamphlet appeared on 31 July 1919 on the front page of *Izvestiya* (see V. Sokol, '"Krik dushi" Leonida Andreyeva', *Izvestiya*, 1919, No. 167, 31 July, p. 1). It opens with the words: 'L. Andreyev has long been silent; he has not written for a long time and it was not known whether he had moved closer to the workers and peasants or remained true to his old "patriotism". It was pleasant to be in ignorance and to think that L. Andreyev was capable of learning something from life. But the bitter truth is better than pleasant delusions.'

[2] 'Neizdannye pis'ma Leonida Andreyeva', *Zveno*, Paris, 1926, No. 164, p. 11.

[3] A. V. Kartashov was Minister of Public Worship in Kerensky's government and subsequently lent his support to the interventionists. Until his death in September 1960 he was a professor at the Russian Theological Academy in Paris.

[4] 'Neizdannye pis'ma Leonida Andreyeva', p. 11.

[5] Cf. V. G. Bogoraz (Tan), '"Zhizn' Cheloveka" vo vserossiyskoy postanovke. K tryokhletiyu smerti L. Andreyeva', *Rossiya*, 1922, No. 3, p. 15.

the English "S.O.S." with the article by Pavel N. I am overjoyed that it is precisely Pavel N. who has written the foreword. In spite of all his "errors", I consider him Russia's greatest statesman, and even on a personal level he commands my strongest affection.'[1] That it was not a spontaneous and short-lived affection is confirmed by his remark in a letter of 7 March 1916 to his brother Andrey: 'What is strange is my affection for this Milyukov. I hate "Rech' "[2] and all the Cadets, but for him I have a certain weakness. He speaks well and he is intelligent and energetic.'[3]

In addition to the wide publicity given to *S.O.S.*, the formation of the 'North-Western Government' in August 1919 in Estonia with General Yudenich at its head served momentarily to raise Andreyev's hopes. Blinded by his hatred of the Bolsheviks, he flung himself into the arms of these people with whom he had so little in common. In a letter of 23 August 1919 to the painter and academician Nikolay Roerich he confided that in spite of his health he was considering taking upon himself the whole responsibility for anti-Bolshevik propaganda and stated his intention of travelling the following day to Helsingfors to negotiate his assumption of the portfolio of propaganda and the press in the newly formed government.[4] He knew that he could expect only the merest pittance for his labours and that the work would mark his 'undoubted end as an artist and living creature', but, as he put it, 'duty obliges one to work for Russia'.[5] His overtures to the 'North-Western Government', however, met with no success. He was curtly informed that his services were not required. From the beginning the attempts to establish a propaganda department were bedevilled by the intrigue which surrounded Yudenich.

Andreyev was perfectly aware of his unsuitability for the task which he had offered to perform. He wrote to a friend: 'I will tell you the truth: if it were not for my sense of *duty*, which compels me to make much of myself, I . . . do not know what I would be. *Personally* I am not interested in all this and I'm pursuing no personal aims. Personally I am simply tired and exhausted by the

---

[1] I. V. Gessen, 'Poslednie dni Leonida Andreyeva', *Arkhiv russkoy revolyutsii*, vol. I, 2nd edn., Berlin, 1922, p. 311.

[2] *Rech'* was a prominent Cadet newspaper published by Milyukov and Gessen.

[3] 'Pis'ma k bratu', *Zalp*, 1933, No. 1, p. 72.

[4] See N. Roerich, 'Pamyati Leonida Andreyeva', *Rodnaya zemlya*, vol. 2, New York, 1921, p. 38.

[5] Ibid.

need and burdensome obligation to live.'[1] He felt his 'exile' from literature even more acutely than his exile from Russia, though there was little that he could do about it. 'It isn't that I have no time to write,' he remarked in a letter of 4 September 1919 to Roerich, 'or that I am ill—nonsense! It is simply that what constituted my creative power has gone, hidden itself somewhere, disappeared together with the destruction of Russia.'[2] Again he identified his own fate with that of his country.

By this time he was a 'threefold exile', as he termed himself,[3] for he had also been compelled to abandon the 'Villa Avance', which, despite his attachment to Russia, had long been his true 'native land'. In the winter of 1918 the family was forced to move, especially after the electricity had been cut off, to the village of Tyursevo, which was situated a few miles inland. They settled in a small but warm cottage built to withstand the Finnish winter. It was there that Andreyev suffered his first heart-attack from which he never fully recovered. 'For a whole year before his death,' writes Vadim Andreyev, 'he remained a semi-invalid; even the presence of small children and very short strolls exhausted him. Almost every physical exertion came to him with great effort.'[4]

Though it was relatively comfortable in the physical sense, he found life at Tyursevo oppressive due to the *émigré* circle in which he was forced to move. Instead of writers and intellectuals he found himself among businessmen, bankers and aristocrats who had formerly held his name in contempt but who now welcomed him as a valuable advertisement to the peoples of Europe of the justice of their cause. His close friend F. N. Fal'kovsky, a writer and theatre critic of *Birzhevye vedomosti*, writes in his reminiscences of this time:

The bankers and Counts began to run to the Andreyevs one after another and invite them to their homes. Alas, the weak heart of Leonid Nikolaevich could not withstand this whirlwind of idolisation, high-sounding phrases, mysterious conferences, highly promising plans, and, above all, the false, repulsive slander of Russia. . . . He somehow merged quickly with the general background of *émigré* life and became as dull and grey as his milieu. And Leonid Andreyev was no more. This was the first death of Leonid Andreyev.[5]

[1] 'Neizdannye pis'ma Leonida Andreyeva', *Zveno*, Paris, 1926, No. 164, p. 11.
[2] Roerich, loc. cit., p. 40.     [3] Ibid.     [4] *VLA*, December, p. 99.
[5] F. N. Fal'kovsky, 'Predsmertnaya tragediya Leonida Andreyeva. (Iz vospominaniy)', *Prozhektor*, 1923, No. 16, p. 28.

While at Tyursevo Andreyev listened with horror to reports of the fate of his fellow-writers in Russia, e.g. Kuprin and Sologub, who had been forced to sell their possessions and books in order to subsist and, as a last resort, to beg Gorky for employment. The employment was granted, but Gorky made little distinction, so far as financial remuneration was concerned, between these professional writers and translators who barely knew the languages from which they were translating. Fal'kovsky writes: 'In general, he (Andreyev) avoided speaking about Gorky and shared his impressions of him only in his narrow circle of relatives and close friends. He did not like Gorky and spoke of him not with animosity, but with the disillusionment with which one speaks of a friend who has gone over to the enemy.'[1] Gessen puts it a little more strongly and speaks of the 'passionate indignation' with which Andreyev referred to his former friend and colleague.[2] Andreyev found it impossible to understand how Gorky could blanket with his name the monstrosities of the new regime. Nevertheless, he besought the writers to bear their hardship. He said to Mariya Iordanskaya in February 1919:

However difficult it is for them, the intelligentsia and the writers must go to Gorky for work. It is a heavy sacrifice, but they must bear it. . . . They have no right to die of hunger; they have no right to extinguish the light which they are obliged to preserve for the people. They must live. The best forces have already died in the bloody struggle. The people are almost headless. Its brain is bloodless because intelligent, progressive, gifted people have been destroyed in thousands. The few who have survived must live. The money of the people is in the publishing organisation of Gorky, and the writers can take it. They will return it to the people by giving them their creative powers when our free country requires it of them. But they must live until this happens![3]

But Andreyev himself did not act in accordance with these sentiments. When an emissary from Gorky visited him with an offer of two million roubles in exchange for aid for the Bolsheviks' 'literary work' he declined it abruptly.[4]

---

[1] Ibid.

[2] See I. V. Gessen, 'Poslednie dni Leonida Andreyeva', *Arkhiv russkoy revolyutsii*, vol. I, 2nd edn., Berlin, 1922, p. 309.

[3] M. K. Iordanskaya, 'Emigratsiya i smert' Leonida Andreyeva. (Vospominaniya)', *Rodnaya zemlya*, vol. 1, New York, 1920, pp. 51–2.

[4] See L. Pasvolsky, 'Leonid Andreyev and the Bolsheviki', *The Review*, vol. I, No. 30, New York, 1919, p. 638. Andreyev wrote subsequently to Burtsev:

He changed his abode twice more before his death. In the spring of 1919 the family left Tyursevo to settle in a large two-storey house on the coast, and finally, in the early days of September, they moved to the village of Mustamäggi, which was further from the frontier, in order to escape from the air-raids which drove him to distraction.[1] They settled in a large wooden house high on a hill overlooking Lake Vammelyarvi (Black Lake) which belonged to Fal'kovsky, who during this period, as Kugel' put it, 'served Andreyev as something in the nature of a factotum'.[2] Far from his friends and losing hope of ever making progress in his still continuing discussions with the 'North-Western Government', Andreyev surrendered to a profound melancholy. He wrote in his diary on 8 September: 'Everything is so repulsive in the world. It is so unbearably tedious to live, speak or write that I have neither the strength nor the desire to write even a few lines. For whom? Why?'[3] Even so, he was engaged in making preparations to spend the following winter in America on a lecture-tour designed to reveal the full horror of life in Russia. In the letter in which he requested Herman Bernstein to arrange the tour he outlined his purpose in the following words:

The fundamental purpose of my trip to America is to combat the Bolsheviki, to tell the truth about them with all the power and conviction within me, and to awaken in America a feeling of friendship and sympathy for that portion of the Russian people which is heroically struggling for the regeneration of Russia. The struggle is hard and painful and the sympathy of the great American people would hasten the victory and would lessen the sufferings of those who are perishing every hour in dark, lewd and bloody Soviet Russia.[4]

---

'You know that they have tried me also—they offered to publish my works very profitably and stated that "everything was there" and that it was senseless for me to be stubborn' ('Zavety Leonida Andreyeva. Otryvok iz predsmertnogo pis'ma V. L. Burtsevu', *Obshcheye delo*, Paris, 1919, No. 59, 9 October, p. 1).

[1] The day before their departure the windows of their house had been shattered by a bomb which dropped barely two hundred yards away (see *VLA*, December, p. 106).

[2] A. R. Kugel', 'Literaturnye vstrechi i kharakteristiki', in his *List'ya s dereva*, L., 1926, p. 86.

[3] 'Poslednie stranitsy dnevnika L. N. Andreyeva', *Zhar-ptitsa*, Berlin, 1921, No. 2, p. 24.

[4] H. Bernstein, 'Death of Andreyev', *The New York Times*, 1919, 9 November, p. 2.

It was also his stated intention to offer *Satan's Diary* to American publishers, arrange productions of some of his latest plays, and then 'return to Russia a millionaire for a venerable old age free from cares'.[1] But the dream was not to be realized.

Death came to him suddenly as it had to his father. On 12 September he suffered one of his fearful headaches and it was followed by a heart-attack. It took his son three hours to fetch the doctor and by the time they arrived he had already been dead two hours. His death passed almost unnoticed in Russia. Few of his real friends had a pass to cross the border to his funeral. Neighbours, refugees, acquaintances made during his last two years—these were the people who followed his coffin to its temporary resting-place, people with whom he had nothing in common. It was his wife's intention that at the first opportunity his body should be buried in Russia; in the meantime the coffin was placed in a small chapel situated in the garden of a local landowner. Five years previously (1914–15) the same house had been used by Gorky after his return from Italy; to the end the lives of the two writers seemed to be linked by invisible threads. When the news reached Gorky, he remarked with tears in his eyes: 'However strange it may seem, he was my only friend. Yes, the only one. . . .'[2]

[1] See Andreyev's letter to Roerich of 23 August 1919 in N. Roerich, 'Pamyati Leonida Andreyeva', *Rodnaya zemlya*, vol. 2, New York, 1921, p. 38.

[2] See K. Chukovsky, 'Leonid Andreyev', in his *Iz vospominaniy*, M., 1958, p. 270.

# POSTSCRIPT

THE main emphasis in this book has been placed on the ideas which lie at the basis of Andreyev's major works and on the variety of ways in which these ideas are embodied in his fiction. Some readers, no doubt, will regret the restrictive nature of this approach and the less detailed treatment accorded to other elements in his stories and plays which may be judged equally, if not more, important. Given the necessity, however, of delimiting one's terms of reference, the selection of this aspect of the writer for special emphasis is, I think, justified.

It has been indicated that most of the debates provoked by Andreyev's works have centred on the two questions of whether they do, in fact, contain a discernible substratum of ideas and, if so, whether these ideas reflect a clearly defined attitude to life. In the present study both of these questions have been answered unequivocally in the affirmative. The great defect of past critical comment on Andreyev has been its failure to appreciate the central role which ideas of a wholly abstract nature play both in his fiction and in his general approach to life, revealing themselves not only in his treatment of problems of individual personality, but even, as we have seen, in his conception of the issues at stake in the First World War. This failure of criticism would seem to be due, at least in part, to an incorrect understanding of Andreyev's position *vis-à-vis* Gorky and the writers associated with *Znanie* and *Sreda*, and to the resultant tendency to judge him by the same yardstick. Even works of an overtly allegorical character, such as the play *Tsar Hunger*, have suffered from criticism which based its demands on the criteria of realism, as evidenced, for example, by the reactions to this play of Lunacharsky and Serafimovich. At the same time criticism of this kind has shown itself to be equally incapable of disclosing the essential meaning of those works in which the scheme of ideas is more deeply submerged in realistic detail, such as *The Governor* and *Darkness*. It is not surprising that it was precisely these and similar works which incurred the severest criticism, for without reference to the underlying abstractions they have little plausibility. Certainly, Andreyev's frequent inability to combine abstraction with convincing motivation is one of his main weaknesses as a writer, and this point emerged perhaps most clearly in our examination of *Darkness* and also the play *Ekaterina Ivanovna*, but this very inability is merely further testimony to his overriding preoccupation with abstract, metaphysical concepts. There is no exaggeration in the claim that ideas as such acquire in his fiction a prominence unsurpassed in the works of any other writer of his generation, not only serving as the point of departure in his creative process, but also investing the seemingly discordant mass of his work with an unusually consistent inner unity. To illustrate the presence of this unity and to investigate its nature have been two of the principal objects of this study.

It may perhaps be argued, of course, that too much stress is placed on this theme and that more attention should have been devoted to those aspects of his works in which the element of consistency is less conspicuous. It must be re-emphasized, however, that hitherto Andreyev has not been credited with consistency in any individual aspect of his art and, above all, it is to his ideas and attitude to life that this quality has most frequently been denied. Within the framework of the tripartite scheme adopted for analysis, it has been shown that the fictional embodiment of his ideas did indeed undergo a considerable evolution, but it has emerged with equal clarity that this evolution signified no change of basic beliefs, and illustration of this fact has been judged the most urgently required task in Andreyev studies.

Naturally, one would have liked to devote more space and attention to questions of style and structure, especially as a more searching consideration of these aspects of his art would have served to reinforce some of the main conclusions reached. Demonstrating the predominance of the abstract over the concrete in his style, as in his thinking, and confirming the verdict of Tsetlin that Andreyev was one of the first prose writers to break with the realistic tradition of Russian literature,[1] it would have illuminated from a different angle that schematic quality of his art which has been revealed in the study of his ideas and which was carried to its ultimate extreme in *The Life of Man* and *Tsar Hunger*. Moreover, an approach to Andreyev based on Professor Leo Spitzer's

[1] Cf. Tsetlin, loc. cit., p. 253. This subject is treated at greater length in my article 'Devices of Emphasis and Amplification in the Style of Leonid Andreyev', *The Slavic and East European Journal*, University of Wisconsin Press, vol. IX, No. 3, 1965, pp. 247–56.

'philological circle'[1] would perhaps help to show just how deeply ingrained were some of those aspects of Andreyev's personality as both man and writer that have been indicated. It does not seem fanciful, for example, to maintain that due emphasis of the contrast between the structural schematicism of most of his major narrative works and the bursts of exuberant prose, overflowing with imagery and hierarchies of clauses, which repeatedly punctuate their flow, would offer a new sidelight on that tension between the man and the thinker which has been traced in the development of his thought, i.e. on the deeper contrast between introvert and extrovert which Andreyev presented to his contemporaries—between the 'spirit of exile' who sought the splendid isolation of a Finnish wilderness and the city-lover who craved companionship and an environment in which he could give full vent to his colourful personality.

Whatever critical approach to Andreyev is adopted, however, it would undoubtedly confirm the validity of our insistence that he be regarded as a wholly unique figure in the literary life of his times. Identifiable with none of the numerous contemporary literary groups, he followed his own independent path with remarkable perseverance, and the solitude which he continually lamented was the price which he paid for it. Yet no less remarkable, as stated, is the degree to which he summed up in his person and in his art so much that was typical of the age in which he lived. The isolation and rootlessness of the intellectual in contemporary Russian society, the intrinsic perils of a predominantly rationalistic culture, the inevitable bankruptcy of an assertive individualistic philosophy of life, the irreconcilability of abstract ideals and mundane reality, the relation of man to his neighbour and to the universe as a whole— these are the problems to which his thoughts were constantly directed, problems which had inspired some of the best-known works of nineteenth-century Russian literature, but which from the turn of the century to 1917 acquired an unparalleled ascendancy in Russian intellectual life. And the level of abstraction to which he raised them was in itself symptomatic of that renewed concern with the metaphysical, as distinct from the social-political, dimension of life which was an important contributing factor in the birth of Russian symbolism and in the general renaissance of art and letters in the two decades before the Revolution, and which, tragically for

---

[1] Cf. L. Spitzer, *Linguistics and Literary History. Essays on Stylistics*, Princeton, New Jersey, 1948.

the future of Russian literature, proved incompatible with Bolshevik aesthetics. The excitement and controversy which greeted almost his every work is evidence of the extent to which Andreyev was inwardly attuned to the spirit of his times. Nor was this a case, as hostile critics have claimed, of a writer pandering to popular taste, for the most salient features of Andreyev's mature art, as we have seen, are already apparent in his earliest stories. He wrote in the only way he knew how on the subjects which dominated his attention, and thereby provided a generation with one of its most representative and intriguing voices.

# INDEX

This Index includes names contained in the text and footnotes, but not in references. Fictional names are not included.